To
The Dairy
        with best wishes,
            Christel Lane
                FS+C 2014

The Cultivation of Taste

The Cultivation of Taste

Chefs and the Organization of Fine Dining

Christel Lane

OXFORD

UNIVERSITY PRESS

Great Clarendon Street, Oxford, OX2 6DP,
United Kingdom

Oxford University Press is a department of the University of Oxford.
It furthers the University's objective of excellence in research, scholarship,
and education by publishing worldwide. Oxford is a registered trade mark of
Oxford University Press in the UK and in certain other countries

© Christel Lane 2014

The moral rights of the author have been asserted

First Edition published in 2014

Impression: 1

Published in the United States of America by Oxford University Press
198 Madison Avenue, New York, NY 10016, United States of America

British Library Cataloguing in Publication Data

Data available

Library of Congress Control Number: 2013950249

ISBN 978–0–19–965165–8

Printed and bound in Great Britain by
CPI Group (UK) Ltd, Croydon, CR0 4YY

Acknowledgements

It has been great fun to write this book. It has involved me in lots of enjoyable conversations and social interactions with old friends and new acquaintances in both Britain and Germany.

My first and largest debt of gratitude is to the forty-four chefs from both countries who have made time in their extremely busy schedules to allow me to interview them. They have been very open and gracious in their responses, and it has been a great pleasure to get to know them and hear about their 'lives in the kitchen', their joy in their job, but also their concerns about the problems it throws up almost daily. I have tried to present both with understanding and sympathy. Most people are very interested in and love to talk about food and restaurants, and some—by no means regular fine diners—even have offered their company when I wanted 'to do fieldwork' in a particular restaurant. I am grateful also to the individuals who let me interview them on the pleasures of fine-dining, as well as to the two representatives of *Michelin Germany* and *Michelin Britain* who willingly answered all the questions I posed.

I additionally owe thanks to many friends, colleagues, as well as former students who have helped me in many ways. They have provided contacts with interviewees, have let themselves be interviewed, made perceptive comments on chapters of the book, have offered me accommodation in Germany or, simply by their lively interest in my research, have provided me with stimulation and encouragement. I am grateful to Doreen Burgin, Peter Burke, Nicky Hart, Julietta and John Harvey, Nahee Kang, Frens Kröger, Christian Morgner, Stephen Mennell, Maria Lucia Pallares Burke, Sigrid Quack, Lars Repp, Michael von Thadden, Andrew and Man Wing Timming, and Anna Wood.

A few people, however, must be singled out for special thanks. Bill Brogan, the catering manager of St John's College, through his industry knowledge and contacts, has generously helped me in numerous ways all through the project. Mike Lane, Jocelyn Probert, and Kate Wright each have read and helpfully commented on several chapters of the book. In Germany, Gunda von Thadden has loyally collected newspaper cuttings on the topic for several years, given me hospitality, as well as explaining to me some intricacies of German culture. Trudi McMahon also has been a very good friend. She has chauffeured me around the Black Forest area to various restaurants, as well as advising me on some translation problems. Last, though not least, I owe special thanks to my husband David Lane. He has often accompanied me on interview trips across Britain, has read and commented on many of the chapters, but, above all, has sustained me with his encouragement and support throughout the long gestation period of this book. This study has even converted him to fine-dining!

Contents

List of Tables

List of Boxes

The pleasures of the table belong to all times and all ages, to every country and every day; they go hand in hand with all our other pleasures, outlast them, and remain to console us for their loss.

Jean Anthelme Brillat-Savarin, *La Physiologie du Goût*, 1825

Introduction

After decades, if not centuries, of neglect of fine food and high-level restaurants in Britain, a massive explosion of interest in food and dining out has occurred. Starting from the middle of the 1980s, and particularly during the 1990s, an astonishing catching-up has taken place in the gastronomic scene. This has occurred in both the restaurant sector in general, as well as its apex. While there is no consensus on how to define the top of the restaurant scene, the award of Michelin stars may be taken as a shorthand for the attainment of consistent impeccable quality and originality of food served in restaurants. Taking the award of Michelin stars as a measure, between the beginning of the awards in Britain in 1974 and today (2013), a dramatic six-fold increase in stars awarded has taken place.[1] While this achievement still lags behind the advances made in comparable European societies and progress remains geographically uneven, it nevertheless constitutes a remarkable culinary transformation. This work charts the process of transformation and, more comprehensively, examines top restaurants at the current time—their chefs and the food they produce, their customers, and the gastronomic arbiters who judge their standards.

My book thus is concerned with high-end restaurants which, for want of a better word, I refer to as 'fine-dining restaurants'. I am aware that this term is a deeply contentious one, laden with largely pejorative meaning. Journalists in particular love to make fun of 'faine' dining and associate it with a snobbish style, poncy waiters, and over-elaborate food. According to Jonathan Meades, a journalist writing for *The Telegraph*,

> the...world of gastronomy has produced few constructions more likely to promote teeth-gnashing, mockery and despairing contempt than 'fine-dining'.[2]

Although interested in good food, critics like Meades[3] declare that they love 'real and honest' food—whatever that is—implying that food served in high-end restaurants is somehow artificial and dupes the unsuspecting diner. They adopt a sneering tone both towards chefs and people who dine in these restaurants which sometimes smacks of inverted snobbery. Many ordinary people, too, think fine-dining restaurants are formal, fancy, and pretentious and would not think of ever dining there. Even people who value high-quality food and good service and have the income to be able to afford it often believe that such restaurants are too elitist or 'out of their league'.

I view some of the above characterizations as now largely outmoded stereotypes and others, while still retaining a grain of truth, as gross exaggerations, often adopted for the sake of polemics. These caricatures no longer apply to the majority of fine-dining restaurants. These restaurants simply serve fine food which exceeds ordinary everyday food both in its taste, aesthetic appeal, and originality. Yes, this food is more elaborate than so-called 'real' food, involves some 'presentational fuss' and therefore inevitably is more expensive, though, I shall show, not necessarily over-priced. But it is also the result of very skilful and imaginative cooking, and together with attentive service and a pleasing ambience, turns a meal into an inspiring 'special occasion'.

My study is a cross-nationally comparative study of restaurants, their chefs, customers, and gastronomic guides in two countries—Britain and Germany. However, occasional cross-national comparisons with other countries place the two high-end restaurant sectors also in an international context. This enables me to appreciate the distinctiveness of the British fine-dining restaurant industry and the problems and opportunities it faces. Most people still equate fine-dining with France, yet a comparison of the British with the German Michelin-starred restaurant sector, for several reasons, makes more sense. Neither society has an indigenous *haute cuisine* and both have come relatively late to fine-dining, as defined by the *Michelin Guide*. Equally important, their top-level restaurant sectors are more nearly comparable in size in that both are appreciably smaller than the French sector. At the same time, the two countries have quite different social institutions and a divergent business ethos which, despite many similarities between the two fine-dining sectors, explain some of the striking differences between them. One of these is the fact that Germany proportionally has more starred restaurants, as well as more restaurants with two and three stars. This poses a research puzzle to be solved in this book.

Fine-dining restaurants revolve around highly skilled and often inspired chefs. Top-level chefs now are familiar to most of us from the many television programmes on food and cooking, but this familiarity remains shallow. Very few people really know what sort of individuals reach the top of the restaurant hierarchy, what drives them to achieve the consistently high standards demanded by restaurant guides and increasingly also their customers, and what psychological and financial pressures they face in their working lives. Yet top chefs have become important figures in the contemporary cultural landscape who have shaped our aesthetic sensibility and taste in food far beyond the confines of fine-dining restaurants. Without the resurgence of fine-dining restaurants and their chefs, we would not have experienced the impressive raising of standards and aspiration around food which go well beyond the confines of the top restaurants. They also have influenced, in recent decades, many lower-level restaurants, food retailing, and much ordinary household food preparation and consumption.

The fine-dining restaurant is not a restaurant one would visit every day or even frequently, and the comparatively high prices for food and wine inevitably surround it with an aura of elitism. However, the alleged snobbish atmosphere and high formality is long gone in the majority of these restaurants, particularly at the one- and two-star levels. Admittedly, enjoying a meal there still presupposes that the diner knows and appreciates good food and is open to surprising and creative interpretations of familiar ingredients. In other words, a fine-dining restaurant invites diners who have cultivated their (gustatory) taste and/or are open to and even looking for its further refinement.

Why do fine-dining restaurants and their chefs evoke such controversy and incite sometimes even quite vitriolic comments? Talking about fine-dining means talking about taste. It involves not simply individual gustatory taste about which, famously, it is not worth having a dispute. More importantly, it concerns taste as a thoroughly social phenomenon which is a much more complex, multi-layered notion. Such taste implies discrimination between types of food, attributes or impugns quality, and involves the rendering of value judgements. These judgements simultaneously situate the person making them in social space. Judgements of taste define social identity. Hence disputes around this notion of taste involve intense cultural conflict about the superiority of one judgement of taste over another and efforts to present one notion of taste as legitimate, while denigrating another. Such judgements of taste concerning fine-dining appear to be a lot more adversarial than judgements attributing high value to a theatre performance or a particular form of art. This is because exquisite food is not seen as a cultural good by many such judges. Consequently, interest in fine food by others, and in the dining experience around it, is denigrated as self-indulgent and elitist conspicuous consumption. In contrast, such comments are rarely made about people cultivating discernment vis-à-vis equally expensive and therefore elitist cultural engagements, such as interest in theatre and opera.

How then are tastes in the field of fine-dining, as discriminating judgements of quality, established? I shall argue in this book that, while top chefs and, to a much lesser extent, knowledgeable diners are to some extent involved in the process of taste making, it is mainly gastronomic guides which shape our notion of what is legitimate taste. While many journalist food critics are deeply devoted to the notion of 'real and honest' food, the gastronomic guides are more concerned with 'fine-dining'. They try to shape our notions of what should be regarded as high-quality and creative food. (This is one of the many reasons why chefs, who pay much more attention to gastronomic guides than to newspaper critics, are sometimes treated with a sneering condescension by the latter.) Among such guides, the *Michelin Guide* (also referred to as the *Red Guide*, because its inspectors' judgements of taste have become highly influential), is (rightly) surrounded with a degree of controversy. The import of the *Red Guide* from France further fuels its vehement rejection in some quarters. Hence the notion of a Michelin-starred restaurant, combined with the notion of fine-dining, causes almost apoplectic rage among some commentators. To quote again from an article by Jonathan Meades:

> One construction which outdoes even 'fine-dining' in its capacity to make the sentient contort themselves wincing is 'Michelin-starred fine-dining'.

When it comes to the working of gastronomic guides which place restaurants and their chefs at the pinnacle of the restaurant hierarchy, most diners and even some chefs remain unaware of the symbolic and material power they possess. The fine-dining restaurants which form the focus of my study in this book are those which have been awarded one or more Michelin stars. Why then, in the face of the many criticisms levelled against the *Michelin Guide* have I selected restaurants and their chefs on this basis? Michelin status initially was simply a sampling device which enables me to make comparisons of like with like, both within and between countries, of restaurants and chefs which, in some essential respects, are legitimate units of comparison. However, I soon realized that, as highly influential arbiters of taste, the *Michelin Guide* and a few other comparable gastronomic guides had to become objects of critical study themselves. Public and even journalistic knowledge of them is even more patchy than it is about fine-dining chefs and their restaurants. Questions such as how gastronomic critics become arbiters of taste, what is the substance of this taste, and what beneficial and negative consequences flow from their judgements of taste therefore also are confronted in this book.

My book aims to dispel some of the prejudices and misconceptions that surround fine-dining restaurants and, in the process, offer a deeper and more rounded understanding of what they represent. In doing so, I am neither just introducing a high-profile occupational group nor a particular type of small business enterprise—although both of these are important—but also an important cultural enterprise which endows food with symbolic value and fosters a particular style of service and type of sociability and may provide customers with a memorable experience.

This memorable experience, however, is produced by a business which, in most of its organizational features, harks back to an earlier stage of social and economic development. High-end restaurants are largely small, owner-managed organizations, devoted to handicraft or artisan production on a small scale. Furthermore, the work organization of high-end kitchens, driven by a variety of often conflicting demands, does not exactly provide a model work experience or environment. A study of top restaurants must concern itself with the many paradoxes which surround those who work in them. Chef proprietors/patrons are driven both by aesthetic passion and have to balance the books (and making a reasonable profit is a continuous struggle). Pecuniary reward for both employees and proprietors or employed head chefs is only modest. Chefs achieve a high symbolic reward but are also exposed to relentless psychological and financial pressure, as well as to a very taxing working environment and long working hours. They simultaneously have to work in an extremely disciplined and almost military manner and be highly creative and even innovative. Front-of-house service staff have to possess a whole range of personal and social virtues. They may be the last 'deferential workers' we encounter in the service sector, yet their earnings and career chances remain far below those possessed by the customers they serve.

When we turn to diners, ambiguities and paradoxes also abound. Diners' wants and expectations are not always consistent—they demand fresh local ingredients, but also crave novelty and exoticism. At the same time as a more highly educated and prosperous population has become more open to the delight and pleasure derived from meals utilizing high-quality ingredients, prepared to perfection and presented with style, a new social ethos has also gained ground. This democratic ethos rejects exclusivity and values a relaxed and more inclusive style of dining. Additionally, many of these diners increasingly refuse to equate good food only with French *haute cuisine* and instead welcome a greater diversity of culinary styles and of levels of refinement. This study therefore explores how change in social mores and habits impacts on fine-dining restaurants and how both chef patrons and Michelin inspectors have had to adapt to diners' widening social and geographical horizons and greater claim to expert culinary knowledge.

I have written this book as a sociologist but have tried to transcend a narrow academic focus. I would like the book to be accessible to all those who have an interest in good restaurants and fine-dining and who would like to learn more about the chef patrons at the centre of them. Chefs are portrayed as part of a complex network, in their relationships with their employees—both in the kitchen and front-of-house, their customers, gastronomic critics, suppliers of food, and even their financiers. I also discuss the historical emergence of high-end restaurants, as well as the current processes of their transformation.

My understanding of fine-dining restaurants and their chefs is based on information I have collected in a series of personal, in-depth interviews in Britain and Germany. Interviews were of about ninety minutes' duration and took place between 2010 and 2012. The most important are twenty interviews in each country with Michelin-starred chefs themselves. These chefs are the chef patrons of, or are employed in a diverse range of starred restaurants, ranging from very small husband-and-wife operations to very large, highly professionalized ones, usually forming part of top hotels. The restaurants are situated in a range of geographical locations, taking in both small and relatively remote villages, as well as large towns, and I have chosen restaurants in all three star categories. Needless to say, I had to sample the food they produce, in at least some of the forty restaurants, and I also visited some of the kitchens. Chefs generously took time out from their hectic schedules and talked to me in a very open and often animated manner. These forty interviews with current *chefs de cuisine* were supplemented by four interviews with former Michelin chefs, among them one of the most important former British three-star chefs—Albert Roux. My interview schedule, containing the many questions I asked chefs, may be found in an appendix of this book. (The interviews of German chefs and diners were conducted in German.) I additionally constructed a database on *all* two- and three-star chefs in the two countries during the 2010–12 period. This is based on a diverse set of secondary sources, such as chefs' books, newspaper articles, restaurant websites, and many other Internet sources.

My interviews with chefs were complemented by thirty-two interviews with restaurant diners, as well as by one interview each with *Michelin Great Britain* and *Michelin Germany*. I make extensive use of the interview material by illustrating topics and sometimes substantiating claims. This greatly enlivens the book by conveying chefs' own perceptions of the many aspects of their activity. Any gaps in my knowledge remaining after the completion of these seventy-eight interviews were filled by a systematic analysis of information contained in the *Michelin Guides* for various years, as well as by study of a large range of secondary sources acknowledged in the endnotes to each chapter. All these sources of information combined, I claim, give me an unprecedented insight into what goes on in Michelin-starred restaurants—what makes their chefs tick, intrigues their critics, and beguiles or annoys their customers.

The many paradoxes which surround the work of fine-dining restaurants are viewed through the theoretical lens of the work of two French sociologists, namely Luc Boltanski and Laurent Thévenot on *Orders of Worth*.[4] Relationships between people at work and coordination of their actions, Boltanski and Thévenot argue, are oriented towards modes of evaluation or normative principles which define what is held to be of value or what counts. These, together with the human qualifications and the nature of the fundamental relationship entailed, are termed 'orders of worth'. They define what is appropriate and fair behaviour in a given situation: that is, they each provide a distinctive moral philosophy which shapes mutual expectations about the right conduct.[5] The authors distinguish between six discrete orders of worth that are applied and often challenged and tested in social interaction: the inspired; domestic; market; industrial; civic; and that of opinion. Table I.1 sets out the contending principles of evaluation used to assess a person's order of worth.

The guiding principles and human qualifications of each order of worth are incompatible with those of the others. Such conceptions of what has value, the authors argue, are made evident mainly when one party to the relationship feels something is going wrong and urges the other to justify the stance he or she has adopted by making explicit the mode of evaluation which has informed their behaviour.

The work of Boltanski and Thévenot is strongly motivated by the perceived conflict between the presence in an interaction of elements from different and incompatible orders of worth. The American sociologist David Stark, in contrast, is intent on showing the productive aspects of such tensions—what he calls a 'resourceful dissonance'[6]—and the way this inspires entrepreneurship and innovation in business organizations. In contrast to both sets of authors, I try to show that, depending on the circumstances, the presence of a multiplicity of orders of worth may generate either conflict or, *more often*, accommodation and relatively stable compromises. While the work of Boltanski and Thévenot represents a culturalist approach to business organizations and the work relations within them, my book also connects these value orientations with repertoires of action and the ensuing logics which structure restaurants as organizational entities.

The explanatory value of these initially somewhat abstract concepts becomes evident when they are applied to various types of interactions

Table I.1. Orders of worth

	Inspired	Domestic	Civic	Opinion	Market	Industrial
Mode of evaluation	Creativeness	Esteem	Collective interest	Renown	Price	Efficiency
Format of information	Emotional	Oral, exemplary	Formal	Semiotic	Monetary	Measurable
Elementary relation	Passion	Trust	Solidarity	Recognition	Profit	Functional link
Human qualification	Creativity, ingenuity	Authority	Equality	Celebrity	Competitiveness	Competency, expertise

Note: The table has been adapted from Boltanski and Thévenot 1999: 368.

7

in fine-dining restaurants. This type of restaurant is oriented towards a strange mixture of modes of evaluations or guiding principles and displays a diversity of organizing logics. On the one side, it is oriented towards a hierarchical form of craft organization (overlapping with the 'domestic order of worth'), dating back to its origins in early nineteenth-century France. This organization additionally has incorporated some modern industrial principles which may stand in contradiction to those of the 'craft' type. On the other side, top-level restaurants are part of the contemporary cultural economy generating products for an affluent society. In this type of enterprise, the aesthetic and inspired value of the product—the restaurant meal and service—are as prominent as the material. Producer creativeness is a very important, if not decisive factor of production and of the whole business logic. At the same time, the restaurant is a market-oriented business, and a profit imperative informs activities side by side with a creative impulse. My book thus explores how chef patrons manage to juggle the associated orders of worth and the performance requirements they entail.

My comparisons between the British and the German fine-dining industry and my explanations of differences encountered are loosely guided by another theoretical approach—the 'varieties of capitalism' thesis.[7] This approach views business organizations—in this case fine-dining restaurants—as operating within national institutional frameworks which partially condition their comparative economic advantage. Institutions have a constraining but not a determining influence on organizational actors such as chefs. Actors may circumvent their constraining effects and engage in organizational innovation, though usually at an extra cost. I have placed considerable emphasis on one institutional complex—the system of vocational education and training. I additionally explore the way in which divergent national financial and political traditions shape the organization of fine-dining.

The book will take you behind the scenes of Michelin-starred restaurants. It will show you how the beautiful and tasty composition on the plate in front of you has emerged out of a complex mix of ambition, anxiety, and creative joy, but also from hard graft, precise and disciplined teamwork between kitchen and restaurant brigades, and sober financial calculation. In sum, by exploring the many paradoxes and tensions outlined above and by throwing light on the processes and people that make up the fine-dining restaurant industry, this book illuminates an important area of our contemporary cultural economy. It shows that restaurant cooking and dining are highly social and cultural activities and provides a more rounded knowledge and understanding of one aspect of contemporary cultural life and of society.

Notes

1. For details, see Chapter 2.
2. J. Meades, 'Blinded by the Michelin Stars in their Eyes', *The Telegraph* (21 February 2012). <http://www.telegraph.co.uk/foodanddrink/9096154/Blinded-by-the-Michelin-stars-in-their-eyes.html>.
3. Meades 2012.
4. L. Boltanski and L. Thévenot, 'The Sociology of Critical Capacity', *European Journal of Social Theory* 2.3 (1999): 359–77; L. Boltanski and L. Thévenot, *On Justification: Economies of Worth* (Princeton: Princeton University Press, 2006) (translation from the French of *De la Justification: Les Economies de la Grandeur*).
5. P. Du Gay and G. Morgan, G. 2012, 'Understanding Capitalisms: Crises, Legitimacy, and Change through the Prism of *The New Spirit of Capitalism*', in P. du Gay and G. Morgan (eds.), *New Spirits of Capitalism? Crisis, Justifications, and Dynamics* (Oxford: Oxford University Press, 2012), 1–40.
6. D. Stark, 'Heterarchy: The Organization of Dissonance', in D. Stark (ed.), *The Sense of Dissonance* (Princeton: Princeton University Press, 2009), 1–34.
7. P. Hall and D. Soskice, 'An Introduction to Varieties of Capitalism', in P. Hall and D. Soskice (eds.), *Varieties of Capitalism: The Institutional Foundations of Comparative Advantage* (Oxford: Oxford University Press, 2001), 1–68.

1

The Fine-Dining Restaurant Industry in Historical Perspective

The historical comparison of British and German Michelin-starred restaurants holds particular interest because it involves two countries *without* an indigenous historical tradition of *haute cuisine* but where a significant sector of fine-dining restaurants nevertheless has developed from the late 1960s onwards. I try to solve the puzzle of why, despite very unpromising culinary traditions, a significant high-end restaurant sector has nevertheless developed in both societies.

Despite basic similarities in their historical development, the British fine-dining sector fares less well than the German in both the overall number of starred restaurants and in the number of multiple-starred establishments. Success in this business is presumed to be due largely to the personal qualities of owners and chefs—particularly the rather elusive qualities of creativity and innovativeness. However, I shall suggest that personal performance is supported and sustained to varying degrees by the two societies' culinary traditions and by their social institutional environments.

This chapter covers four related topics. The first is an examination of the historical antecedents of present-day Michelin-starred restaurants. This requires familiarization with the French traditions of classical and *nouvelle cuisine* on which both British and German high-end restaurants have been heavily dependent. In the second part of the chapter, I trace the emergence, in each country, of more home-grown fine-dining restaurants during the period of 1967 to 1990. In the concluding section, I place my findings in a wider international context by making comparisons with both other European high-end restaurants and with American and Japanese ones.

Social and Cultural Histories of Fine-Dining in the Nineteenth and Early Twentieth Centuries

The rise and development of fine-dining restaurants in Britain and Germany has to be seen against the background of the long cultural tradition of fine-dining in France. French *haute cuisine* restaurants and chefs have exercised a strong and pervasive influence on the emergence and the character of *haute cuisine* restaurants and professional chefs in other developed societies. Whereas in Europe the French influence dominated aristocratic dining from the mid-nineteenth century, in the USA it became established at the end of that century.

The Rise and Development of the Fine-Dining Restaurant in France

Britain and Germany historically both had their own indigenous food ways and regional cuisines but *haute cuisine* in fine-dining restaurants has long been the monopoly of France. All aspects of British and German fine-dining restaurants—the choice and preparation of the dishes, the training of chefs and the organization of both the kitchen and front-of-house, as well as the ambience and social ethos of restaurants—have been and continue to be strongly shaped by the French historical precedent.

In French society, fine-dining is accorded a high value and has been an integral part of culture and national identity for several centuries. The sociologist Stephen Mennell has connected this phenomenon with the special character of French court society during Louis XIV's *Grand Siècle*, particularly its strong focus on the royal court in Paris.[1] The high degree of concentration of courtiers in the capital, rather than in the shires or regional dukedoms, induced a highly competitive striving for status. This expressed itself in conspicuous refinement in manners, clothing, and entertaining. In this context, a refined style of cooking and serving food became one of the media to signal status and promote advancement at court. This model of gastronomy entailed an early rise of a corps of highly trained chefs who cooked both at court and in the various aristocratic households and provided the material basis for the evolution of an *haute* or *grande cuisine.* Mennell dates the beginning of French leadership in the field to 1651, the year when La Varenne—a cook in a noble household—published his book, *Le Cuisinier François.*[2]

Cooking and dining in public restaurants, however, marked a radical change in organization and social interaction which arose only from around the last quarter of the eighteenth century. The word 'restaurant' is derived from the French word '*restaurer*'—to restore/revive—with a 'restaurant' being a health-restoring broth, served in a variety of environments, initially not serving food. Over time, however, the restaurant became the place where you were served the broth and also some food. It became distinguished from other, older places of (mostly collective) food consumption, such as *traiteurs* (retail caterers) in France and cook shops, inns, and taverns in Britain, by a number of quite radical innovations. The restaurant, as it first appeared in Paris, came to be regarded as a well-appointed place where small dining parties sat around individual tables, chose their food and drink from menus according to purchasing power and culinary inclination, and were able to expect personal and attentive service. Restaurants thus afforded the diner individual privacy and choice.

The first restaurant was opened in Paris in 1765 when a baker first served restorative drinks with food.[3] When Beauvilliers opened his restaurant in 1780 he named it *La Grande Taverne de Londres*, indicating the influence English taverns had at this time in France.[4] Further restaurants opened in the 1770s and 1780s—mainly in the Paris area around the *Grand Palais*—under chef proprietors such as Robert, the brothers Véry, and Les Trois Frères Provencaux.[5] However, the transformation from cooking fine food in aristocratic households to its public provision in restaurants gained pace only after the French Revolution in 1789. The dissolution of the *ancien régime*, of court society and its status competition also swept away luxurious and refined aristocratic household entertainment, thus leaving many highly accomplished chefs without employment. For chefs, the move from cooking in noble households to restaurant cooking was aided by two other contemporaneous developments: the loosening of the guild system and the abolition, by a royal edict of 1776, of the monopoly on public food provision by *traiteurs*,[6] as well as by the rise of an *haute bourgeoisie*, particularly in Paris, interested in and able to afford eating out. The significant expansion of restaurants is widely ascribed to the period after the Revolution, particularly to the Napoleonic and Restoration periods at the beginning of the nineteenth century, when their number is said to have grown exponentially.[7] They became distinguished by their refined food, together with the provision of elaborate service and a luxurious environment, as well as the requirement that diners observe a commensurate dining etiquette and decorum. Last but not least, fine-dining as a significant symbolic marker of high social status was reaffirmed.

Haute cuisine, consisting of refined, labour-intensive and therefore expensive dishes gradually became institutionalized. This development was furthered by the systematic provision of time-serving apprenticeship training for aspiring cooks, spent under the strict supervision of master chefs. As Mennell observes,[8] the establishment and increasing cohesion of a professional elite of cooks, sharing a common repertoire of methods and even recipes, goes a long way towards explaining the early spread of *haute cuisine* in France, though at first mainly in Paris. Apprenticeship training also for allied trades, such as butchers and patissiers greatly strengthened the supply side for top restaurants. The rise of restaurants was also accompanied by the rise of the 'bourgeois gastronome, the expert on and publicist of the art of eating'.[9]

Freed from their dependence on aristocratic households, master chefs gained the chance to become independent restaurant proprietors although many at first remained employed by restaurateurs. In the top ranks, chefs managed to transform their social status from unknown domestic servants into a professionalized elite of chefs. They turned out culinary master works, admired around the western world. Public fine-dining became a central part of first French metropolitan and gradually also provincial life.

This process of institutionalization was greatly advanced by the emergence of a number of great chefs and food writers who systematized and codified culinary knowledge and techniques, such as Grimod de la Reynière (1758–1838), Carême (1784–1833), Brillat-Savarin (1755–1826) and Escoffier (1847–1935), who addressed both each other and the educated public. While Grimod de la Reynière addressed a gradually evolving fine-dining public, the essays of Brillat-Savarin raised more weighty issues around taste, aesthetics, and social mores. The name of Carême, in particular, became closely associated with the transformation of the aristocratic cuisine of the *ancien régime* into the cuisine of the nineteenth-century bourgeoisie. He purged the aristocratic cuisine of some of its extravagance and rationalized the process of culinary production.[10] In his *Philosophical History of Cuisine* (1833), he was the first to create a vision of *grande cuisine* as both art and science.[11] In the late nineteenth and early twentieth centuries, Escoffier initiated the renewal of French cuisine. He also was the first chef to develop an international career and his example intensified the export of French cuisine to Europe by emigrant professional chefs. According to Mennell,[12] his *Guide Culinaire*, first published in 1903, 'acquired a biblical or paradigmatic status among chefs'. It essentially reflected the cooking of the new *grands hôtels*, as well as evolving a model of their kitchens' organization with a lasting impact on all professional kitchens. His writing formed the body of what became known as French 'classical cuisine' which even today remains a central text in the training of professional cooks.

The pervasive recognition and appreciation of fine food and good cooking among the upper-classes—the cultivation of good taste in its literal sense— also reflected and further enhanced the centrality of good food and elaborate cooking in relatively ordinary bourgeois households and in the food markets and shops catering for them. It thereby created knowledgeable and discerning customers for the *grands restaurants* and ensured the centrality of food in French culture in general. The introduction of the *Michelin Guide* in the early twentieth century, following the rise of the automobile, became the logical culmination of this pervasive love of and respect for *haute cuisine* and fine-dining.

The luxurious Paris *grands restaurants*, publicized by culinary magazines, food writers, and critics, attracted not only French bourgeois diners but also upper-class tourists from all over Europe and the USA. Visiting France, from the nineteenth century onwards, became synonymous with indulging in fine-dining, along with the other luxury products in which France came to specialize. Brillat-Savarin,[13] while rejoicing about the revenue it brought to the French economy, comments on this influx in a satirical vein: 'When the Britons, the Germans, the Teutons, the Cimmerians, and the Scythians poured into France, they brought with them a rare voracity and stomachs of uncommon capacity.'

French high-level chefs had become a valued commodity, and, from the early nineteenth century, were hired by rich noble households and finance houses all over Europe,[14] including Britain and Germany. But it took some further decades—from the middle of the nineteenth century onwards (during the Directory and the Empire)—until French chefs came to head the fine-dining restaurants of the new luxury hotels, and to a much lesser degree, to open their own restaurants, in the metropolises of Britain, Germany, and the USA. In Britain (mostly in London), by 1890, there were said to be around five thousand French chefs cooking in elite households, clubs, hotels, and restaurants.[15] This early export of French culinary culture and chefs gradually— with interruptions during times of war and the Great Depression—became a stream of ideas, techniques, organizational forms, and people, indelibly shaping the fine-dining industry in receiving countries up to the present day. In the words of one French chef, writing in the *The Epicure* in 1903: 'So-called German [and] English cookery was not cookery at all. There only existed one "cuisine"—*la cuisine*—invented by France.'[16]

French cuisine not only influenced most European countries but also the USA (where the large luxury hotels opened even earlier than in Europe), and, a little later, it also infiltrated other continents.

Classical cuisine reigned supreme in France until the late 1960s/early 1970s. At that time it was challenged by culinary and organizational innovations, first introduced by some of France's top chefs—Paul Bocuse, Michel Guérard, the Troisgros brothers, and Alain Chapel. Arising during a time of general social and political change, the challenge was taken up by the journalists Gault and Millau who theorized and propagandized the new approach to *haute cuisine* under the label of *nouvelle cuisine*. Together, the chefs and their journalistic propagandists created a new culinary rhetoric, rules of cooking, archetypical ingredients, role of the chef, and organization of the menu.[17] The dishes became lighter, and fruits, vegetables, and herbs were used more prominently; the original taste of the basic ingredient—the fish or meat—became preserved and even enhanced, rather than being masked by sauces. The rebel chefs introduced more adventurous contrasts in ingredients (e.g. mixing meat with fish), as well as importing exotic foodstuffs, to set surprising and intriguing accents and to design aesthetically pleasing compositions. Shorter menus, requiring lower stores, introduced greater economy.[18]

Service through the plate, as opposed to the earlier presentation of food in serving dishes on the table, also upgraded the role of chefs vis-à-vis waiters. The play with colours and contrasting textures afforded *nouvelle cuisine* chefs the opportunity to 'paint pictures on the plate' and to appeal to all five senses. This feature, together with the other changes, provided chefs with a broader scope for invention and creativity. Although the notion of the chef as artist had already been asserted by Carême, this claim received further impetus and support at this time. By turning chefs from interpreters of classic texts into inventors and creators, the *nouvelle cuisine* movement enhanced their autonomy and status. It ushered in the chef patron and thereby paved the way for the later emergence of celebrity chefs.

Nouvelle cuisine did not totally supersede classical French cuisine. Instead, an erosion of the boundaries of the two types and a creative recombination of elements of the old with the new culinary style occurred.[19] It not only gained relatively quick and enthusiastic acceptance in France[20] but also created waves of excitement in other European countries. In both Britain and Germany, it eventually became an essential part of the revival of *haute cuisine*, initiating the growth of an indigenous and more widely embraced fine-dining restaurant sector.

During the 1980s and 1990s, the term *nouvelle cuisine* fell into disrepute. Over time, it had become interpreted and reinterpreted in such a way to trivialize its essence. In the words of chef Raymond Blanc:

> Nouvelle cuisine began as a revolution filled with promise but turned into a nightmare. The philosophy was misinterpreted. The design element seemed to power everything. Insane combinations were presented on plates. It would become 'a freak show'.[21]

Or, as one British chef tells me: 'it came to mean "French cuisine with a slice of Kiwi on top" and it became a disadvantage to call yourself an adherent of nouvelle cuisine'.

Additionally, the public came to perceive *nouvelle cuisine* as a tiny amount of food on very large plates. The term *nouvelle cuisine* therefore is now rarely used by chefs. However, its principles and practices, as outlined above, have endured to the present day, even if many younger chefs no longer are aware of the culinary origins of their practices. As a German chef tells me: 'One falls back on *nouvelle cuisine* without being conscious of doing so.'

More recently, French *haute cuisine*, as celebrated by the *Michelin Guide*, has again been challenged both from within and without France. Cammas and Rubin were significant native food critics. In 2000, they launched a new guide, the *Fooding* guide, which criticizes both the food itself and what they perceive to be the conservative cultural stance behind it. What is more, the new guide sought to save French cuisine from terminal decline by advocating a new approach which extolled informality, novelty, and above all fun. Their critique was taken note of by the daily French newspaper *Le Figaro* which claimed that French food was now divided into two families, each with its own public and cultural identity:

> On the one side, *Michelin*, with its century of cultural expertise; on the other the *Fooding* guide, born ten years ago in an attempt to break the codes and finally offer real change to a gastronomy that its authors judge to be outdated.[22]

As American food writer Adam Gopnik points out, Cammas and Rubin's objectives are too diverse and insufficiently clearly defined to usher in the new epoch of French cuisine they advocate. Nevertheless, the critique has a serious core which has found many echoes outside France. It has removed the gloss of French *haute cuisine* though has not finally undermined the 'model' function it still enjoys among many British and German chefs.

The Historical Development of Fine-Dining Restaurants in Britain and Germany, 1850–1950

Public places of various kinds for food consumption existed in both societies from at least the Middle Ages, and in the case of London taverns—the nearest equivalent to a restaurant—well preceded the rise of restaurants in France. However, restaurants, as we now know them, emerged only relatively recently (i.e. from the mid-nineteenth century onwards).[23] They were the product of a market society and of increased geographical and social mobility. The emergence of fine-dining restaurants crucially depended also on the existence of a strong culinary tradition, a culture of enjoying good food and cooking, and the existence of a body of professional cooks. For most of these cultural and material stimuli, as pointed out above, both countries had to rely on an input from France.

From around the 1850s onwards, high-level restaurants became a feature of urban life in the larger cities of Western Europe other than those of France.[24] In Britain, restaurants emerged from the 1860s onward,[25] to become widely diffused and very popular with the upper- and upper middle-classes at the turn of the nineteenth century. Germany followed suit during the last decades of the nineteenth century, and the growth of restaurants accelerated from the 1890s until the First World War—a relatively peaceful and affluent period for the expanding German middle-classes.[26]

The Development of Fine-Dining Restaurants in Britain

Up to the end of the eighteenth century, Britain had its own culinary traditions, based on the farmhouse cooking cultivated by prosperous farmers and adopted also by the gentry. There was a rich diversity of ingredients and dishes in both farmhouses and, to a lesser degree, bourgeois homes.[27] Indeed, up to then visitors to Britain often remarked on the superior quality of its ingredients, particularly its meat. The British, too, prided themselves on 'O the roast beef of Old England'. Middle and upper middle-class country women and some of the lower gentry were in charge of their own domestic arrangements and also were behind most of the cookery books written in this period.[28] This cooking favoured good basic ingredients and plain, rather than refined preparation of food, but nevertheless is said to have been more varied and interesting than it became in later centuries. However, despite this culinary tradition, its great wealth, and early cosmopolitanism, Britain did not develop an indigenous *haute cuisine*. To the contrary, the quality of its restaurants and hotels has periodically attracted scathing comments which have only abated in recent decades.

The nineteenth century in particular saw a radical decline in culinary standards, particularly in the large industrial towns and in London. The social historian Roy Strong[29] suggests: 'By 1900 the English had totally forgotten that they had ever had a cooking tradition, accepting that when it came to the culinary arts, they were inferior.' A number of reasons both for the initial decline and subsequent further degeneration—all implicating class—have been advanced in the literature. These may be considered complementary, rather than alternative explanations.

The first explanation is favoured by the sociologist Mennell who points at the greater decentralization of upper-class power in Britain, as compared with France. The consequent absence of a developed court society, resorting to conspicuous consumption to signal status to compensate for lack of real power, meant that an aristocracy-supported *haute cuisine* did not develop. Court circles consequently shaped the development of cuisine to a much lesser degree than was the case in France.[30] Where the most wealthy aristocratic households did aspire to fine-dining, they employed immigrant French chefs.[31] By 1850, the hegemony of French chefs over both royal and upper-class private dining was complete.[32] French influence also extended over some of the upper-class private members' clubs. The fashion for French food remained confined to this small upper circle of English society. The hegemony of French cuisine and gastronomy over the highest levels of society, for Mennell, meant that cookery in England became 'decapitated'.[33] This process was set to negatively also affect other classes and the nature of public dining, as it eventually evolved.

A second explanation suggests that an indigenous culinary tradition, by the beginning of the nineteenth century, had become coarsened and eventually undermined by land enclosure and the ensuing rapid urbanization, as well as by industrialization. Enclosure and the abrupt expulsion of village people from the land disrupted the transfer of culinary lore and practices between generations and came 'to erase the English rural *cuisine*'.[34] It is the disappearance of a peasantry and the early and quick rise of a working-class which distinguishes Britain from continental societies, such as France and Germany and, in the process, largely undermined its culinary traditions.[35] Rapid urbanization and industrialization meant the end of self-sufficiency and the development of a market society. It favoured the emergence of mechanized and standardized food production and came to affect British food and food culture in a very negative manner. In the words of food writer Clarissa Dickson Wright: 'The Industrial Revolution...broke the close ties between growing, cooking and eating—and generations have grown up who either don't want to cook or don't know how to, or both.'[36]

A third explanation of the decline during the nineteenth century implicates the relatively large urban bourgeoisie. It is said to have played a significant role in the decline of culinary traditions and the quality of food provision. Although the bourgeoisie, in its home cooking, held fast to English food traditions much longer than the aristocracy and *haute bourgeoisie*, it was unable to provide leadership in either preserving the eighteenth-century farmhouse tradition or in developing a refined urban cuisine. The vast majority of upper and lower middle-class households practised a debased version of the native tradition. Women were totally reliant on domestic employees of working-class or rural origin whose own culinary tradition and skills had become impoverished by enclosure and industrialization.[37] The bourgeoisie therefore failed to develop a distinctive bourgeois cuisine in the home. Cookbooks of the time, catering for this expanding class 'reveal palates which were not only unsophisticated but ignorant'.[38] Mrs Beeton's cookery books are viewed as both reflecting and reinforcing the impoverished food tradition of Victorian society. However, up to 1880, cookbooks always recommended English dishes,[39] and the cooking of the middle-classes was hardly influenced by the French paradigm. The average middle-class diet remained 'plain roast and boiled'. While plenty of academic sources thus emphasize deficiencies of bourgeois household cooking during the nineteenth century as one of the reasons for an absence of an indigenous refined cuisine in households and restaurants, a few authors talk about the good food enjoyed in some bourgeois households, such as that of Charles Dickens, for example.[40]

Food consumption both at home and in restaurants was negatively affected also by the early industrialization of agriculture and commercial food provision. Early concentration of agriculture and the ensuing standardization of animal breeds had deleterious effects on the supply of produce, as did the rise, during Victorian times, of large food manufacturing firms. The bulk production of more standardized food, together with a move to national rather than regional distribution, negatively affected standards and taste. Moreover, the national homogeneity of food supply came to undermine the preservation of regional specialities and cooking. Regional cuisines, said to have been pronounced until the end of the eighteenth century, became seriously impaired during the last quarter of the nineteenth century. The regionalism of the British diet began to decline.[41]

A much earlier development with a negative impact on food production was the withering away of the guild system during the seventeenth century— a consequence of Britain's early political and economic liberalization. This compromised and eventually eliminated the apprenticeship training systems of crafts, such as cooks, patissiers, bakers, and butchers whose members previously had upheld quality standards in food production. This, in subsequent centuries, was to exercise a fundamental negative influence on the supply side—that is of well-trained cooks and supporting food-producing artisans.

The loss of an appreciation for good and varied food which had occurred during the nineteenth century in most British homes at all but the highest levels necessarily came to influence the cuisine in restaurants when they came to be developed during the second half of that century. It is not known when the term 'restaurant' first received currency in Britain. It was from the 1860s onwards, that French and other continental cuisines became available in the luxury hotels and in a small number of foreign-owned restaurants in London—the latter mainly in the areas of Soho, the Strand, and Regent's Street. For restaurants in luxury hotels, 'Cesar Ritz and Auguste Escoffier stood behind the eating-out boom in Victorian and Edwardian London'[42] that developed in the closing decades of the nineteenth century. In addition to hotel and independent French restaurants, there also were a number of Italian ones. These were largely connected with the early immigration from the Emilia Romagna area of Italy. (Later Italian immigrants came more from southern Italy.) But, from this time up to the present time, Italian restaurants were rarely found at the top level of the restaurant industry. Instead, they 'mopped up more popular types of catering'.[43] The best-known London restaurants at this time were the *Café Royal*, *Romano's*, the *Criterion*, *Kettner's*, and *Frascati*. They became fashionable London meeting points for men and women of the affluent classes. However, there also existed at this time three restaurants with English menus, namely *Rules*, *Simpson's*, and *Scott's*.[44] They have remained popular among those in search of traditional English food or, at *Scott's*, of seafood and oysters, and *Simpson's* was among the first to earn a Michelin star in 1974.

By 1880, large capital was beginning to be attracted to the hotel industry, with, amongst others, the establishment of the Savoy (1889), Claridge's (rebuilt in 1897), and the Ritz (1905). The hotel restaurants mainly had French chefs—Escoffier cooked at the Ritz—and were widely held to offer the best food in London. The other famous names of chefs connected with the wider diffusion of French cuisine were Alexis Soyer (1809–58) and British-born but French-trained Charles Francatelli (1805–76).

According to Burnett,[45] late Victorian and early Edwardian England was a golden age for the wealthy gourmet. Driver takes a dimmer view of this development when he says: 'The British middle and upper classes of the late nineteenth century were left dependent on foreign craftsmen and entrepreneurs for restaurants and hotels, that is for the whole public dimension of eating and entertaining.'[46] These good times came to an end with the outbreak of the First World War. Rationing from 1917 greatly reduced what food was available to both households and restaurants. Nevertheless, the food situation remained better than on the Continent.[47]

Neither were the early twenties a good time for the high end of the hospitality industry. Yet by the end of the twenties, it experienced a revival and even a considerable expansion which lasted right up to the beginning of the Second World War. However, the reliance on French chefs and restaurateurs, as well as on some Italians, continued in the same way as in the nineteenth century. Among the grand new hotels built from 1927 onwards, were the Mayfair, the Park Lane Hotel, and the Dorchester. Among the notable new restaurants were *Quaglino's*, *The Ivy*, *Quo Vadis* (still in Soho today), *Boulestin's*, and *Prunier's*. *The Ivy* was founded in 1917 by two Italians, one of them being Mario Gelati, a former head waiter at *Romano's*, but at this time it served mainly French food. The two French restaurants, *Boulestin's* and *Madame Prunier's*, both owner-managed, became particularly famous. Boulestin became 'an icon of the age', both as a chef and cookery book writer.[48] His writing popularized French cooking in Britain and is said to have influenced Elizabeth David's writing. Even at this time though, the style of Escoffier no longer held a monopoly, and many other national cuisines flourished, including Indian and Chinese, though not at the higher levels of the industry.[49] Christopher Driver, a former editor of the *Good Food Guide*, comments on the predominance of foreign high-level chefs during this period in his characteristically sardonic manner: 'We brought into our cookery what had always been our boast in other fields: our prowess on the global markets as borrowers, opportunists, cultural saladiers.'[50]

In the inter-war years, the phenomenon, still evident today, of talented British amateur chef proprietors first emerged. At this time, good restaurants were also established in a few country towns and some villages, mainly by people with a love of cooking and with the imagination and dedication to produce good and interesting food. Burnett mentions the *Hind's Head* in Bray (now owned by Heston Blumenthal), the *Miller of Mansfield* in Goring-on-Thames, and the *Spreadeagle* at Thame in Oxfordshire.[51] The chef proprietor of the latter, John Fothergill, was particularly well known, both for the quality of his cooking and his temperament. The appearance of these restaurants gave hope for a revival of the reputation of provincial restaurant cooking, but this proved too optimistic. The number of restaurants was too small for them to counteract, on their own, the tradition of dreary and monotonous cooking. The decline of regional cooking was not reversed. The effort of food writers to achieve such a reversal and to demonstrate the 'Englishness of English food', described by Driver as 'rescue archaeology',[52] also attained only limited success.

During this period from the end of the nineteenth century up to 1940, standards in restaurant and hotel dining further declined. Mennell attributes this decline to the fact that the British saw cooking as a mere craft and showed more interest in hotels than in restaurants. This phenomenon probably was a consequence of the early establishment in the hospitality industry of 'big capital'.

However, as shown above, there existed islands of excellence in this sea of mediocrity. During the early 1930s, the Wine and Food Society, founded by André Simon (1877–1970), was drawing its membership from the professional classes, though mainly in London. Its main aim was to raise the standard of good cooking in Britain, as well as the level of appreciation of good wine. Simon regretted that in England, unlike in France, the more homely *cuisine bourgeoise* of the provinces had not developed.[53] Simon's Society created the template which, in the early 1950s, was revived by Raymond Postgate, the founder of the *Good Food Guide*.[54]

The Second World War put a brake on the supply of ample and varied food and on fine-dining. But the turn to austerity and the ensuing food shortage was not as deep as in Germany.[55] Despite rationing, most of the restaurants kept going. Diners were served such delicacies as Creamed Spam Casserole in *Simpson's*, or, at *Prunier's*, Sardine with Potatoes Land Girls (mashed potatoes with dried egg powder).[56] However, most of the French chefs in Britain (unlike the Italians) went back to France at the beginning of the war to fight for their country, to return only from the 1960s onwards.

The war years also inspired further significant standardization of food supply. The 1947 Agriculture Act encouraged farmers to specialize to raise yield and thereby led to a reduction in the range of what was produced. It brought the near extinction of a range of animal breeds, particularly of pigs. The early rise of supermarkets (in the early 1950s), compared to Germany, also was complicit 'in this drive for uniformity and the loss of variety and of traditional foods'.[57]

When the war was over, high hopes arose for a return to the state of plenty of the pre-war years, but this hope could not be realized until the last rationing measures were removed in 1954. This was particularly hard to bear when, in vanquished Germany, rationing had been discontinued four years previously. Nevertheless, from the mid-1950s onward, a very slow revival of up-market restaurants occurred, often under foreign ownership. The small restaurants run by British amateur chefs also returned (Box 1.1).

A high point of the 1950s was the publication, in 1951, of the first edition of the *Good Food Guide* by Raymond Postgate. Sales of 5,000 copies at first raised hopes about a culinary awakening of the British people. Yet the figure also showed that, at this point in time, people interested in good food and in eating out were still a tiny minority. A survey in 1958 established that eating out for pleasure in the evening was rare, with only 5 per cent of the population doing so in summer and a mere 2 per cent in winter. Tastes in food for home cooking had remained traditionally English.[58] The provision of good restaurants remained very patchy, and the conditions for the revival of an indigenous fine-dining sector continued to be lacking. British restaurant food, during the inter-war years and the immediate post-war years up to the end of the 1950s, was characterized as follows by Driver, a later editor

---

Box 1.1 GEORGE PERRY-SMITH: AN OUTSTANDING CHEF OF THE EARLY POST-WAR DECADES

The most admired and most influential of these restaurants was that of George Perry-Smith, the *Hole-in-the Wall*, opened in Bath in 1952, which remained under his ownership for twenty years. Perry-Smith was a Cambridge graduate in Modern Languages whose post-degree travels had taken him for a long period to France where he fell in love with food and cooking. His cooking therefore was largely French. (Perry-Smith borrowed a large number of his recipes from Elizabeth David's cookery books.) But he was open, too, to other continental cuisines, particularly the Italian, and he also made bows towards an English culinary tradition. His style of cooking and restaurant management became very influential. His food, although not original, was considered of the highest quality. It has been described as 'real' food, close to superior home cooking. He already championed local sourcing. Furthermore, Perry-Smith practised work rotation between kitchen and service staff, in order to overcome the traditional division and ensuing animosity between the kitchen and front-of-house. Perry-Smith's style appealed to many upcoming chefs. Driver[a] has traced thirteen chefs who wholly or partly were inspired by Perry-Smith. He must be regarded as one of the people who greatly influenced the revival of *haute cuisine* in provincial Britain. Some commentators even associate him with an alternative tradition of gastronomy to that later introduced by the Roux brothers, which was linked to a more formal and more hierarchical style, as well as with more showy dishes.

[a] Driver 1983: 191.

of the *Good Food Guide*: 'The first picture that anyone has of British cooking, outside the home, is of dullness and incompetence; and of British service, it is of ineptness or downright surliness.'[59] Neither the demand- nor the supply-side, despite a few notable exceptions, encouraged a significant fine-dining sector at this point in time.

The social institutional environment during this period also placed strong impediments upon the evolution of an indigenous British *haute cuisine*. The reasons are first, the baleful influence of large hotels. Large capital had been attracted into the industry, encouraged by the ease with which limited liability companies could be formed,[60] and by the stock market-centred financial system. From the 1880s, this system encouraged gigantism and, eventually, the development of chains in the hospitality industry. Even though small entrepreneurial enterprises existed, financial concentration shaped the ethos of the industry. Second, and related to this, was the development of a catering industry which elevated the business aspects of providing food above the development of craft, let alone, art, in the provision of meals.[61] A third institutional deficiency was an inadequate training system. At best, it was highly skewed in terms of both target groups and objectives and, at worst, completely ineffective in reaching entrepreneurial restaurateurs. A consequence of this was an absence of well-trained chefs and also a shortage of supplier craftsmen, such as butchers and bakers. The standard of British cuisine at the end of the 1950s elicited sentiments ranging from regret to derision. In a later section, I will examine how a slow, but cumulatively significant transformation of the high-end restaurant sector and cooking nevertheless was accomplished.

The Development of Fine-Dining Restaurants in Germany

Germany, for political and cultural reasons, developed no national cuisine, but many different regional kitchens.[62] These sometimes refer to farm and sometimes to bourgeois cooking. As far as any *haute cuisine* existed, until the end of the nineteenth century, it remained mainly French. As in Britain, French cooks emigrated to Germany after the French Revolution and exported the *grande cuisine*, as well as the idea of the restaurant. Private chefs in great noble households, as in Britain, were French, as were the cooks of Prussian kings and German emperors right up to the First World War.[63] The cultural historian Teuteberg dates the real growth of German restaurants as starting only from the 1870s.[64] In Germany, as in Britain, restaurants achieved their fullest form first in hotels, such as Hamburg's Vier Jahreszeiten, opened in 1897.[65] Some of the first restaurateurs in Germany were Frenchmen.

Gastro-nationalism thus was not aspired to in the nineteenth century. However, some exceptions to this rule may be noted. The German chef to

Friedrich August III (first the prince and later the king of Saxony) Ernst Max Pötzsch, assembled a collection of his own (745) recipes five years before Escoffier published his *Guide Culinaire* in 1903. These recipes, written in German, not only show that Saxony had a tradition of exquisite cuisine but also that the influences on this cuisine were by no means all French ones.[66] A few high-end and famous German restaurants also existed from the middle of the nineteenth century onwards, particularly in Berlin, such as *Dressel*, *Hiller*, the *Kaiserhof*, and *Borchardt's*. They were patronized mainly by a wealthy upper middle-class and by foreign visitors.[67]

The German bourgeoisie, particularly the *Bildungsbürgertum* (highly educated middle-classes and higher civil servants), never became as integrated into the aristocracy as was the case in Britain. The dominance of the French influence over *household* cooking began to wane by the middle of the nineteenth century. Furthermore, due to Germany's delayed industrialization and the absence of an industrialized agriculture, particularly in the west of the country, industrialization and standardization of food did not emerge to the same high degree as in Britain during the nineteenth century. Because of the preservation of craft production of food, particularly of bread and meat, and of smaller food retailers, the quality of food did not deteriorate to nearly the same degree as it did in Britain. Towards the end of that century, many cookery books on good bourgeois cooking were published. They recommended *Hausmannskost*, i.e. simple hearty dishes, as commonly enjoyed in families of the middle-classes. During this period the *Biedermeierzeit*—home entertainment of distinguished guests—was still the cultural norm.[68] The culinary tradition of the bourgeoisie came to form a counterweight to the fine *cuisine* of the nobility which, until then, had dominated cookbooks. From 1890 onwards, in contrast to the situation in Britain, culinary terminology was translated into German.[69]

An indigenous German *haute cuisine* nevertheless failed to emerge. A number of explanations for this come to mind. Economic factors, such as comparatively late industrialization and urbanization, and a relatively low diffusion of wealth were of considerable importance. But the literature puts a lot of weight also on a philosophical tradition, based on Immanuel Kant and embraced and perpetuated by the *Bildungsbürgertum*. Kant's philosophy relegated the sense of taste to the lower senses and discouraged sensual gratification. The *Bildungsbürgertum* defined itself by a concept of culture that did not recognize a culinary art, and cooking had a hard job establishing itself as something amenable to aesthetic perfection.[70] Such a culture put a strong brake on the emergence of an indigenous *haute cuisine*. Some important writing in the nineteenth century in the gastrosophic tradition (philosophical gastronomy) by Rumohr (1832) and Vaerst (1851) offered a polemic against French domination, as well as promoting the bourgeois concept of cuisine.[71]

However, these writers remained 'voices in the wilderness' and no widespread change occurred. The Germans, Rumohr suggested, were not yet ready to enjoy good food.[72]

During the first half of the twentieth century, prolonged periods of extreme economic deprivation, disruption of agricultural supply, imposition of drastic economies in food consumption, and even widespread hunger became additional factors retarding the spread of fine-dining. This started with the period from 1918 to 1923 and resumed during the depression of 1929–32. The near compulsory 'Stew Sunday' during the latter years of the Second World War did nothing to enhance German cuisine. The attendant shortage economy turned into real deprivation during the post-war period, lasting until about the middle of the 1950s. In contrast to the situation in Britain, the years between 1945 and 1949 constituted a nadir of widespread real hunger. It forced remaining restaurateurs to fight for their survival, and no innovation occurred during this period.[73] However, these hard times periodically returned consumers to their German (and usual regional) culinary roots. They additionally engrained in the population an economy-mindedness suffusing behaviour relating to food consumption and a corresponding rejection of the consumption of luxury foods. At the end of this period, a disdain for the enjoyment of fine-dining by the educated middle-classes was again articulated at the intellectual level. The 1970 work of the sociologist Theodor Adorno (1903–69), *Aesthetic Theory*, perpetuated the Kantian attitude that food satisfies bodily demands and thus can appeal only to the lower senses.

Germany, unlike Britain, did not abolish its craft guilds until the middle of the nineteenth century (in 1868). It retained and later even revived many core aspects of the system to sustain a highly respected apprenticeship system and a large artisan sector.[74] There existed therefore no shortage of trained cooks, nor of well-qualified bakers/pastry makers and butchers, to secure local supplies of good food (Box 1.2). Hence the industrial degradation of food set in much later in Germany than it did in Britain and never reached the same high level.

The time from the late-1950s to the mid-1970s was a catch-up period during which over-compensation for prolonged deprivation of special and luxurious foods resulted in a so-called *Fresswelle* (wave of gorging), antithetical to fine-dining. In Germany, too, the growth of the supermarkets from the second half of the 1950s homogenized the food supply across the nation. Yet it introduced individual consumers also to a much wider choice of foods, many of which were new to the German market. From the 1960s onwards, American fast food established itself in Germany and was widely embraced. It symbolized the American dream of abundance and of technological development, as well as a revolt against bourgeois conventions of meals around the family table.[75] In the Soviet zone of Germany and the later German

---

Box 1.2 ALFRED WALTHERSPIEL

One famous chef, Alfred Waltherspiel (of the Berlin *Adlon* and the Munich *Vier Jahreszeiten*), emerged during the Roaring Twenties (1923–29). He managed to create for the first time what was recognized as a German *haute cuisine*, albeit one with roots in classical French cooking.[a] Waltherspiel took up German regional cooking and married it to the classical principles of Escoffier and the elegance and simplicity of Ferdinand Point.[b] However, by the end of the 1920s, Waltherspiel's influence on German cuisine and restaurants became curtailed by the severe economic downturn. Yet he had provided an example to which German chefs could turn in the later post-Second World War decades.

[a] K. Moeckl, 'Die grosse deutsche Kueche. Formen des Essverhaltens seit den siebziger Jahren', in W. Protzner (ed.), *Vom Hungerwinter zum kulinarischen Schlaraffenland. Aspeckte einer Kulturgeschichte des Essens in der Bundesrepublik* (Wiesbaden: Karl-Steiner Verlag, 1987), 49–64 (53).
[b] Barlösius 1988.

Democratic Republic, the forces arraigned against the emergence of an *haute cuisine* and fine-dining restaurants were formidable.[76] The shortage economy, together with the absence of private enterprise and an ideological opposition to bourgeois fine-dining, lasted right up to and even well beyond the time of the Republic's demise in 1989.

In the western parts of Germany, isolated talented chefs existed who had been trained in Germany during the early post-war years. Significantly, chefs such as Waltherspiel, Katzenberger, and Gietz all worked in southern Germany (Baden and Munich).[77] The southern German states (*Länder*) are widely associated with a more developed and refined cuisine, due to both their natural endowments and their proximity to France and Switzerland. However, Katzenberger did not imitate French cuisine but focused strictly on regional Baden specialities.[78]

German bourgeois cuisine during the 1960s and 1970s was judged dull and without refinement, particularly in relation to French cuisine. Germany was regarded by many as a 'culinary developing country' and its cuisine as being 'without profile'.[79] It thus was deemed unable to inspire the birth of an indigenous *haute cuisine*. However, standards of food quality never fell as low as in Britain at this time, and artisan-produced ingredients were widely available. Moreover, German bourgeois cooking had a much more developed repertoire of techniques of food preparation and dishes, with soups, sauces, and dressings playing a much bigger role than in Britain. Meat preparation—probably conditioned by shortages of good cuts—was more elaborate than in Britain. A wide range of refined cakes and gateaux and a diversity of breads and rolls were produced, presenting a striking difference to the homogenized industrial white and brown (and usually sliced) loaves sold in Britain during the

1960s and 1970s. Thus, it was more the hearty character of a lot of German food, rather than its poor quality, which presented an obstacle to the development of fine-dining.

The same precipitous decline in the quality of food supplies as in Britain had not occurred in Germany, nor had regional differences in taste undergone such a comprehensive demise. However, impediments to the creation of an indigenous fine-dining industry during the post-war period—mainly cultural in nature—nevertheless were considerable.

The Rise of an Indigenous Michelin-Starred Restaurant Sector from the mid-1960s to the 1990s

Despite multiple obstacles in both societies to the emergence of a significant high-end restaurant sector, from the late-1960s onwards, fundamental transformations began to occur, first in Germany and somewhat later and more hesitantly in Britain. By 2013, both British and German high-end restaurants had gained significant success in terms of Michelin accreditation, and it is instructive to trace their gradual transformation during the twenty-odd years at the end of the twentieth century. The twenty-year period of 1966–1986 has been selected for study, because 1966 formed the start of Michelin awards in Germany (as against 1974 in Britain), and 1986 was the year when a second British restaurant was awarded three stars. The figures in Table 1.1 convey the very different developments in the two countries during this period.

Table 1.1 shows a number of interesting contrasts between the two countries. First, the award of stars in Germany started in 1966, eight years earlier than in Britain, and there immediately was critical mass—sixty-six awards of one star. By the time twenty-four British restaurants (England, Scotland, Wales, and Northern Ireland) were awarded their first star in 1974, the number in Germany already had risen to 169. Second, the number of German

Table 1.1. Michelin recognition of German and British restaurants, 1966–1986[80]

	Germany				UK			
	1 star	2 stars	3 stars	Total	1 star	2 stars	3 stars	Total
1966	66	0	0	66	0	0	0	0
1970	189	0	0	189	0	0	0	0
1974	169	7	0	176	24	0	0	24
1978	129	8	0	137	24	4	0	28
1982	149	9	3	161	27	5	1	33
1986	173	9	3	185	24	4	2	30

one- and two-star awards grew continuously in the period covered, whereas the growth of comparable restaurants in the UK remained almost stagnant between 1978 and 1986. Third, three stars were awarded very sparingly in both countries. Only three German restaurants had three stars in both 1982 and 1986. Significant increases would only come with a new generation of German chefs coming of age in the 2000s. This nevertheless rapid upswing in Germany's high-end restaurant sector attracts the following comment from one of the columnists of *Der Spiegel*, an important weekly magazine: 'Germany has changed in the last forty years from a culinary desert to a Schlaraffenland for gourmets.'[81]

In the UK, too, the first three-star restaurant emerged only in 1982—namely London's *Le Gavroche*. Its chef proprietor was French-born chef Albert Roux, and in 1986 his brother, Michel Roux, of the *Waterside Inn* in Bray, Berkshire, received the same honour. The number of three-star restaurants has remained relatively low right up to the current time. However, the huge concentration of starred restaurants in London, together with the very vibrant restaurant sector just below the top level, has created a pervasive impression that the renaissance in Britain of *haute cuisine* has been more significant than has actually been the case. In view of these divergent national development trajectories, it would be fair to say that the British Michelin-starred restaurant sector took shape only from 1990 onwards, whereas the German beginnings took place twenty years earlier, in the early 1970s. The reasons for these divergent developments in the two national high-end restaurant sectors will be explored in the following sections.

The Rise of a Michelin-Starred Restaurant Sector in Britain, 1972–1990

Given the mostly dismal picture painted above of the British restaurant industry and the food it provided during the nineteenth and early twentieth centuries, how did it become possible for a Michelin-starred sector to emerge in Britain? Who were the people who initiated the transformation?

The small number of high-end restaurants which emerged in the 1970s and 1980s were run by two different groups of restaurateurs/chefs, circumventing the obstacle of a poor training system and an insufficient supply of skilled chefs in different ways.

First, a number of hotel and restaurant kitchens, as in earlier periods, were run by gifted and entrepreneurial immigrant chefs. Most of these chefs were French, and the two Roux brothers, Albert and Michel, stand out among them. They arrived in Britain in 1953, but, until 1967, worked as chefs in private houses. By training a large number of young chefs from 1967 onwards, Albert and Michel Roux put their indelible stamp on the top-end restaurant sector. They have trained three generations of chefs, among them Marco Pierre White, Gordon Ramsay, Rowleigh Leigh, Paul Rankin, Bryn Williams, Martin Wishart, and Andrew Fairlie. In 1985, they instituted the Roux scholarship which allows the winner, all costs paid, to choose an internship (a *stage*) in almost any famous kitchen, in any country.[82] The brothers also were among the first to be awarded Michelin stars from 1974 onwards. Together with *The Box Tree Inn*, Ilkley and the restaurant at *The Connaught*, they were the first recipients of two stars in 1978. They remained the lone holders of three stars, until, in 1993, one of their trainees, Marco Pierre White, received three stars. In addition to the Roux brothers, Frenchmen Raymond Blanc and Pierre Koffman, Swiss Anton Mosimann (*The Dorchester*) and Germans Anton Edelmann (*The Savoy*) and Peter Kromberg (*The Intercontinental*), also made very significant contributions to the rebirth of a high-end British restaurant sector from the late 1970s onwards. These latter industry doyens are now much less talked about. Nevertheless, their introduction of excellent continental training systems to the very large restaurant kitchens of London's luxury hotels made a huge contribution to their improvement, if not rescue, at the time. These Swiss and German chefs, too, trained quite a few future British Michelin-starred chefs, such as, in my sample of chefs, Andreas Antona, Shaun Hill, and Marcus Wareing.

The shortage of British chefs in this early period was severe also at the lower levels of the kitchen brigade. Shaun Hill, of the *Walnut Tree Inn* in Llandewi Skirrid, in an interview with author Simon Wright, remembers his first kitchen in the mid-1960s:

> At that point you got the odds and ends of Europe there, anybody with work permit difficulties or psychiatric or alcohol problems would be sort of compressed into this, and in that way it was quite fascinating.[83]

During the 1980s, as Wright points out, 'British chefs had largely taken their lead from France and particularly from the grander style of cooking.'[84] While *nouvelle cuisine* also made a big impact in London, particularly among the French chefs, it did not seem to unleash the same big wave of enthusiasm it did in Germany. When people reminisce about *nouvelle cuisine* today, it is usually in a deprecating manner. They mainly refer to the 'overpriced silliness' it became among less well-trained chefs outside London.

Single stars during the 1970s also were gained by a small number of restaurants in country house hotels, such as Sonia Stevenson's *Horn of Plenty* in Gulworthy, Devon and *Sharrow Bay* in Cumbria. Kenneth Bell, after a short spell in the early 1960s at *The Elizabeth* in Oxford, subsequently cooked for twenty years at the country house hotel *Thornbury Castle* in Gloucestershire. He must be considered another notable early influence on fine-dining in Britain. His fusion of British and French dishes earned him early Michelin stars.

Second, many of the smaller restaurants in different parts of Britain, but particularly in the south-west, were started up by British-born, talented middle-class (often graduate) amateur cooks. According to the social historian Burnett,[85] of the people held to have exerted an influence on British cooking and eating, few had received conventional training as chefs: they had learned by experience, as gifted amateurs with a flair for communication. Among the talented restaurateurs in this period was Michael Lawson of *The Boxtree Inn*, Ilkley 'who had dined in all the two- and three-star restaurants of France'.[86] (Marco Pierre White, the star of the late 1980s/1990s, received his early training there.) In London, during the 1960s and 1970s, Robert Carrier, a Francophile former journalist, made an impact. Other, slightly later pioneers, some of them inspired and/or trained by Perry-Smith, were Tim and Sue Cumming and Joyce Molineux, of the *Carved Angel*, Dartmouth.

On the demand side, the following developments were levers for change: rising levels of affluence and education; greater middle-class foreign travel and experience of the superior French and Italian cuisine; and the spread of good cookery books, starting with Elizabeth David's *Book of Mediterranean Cooking*. One-star chef Shaun Hill is very aware of the link between the right customer base and the success of a restaurant:

> For restaurants to thrive, you need the soil for them to thrive in. I was the first in Ludlow [where he owned the Merchant's House]. A large constituency of affluent people sustained me.

But during the 1970s, according to Albert Roux,[87] the general interest in good food still was quite low: 'Customers were not abundant...The population had no concept of and desire for good food.' Roux's comments are, of course, an over-generalization as many middle-class households knew by then how to appreciate and prepare good food, even if they did not yet appreciate Michelin-style *haute cuisine*.

Supermarkets have also played a crucial part in expanding the culinary horizons of the nation, making fresh ginger and basil available to all. Cookery books published by supermarkets, together with their increasingly more adventurous stocking policy, taught the average middle-class consumer how to use the newly available ingredients for more elaborate and often foreign dishes. The launch, in 1979, of a range of high-class cooked and chilled recipes by Marks & Spencer, was another highly significant step forward in the wider dissemination of interesting and well-prepared food.[88] However, even this staunchly British institution had to rely on the consultancy services of a French-born chef, Albert Roux.[89]

A third and last factor to stimulate and reflect the rise of a fine-dining sector was the mounting influence of Raymond Postgate's *Good Food Guide (GFG)* which was published annually from 1963. It gradually came to influence both restaurateurs and the middle-class dining public. The *GFG* rewarded effort and ingenuity among restaurateurs and, by creating a market for fine-dining, it raised diners' expectations and powers of discrimination. Over time, the *GFG* became embraced by the British middle-class dining public, thus creating a culinary public for chefs. In 1970, the *GFC* sold 100,000 copies and received more than 40,000 reports from members.[90] In this year, the *GFG* listed twenty high-level restaurants in London—among them *Carrier's* and *L'Etoile*—and fifty in the provinces. From 1974 onwards, the good work started by the *GFG* was amplified by the *Michelin Guide*. But the *Michelin Guide* found rather fewer high-end restaurants, that is restaurants worth a star, and it mainly motivated British chefs to aspire to higher levels of perfection.

During the 1970s, despite all these encouraging changes in aspirations and the emergence of enlightened champions of good food, the achievement of real changes in food culture and habits was slow. Chefs still faced an uphill struggle. Albert Roux likens the development of a British fine-dining industry during that time 'to a small snowball rolling down from the top of a mountain, picking up snow on the way'.[91]

Chef Raymond Blanc, when first arriving in Britain in the 1970s, mainly perceived the industry's relative backwardness and vividly expresses his immediate impressions:

> I was about to enter a culture that was so different to the one I had known and adored...Much of it [the food] was either frozen or came out of a bottle or jar. There was white sliced bread and white rolls, straight out of a factory. The chef at the *Rose* [his first place of employment] used frozen fish and he was no different from other chefs of that era.[92]

And Albert Roux confirms: 'It was a constant battle to get provision'—a situation which Roux managed by importing a great part of the ingredients he needed from Paris.[93] For the social historian Burnett, in contrast, the food revolution started in the 1970s when one could own up to interest in good food and a vocabulary of appreciation of fine food became acceptable.[94] The figures on Michelin stars for the 1970s, an indication of the low degree of advance achieved in the high-end dining sector, lend more support to Albert Roux than to Burnett.

By the mid to late 1980s, however, change began to assume greater momentum, particularly in London, where restaurants like Marco Pierre White's (MPW) *Harvey's*, the *River Café*, and Simon Hopkinson's *Bibendum* (Conran-owned and -designed) caused a stir. The latter two introduced also a new, more relaxed and less exclusive dining style. Yet overall, the number of Michelin-starred restaurants still remained small—there were only twenty-eight in the whole of the UK in 1986.

It was only in the later-1990s/early-2000s that there had developed sufficient change among both the providers and the consumers of *haute cuisine* to allow the development of a nationally significant Michelin-starred restaurant sector. From that time onwards, there emerged a number of talented British chefs, trained by the earlier pioneers, as well as, in some cases, by a spell in French kitchens. As Phil Howard, a London two-star chef tells me: 'I started at the beginning of the food revolution. Roux brought the idea of good food into England, and, in the early 1990s, MPW made it rock and roll.' The two-star chef of a gastro pub confirms: 'It is only since the arrival of MPW that we found our feet.'

Marco Pierre White is viewed by many chefs and critics as *the* most important chef to stir up the British restaurant landscape and to galvanize other, particularly younger chefs into raising their standards. This was both because he was the first outstanding British-born professional chef and because he had real talent, backed up by tremendous drive. *The Telegraph*'s Jasper Gerard considered him a 'genius who shaped the starched linen landscape of Britain'.[95] His former head chef, three-star Albert Roux, too, pays White a generous tribute in the foreword of his book *White Heat* when he says: 'His genius is reflected on the plate.'

In addition to French-trained White, in the late-1980s/early-1990s there also emerged a 'new wave' of chefs, such as Rowley Leigh, Alistair Little, Gary Rhodes, Fergus Henderson, Shaun Hill, and John Burton-Race. They moved away from grand French cooking and developed what came to be referred to as 'a more earthy and honest approach to cooking', called 'Modern British'.[96] These chefs rediscovered the virtues of native meats, fish, game, and poultry, unpretentiously presented, seasonal vegetables and fruits from local sources, and traditional pies and puddings.[97] The extent of the change that eventually occurred still gives some people cause for wonder. Thus Raymond Blanc comments in 2008: 'A couple of decades ago, to suggest that such riches might one day descend upon us would have seemed risible.'[98]

The very slow pace of change in Britain, as compared with Germany, was due to a number of interacting factors. The nadir reached in the quality of food and cooking in the early post-war decades had been particularly low. Even when consumers' and chefs' aspirations began to rise, a number of lingering impediments—both cultural and institutional—delayed the emergence of a sizeable top-end restaurant sector. An inadequate training system remained an important obstacle. It resulted in an undersupply of well-trained chefs and perpetuated a reliance on foreign chefs, mainly from Europe. This lack created a shortage of people with the disciplined skill needed to fulfil the high Michelin requirement of consistent excellence, that is, excellence day after day. According to a British Michelin inspector: ' "Consistency" is the number one thing why we do not have more stars in this country. Chefs may fall down on one course.'

Also the resurgence of fine-dining restaurants happened disproportion-ately in the capital, reflecting Britain's political and cultural centralization, as well as the much greater inequality of wealth between different parts of the country, as compared with Germany. A British Michelin inspector regrets that, in Britain, 'there are whole swathes of the country without a Michelin star'.

Another disadvantage faced by aspiring British restaurateurs has been the fact that, due to the absence of any systematic local authority zoning regulation and the prolific development of large companies in the restau-rant industry, high streets became occupied by big brands, and rents became unaffordable for chef patrons. A British Michelin inspector comments: 'Local authorities could do more to encourage good restaurants. Other Europeans are not as obsessed with having brands in the High Street. Rents are too high in London.'

Yet another impediment to the development of a buoyant fine-dining sec-tor was that, during the 1970s, the food supply situation still was in a dire state. Many of the ingredients needed for *haute cuisine*, such as olive oil, fla-voursome free-range chickens, and good bread, simply were not yet available. There also was a lack of variety and quality in vegetables, mushrooms, herbs, and seafood. According to Raymond Blanc:

> the biggest challenge in 1977 was to get quality produce. England had become an industrial intensive garden, farmers solely dependent on pesticides...It took many years to secure a supply—it was a gigantic struggle—and initially we had to secure a lot of produce from France.[99]

The Development of a Michelin-Starred Restaurant Sector in Germany

Once the deprivations of the early post-war period were overcome and wide-spread affluence had occurred, there emerged, from the late 1960s onwards, a small number of talented chefs, trained in the French classical tradition. Affluence also encouraged mass tourism of Germans to countries like Italy and France where new and more sophisticated tastes were developed by middle-class travellers. This was also the time when magazines concerned with fine food and dining, such as *Der Feinschmecker* and *Gourmet* first appeared.

In Germany, the early emergence of a small group of talented chefs appears to have been the main driver of developments, while consumers with refined palates and ready to embrace new culinary developments are said to have followed more hesitantly behind. These were professional chefs, trained both in Germany and in Austria. A number of outstanding restaurants, such as *Der*

Erbprinz in Ettlingen, Baden-Württemberg and Rudolf Katzenberger's *Adler* in Rastatt were already known in the 1960s. They were recognized as top restaurants, together with others, by the *Michelin Guide*'s award of sixty-seven stars in 1967—well before any such development in Britain.

However, a major breakthrough came only a few years later, in 1971, when a forward-thinking gourmet, Fritz Eichbauer, met with a talented chef, Eckart Witzigmann. Eichbauer, a wealthy Munich building contractor, had travelled and eaten a lot in France and wanted to introduce what he enjoyed in France to Germany. He therefore financed and opened the restaurant *Tantris* in Munich and recruited as his head chef a man who was then believed to be the best chef in the German-speaking world—Eckart Witzigmann. Witzigmann introduced *grande cuisine* to the *Tantris*. He was very internationally oriented and had not only worked with Haeberlin and Bocuse, but also in London's *Café Royal* and in Brussels, Stockholm, and Washington. According to the magazine *Der Feinschmecker*,[100] Witzigmann initiated the German *Küchenwunder* (kitchen wonder). His contribution to *haute cuisine* in Germany has been recognized not only by Michelin who awarded him a third star in 1979—he was the very first chef to receive three stars—but later also by the French government. In 1991, they bestowed on him the *Ordre des Arts et des Lettres*. In 2011, Witzigmann's 70th birthday was marked in grand style in the *Tantris*, and he and his work were widely celebrated in the German media. Munich one-star chef Jacob Stüttgen comments on his importance for the profession: 'Witzigmann, the godfather of German cuisine. He was more an initiator than a creator. We could not work, as we do today, if he had not opened the door for us in Germany as he did.'

Witzigmann's cooking, however, did not immediately take Germany by storm. Both the majority of chefs and German diners continued to favour the unimaginative 'good bourgeois' German cuisine. According to Witzigmann, 'one had to educate the Germans, and it took quite some years to make them understand that there was something beyond Schweinshaxe and Rouladen'.[101] During the early years, his restaurant, the *Tantris*, consequently experienced deeply red figures, with Eichbauer absorbing the losses.

The catalyst for more widespread change was provided by the visit to Germany, in 1977, of one of the leaders of French *nouvelle cuisine*, Paul Bocuse. By then, however, French *haute cuisine* already had found a larger following among German chefs. In 1974, 169 chefs had received one star, and seven had achieved two stars. In addition to Witzigmann, other well-known chefs of that time were Rudolf Katzenberger, Lothar Eiermann, Frenchman Henri Levy, and, a little later in the 1970s, Dieter Müller, Heinz Winkler, and Jean-Claude Bourgueuil. Witzigmann is said to have raised the first generation of German chefs. He unfortunately retired early from restaurant cooking, following a drug offence. Two further generations of top chefs were to broaden and solidify *haute cuisine* cooking in Germany in the years to come. (In the longer run, it is Harald Wohlfahrt—he received his first star in 1977—who has shaped the German industry most profoundly. Among current Michelin-starred chefs, five three-star, six two-star, and thirty-five one-star chefs have been trained by him.) Thus when Bocuse did his famed show-cooking in Germany, he could rely on a sizeable and knowledgeable audience of chefs. This visit proved very inspirational and prompted an upsurge in the adoption *of nouvelle cuisine*.

The arrival of *nouvelle cuisine* turned out to constitute a real turning point. It was avidly adopted by top chefs and was said to be in great demand by the fine-dining public. It also received generous support from the newly active restaurant critics. According to chef-author Vincent Klink,[102] Germans learnt at last that mass is not necessarily class but that enjoyment has a lot to do with moderation.

In contrast to the situation in Britain, it was German rather than immigrant French chefs who embraced *nouvelle cuisine*. A well-developed training system supplied the necessary skilled chefs. Moreover, the embrace of *nouvelle cuisine* went hand-in-hand with a resurrection of Waltherspiel's culinary philosophy and with a turn to regionalism in food and cooking. Many chefs sought to combine a focus on fresh local ingredients with some of the central tenets of *nouvelle cuisine*.

Despite the enthusiastic reception of *nouvelle cuisine* suggested by the literature, German diners generally are portrayed as having been reluctant to convert from *gut bürgerliche Küche* to *nouvelle cuisine*. But this ungenerous assessment cannot be taken at full face value. First, from the early 1960s onwards, newly affluent Germans enthusiastically embraced foreign travel and, with it, foreign cuisine, particularly that of Italy and France. Furthermore, a sizeable minority of people must have dined in the 176 Michelin-starred restaurants which existed by 1974. The lively writing of several noted gastronomes during this period must additionally have relied on more than a very small niche dining and reading public.

Another impediment, slowing up the development of an indigenous *haute cuisine* in Germany during the 1970s, was a lack of high-value or specialist products that chefs could source for their meals. Produce such as *crème fraîche*, basil, maize-fed chicken, and scallops is said to have been in short supply. As in Britain, chefs crossed the border to France and often personally imported the desired products. The well-known *Rungis Express* which made available products from the Paris *Rungis* market in other European countries is a German enterprise founded in 1978. However, the domestic food scene was not nearly as impoverished as in Britain during the 1960s and 1970s. Chefs were able to draw on the products of an army of artisan bakers, confectioners, and butchers, and many farms were still run along less industrial lines than in Britain.

As in Britain, several keen gastronomic critics and journalistic promoters of good food and restaurants had also emerged, along with several publications devoted to these tasks. Among the critics, the following three were particularly prolific and widely read: Klaus Besser (1919–95), Gert von Pazcensky (1925–), and Wolfram Siebeck (1928–). Besser, a journalist and editor, writing initially just on labour issues, devised the first annual award of a prize for German culinary art—*The Golden Pepper Mill*. In 1978, he also founded *Besser's Gourmet Journal* which eventually became the influential contemporary magazine *Der Feinschmecker*. Von Pazcensky, a prominent newspaper and radio journalist and editor, as well as the author of academic works on colonialism and developing countries, became a popular restaurant critic. He mainly wrote for the magazine *Essen und Trinken*. His gastronomic criticism, devoted to improving Germany's eating culture, was widely admired for its fine writing. Wolfram Siebeck, after an early career in the artistic field, became a gastronomic columnist in the late 1950s, working for *Der Stern*, *Die Zeit*, and, most recently, for *Der Feinschmecker*. Siebeck now mainly writes polemics against fast food, ready-prepared dishes, the food discounters, and deficient animal husbandry. Between them, these three critics put German chefs and their interpretations of *nouvelle cuisine* on the map, as well as initiating some of the institutions which have sustained fine-dining up to the present time.

Thus, despite continuing impediments to the emergence of a vital and original *haute cuisine* in Germany, by 1990 developments in Germany were well in advance of those in Britain. Solid foundations for the emergence of a sizeable and less French-dominated fine-dining sector during the twenty-first century had been laid.

Notes

1. S. Mennell, *All Manners of Food: Eating and Taste in England and France from the Middle Ages to the Present* (Oxford: Basil Blackwell, 1985).
2. Mennell 1985: 198, 71.
3. J.-R. Pitte, *Gastronomie française. Histoire et géographie d'une passion* (Paris: Fayard, 1991), 157.
4. J.-R. Pitte, 'Du bon usage scientifique du restaurant', in A. Huetz de Lemps and J.-R. Pitte (eds.), *Les Restaurants dans le Monde et à travers les Ages* (Paris: Editions Glénat, 1990), 15.
5. J. Burnett, *England Eats Out: A Social History of Eating Out in England from 1830 to the Present* (Harlow: Longman, 2004), 11.
6. I. Terence, *Le Monde de la Grande Restauration en France* (Paris: L'Harmattan, 1996).
7. Mennell 1985; Pitte 1991; Terence 1996; P. Ferguson, 'A Cultural Field in the Making: Gastronomy in Nineteenth Century France', *American Journal of*

Sociology 104 (1998): 597–641; A. Trubek, *Haute Cuisine: How the French Invented the Culinary Profession* (Philadelphia: University of Pennsylvania Press, 2000); A. Drouard, 'Chefs, Gourmets and Gourmands', in P. Freedman (ed.), *Food: The History of Taste* (London: Thames & Hudson, 2007), 263–300; Burnett 2004: 10.

8. Mennell 1985: 67.

9. Mennell 1985: 134.

10. P. Ferguson, *Accounting for Taste: The Triumph of French Cuisine* (Chicago: University of Chicago Press, 2004).

11. C. Fischler, *L'Homnivore. Le goût, la cuisine et le corps* (Paris: Editions Odile Jacob, 1990 and 1993), 247f.; Pitte 1991: 192f.; H. Rao, P. Monin, and R. Durand, 'Institutional Change in Toque Ville: Nouvelle Cuisine as an Identity Movement in French Gastronomy', *American Journal of Sociology* 108.4 (2003): 795–843.

12. Mennell 1985: 157.

13. J.-A. Brillat-Savarin, *The Pleasures of the Table* [1825] (London: Penguin, 2011), 81.

14. Trubek 2000: 9.

15. Trubek 2000: 47.

16. Cited by Trubek 2000: 64.

17. Rao et al. 2003.

18. C. Fischler, *L'Omnivore: Le goût, la cuisine et le corps* (Paris: L'éditions Odile Jacob, 2nd edition, 1993); Rao et al. 2003.

19. H. Rao, P. Monin, and R. Durand, 'Border Crossing: Bricolage and the Erosion of Categorical Boundaries in French Gastronomy', *American Sociological Review* 70 (2005): 968–91.

20. Pitte 1991: 202f.

21. R. Blanc, *A Taste of My Life: One Man's Hunger for Perfection* (London: Transworld Publishers, 2008), 313.

22. Quoted in A. Gopnik, *The Table Comes First: Family, France, and the Meaning of Food* (New York and Toronto: Alfred Knopf, 2011), 244.

23. Mennell 1985; Burnett 2004; C. Drummer, 'Das sich ausbreitende Restaurant in deutschen Grossstädten als Ausdruck bürgerlichen Repräsentationsstrebens 1870–1930', in H.-J.Teuteburg, G. Neumann, and A. Wierlacher (eds.), *Essen und kulturelle Identität* (Berlin: Akademieverlag, 1997), 303–22; A. Jenn, *Die deutsche Gastronomie. Eine historische und betriebswirtschaftliche Betrachtung* (Frankfurt: Deutscher Fachverlag, 1993).

24. R. Strong, *Feast: A History of Grand Eating* (London: Jonathan Cape, 2002), 287.

25. Burnett 2004: 80.

26. Drummer 1997: 304.

27. Mennell 1985; C. Spencer, *British Food: An Extraordinary Thousand Years of History* (London: Grub Street, 2002); C. Dickson Wright, *A History of English Food* (London: Random House, 2011).

28. Mennell 1985: 95.

29. Strong 2002: 286.

30. Mennell 1985: 108.

31. Burnett 2004; Dickson Wright 2011.

32. Strong 2002: 285.

33. Mennell 1985: 135.
34. Spencer 2002: 246; Strong 2002.
35. Spencer 2002.
36. Dickson Wright 2011: 440–1.
37. Spencer 2002: 246.
38. Strong 2002: 286.
39. Mennell 1985: 206; Burnett 2004: 70.
40. C. Tomalin, *Dickens: A Life* (London: Penguin, 2012), 229.
41. C. Driver, *The British at Table, 1940–80* (London: Chatto & Windus, 1983); L. Chaney, 'A Meal for a Millennium', in I. Day (ed.), *Eat, Drink and be Merry: The British at Table 1600–2000* (London: Philip Wilson Publishers, 2000), 149–54 (149).
42. Driver 1983: 148.
43. Driver 1983: 148.
44. Burnett 2004.
45. Burnett 2004.
46. Driver 1983: 175.
47. Burnett 2004: 187.
48. Burnett 2004: 198; Driver 1983.
49. Driver 1983.
50. Driver 1983: 1.
51. Burnett 2004: 214.
52. Driver 1983: 10.
53. A. Simon, *The Art of Good Living* (London: Constable and Co., 1929), 4.
54. Driver 1983.
55. Burnett 2004; Driver 1983: 17.
56. Driver 1983: 239.
57. Dickson Wright 2011: 438–40.
58. Driver 1983: 258.
59. Driver 1983: 52.
60. Mennell 1985; Burnett 2004: 98.
61. Mennell 1985.
62. G. Hirschfelder and G. U. Schoenberger, 'Germany: Sauerkraut, Beer and So Much More', in D. Goldstein and M. Merkle (eds.), *Culinary Traditions of Europe: Identity, Diversity and Dialogue*. Presented by DG of Education, Culture and Heritage of the Council of Europe (Strasbourg: Council of Europe, 2005), 183–94 (184).
63. J. Teuteberg, 'The Rising Popularity of Dining Out in German Restaurants in the Aftermath of Modern Urbanization', in M. Jacobs and P. Scholliers (eds.), *Eating Out in Europe* (Oxford and New York: Berg, 2003), 281–300.
64. Teuteberg 2003.
65. Drummer 1997: 323.
66. *Slow Food Magazine* 20.3 (June 2012): 73.
67. Jenn 1993; Drummer 1997.
68. Jenn 1993.

69. K. Schlegel-Matthies, 'Regionale Speisen in deutschen Kochbüchern des 19. und 20. Jahrhunderts', in H.-J. Teuteburg, G. Neumann, and A. Wierlacher (eds.), *Essen und kulturelle Identität. Europäische Perspektiven* (Berlin: Akademie Verlag, 1997), 212–27.

70. E. Barlösius, 'Soziale und historische Aspekte der deutschen Küche', postscript to S. Mennell, *Die Kultivierung des Appetits. Die Geschichte des Essens vom Mittelalter bis heute* (Frankfurt: Athenäum, 1988), 33–44.

71. K.-F. von Rumohr, *Der Geist der Kochkunst* [Leipzig, 1832]. Translated by Barbara Yeomans as *The Essence of the Art of Cooking* (London: Prospect Books, 1993); E. von Vaerst, *Gastrosophie oder die Lehre von den Freuden der Tafel*, 2 vols. (Leipzig: Avenarius & Mendelssohn, 1851).

72. Von Rumohr [1832] 1993.

73. Jenn 1993: 63.

74. C. Lane, 'Industrial Reorganization in Europe: Patterns of Convergence and Divergence in Germany, France and Britain', *Work, Employment & Society* 5.4 (1991): 515–39.

75. J. Tanner, 'Kulinarische Neologismen in der deutschen Gegenwartssprache', in Alois Wierlacher, Gerhard Neumann, and Hans Juergen Teuteberg (eds.), *Kulturthema Essen* (Berlin: Akademieverlag, 1993), 269–77.

76. Jenn 1993; R. Horbelt and S. Spindler, *Die Deutsche Kueche im 20. Jahrhundert* (Frankfurt am Main: Eichhorn AG, 2000).

77. A. Jenn, *Die deutsche Gastronomie. Eine historische und betriebswirtschaftliche Betrachtung* (Frankfurt: Deutscher Fachverlag, 1993).

78. V. Klink, *Sitting Küchenbull. Gepfefferte Erinnerungen eines Kochs* (Reinbeck and Hamburg: Rororo, 2009), 130.

79. Jenn 1993: 77; Barlösius 1988.

80. Based on own calculations from figures provided by Michelin Germany and Michelin Great Britain.

81. <http://www.spiegel.de/sptv/dokumentatio/0,1518,749228,00.html>.

82. Interview with Albert Roux, 2012.

83. S. Wright, *Tough Cookies: Tales of Obsession, Toil and Tenacity from Britain's Culinary Heavyweights* (London: Profile Books, 2006), 14.

84. Wright 2006: 123.

85. Burnett 2004: 274.

86. M. P. White, *White Heat* (London: Pyramid Books, 1990), 10.

87. Interview with Albert Roux, 2012.

88. P. Russell, 'The Sainsbury Cookbook Series 1978–1994', *Financial Times Magazine*, 16/17 February 2013: 35.

89. Interview with Albert Roux, 2012.

90. Burnett 2004: 277.

91. Interview with Albert Roux, 2012.

92. Blanc 2008: 143, 150.

93. Interview with Albert Roux, 2012.

94. Burnett 2004: 288.

95. *The Telegraph* (26 December 2009): W28.

96. Wright 2006.
97. Burnett 2007.
98. Blanc 2008: 9.
99. Blanc 2008: 165, 187.
100. *Der Feinschmecker* 12 (2011): 43.
101. <http://www.spiegel.de/sptv/dokumentatio/0,1518,749228,00.html>.
102. Klink 2009: 191.

2

The Michelin-Starred Restaurant Sector Today

The Size and Composition of the Sector

In both Britain and Germany, the restaurant sector in general has responded to growth in affluence and leisure, as well as to increasing female labour force participation, by vigorous expansion. In both countries, it is an extremely large industry in terms of the number of establishments, employees, and extent of turnover. Its top-end restaurants—the Michelin-starred establishments—have grown along with the industry. In Germany, an increase of 45 per cent (from 176 to 255) in the number of Michelin-starred restaurants has taken place during the last thirty-nine years, i.e. between 1974 and 2013. In Britain, the increase has been much more dramatic, albeit from a much lower base. There has been a six-fold (or 576 per cent) increase (from twenty-four restaurants in 1974 to 162 in 2013) (own calculations from figures provided by *Michelin Great Britain* and *Michelin Germany*). Nevertheless, fine-dining restaurants continue to form only a small part of the industry as a whole.

Table 2.1 provides the numbers for both countries in 2013. The table shows the significantly larger number of starred restaurants in Germany. Germany, of course, has a larger population, but when one considers that Michelin restaurants are mainly found in the old West Germany—there were only sixteen in the former German Democratic Republic in 2013—then the population size is only slightly higher in Germany, that is 67 million versus 61 million in Britain.

Further facts evident from the figures in Table 2.1 are that, in both countries, one-star restaurants form the overwhelming majority, and two- and particularly three-star establishments constitute a small elite. German restaurants show superior performance in all three categories, but the difference is most striking in the two- and three-star categories.

Table 2.1. Number of Michelin stars awarded in 2013

	UK (number)	UK %	Germany (number)	Germany %
One star	138	85.00	209	82.00
Two stars	20	12.00	36	14.00
Three stars	4	2.5	10	4.00
Total	162	99.5	255	100

Source: Own calculations from data in *Michelin Great Britain 2013* and *Michelin Deutschland 2013*. Percentages have been rounded up/down.

The Cultural Support for the Growth of the Fine-Dining Sector

To what extent is the growth of the Michelin sector in both countries a response to increased demand, and to what extent has it been stimulated by the growing supply of highly qualified chefs? These two developments clearly have interacted but the answer nevertheless differs between the two countries. Whereas in Germany the growing supply of chefs appears to outstrip demand from consumers, in Britain the opposite scenario prevails.

The vigorous growth of Michelin-starred restaurants in Germany therefore is not uniformly welcomed by chefs who fear that competition might prove ruinous. An expatriate German chef, now running London's *Zuma*, takes a very pessimistic view of the situation in Germany:

> With high staff costs, the restaurant has to be booked out for lunch and dinner all through the week. This is possible in London but would not work in Germany. Sunday to Tuesday are weak days when people [in Germany] do not go out to dine as frequently as elsewhere, and the lunch business is almost absent. It is also difficult to get two seatings per night accepted...Germany, in comparison to London, has less international tourism and less purchasing power.[1]

A former German two-star chef, now Executive Chef for Volkswagen's *Casino* restaurant, agrees:

> Going out to eat, most people would visit a starred restaurant only at the weekend. Most chefs have problems during the week. The weekend then forces you to make up for the week's lack of business. In Germany, you go [out] mainly for a special occasion and mainly for showing off.

Joachim Wissler, a three-star chef, has similar concerns about an oversupply of Michelin-starred restaurants: 'German cuisine has changed incredibly, but people do not make sufficient use of this. The number of guests did not increase with the number of starred restaurants. There has been a lack of growth in demand.' This is confirmed by his colleague Sven Elverfeld: 'There are significantly more starred restaurants in Germany than there used to be, but there has been no increase in German guests.'

This situation has been worsened by the fact that, except for very top managers, firms have cut back on expense account dining out since the start of the current financial crisis. This has negatively affected those urban starred restaurants which rely on this type of business customer. *Gault Millau* refers to this development as politically sanctioned social envy which is destroying lunch-time trade and therefore causes many chef proprietors to keep their restaurants closed at lunch time.[2] The resulting oversupply of chefs also means that Germany turns out high-level chefs 'for export' as one of my British respondents who once worked in Germany notes: 'Germany produces chefs for export. There are many German expatriate chefs.' Examples of chefs with multiple stars are: Heinz Beck in Rome, Dieter Koschina in Portugal, Silvio Nickol in Vienna, Oliver Glowig on Capri, as well as London's Rainer Becker, owner of the highly successful restaurant *Zuma* and several clones of its concept around the world.

In Britain, in contrast, an under- rather than an over-supply of fine-dining chefs and restaurants is the problem in many parts of the country (see regional breakdown, Table 2.3). There is such a shortage of high-level chefs that, at the level of *chef de cuisine*, a high proportion are foreigners. London two-star chef Phil Howard comments:

> But in the last 30 years far more restaurants opened than there are resources for in terms of staff...it is still very hard to find good cooks. There is no disciplined process and structure for trainees in this country. The expansion [in the restaurant sector] was too rapid to train all new chefs—there was a vacuum. We need a better training system. Even for young people who have received training, there is insufficient people and time to provide further training, everything is too hurried.

Nevertheless, in London, competition is an issue but it is of a different kind than that experienced in Germany. In London, there is a wealth of exciting restaurants serving all manner of foreign food just below the Michelin level. Increased competition from this sector and doubt about a continuation of recent growth in the top Michelin-starred sector is perceptively noted by one two-star chef:

> The world of fine-dining is shrinking...there now are so many other ways to get good food, e.g. in the *River Café* (very informal); in *Nobu* (very animated and noisy), or in *Hakkasan*. There is a much bigger variety of places to choose from now.

A gauge of the perceived support for Michelin restaurants from potential diners is obtained from chefs' responses to my question *Do you consider British (German) culture supportive of fine-dining restaurants and their chefs?* Whereas the majority of the British chefs feel supported, most of the German chefs do not consider German culture to be supportive or, in several cases, they see support balanced by negative attitudes. A number of German chefs feel quite strongly about this and respond at much greater length than my British respondents. In both countries, however, food culture is viewed still as well behind the unquestioning support for fine food found in France. Thus, German chef Sven Elverfeld remarks a little wistfully:

> The French spend more for produce, even in supermarkets. The French, Spanish, and Italians have a developed food culture...At Michel Bras's place you see many small cars parked outside, and guests come dressed in jeans.

The main grievance chefs hold against diners in Germany is that they do not visit restaurants with sufficient frequency. Furthermore, they are not prepared to spend the amount of money needed to finance a visit to a Michelin-starred restaurant. It is notable that the strongest complaints come from chefs with multiple stars, i.e. of restaurants with the most expensive menus. Although some chefs acknowledge that Germans have become much more knowledgeable and discerning regarding food consumption, eating out in a good restaurant still comes much lower in their order of budgetary priorities than owning a luxury car. A one-star and a two-star chef express what several other chefs indicate:

> Germans read the menu from right [the price] to left. Germans have the following order of priorities: the car, their holidays, their flat, their family, and only then comes food.

> [They are] not really [supportive]. The proportion of people for such restaurants is minor. It is not common in Germany and will not change. Their goal is different—Germans would rather adopt a car as a status symbol.

I received no equivalent complaints from British chefs.

Much competition, particularly at the two- and three-star levels, is now international. Several German chefs point out that, while the governments of countries like Spain or Denmark and Sweden support their high-level chefs, the German government remains totally focused on manufacturing industry:

> The Spanish government spends 50,000 euros so that three chefs can present their cuisine for the Pellegrino list a night before the voting. In Scandinavia governments have written concepts, have organized show cooking and invited journalists. All this is unthinkable in Germany. If, however, you wish to present a car, then there is no problem.[3]

What is more, the disdain for spending on good food makes it impossible for members of the government to lend personal support to Germany's *haute cuisine*. A three-star chef complains:

> Germany sees itself as an industrial nation, and agriculture does not receive the support it does in France. Thus politicians cannot be seen to eat in expensive restaurants. Food is not a cultural good—it is different from France and Spain. It is a typically German behaviour.

A two-star chef perceives the same problem:

> If a French minister goes with his guests into a three-star restaurant then it is quite normal, whereas here in our country it will be perceived as a negative signal, a black mark.[4]

Another three-star chef bemoans the lack of support from the German press:

> No, [there is] not enough [support]. The press does not support us sufficiently. Both in Spain and in the Netherlands the press is proud of its starred restaurants. In Germany, in contrast, everything is torn to pieces. It is a general German trait.

The above diagnoses of cultural attitudes towards fine (and expensive) food and dining therefore still echo the cultural orientations of the *Bildungsbürgertum* in the nineteenth century. The shadow of Kantian ethics still hovers over consumption of fine food, and its enjoyment does not yet find full cultural endorsement.

Not all chefs agree with these negative views about German dining culture, and a minority hold a more balanced view. Italian-born one-star chef Gamba believes: 'The Germans have discovered delight in eating and a sense of beauty, as well as the quality of the product. The cultural level has risen through travel.'

Some of the negative evaluations of German dining culture by chefs contrast with other evidence available. Thus a small stratum of younger professional people are said to take a very keen interest in good food and/or healthy eating of local foods. Such an interest in food and cooking among young German managers is confirmed by VW executive chef, Niels Potthass—a former Michelin-starred chef—who teaches young managers to cook: 'Concerning customers [of high-level restaurants], there now exists a stratum which likes to cook well. These are young people who have their first professional success—young managers—and who find it fun.'

Another indicator of considerable interest in good food and dining is the comparatively large number of magazines on sale to do with fine food (as well as wine) and dining. Significantly, some of them—e.g. *Effilée* and *Port Culinaire*—also engage with food at the intellectual level and continue the 'gastrosophic' tradition started by Karl-Friedrich von Rumohr[5] in the

45

nineteenth century. I have found no equivalent magazine in Britain, nor is the number of food and restaurant (rather than cooking) magazines as large and as varied.

In Britain, by contrast, the complaints from chefs are not about tight-fistedness when it comes to expenditure on fine-dining. Instead they focus more on the traditional lack of appreciation of good food. However, the majority of chefs underline the tremendous progress in this respect in recent decades. Thus London two-star chef Phil Howard:

> In general, there is very little food heritage in Britain. There is no inherent under-
> standing of food passed down through families—no genuine understanding by
> the public of food. But attitudes towards food have transformed beyond recogni-
> tion. There has been a massive explosion in interest for eating out and for new
> restaurants.

One-star chef Shaun Hill makes a similar point: 'It [British culture] is gradu-ally moving in the direction of support. Television chefs have drawn them in. But it is concentrated on the South East and London. In the provinces, the restaurants draw less on the local population.' An article in *The Financial Times Magazine* on the new support by the middle-classes for good food at all levels notes: 'For food lovers all this constitutes a national catching up...a readjustment after generations of neglect.'[6]

But in Britain, too, there are a few non-London chefs who are sceptical of the notion that British culture supports 'fine-dining'. A northern one-star chef expresses this view: 'The average British person will not seek culinary excel-lence. They will be happy with what they are getting and will not demand the best.' Another one-star chef makes a similar point: 'They go for volume, less for quality in the UK. The food culture in France and Italy is much more advanced.'

In Britain, too, there are a few chefs who are worried about filling the res-taurant every day. But equally there are others who, despite a prolonged recession, have not noticed any falling off of business. Thus one-star chef Phil Thompson, of *Auberge du Lac* in Welwyn informs me: 'We are the high end of the economy and have not yet been affected by the recession. The recession sorts out the bad from the good.'

The Internal Differentiation of the Sector

Michelin restaurants, in each country, are a highly diverse category. They may be free-standing restaurants, or they may form a part of large high-end hotels. The free-standing restaurants mostly are independents, that is, they are owner-managed whereas this is rarely the case for hotel restaurants. In most establishments, the *chef de cuisine* is the chef proprietor, but in a very small proportion of restaurants, in both countries, the owner acts merely as restaurateur or silent financial partner. The independent establishments, in turn, consist of bistros, gastro pubs/rural inns (*Landgasthöfe*), and conventional restaurants.

Bistros, British gastro pubs, German *Landgasthöfe*, as well as establishments with a relatively low level of comfort/elegance (receiving only one knife and fork from Michelin) have been deemed worthy of the award of stars only during the last decade or so. In both countries, they still form a small minority of all starred establishments. While such simpler establishments were only awarded one star at first, the award, in 2012, of a second star to Tom Kerridge's Marlow gastro pub, *Hand & Flowers*, caused a minor sensation. All four types of establishment have received much attention from the press in recent years. Awarding them stars is rightly seen as constituting a new approach by Michelin which was emphasized again when the new 2013 guides appeared. In her comments on the 2013 British awards, the editor-in-chief, Rebecca Burr, speaks about the diversity of restaurant styles now supported: '[Restaurants] can range from a busy Chinese restaurant like Hakkasan or a Japanese restaurant like Nobu serving three hundred covers a night to the Hayward Arms [a gastro pub], through to a luxury dining experience.'[7]

The editor-in-chief of *Michelin Germany*, Ralf Flinkenflügel, makes a similar observation about the 2013 awards, noting that the trend towards a more relaxed dining style is quite evidently spreading: 'one has found many small restaurants, in which it [the atmosphere] is relaxed, laid-back and cheerful, and offering value for money'.[8] The *Michelin Guide*, in both countries, has followed the cultural change among diners who now more often seek an informal dining environment.

Pubs have been a central British cultural institution because their low degree of formality—particularly the absence of service at tables and of a dress code—has endowed them with a classless and non-intimidating character. There are currently (in 2013) thirteen starred pubs in Britain. In Germany, eleven establishments in the 'standard comfort' (the lowest) category for ambience, i.e. one knife and fork, have been starred.[9] These might be considered as a rough equivalent to pubs in their low-key physical environment and often extremely relaxed style. These are mainly urban establishments and include bistros. Examples of such laid-back restaurants with one star are Munich's *Tramin* and Frankfurt's *Weinsinn*. There exist many more *Landgasthöfe*, however, which, though often quite simple, must exceed the requirements of the 'standard comfort' category in terms of their ambience and physical appearance. As their provenance in many ways is similar to that of gastro pubs, both merit more attention.

Initially pubs in Britain were converted into high-quality restaurants simply because chefs found the premises cheaper to buy and also did not need to apply for planning permission. However, over time the word 'gastro pub' became a stylistic concept, albeit a somewhat vague one. It receives different interpretations by different owners and gastronomic constituencies and remains a contested notion. At the very least it presupposes an establishment which continues to serve customers beer (on tap) by itself, either from the bar or from an area preserved for 'drinking only' customers. Dining customers, however, are usually served by waiting staff just as in a restaurant although there are no sommeliers. In some gastro pubs, the menu offers up-market pub food, besides a more ambitious fine-dining menu. Yet the gastro pub provides a fairly simple and informal dining environment, the main distinguishing feature of which is a lack of table cloths. On the down side for their owners, these establishments are expected to keep their prices below those of restaurants.[10] Awarding stars to pubs, which will be considered in greater length in later chapters, has given rise to some confusion among customers and, occasionally, even to some backlash.

Bistros are in vogue again and are frequently held up as preferable alternatives to and competitors of fine-dining restaurants, particularly by people who decry what they see as the elitism of the latter, including their alleged stiffness and pomposity. It is, however, no longer that easy to draw clear distinctions between the two types of restaurants. Bistros are seen to differ from restaurants in virtue of their lack of table cloths, their simpler furnishings, and their less elaborate food. Bistros are said to provide an uncomplicated kind of enjoyment, contrasted with what are deemed to be the more capriciously refined dishes and heavy starched table cloths which abound in the clichéd notion of a 'temple of gastronomy'. From the chef proprietor's point of view, bistros additionally are distinguished by the fact that there usually are several sittings, thus providing the owner with a much larger turnover. Scottish one-star chef and brasserie owner Martin Wishart explains: 'A brasserie is a very different way of working. You need a large number of staff to do 125 people in one sitting. It has a larger menu and does not have to be as creative. Prices are lower…'

We find both bistros converted to Michelin-standard restaurants and self-consciously separated and simpler establishments, kept by Michelin chefs to improve the flow of profit. A bistro as a second restaurant is particularly frequently found in high-end hotels, to provide guests with an alternative and less demanding venue for eating.

German *Landgasthöfe* are simple rural establishments which usually have been family-owned for several generations. They cultivate the same unpretentious dining environment as pubs but do not serve drinks only at the bar. Yet like pubs they have a cross-class appeal. *Landgasthöfe* seek to preserve a more traditional and, mostly, regional food culture. They often offer two parallel menus: a fine-dining menu which reaches the same standard as urban restaurants and a menu with regional favourites, prepared at a higher than average level. One example of such an establishment is the one-star *Zum Storchen* in the small, relatively remote and not touristified Baden village of Schmidhofen. The building is very simple and functional—you would walk past it if you did not know about it—but inside it is very comfortable and above pub standard, though not akin to an elegant restaurant. In addition to the gastronomic menu, they offer a second menu, entitled 'Local Cultural Heritage—Enjoyment from the Three Countries Triangle'. A second example is Markus Nagy's *Zum Löwen*, a one-star *Landgasthof* in Eggenstein, another Baden village. Nagy, too, serves more traditional food, such as *Kohlrouladen* (minced meat wrapped in cabbage leaves), to guests who do not want the fine-dining menu.

In Germany, you find more fine-dining restaurants in hotels than in Britain. In Britain, by contrast, independent restaurants predominate, and hotel restaurants are found mainly in London and in a handful of country house hotels in tourist areas, like Cumbria, Yorkshire, and the West Country. The average size of restaurants, measured in terms of covers, is significantly smaller in Germany than in Britain. In Germany, quite a polarized industry structure exists, with large hotel restaurants, on the one side, and predominantly small independent ones, on the other (Boxes 2.1, 2.2). You get owner-managed restaurants with only five employees, as well as restaurants in luxury hotels with forty chefs in the kitchen.

Among the twenty German restaurants I visited, twelve have fewer than fifty covers and only two cater for over seventy guests. In Britain, the majority of restaurants in my sample have between fifty and seventy covers, with only two exceptions at the top end of the spectrum, with around 130 covers. The

---

Box 2.1. A SMALL GERMAN RESTAURANT

One of the smaller restaurants I visited is one-star *Halbedel's Gasthaus* in Bonn-Bad Godesberg. The twenty-five covers (for dinner only) are serviced in the kitchen by Mr Halbedel, two further chefs, and two apprentices. The *chef de cuisine* also acts as sommelier and waiter in that he personally introduces each course to all his guests. Restaurant service more generally is provided by Mrs Halbedel—the restaurant manager—and two young girls, trained by her. Despite its name, the restaurant has little in common with a *Gasthaus*, being situated in a beautiful *fin-de-siècle* white villa and with an extremely elegant interior. Mr Halbedel proudly tells me that the house has been fully paid for and that he is making a good profit. During the early part of the day, he and his wife look after their own (vegetable and herb) farm in the Eiffel mountains.

Box 2.2. A LARGE GERMAN RESTAURANT

At the other end of the scale, Berlin two-star restaurant *Fischer's Fritz* in the Regent Hotel has ninety covers and two daily services. Christian Lohse, the *chef-de-cuisine*, commands forty-five chefs (of whom around five are apprentices) in the kitchen, among them several head chefs. Guests are taken care of by forty-five full-time, highly polished and internally stratified restaurant staff.

Box 2.3. THE *RIVER CAFÉ*: A LARGE BRITISH RESTAURANT

'We seat around 300 for the day, more in the evening than at lunch time. In 2010, we fed 87,000 people during the year.' The restaurant has 120–150 covers and mostly does two services. Its kitchen is staffed by twenty chefs, five of whom are head chefs. In the restaurant, customers are served by forty staff although quite a few of these work part-time. Although the *River Café* prides itself on its relaxed atmosphere this certainly does not translate itself into haphazard service.

---

average size of the restaurants I visited is forty-one covers in Germany and sixty-four covers in Britain.

An example of a very large British restaurant is the one-star *River Café*. The figures in Box 2.3, supplied by its restaurant manager, illustrate the scale of their catering operation.

I have no small independent restaurants in my British sample, but according to the trade magazine *Restaurant*,[11] there exist a few very small and highly exceptional starred restaurants—so-called Lone Rangers. One such Lone Ranger is Marc Wilkinson with his one-star restaurant *Fraiche* in the Wirral, in north-west England (Box 2.4).

Another very small restaurant, run by husband-and-wife team Russell and Elena Brown, is the sixteen-cover one-star *Sienna* in Dorchester in Dorset—the only starred restaurant in Dorset. The restaurant does both lunch and

---

Box 2.4. A VERY SMALL BRITISH RESTAURANT

The restaurant has only sixteen covers, and chef proprietor Marc Wilkinson runs it almost single-handedly. He manages all the kitchen work and cooking by himself, and at service time, regards himself as a 'flying solo'. Wilkinson employs only one person as front-of-house. In addition to the cooking, he does the many other tasks a restaurateur faces, from washing-up to doing the accounts. Although the restaurant is usually full, Marc Wilkinson makes very little money. He is thinking of moving to a larger place where he could add a small number of hotel rooms to the restaurant, in order to increase his income.[a]

[a] <http://www.thestaffcanteen.com./the-staff-canteen-meets/marc-wilkinson-chef-patron-resta urant-fraiche-oxton-the-wirral/>.

---

dinner. In addition to Russell, there are another two chefs in the kitchen. They employ also two part-time people who double as kitchen porter and waiter. The only way the couple can make 'a modest living' is to work extremely long hours, with Russell doing up to 90 hours in the kitchen and Elena up to 70 hours in the restaurant. These are longer hours than put in by any of the chefs I interviewed. The couple know that the only way forward is to look for larger premises where they can more than double the number of covers.[12]

In addition to organizational form and size, restaurants differ significantly according to the number of stars they hold. Multi-star restaurants differ from those with only one star. This applies particularly to the more stringent testing procedures they follow in the kitchens, the originality and complexity of their dishes, and the elaborate and often beautiful nature of their presentation. As Michelin are very sparing with the award of a third star, the chefs who have received them form a small elite both within their own country and also in Europe. However, as far as style and etiquette are concerned, two- and three-star restaurants no longer necessarily differ drastically from those with only one star. Diners' demands for greater informality have also penetrated this small elite of restaurants. Of the four German three-star chefs I interviewed all aim for the creation of a relaxed restaurant ambience although most still preside over an elegant, if not necessarily luxurious house.

The Socio-Spatial Distribution of Restaurants

The spatial demarcations found in Britain and Germany, shown in Tables 2.2 and 2.3, largely reflect the divergent degrees of political and cultural de-centralization and the accompanying preservation or loss of regional

Table 2.2. Distribution of Michelin-starred restaurants between the German federal states, 2012

Berlin	16	Niedersachsen	13
Baden-Württemberg	58	Nord Rheinwestphalen	40
Bayern	40	Rheinland Pfalz	25
Brandenburg*	2	Schleswig-Holstein	14
Bremen**	1	Saarland	5
Hessen	17	Sachsen*	3
Hamburg**	9	Thüringen*	2
Mecklenburg*	8	Sachsen-Anhalt*	1

States of the former GDR have been marked by the author with a *. States marked with two ** are city states.

Source: 'Die Sterne Restaurants Deutschland 2012', <http://www.kochmesser.de/component/name. Die-Sternerestarants-Deutschland-2012_340063.hmtl>.

Table 2.3. Distribution of British Michelin-starred restaurants between the English counties/UK regions, 2012

Bedfordshire 1	Herefordshire 1	Somerset 2
Bromley 1	Hertfordshire 1	Surrey 3
Bristol 1	Jersey, Isle of 3	Sussex 3
Buckinghamshire 3	Kent 3	Warwickshire 1
Cambridgeshire 1	Lancashire 1	Wight, Isle of 1
Cheshire 1	Merseyside 1	West Midlands 3
Cornwall 2	Norfolk 2	Wiltshire 2
Cumbria 3	Nottinghamshire 1	Windsor and Maidenhead 3
Derbyshire 1	Oxfordshire 2	Yorkshire 6
Dorset 1	Reading 1	London 52
Gloucestershire 3	Rutland 2	*Scotland 16*
Hampshire 3	Shropshire 1	*Wales 4*

The non-English regions are rendered in italics. Northern Ireland has no starred restaurants. Counties with no starred restaurant are omitted.

Source: Own calculations from figures provided by *Michelin Great Britain 2012*.

cooking. But spatial concentrations are also indicative of geographically based social inequality and, in Germany, of divergent political traditions.

In Germany, in 2012, only sixteen, or 15.5 per cent, of Michelin-starred restaurants were in Berlin, while regional capitals like Munich, Hamburg, Stuttgart, Düsseldorf, Frankfurt, and Cologne did not come far behind in the number of starred restaurants. Munich (an economic, political, and cultural centre) comes a close second with eleven restaurants, while Hamburg (an important centre of foreign trade, with a high level of per capita GDP), comes third in the list with nine starred restaurants. They are followed by Stuttgart and Düsseldorf (both are business centres) with eight each, Cologne (a business and tourist centre) with seven, and finally Frankfurt (the financial centre), with six starred restaurants. Germany's capital thus is not at all comparable to Britain's. However, since reunification in 1989, Berlin's restaurant scene has developed a great deal, particularly in recent years. Some commentators now rate it as coming third among Europe's capital cities, after Paris and London, in its provision of dining and other entertainment.

In Britain, in contrast, the capital London holds an overwhelming share of restaurants. Thus, in 2012, fifty-two, or 33.66 per cent, of all Michelin-starred restaurants in the UK were located there. Large regional centres of population, in contrast, support only a very few or even no such restaurants. In 2012, there were three starred restaurants in Birmingham, with one each in Sheffield, Nottingham, and Bristol. There were no starred restaurants in large northern cities like Manchester, Liverpool, or Leeds. With respect to Manchester, Michelin chef Raymond Blanc comments as follows:

I cannot believe that the second biggest city in Britain cannot sustain a quality restaurant…All the great European cities are judged on their restaurants as much as any part of their culture and, if you look at Manchester's record, it is appalling.[13]

In Germany, Michelin-starred restaurants are strongly represented in small towns and even villages, with rural locations particularly prevalent. The frequent use of restaurant names, such as *Landhaus, Gutshof*, or merely *Hof*, serves to indicate the rural ambience restaurateurs try to simulate. The many small spa towns all over Germany have been particularly successful in attracting Michelin-starred restaurants. Thus, out of 249 places where there were starred restaurants in Germany in 2012, less than 50 per cent were situated in large towns. The others were in smaller towns in more rural areas, and some in very small villages. The remote Black Forest village of Baiersbronn, for example, has three Michelin-starred restaurants, two of which have three stars, while the small Westphalian town of Bergisch Gladbach (5,000 inhabitants) has a three- and a two-star restaurant. A British Michelin inspector interviewed in 2011 implicitly ascribes the willingness of German chef proprietors to settle in smaller towns to the greater attractiveness of these towns, compared with their British counterparts: 'Small provincial towns in Germany have a livelier scene than in Britain. Our High Streets all look the same.' However, in Britain, too, Michelin-starred restaurants in the provinces are frequently found in smaller towns and villages. But the culture of spas—still prevalent in Germany—is defunct in Britain, and as a result the number of locations where starred chefs may expect ready custom has been reduced.

In both countries, the geographical distribution over the regions/counties is uneven, with a particularly striking imbalance between northern and southern locations. For Britain, this is readily explained in terms of the high degree of political, financial, and cultural centralization in London as well as the decline of northern industries and the resultant significantly lower average income of people residing in the north. In Germany, however, such explanations hold less readily, and cultural factors need to be considered. The southern state of Baden-Württemberg (particularly Baden) had the largest number of starred restaurants, namely fifty-eight, or 23 per cent, of all restaurants in 2012. Beyond its relatively greater industrial wealth, several other influences may be considered as equally if not more important. First is its natural environment and the culinary heritage that that has shaped—ample fruit, vegetables, and wine and a historical concentration on *Teigwaren* (pasta). Second, and of equal importance, must be its geographical and cultural proximity to France, particularly to Alsace-Lorraine—a stronghold of French *haute cuisine,* albeit with some Germanic characteristics. Baden in particular has long been a centre of good cuisine and, together with Munich, led the culinary revival from the 1960s onwards. Bavaria (Bayern) has the second largest concentration, with forty awards. *Bayern*, too, has a strong indigenous food tradition which, however, often overlaps with that of Austria to its south.

The distribution of restaurants across the different *Länder* (federal states) shown in Table 2.2, however, is not nearly as uneven between the south and the north of the country as that in the UK. Thus states like Schleswig Holstein, Nordrhein-Westphalen, and Niedersachsen, said to be without a heritage of fine food, now have a significant concentration of starred restaurants. You even find an outstanding three-star restaurant in the less than promising location of Volkswagen's Autostadt in Wolfsburg.

There is a noteworthy geographically configured but primarily political imbalance in Germany between the eastern *Länder* of the former German Democratic Republic (GDR) and the western *Länder* of the former Federal Republic of Germany (FRG). Of the 249 starred restaurants in 2012, only sixteen were in the new federal states, 217 in the western states and sixteen in Berlin (it is difficult to divide the latter between the two former political spheres) (see Table 2.3). This stark difference, apart from the much lower population density and level of affluence, may additionally be attributed to the legacy of GDR culinary culture and training. By encouraging uniformity, training did not generate 'star cooks', nor did the erratic supply situation and dominant ideology permit the evolution of high gastronomy.[14] The suppression of entrepreneurialism and a high degree of isolation from the western world have been additional shaping factors. Thus, during the time of the GDR, there existed neither restaurants of an international standard, nor any top chefs.[15] In the years immediately after unification, people spent their money on catch-up purchases of durable consumption goods, and eating out received a low priority. Even today, there is a perception of weak cultural support for fine-dining although this is seen to be changing among the younger generation.

Many of the new restaurants established in the east during the last decade or so have been opened by individuals from western Germany and may be found in holiday destinations (the island of Rügen) or in important towns in Saxony, such as Leipzig (trade fair town) and Dresden (cultural centre and tourist destination). A restaurateur in a very rural part of Mecklenburg (whose father-in-law had come from the west to buy what used to be a Young Pioneers holiday home and turned it into restaurant with rooms) comments:

> But [there is] less [support for fine food] here in Mecklenburg because of a lack of tradition, prejudice and because we have no small and medium-sized business entrepreneurs. But the younger people in Mecklenburg already have less of a problem with fine-dining. They come and bring their parents and then you see the difference [between the generations].

Of all 136 Michelin-starred restaurants in Britain in 2012, 121 were in England (of which fifty-two were in London), sixteen in Scotland, four in Wales, and none in Northern Ireland. Most of those situated outside London are in the southern counties and in the south-eastern and south-western parts of the country. One exception is Yorkshire—a tourist destination—where one finds six starred restaurants in smaller towns and villages. Of the provincial large towns, only Edinburgh in Scotland now has a significant concentration of fine-dining restaurants, and Birmingham—which has an excellent College of Food—hosts three. Many counties have only between one and three starred restaurants (see Table 2.4), and eighteen counties, such as, for example, Greater Manchester, Essex, Staffordshire, and Suffolk, did not support any Michelin-starred restaurants at all in 2012. Thus the new culture of fine-dining which has gained a foothold in Great Britain since the 1990s has not yet penetrated the country as a whole.

The extremely strong concentration of Michelin-starred restaurants in London, fifty-two, or around one-third, of all restaurants, has already been mentioned. Together with the marked presence in the capital of strong foreign culinary influences and a sophisticated and demanding clientele, this generates a creative space, with great opportunities for innovation. Such concentration creates very intense competition, conducive to both weeding out the weaker restaurants and spurring on the stronger ones to distinguish themselves by innovation in cooking and ambience. One would therefore expect a high number of multi-starred restaurants in London. It is, however, notable that of the eighteen two- and three-star restaurants in Britain in 2012, nine were outside London which does not support the hypothesis that dense geographical concentration by itself creates innovation-fostering networks. Innovation is thriving, however, in London's middle- and upper-middle restaurant sector.

The Changing Face of *Haute Cuisine* in British and German Starred Restaurants

Have the continuous expansion of the two Michelin-starred restaurant sectors and the new confidence of both customers and chefs also brought efforts to change the identity of *haute cuisine* in the two countries? While an extended answer to this question will be provided in Chapter 6, a preliminary and more summary response is provided here. In neither country did an indigenous *haute cuisine* come to the fore during the last decades of the twentieth century. During the first decade of the twenty-first century, however, efforts towards emancipation from French *haute cuisine* have become noticeable. Yet these new departures have emerged just at the same time as a trend towards a more global food culture has taken hold. Such attempts to create an indigenous culinary culture have been a hesitant and challenging undertaking for chefs, giving rise to complex and ambiguous outcomes. As chefs in the two countries have built on slightly different food traditions, new developments also have diverged.

Britain

In Britain, traditions of French cuisine—both classical and the principles of *nouvelle cuisine*—are still quite strong. According to one British chef, 'there is still too much leaning on Franglais'. This is due, on the one side, to the presence of several influential French-born chefs at the apex of the restaurant hierarchy and, on the other and related to it, the weakness of both indigenous national and regional fine food traditions. The underlying principles of French cuisine have not been abandoned. According to one-star chef Shaun Hill: 'The structure of the kitchen is still French. Thus, according to Escoffier, you make stocks from more inferior cuts to put sauce on top of prime cuts.'

The claims which periodically arise about a revival of British cuisine imply a regionalism in the cooking of high-level restaurants. Christopher Driver, a past editor of the *Good Food Guide*, pronounced the implied regionalism as 'slenderly supported outside the ranks of tourist boards and cookery writers'.[16] There have been quite a few writers and food specialists undertaking 'nostalgic journeys round the country looking for food we have lost'.[17] On the whole, they find their search for the holy grail of a regional revival disappointed or, where they detect an increased engagement with the idea of regionalism, find it to be much less developed than in France, Italy, or Germany. It is in any case doubtful whether an *haute cuisine*, mainly centred on the capital London, can be rooted in the locality in its sourcing practices—one central tenet of the new regional *cuisine* in Germany. Thus a Hertfordshire-based chef says: 'We are close to London. In this country, "regional" means northern.' However, isolated pockets of regional Michelin-starred cuisine in some parts of Britain do exist.

This absence of a strong indigenous tradition has been perceived as a grave lack which has caused deep regret. However, among many food writers, it has also inspired a determination to dig for a meaningful culinary past and to harness it to current endeavours. Consequently, almost every decade a small wave of apparently British fine food and cooking has arisen, and a few individual chefs, such as Gary Rhodes and Fergus Henderson, have called their cuisine Modern British. The characteristic content of Modern British Cooking, according to the social historian Burnett,[18] has been minimally defined to consist of good, seasonal vegetable cooking, native meats and plain roasts, game and poultry, and traditional puddings and pies, locally sourced and unpretentiously presented. However, a renewed turn towards Britishness has arisen which is particularly prominently expressed in a move towards local sourcing. One-star Yorkshire chef Frances Atkins is one example of this practice: 'regional to me means using fresh local produce, with a Yorkshire accent. For example, I use a lot of game when in season.' Other forms of regionalism and/or a British culinary style will be explored in Chapter 5.

Altogether, there have been growing efforts to throw off the supremacy of French cuisine. According to Heston Blumenthal:

> chefs are now thinking that they don't have to cook French food. They are using their own style with these [molecular] techniques and local ingredients and cooking something that sings the praises of their own country.[19]

However, even the sum of these efforts, although remarkable, does not come anywhere near to resurrecting what has been neglected over decades. In many places, traditional British or regional cuisine for discriminating palates has become almost completely extinguished. These attempts therefore are still too few and scattered to create a new British cuisine. Instead, this current—the search for British roots—takes its place among the many other national/ethnic cuisines—the global kaleidoscope of culinary styles—which now characterizes British, and above all London dining.

These global influences have emanated from first, Britain's past colonial status and second, its long-time and continuing openness to foreign trade, investment, and migration and the ensuing status of London as a world city. The resulting multiplicity of foreign influences has led to great variety in ingredients and tastes: 'London has a lot of other styles to offer—a whole variety. It is very cosmopolitan' (two-star Marcus Wareing). Another British chef, contrasting the British culinary scene with the German, comments as follows: 'Ethnic cuisine is very important in Britain, whereas Germany has the quality.'

However, the huge variety of ethnic and national foods and the vibrancy it lends to London dining, by and large, occurs below the top level of restaurants. There are a few excellent Michelin-starred ethnic restaurants at the one-star level, doing Modern Indian, Chinese, and Thai food. But their number is still small, and none of them have progressed to the two-star level. The chef-patron of one of the two Indian restaurants I visited feels that Michelin do not sufficiently recognize the ethnic diversity of cuisine in Britain: 'Michelin should consider how varied and diverse British chefs are. Other nationalities—the French and the Germans—would not have left their comfort zone like this.'

But Indian food, although well liked by the British population and available as ready-cooked supermarket dishes, probably has become inextricably linked with low culinary status. This is hard to overcome, even for such excellent chefs like Atul Kochhar and Sriram Aylur and their elegant modernized restaurants *Benares* and *Quilon*, respectively. They and several other high-level Indian chefs are said 'to have made London the epicentre of Indian food outside the subcontinent—and arguably the most exciting place to eat India food in the world'.[20]

Germany

Haute cuisine in Germany, too, still bears the unmistakable imprint of its French origins. Both the impact of the French model in professional training and the geographical proximity to France in the south-west of Germany have kept this cuisine alive, even if there now are very few French-born Michelin chefs in Germany. In comparison with Britain, German chefs started earlier to try to escape French influence, cooking both in a Mediterranean style (absorbing both French and Italian influences) and looking towards German regional and national traditions. The fact that a return to a German style has been hesitant and slow is not, as in Britain, due to the dearth of regional and national traditions. Nor is it a consequence of the absence of good regional and craft produce. In Germany, such a return to domestic traditions was hampered mainly by the nature of German cooking itself—it is predominantly hearty, filling food—the very opposite of fine food and *haute cuisine*. Such food also is often referred to as *bodenständig*, that is, food rooted in the locality.

Nevertheless, a greater shift towards German (national and regional) traditions has become notable during the last decades. A third generation of German-trained chefs now has the confidence to question the French supremacy and to search for ways to further weaken its influence. Both two-star Eric Menchon and Christian Lohse tell me: 'But now the upswing has happened—there is no longer much dependence on France' and 'Now there are new chefs who are less dependent on French style.'

The revival in Germany of gastro-regionalism, amongst others, by some Michelin-starred chefs, has responded to consumer demand. A focus on indigenous cuisine, as a reaction against foreign influences from the early 1980s, symbolized a reaction against standardized international cuisine.[21] Overall, regional dishes have experienced a strong revival and are much more widely embraced by the population than is the case in the UK. However, a search for simple, but well-prepared dishes in traditional rural inns (*Landgasthöfe* and *Gaststätten*) exists side-by-side with a demand for *haute cuisine*. Yet during the new century, a more confident and wider embrace of local produce and culinary traditions has come about. This will be explored in detail in Chapter 6.

What is German Michelin-starred chefs' attitude to non-European ethnic cuisine? From the later 1960s onwards, Germany, too, has become host to a large number of immigrants from a variety of other cultures. Many Germans have experienced foreign cultures and their food also by way of travel, with gourmandizing travel a new preoccupation. Foreign speciality restaurants have become very popular. However, unlike in Britain, such foreign speciality restaurants exist alongside restaurants serving German regional dishes and starred restaurants. As in Britain, there are very few Michelin-starred restaurants serving a non-European cuisine. I have come across only one starred Thai restaurant and another one-star restaurant—the Hamburg restaurant *Piment*—where the Moroccan chef proprietor Wahabi Nouri harmoniously combines Moroccan and French cuisine into delicately spiced dishes, with a very accessible exoticism. Additionally, two-star German-born Berlin chef Tim Raue provides a strongly Asia-oriented cuisine, serving, amongst other dishes, Chinese Dim Sum.

What is particularly notable about culinary identity in both Britain and Germany is that many chefs have become very reluctant to pigeon-hole themselves in terms of any national style, be it French, British, or German. This is well expressed by German three-star chef Elverfeld:

> The word 'style' from my perspective is always difficult to define. I like to allow my creativity free rein without having to consider if a new inspiration 'goes with' my current way of cooking, my style, or not.

There are two reasons, I believe, for this reluctance to declare allegiance to a particular culinary current or even long-time tradition. First, in both countries, chefs now borrow spices and ingredients, and sometimes also techniques, from more than one culinary tradition, in order to integrate them in their own individual manner. The result is not a global mish-mash but mainly constitutes the integration of a few elements—a sauce, a spice, an exotic fruit, or a vegetable—into what remains fundamentally a European dish. Moreover, it remains predominantly a dish cooked using French technique as its basis. Second, two- and three-star chefs in particular view themselves as creative and, often, innovative artistic craftspeople who do not wish to undermine this image by professing subordination to a particular national style. Thus a Joachim Wissler or a Marcus Wareing wishes to portray himself as having a style of his very own, that is to cook like Wissler or Wareing. But at the same time, chefs often find it very hard to define their cuisine in a way which renders it distinctive. They often ended up by describing to me the dishes they had created recently. Thus even the British chefs who draw on native historical tradition and the German chefs, subscribing to *Neue Deutsche Küche*, will not spontaneously describe their style as British or German. Even though a few British (e.g. Sat Bains and Simon Rogan) and German chefs (e.g. Sven Elverfeld and Daniel Achilles) frequently make use of molecular techniques—i.e. they use knowledge of a food's molecular structure to manipulate it—they are at pains not to define themselves by reference to molecular cuisine.

In conclusion, in both countries, some distancing of chefs from the style of French cuisine—though not from French basic techniques—has taken place. The emerging new styles are too diverse and too ill-defined to make it possible to speak of the emergence of a unified distinctive style. In this they differ from currently hegemonic chefs—i.e. those highly rated by the Pellegrino Awards—who refer to themselves as Nordic, Spanish, or French chefs.

Finally, despite the great diversity of cuisine *within* countries, one nevertheless can identify some general features characterizing each *national* cuisine. The more complex 'compositions on the plate' by some German chefs show the same degree of 'over-engineering' as is found in manufacturing industry. It provides an outlet for the high level of skill of the labour force. Conversely, a greater preference for simpler dishes/plates in Britain also may be related to the less developed training for chefs. Additionally, it is more compatible with the slightly lower staffing levels (see Chapter 3) in predominantly independent restaurants.

The Competitive Position and Outlook for the Future of British and German Michelin-Starred Restaurants

Given the much greater endowment of stars in Germany and the phenomenal rise particularly of two-star restaurants in recent years, it is not surprising that chefs and other commentators think that *haute cuisine* in Germany, in comparative terms, has now reached a very high international status. Even the former French chief executive for Michelin Publishing, Luc Naret, acknowledges German chefs' achievement: 'The best chefs in Germany cook today in the way the Germans build cars: on an absolutely perfect level.'[22] Some commentators even put it level with French cuisine. Thus a two-star chef states: 'We no longer have to drive to France to eat well', while a three-star chef claims: 'In Germany we now cook in a more refined (*raffiniert*) manner than in France. The French cuisine has lost a little.' A British Michelin inspector, too, acknowledges the superiority of German *cuisine*, as compared with Britain's: 'There is a higher standard in general in the [German] industry [as compared with Britain].'

This perception of excellence, together with German restaurants' relatively reasonable prices, now attracts foreign diners from France, Belgium, and the Netherlands in the west and from Denmark and Sweden in the north and north east of the country (information from chefs). German starred restaurants are said to be cheaper than those in Britain and, more so, in France, and the proportion of restaurants awarded a Michelin bib gourmand (to reward good value for money) is also significantly higher than in Britain. In 2012, there were 435 awarded to German restaurants, as opposed to only 117 in the UK.[23]

Yet, paradoxically, German cuisine has not yet received the international acknowledgement it merits, and the old stereotypical image of hearty German food endures abroad. Three-star Joachim Wissler regrets that 'wherever you are in the world, everywhere they talk about Frankfurters, Eisbein and Sauerkraut. This is an enormous handicap.'[24] A few of my respondents are a little bitter about this lack of recognition, particularly in international competitions like the Pellegrino Awards. They feel that more guests from abroad would be necessary to offset what they see as a relatively weak demand at home. Cologne two-star chef Hans Horberth comments:

> German cuisine is undervalued at the international level. Yet it is nearly always of outstanding quality. Internationally, the German starred cuisine is not being noticed. People have not even tried it.

Also three-star Sven Elverfeld/Aqua says: 'If we get 5 per cent of foreigners in Germany [among the guests] then that is a lot.'

However, this low percentage of foreign customers does not apply to all German restaurants. In big cities like Berlin, Munich, and Cologne, chefs speak of 20–30 per cent of guests coming from abroad, and one chef in the north German border town of Glücksburg receives half of his customers from Scandinavia where good food is a lot more expensive.

Nevertheless, a high level of Michelin recognition does not necessarily translate into being well known internationally, particularly if the restaurant is located off the tourist or business trail. Furthermore, high quality does not automatically translate into innovative 'on trend' food of the kind rewarded by the international Pellegrino Awards. Thus, German three-star chefs of long duration are hardly known among British chefs who instead look more towards Spanish, Scandinavian, American, and French chefs. German chefs, in contrast, tend to know the second layer of London's cuisine better, particularly innovative ethnic cooking such as *Hakkasan's* or *Zuma's*. Nor do German chefs enjoy recognition from American chefs and gastronomes. Well-known American food writer Adam Gopnik, for example, perpetuates this amazingly ill-informed view on German cooking:

> when Spanish cooking is everywhere sanctified and even English cooking, for the first time, canonized, not many people are making a case that German cooking is much more than fish and potatoes and sauerbraten.[25]

Another problem which affects the competitiveness of German starred restaurants is the changed tax regime for business customers eating on expense accounts. This has led many starred restaurants to close at lunch-time and is viewed as such a significant problem that the 2013 edition of the *Gault Millau* guide devoted a special two-page feature to it: 'Ever since those eating on expense accounts stay away, due to a social envy sanctioned by the state, more and more top chefs focus exclusively on the dinner business.'[26] The sanctions by the state referred to are two-fold. First, claims for tax relief on expense account entertaining are now much more closely scrutinized than in the past. Second, only 70 per cent of expenses incurred are now tax-deductible. Hence companies have become less permissive about visits particularly to three-star restaurants.

In Britain, too, a huge pride in its top-level restaurant sector now exists. This discourse often articulates the tremendous progress made since the mid-1990s and justly comments on a truly amazing overall transformation of the culinary scene. This admiration and praise singles out the status of London as an exceptionally vibrant and rich international dining destination. It is, however, often forgotten that the progress has occurred overwhelmingly in London and that the country as a whole has not fully benefited from it. Thus, when a lead article in *Observer Food Monthly*, entitled 'Foodie Nation', claims that 'our restaurants are the envy of the world', they have a point as far as London is concerned.[27] They show blissful ignorance, however, of what goes on in the rest of the country. Indeed, there are wide stretches of the country where there is very little outstanding restaurant food to be eaten and where you need your gastronomic guide to locate the few places that do exist. However, these critical observations do not imply that no progress has been made outside London. A small yet growing number of excellent British chefs outside London have achieved remarkably high standards in an often unpromising environment and without the stimulus of other local Michelin-starred establishments. However, their number is still too small to create critical mass in the counties, and in several counties not a single starred restaurant may be found. As far as recognition of British restaurant food abroad is concerned, it is principally American commentators who have remarked on the big transformation that has occurred, particularly in London.

Moreover, the enthusiasm and satisfaction about the transformation achieved in Britain also overlooks the fact that British restaurants have been awarded relatively few multiple stars. The development of three-star restaurants has remained stagnant for decades. Furthermore, the fact that many of the restaurants with multiple stars are run by French immigrant chefs— Raymond Blanc, Claude Bosi, Helen Darroze, Alain Ducasse, Joel Robuchon, and last, but not least, Michel and Alain Roux—also attracts little comment.

However, in contrast to the situation in the past, excellent British-born chefs now form a significant counter-weight to the domination by foreign chefs. Finally, it is overlooked that many of the restaurants which make London into an exciting destination for food lovers are ethnic or concept restaurants at a level below fine-dining ones. They have innovative concepts and interesting and diverse food (but also American diner-style greasy and high carb food, such as 'luxury' burgers), but they do not offer the impeccable and reliable quality of Michelin-starred restaurants.

This cosmopolitan and innovative restaurant scene in London may also benefit starred restaurants. Yet there is, at the same time, more competition from below from middle-level small chain restaurants and upper-middle-level concept restaurants than in half-way comparable German cities. British Michelin chefs, too, report highly varying percentages of foreign customers. While many in the provinces speak of only 5 per cent, two London chefs and one Edinburgh chef report a figure of 50 per cent. In Britain, however, no chef expresses a concern about a low proportion of foreign customers. Presumably, given the low density of starred restaurants outside London, they attract sufficient British diners to fill the restaurant.

British and German High-End Restaurants in an International Comparative Perspective

To put the remarkable transformation of the fine-dining scene achieved in Britain and Germany into perspective, I now briefly examine their main international rivals, both in Europe and in the US and Japan.

One way of assessing the relative importance of British and German Michelin-starred restaurants in a wider context is to compare their ratings by Michelin with those of French, Italian, Spanish, Scandinavian, US, and Japanese restaurants. Another way to compare is to contrast all these Michelin ratings with those of the international Pellegrino Awards (founded in 2002 by the British trade magazine *Restaurant*) to restaurants in the same countries. Before making these comparisons, however, a brief contrast of the Michelin organization's rating process with that of the Pellegrino Awards is necessary.

Michelin mainly take into account the *consistently high quality* of the food and, for the award of two and three stars, also originality or personal signature. There are no agreed criteria for the Pellegrino selection of the World's 50 Best Restaurants. However, selection is mainly based on originality and/or innovativeness. The latter appears more and more like novelty, that is, the Pellegrino Awards are focusing on the current stars. The impression of setting the latest trend and providing the shock of the new arises because chefs who one year have figured among the top ten a few years later may have descended to a place between thirty and fifty, or may even have fallen out of the World's top fifty altogether. Moreover, recent top runners all have been engaged either in molecular (also referred to as techno-emotional) cuisine, or, like the 2012 chef in first place—Danish René Redzepi—practise molecular cuisine *together with* extreme localism. In contrast, Michelin have rewarded German chef Harald Wohlfahrt's persistent quality and perfect execution with three stars since 1992, and the British *Waterside Inn* in Bray, run by Michel and, since 2004, by his son Alain Roux, has held three stars ever since 1985.

These contrasting results are influenced by the selection process. Michelin's anonymous professional inspectors select restaurants for awards after prolonged observation and, if considering selection for two or three stars, after repeated visits. In contrast, the Pellegrino Awards are made by chefs' peers once a year in a more snapshot manner. Judges just have to declare that they have eaten in the restaurant of their choice during the course of the preceding eighteen months and that they think them worthy of inclusion in the Pellegrino list. Thus chefs from highly visible places like New York and London are more likely to be voted for than those cooking in a small village. Despite some overlap in the awards between the two rating bodies, striking differences in evaluation also have emerged. (The selection process is discussed in more detail in Chapter 10 which deals with gastronomic guides and other rating processes.)

Table 2.4 provides data on Michelin stars awarded for 2013 in several European countries, plus the USA and Japan, while Table 2.5 analyses the Pellegrino top fifty in terms of country of origin in 2012.

Table 2.4, interpreted at face value, shows that in Europe, both British and German chefs, despite their recent progress in attaining stars, are still a long

Table 2.4. Numbers of Michelin-starred restaurants in selected European countries, and in the USA and Japan, 2013

	One star	Two stars	Three stars	Total number of stars
France	487	82	27	596
Britain	138	20	4	162
Germany	209	36	10	255
Italy	261	39	7	307
Spain	123	17	5	145
Denmark*	12	1	0	13
Sweden*	10	2	0	12
USA*	103	17	10	130
Japan*	224	61	32	317

A * denotes that the figures are for 2012. It additionally draws attention to the fact that, in these four countries, stars have been awarded only for restaurants in a small number of large cities.

Source: Figures have been taken from a large number of websites.

Table 2.5. The Pellegrino Awards in 2012: the World's 50 Best Restaurants, by country

Country	Number of chefs in top 50
France	7
Italy	3
Germany	2
Britain	3
Spain	5
Denmark	2
Sweden	3
Japan	2
USA	9

Source: 'The World's 50 Best Restaurants 2012 and 10 years of global gastronomy', *Restaurant* (March 2012): 62–78. Own calculations.

way from the position of French chefs, both in terms of the overall number of stars and in terms of three-star chefs. As far as Michelin is concerned, French cuisine has *not* lost its supremacy in Europe. However, some critics view the *Red Guide* as deeply old-fashioned.[28] (For an extended critique of the *Michelin Guide* and the organization behind it, see Chapter 10.) Table 2.4 additionally reveals that, in Europe, Germany comes second in terms of the number of three-star chefs. However, Italian restaurants have won more single and slightly more double stars (thirty-nine as compared to thirty-six) than German ones. This more uneven performance in different star categories in Italy is said to be due to this country's deeply traditional and therefore less experimental and original cuisine. Spain, whose chefs are among the current stars in the Pellegrino league table, has a relatively low overall profile in terms of Michelin stars, being similar in the number of two- and three-star chefs to Britain, but coming well behind Germany. Its high profile in the Pellegrino Awards has been established mainly by a handful of both Catalan and Basque chefs—many of whom are followers of Ferran Adria's techno-emotional cuisine. The rest of the country is less well served by high-end cuisine, with Madrid hosting very few starred restaurants. Last, the two Nordic countries Denmark and Sweden still appear overall as underdeveloped in culinary terms. However, both countries have evolved a few very high-profile chefs who have put Nordic cuisine on the world's culinary map. As the Pellegrino Awards for 2012 in Table 2.5 show, Copenhagen chef René Redzepi was rated number one, and other Danish and Swedish chefs occupy relatively high positions, while Michelin still deny Redzepi a third star.

Table 2.4 also reveals that Japanese chefs, rated since 2003 and only in their larger cities, have really put European and, more so, French, particularly Parisian, cuisine into the shade. The world's top culinary city is now Tokyo.

65

With its 247 starred chefs (among them sixteen three-star chefs), it eclipses Paris with only seventy chefs awarded stars and only ten of these three stars.

The Pellegrino Awards, however, do not properly reflect Japanese culinary excellence, thus casting doubt on the adequacy of the voting system. Japanese cuisine is said to have purity, rigour, and beauty of presentation and is seen to excel by its 'intricate flavours; the layering of textures from crunchy to slimy; and the mixture of temperature'.[29]

Japanese restaurants tend to be quite small, with chefs devoting infinite care to a single dish for every customer. These accomplishments and attitudes require a long apprenticeship and a very high level of skill. Japanese *haute cuisine* is uniformly singled out for admiration both by my British and German interviewees and has come to influence European top-level cooking in many subtle, though never determining ways. For example, German three-star Sven Elverfeldt says: 'Yes, the Japanese model has influenced me in my plate arrangements—the linear and the minimalist way' and British two-star Sat Bains reports that 'I have been to Japan and have taken the purity of taste from there, the essence of an ingredient.'

The USA also stands out in Table 2.4, both for its low overall number of stars and its relatively high number of three-star chefs. The low overall number is due to the fact that Michelin rate the cuisine of only a few of America's large cities, namely New York, Chicago, and San Francisco/Californian Bay and Wine areas. (The rating of restaurants in Los Angeles and Las Vegas was discontinued.) One may well imagine that there are vast stretches of the country which are total culinary wastelands. As in Britain, American high-level cuisine developed relatively late, from the early 1990s onwards. High spatial concentration in a few big cities and intense competition are forcing chefs both to differentiate themselves and to become business persons as much as chefs. Just as in Britain, there are a significant number of middle-class 'gifted amateurs' among American chefs, as well as quite a few foreign-born chefs. New York chefs are evaluated particularly highly by Michelin, with seven three-star, seven two-star, and fifty-one one-star restaurants in 2013. This high evaluation is echoed also by the 2012 Pellegrino Awards where five of America's eight restaurants, included in the World's 50 Best Restaurants, are in New York. This places New York not far behind Paris. It may explain why American food writers and academics, such as Steinberger, Gopnik, and Johnston and Bauman,[30] now denigrate French cuisine and restaurants. They often hold a rather stereotypical idea of stiff, opulent temples of gastronomy, serving food submerged in cream and butter. New York chefs themselves though do not necessarily concur with this evaluation. In a recent academic study by Leschziner,[31] they are reported as naming a significant number of French chefs among those with whom they would have liked to work, and many of New York's three-star chefs are French-born in any case.

While the rise to global prominence of Japan and particularly Tokyo may be attributed to a very focused national cuisine, prepared by Japanese chefs for a small number of diners, the situation in New York restaurants is more complex. First, there is relatively little that could unambiguously be defined as American cuisine. Indeed, a considerable number of New York's top chefs are not American, but are foreign-born, particularly from France and Switzerland (e.g. Eric Ripert of *Le Bernadin*, Daniel Humm of *11 Madison Park*, and Daniel Boulud of *Daniel*). Top chefs also hail from Austria (Wolfgang Puck), Korea (David Chang), and Japan (Masa Takayama). Restaurants are viewed as businesses where a good profit is secured by a comparatively large number of covers. British food writer and journalist Nicolas Lander comments:

> the ability to scale up, to handle large numbers of customers every day, seems to be a particular trait of American restaurateurs—an extension of their management skills, and perhaps also a reflection of the work ethic of the large workforce from Mexico and South America.[32]

Ownership of multiple restaurants is common. Danny Meyer, for example, operates five top-end restaurants, Wolfgang Puck runs eighteen, and Joe Bastiano and Mario Batali altogether have twenty-five restaurants. Like London, New York is a world city which, because of a sophisticated (America's cultural avant garde) and rich (working in the financial sector) clientele, attracts chefs both from other parts of the country and from abroad. It is not a city with deep culinary traditions that nourish excellent chefs. Because of the need for differentiation, New York high-end restaurants invest significant sums in restaurants' cutting-edge design which enhances their aesthetic attraction. This may partly account for the anomalous rating, in the Pellegrino Awards, of Thomas Keller's two restaurants. Whereas his Californian *French Laundry*, in 2012, had descended to place forty-three in the rankings, his New York restaurant *Per Se*—a much more recently opened and excitingly designed restaurant—sat at place number six.

Nordic restaurants' high ranking in the Pellegrino Awards, despite a low number of Michelin-starred restaurants in those countries in general, is a more recent and different phenomenon. It started only in the mid-2000s, after Copenhagen's *Noma* attracted global attention. *Noma*'s chef Redzepi has devised a highly original way of cooking which owes few debts to the French model. Situated in a relatively lowly urbanized country and surrounded everywhere by sea, Redzepi's extreme localism makes a lot of sense. It has manifested itself in a foraging for wild herbs and vegetables from sea shore and land. His skilful combination of this localism with techno-emotional techniques has resulted in highly distinctive and deeply unusual dishes which, in both appearance—they are sparse and starkly modern yet beautiful—and taste have genuinely extended the boundaries of western cuisine.

Thus, the high-end restaurant scene in west European countries has experienced considerable change in recent decades, and French culinary hegemony has been undermined, though the paradigm is still influential. Italy, too, has a long tradition and retains its independence in defiance of the search for constant novelty elsewhere. This partly explains its relatively low number of three-star establishments and the only middling standing of its chefs on the Pellegrino list. The changes in Britain and Germany are part of this general culinary transformation in developed society, but have occurred earlier than in Spain and the Nordic countries. In the case of Germany, the development of *haute cuisine* has also preceded that in the USA and has been much more evenly spread across the whole country. Japan's *haute cuisine*, of course, is much older and has a significantly longer tradition than classical French cuisine but has only been 'discovered' by western guides and individual travellers in the course of a general cultural globalization.[33] Restaurants appeared already in the Edo period, well before Japan opened up to westernization during the Meiji period. In commercial and cultural centres like Kyoto, Osaka, and Edo (now Tokyo) restaurants opened in the second half of the seventeenth century. These luxurious and costly restaurants offered the so-called 'cuisine of the tea houses'.[34]

My comparative study of fine-dining restaurants in Britain and Germany therefore does not aim to show their exceptional and outstanding nature in an international context. However, their radical culinary transformation and the many divergences between the two countries, despite similar starting positions, pose an interesting research puzzle worth a comparative study in its own right.

Notes

1. *Der Feinschmecker* 1 (2012): 54.
2. *Gault Millau Deutschland* (2013): 35.
3. Interview of three-star chef Joachim Wissler in Süddeutsche Zeitung 154 (6 July 2012): 9.
4. Interview of two-star chef Niels Henkel in Süddeutsche Zeitung 154 (6 July 2012): 9.
5. K.-F. von Rumohr, *Der Geist der Kochkunst* [Leipzig, 1832]. Translated by Barbara Yeomans as *The Essence of the Art of Cooking* (London: Prospect Books, 1993).
6. *Financial Times Magazine* (14/15 May 2011): 39.
7. <http://www.bighospitality.co.uk/Business/Michelin-Guide-2013-What-ma kes-a-Michelin-starred-restaurant>, 5 October 2012.
8. *Süddeutsche Zeitung* 258 (8 November 2012).
9. Information from *Michelin Germany*.

10. *Restaurant* (July 2011): 46–52.
11. *Restaurant* (May 2010): 26–7.
12. *Restaurant* (May 2013): 30.
13. *The Guardian*, G2 (28 July 2009): 11.
14. R. Horbelt and S. Spindler, *Die Deutsche Küche im 20. Jahrhundert* (Frankfurt am Main: Eichhorn AG, 2000), 246. A. Jenn, *Die deutsche Gastronomie. Eine historische und betriebswirtschaftliche Betrachtung* (Frankfurt: Deutscher Fachverlag, 1993).
15. A. Jenn, *Die deutsche Gastronomie Eine historische und betriebswirtschaftliche Betrachtung* (Frankfurt: Deutscher Fachverlag, 1993), 225.
16. C. Driver, *The British at Table, 1940–80* (London: Chatto & Windus, 1983), 108.
17. W. Black, *The Land that Thyme Forgot* (London: Corgi, 2006), 18, 375; H. Ellis, *Eating England* (London: Mitchell Beazley, 2001); C. Dickson Wright, *A History of English Food* (London: Random House, 2011).
18. J. Burnett, *England Eats Out: A Social History of Eating Out in England from 1830 to the Present* (Harlow: Longman, 2004), 307.
19. Heston Blumenthal, cited in *Restaurant* (May 2012): 53.
20. *Restaurant* (July 2010): 25–8.
21. E. Barlösius, 'Soziale und historische Aspekte der deutschen Küche', postscript to S. Mennell, *Die Kultivierung des Appetits. Die Geschichte des Essens vom Mittelalter bis heute* (Frankfurt: Athenäum, 1988), 433–44.
22. <http://www.spiegel.de/sptv/dokumentatio/0,1518,749228,00.html>.
23. *Michelin 2012 Britain* and *Michelin 2012 Deutschland*.
24. Joachim Wissler, cited in *Süddeutsche Zeitung* 154 (6 July 2012): 9.
25. A. Gopnik, *The Table Comes First: Family, France, and the Meaning of Food* (New York: Alfred Knopf, 2011), 200.
26. *Gault Millau Deutschland* (2013): 35.
27. *Observer Food Monthly* (15 May 2011): 29–36.
28. For example, Gopnik 2011 and M. Steinberger, *Au Revoir to All That: Food, Wine, and the End of France* (London: Blomsbury, 2009).
29. R. Blanc, *A Taste of My Life: One Man's Hunger for Perfection* (London: Transworld Publishers, 2008).
30. Steinberger 2009; Gopnik 2011; J. Johnston and S. Bauman, *Foodies: Democracy and Distinction in the Gourmet Foodscape* (New York and Abingdon: Routledge, 2010).
31. V. Leschziner, 'Kitchen Stories: Patterns of Recognition in Contemporary High Cuisine', *Sociological Forum* 22.1 (2007): 77–101.
32. N. Lander, *The Art of the Restaurateur* (London: Phaidon, 2012).
33. N. Ishige, 'Développement des restaurants Japonais pendant la période Edo', in A. Hutz de Lemps and J. R. Pitte (eds.), *Les Restaurants dans le Monde et à travers les Ages* (Paris: Editions Glénat, 1990), 79f.
34. Ishige 1990: 80.

3

Vocation or Business? Competing Organizational Logics and Work Orientations of Chefs

A fine-dining restaurant is a business organization, and like all such organizations has to take account of economic principles. However, many businesses are guided by additional conceptions of what has value. For top restaurants, the cultural infusion of their products and services defines their very identity, and multiple and often opposed conceptions of what constitutes value or worth for an organization form their organizational fabric. However, in top restaurants the existence of a plurality of guiding principles goes beyond the mere tension between the economic and the aesthetic that is emphasized in much cultural economy writing. Rather, a larger variety of conceptions of what has value or counts and related organizational logics and repertoires of action may be identified. In different situations and contexts, these either cause friction and stress or, more often, have settled into compromise solutions which are hardly any longer recognized as such by chefs.

The fine-dining restaurant is oriented towards a strange mixture of guiding principles or orders of worth.[1] It displays a diversity of organizing logics and organizational forms, each with different modes of evaluation and performance requirements. On the one side, it is oriented towards an archaic form of craft organization (overlapping with the domestic order of worth), dating back to its origins in early nineteenth-century France, but this organization also has incorporated some modern industrial principles. On the other side, top-level restaurants are part of the contemporary cultural economy generating products for an affluent society. In this type of enterprise, the aesthetic and inspirational value of the product—the restaurant meal and service—are as prominent as the material. Producer creativeness is a very important, if not decisive factor of production and of the whole business logic. At the same time, it is a market-oriented business, and a profit imperative informs activities side-by-side with a creative impulse. This chapter details the diverse organizational forms and professional identities associated with these four different approaches to production. I explore how they have become integrated or, conversely, compete and even conflict with one another. The comparison between British and German restaurants seeks to establish whether restaurants in the two societies are oriented to different constellations of these orders of worth.

Craft-cum-Industrial Production or Artistic Enterprise?

Craft Production and the Domestic Order of Worth

In this age of large, highly bureaucratized organizations, devoted to mechanized and increasingly automated mass production of standardized goods and services, the fine-dining restaurant appears to be an oddity. It is devoted to petty commodity production, linked to small-scale service provision. Its production line—the kitchen—preserves many features of handicraft production, including a personal form of control, embodying principles akin to those constituting the domestic order of worth.[2] In the restaurant kitchen, skilled craftspeople produce individual products by hand, with technology playing only a subordinate, largely supporting role. High and consistent quality of the food they serve, together with a pleasing and even exciting taste and appearance, are the main objectives. This quality is attained through careful produce sourcing, a high level of skill of kitchen staff, and by the kind of work organization that prevails. When asked to choose the term which best represents their personal identity—artisan/craftsperson, artist or business person—the large majority of chefs (nine in Britain and thirteen in Germany) put artisan/craftsperson in first place. However, in Britain, a few chefs demur that they are simply chefs.

The traditional notion of craftsmanship implies a high level of skill, acquired during an apprenticeship and devoted to attaining persistently high product quality; the completion of a product from beginning to end; and, based on this, a high level of autonomy in the production process. Traditional craft occupations also entail a gradual progression from apprentice to master craftsperson, based on both time-serving and a process of certification. Given the common origin of this craft tradition in nineteenth-century France, we find many similarities in the organizational approach of British and German Michelin restaurants. However, a close analysis of work organization in their kitchens reveals one very consequential difference in the interpretation of the craft paradigm by British and German chefs, centring on the notion of skill.

71

In both countries the craft paradigm has become interwoven with industrial organizational principles, as we will see in a later section.

A feature of work organization, common to British and German kitchens, is the retention of the nineteenth-century notion of a patriarchal management style and a hierarchical organization of the kitchen 'brigade'. It resembles that used by the military but also is found in the domestic order of worth (presuming a generalized notion of the traditional family and of kinship values and relationships). This hierarchy comprises several ranks, bearing French job titles. It ranges from apprentice (in Germany) to *commis* chef (both mainly engaged in basic preparatory work and in expediting), via *demi-chef* and *chef de partie*, to *sous chef* (the head chef's deputy who also oversees the *chefs de partie* and deals with staffing issues), and finally to head and/or executive chef—the *chef de cuisine*. Right outside the craft hierarchy and below even the *commis* chef is the unskilled kitchen porter (referred to also as 'the donkey' in Britain). He or she carries out the most unpleasant and arduous kitchen work (washing pots and carrying heavy loads, but increasingly also preparing food), who usually is not even eligible for advancement in the hierarchy.

The domestic order of worth also permeates other aspects of work organization. The *chef de cuisine* is a figure of unquestioned authority, based on his or her superior skill, creativity, and often even renown. The members of the brigade are required to show loyalty and obedience, and strict discipline is expected of them. All worth is assumed to rest in the figure of the *chef de cuisine*. The continual shout of 'Yes, Chef!', directed at the *chef de cuisine* to acknowledge the receipt of his or her order, is only one of the many illustrations of this hierarchy. When asked about their management style, quite a few chefs in both countries cheerfully own up to an authoritarian and/or autocratic management style although they usually link it to compensating qualities: 'Authoritarian, but very decent and warm. Also fair. I make high demands' (German chef); 'Friendly and autocratic' (British chef).

Allied to taxing working conditions in many kitchens, the often authoritarian management style sometimes adds up to what an older German chef calls 'absolutely feudal conditions'.[3] Former three-star chef Marco Pierre White, talking about his kitchen in *Harvey's* during the late 1980s, paints an equally extreme picture: '*Harvey's* is the hardest kitchen in Britain, it's the SAS of kitchens. But you don't get to the top by being pampered.'[4]

Many contemporary chefs, though, have moved away from some of the most negative features of authoritarian management. Authoritarian hierarchical command—the domestic order of worth—now comes up against demands founded in the civic order of worth, that is, a more egalitarian form of coordination and more civil tones of interaction. Two of the German one-star chefs have even abandoned hierarchy altogether: 'In this kitchen there is no need for authority—we have a flat hierarchy', one said, while the other claimed that 'we have no hierarchy'. However, both chefs manage relatively small kitchens, with only five staff each and thus are somewhat atypical.

Even if naked authoritarianism is no longer widely regarded as 'fair and appropriate behaviour', the demand for strict discipline has not been abandoned. It is seen as integral to the work organization of a fine-dining restaurant kitchen, designed to achieve the tight coordination between functionally specialized chefs and the maintenance of standards. Nearly all chefs stress the necessity for work discipline. One British two-star chef describes it in the following terms: 'It is a military-type organization—you have to have discipline, respect and organization. You have to have discipline before you can get creativity. You have to have boundaries and rules.' A British one-star chef agrees: 'Yes, you have to be disciplined. I insist on clean uniforms and clean shoes.'

However, a number of chefs in both countries try to convey that the demand for discipline is balanced with other aspects of management, expressing a positive involvement with employees, such as giving them encouragement or eliciting enthusiasm. Two German two-star chefs describe their management style as follows: 'Clear leadership, but very human. If they bring the quality it is very relaxed. I demand things of them, but also promote them'; 'Work is very disciplined, but at the same time it is nice and friendly, not the old-style shouting.'

A few chefs even try to combine their demand for discipline with a 'fun' approach:

> My colleague Sat Bains runs his kitchen with military precision. It is like the Royal Navy. We are more like Somalian pirates. I don't mind if it is a bit rough round the edges. For instance, my chefs wear T-shirts, instead of chefs' jackets. But work organization is structured. (British two-star chef Tom Kerridge)

Indeed, a patriarchal concern for the well-being of their employees is expressed by some of my interviewees, such as: 'It is like a family. We stand together for 12 or 14 hours in the confined space of the kitchen. You get to know a lot about each other' (German one-star chef Anders); 'We exist in a big city and have to...take care of the people we employ' (German two-star chef Lohse); 'I worry for my staff and love them' (British two-star chef Kerridge); 'I look after the chefs who work for me' (British one-star chef Phil Thompson).

The fourth and last surviving traditional craft feature of kitchen organization is the long process of learning and skill acquisition, going well beyond the apprenticeship process. A high level of technical skill is required to ensure the top quality of all products, i.e. of the dishes produced in the restaurant kitchen. Thus, following a completed apprenticeship (Germany) or NVQ training—formerly City & Guilds (Britain)—the humble *commis* chef tries to perfect his or her skill by moving from the kitchen of one highly reputed and possibly even famous *chef de cuisine* to another, either in the form of short (a few months) unpaid internships (*stages*) or, more commonly, of low-paid employment.

The notion of craft skill has had a very different history and institutionalized form in Britain and Germany. In Britain, the handicraft form and the related modes of organization died out with the guild system early on in the process of industrialization. The notion of craft which survived in some industries into the earlier post-Second World War decades was prominent particularly for its translation of autonomy into worker control over the labour process. Skill was often a socially constructed notion, rather than one solidly based on formal certification of training. A progression from apprentice via journeyman to the level of master craftsperson also went out with the guild system. In Germany, in contrast, the abolition of guilds occurred much later and forms of handicraft were kept alive and institutionalized in a whole range of occupations, even after the end of the guild system. Hence the notion of skill remains strongly connected with craft knowledge and competence, acquired in a prolonged process of training and always certified. The notion of certified craft skill, which transferred also into industrial and service occupations, has turned into a key and strategic component of German business life, as well as of culture more generally. In Britain, in contrast, widespread skill shortages, despite or perhaps because of periodic political 'quick fixes' to remedy the situation through new methods of training, have remained endemic in the economy. The concept of skill consequently has a much lower cultural validation. Given these divergent histories and organizational and cultural understandings of the notion of craft skill in the two societies, they also have entered the fine-dining restaurant in different constellations.

Although skill training receives a strong weight in both countries, the divergent manner in which it is accomplished merits particular attention. In Germany, aspiring chefs invariably still execute the time-served apprenticeship. The majority of the German chefs I interviewed still provide systematic apprenticeship training to one or more apprentices. Many chefs—30 per cent of my sample—also acquire a Master Chef qualification. This striving for a high level of craftsmanship is illustrated by the following quotations from two German three-star chefs, Sven Elverfeld and Harald Wohlfahrt respectively:

> I cannot imagine working at something that does not challenge me intellectually, physically or with regard to craftsmanship. I believe in perfectly executed craftsmanship.

> [There is constant striving for] unconditional precision. (Interview notes 2011)

Chefs are very proud of the quality of training still to be found in Germany: 'The level of vocational training in Germany is very high, particularly in the Michelin-starred sector. They are nearly the best in the world' (German one-star chef).

In addition to the structure of training in Germany, its content also differs. Chefs are trained to be competent not only in the kitchen but also in the area of service and interaction with customers. Additionally, the learning of a foreign language forms part of the syllabus in all three years of apprenticeship.[5]

In Britain, in contrast, apprenticeship training has long given way to college-based NVQs (national vocational qualifications). Practical experience in a commercial restaurant kitchen during training is not part of the course in most colleges. While German apprentice chefs follow a national, legally binding curriculum, thus guarding the quality and consistency of the training given, this is no longer the case in Britain. There is no national curriculum. The content and quality of training is highly uneven between colleges, depending on very variable training kitchens and staff. The best British colleges have their own competently staffed kitchens catering for a variety of functions, and several of them have started an apprenticeship course. However, there exists only a handful of training institutions with a high reputation in the industry (based on Ofsted rating), among which the following stand out: Westminster Kingsway College's School of Hospitality, Birmingham College of Food, and the Department of Hospitality in Kendal College, Cumbria.[6] Hence *chefs de cuisine* cannot draw on a wide and assured skills base, and training in British restaurant kitchens mostly has to occur on a more informal basis. Indeed, most British chefs say that the completion of formal training is not considered a necessary precondition for employment. Older British *chefs de cuisine* had enjoyed training under the City & Guilds scheme which was widely rated as excellent, and many of these chefs regard the current NVQs with scorn:

> City & Guilds provided you with the perfect skills base—you just lacked experience. When they switched to NVQs it all changed. Today it's all about money. (Former three-star chef)

> It is still very hard to find good cooks. There is no disciplined process and structure for trainees in this country. The expansion [in the profession] was too rapid to train all new chefs—there was a vacuum. (British two-star chef)

One skill which is said to be a dying art in Britain, according to Michel Roux Jnr., is *patisserie*. Becoming a pastry chef requires more skill and longer training than is required for other kitchen specialisms, and even many Michelin-starred kitchens are no longer prepared to make this costly investment. Instead they deploy young chefs without the necessary skill base. Furthermore, young British chefs do not have the same incentives as German chefs to learn *patisserie* as there exist hardly any high-level pastry shops in Britain which would supply alternative employment and ownership routes. Making and buying delicate and intricate pastries has not been a part of British food culture in recent centuries and constitutes another instance of an insufficiently supportive structural and cultural environment.[7]

Instead, British head chefs put a high value on applicants' readiness and willingness to learn from those above them in the hierarchy. In both countries, recruiting head chefs put strong emphasis on the right personality which promises that the applicant becomes a disciplined team player. But in Germany this is a requirement additional to a completed apprenticeship which is taken for granted. In Britain, in contrast, certified training is not considered a necessary prerequisite for employment by all head chefs. Thus the manager of a large London one-star restaurant states: 'We look for commitment and interest in Italian food. It is not necessary to have formal training.' A London two-star chef says: 'I look at their experience, but the CV means nothing. I look at the human being first and foremost.' And a one-star chef of an Indian restaurant states: 'Above all, I look for a passion for food. They should positively want to do the job. I look for very basic skills and techniques. They could be self-taught.'

Also it is only in Britain that one still finds a number of *chefs de cuisine* without any formal training, among them such renowned chefs as three-star Heston Blumenthal, two-star Raymond Blanc, two-star Phil Howard, and one-star Ruth Rogers of the *River Café*. Among my British respondents, six chefs have not received any formal vocational training.

These and most other British restaurants therefore have to put a lot of effort into on-the-job training which significantly adds to their staff costs and makes the quality and breadth of training uneven. In Germany, in contrast, the invariable employment of *commis* chefs with an apprenticeship, completed to nationally binding standards, obviates such extra investment. Moreover, the generally lower and less reliable level of skill at lower levels of the hierarchy in British restaurants makes it harder to reach the consistency of quality looked for by Michelin inspectors. However, even in Germany some feeling is expressed that the standards of training in vocational schools (*Berufsschule*)—one part of the dual system—have slipped in recent years, due to the obligation to provide a chance to educationally challenged youngsters. It is also recognized that some head chefs want apprentices for their cheapness and will not necessarily have a high commitment to the training required.[8]

The Industrial Order of Worth

Anyone watching chefs during the peak of a lunch or dinner service will be struck by the speed with which they have to perform, as well as by the high degree of coordination between them that is required. Dishes have to arrive at the pass (the place where the *chef de cuisine* carries out the last check on the meticulous execution of his or her vision) in the right number and combination, exactly as ordered by any given table. This requires both high discipline and high speed, and the head chefs at the pass make sure that every plate is turned out to the high degree of perfection specified by them.

In both countries, therefore, craft principles are intertwined with and partially subverted by industrial modes of evaluation, in the way first introduced by the writing of Auguste Escoffier at the beginning of the nineteenth century. Skill, except at the apex of the organization, is not accompanied by craft autonomy in restaurant kitchens.

A consequential departure from the traditional understanding of craft is the abandonment of the holistic view of making products, i.e. the completion of a single product from beginning to end. The craft principle gave way to an industrial-style division of labour, designed to increase efficiency of output. This resulted in the creation of *chefs de partie*, specializing in a particular aspect of the food preparation process. The head chef prepares the overall plan for the day, and the other employees have to stick to the fairly formal organizational rules laid down in most kitchens. Work organization thus is structured by the more instrumental 'efficiency' mode of evaluation where individual competency is the main consideration, as stipulated by the industrial order of worth.

In larger kitchens, there is considerable horizontal differentiation between various *chefs de partie* and even *demi-chefs de partie*, devoted to the preparation of different types of foods. This may include the following: the *garde-manger* (cold dishes), *entremetier* (vegetables, potatoes, and rice and pasta), the *saucier* (meat), the *poissonier* (fish), as well as the *patissier* (desserts and bread). Consequently, the predominance of lateral differentiation is combined with insistence on team work. Team work is regarded as a functional imperative in order to achieve the lateral coordination. A large number of *chefs de cuisine* make it explicit that they look for the ability to work in a team as the main condition for employment, sometimes (particularly in Britain) ranking it above a high level of skill.

As observed by Wright—a writer and former restaurant AA inspector—the skill that is most cherished in the formal fine-dining kitchen is the willingness to obey orders: 'A chef's first responsibility is to learn a task and keep repeating it in exactly the same way to precisely the same standard.'[9] Hence *chefs de cuisine* are very wary of taking on staff who do not have the required personality characteristics: 'They have to fit the kitchen dynamic. This is more important than competence. I don't need egomaniacs' (British two-star chef); or as a German three-star chef puts it: 'They should be team players and should not have an inflated ego.'

Several other chefs—five in each country—specify that staff should be team players, and a preference for personality traits like 'complete dedication' and 'the will for hard work' also figures large in both countries. However, one exceptional German *chef de cuisine*—two-star chef Christian Lohse—is looking for people who think for themselves and stipulates the following character traits for his employees: 'personality; intelligence; strong character; being able to use freedom granted'. Strict discipline, allied to team work, consequently still are considered indispensable parts of kitchen work organization, without which the plates with all their components would not arrive on time at the pass and on the customer's table. Chefs have to prepare in a coordinated manner what has been ordered by a given table at a given time. This usually comprises several different versions of a starter, a meat or a fish dish, each requiring different vegetables and garnishes. It is this simultaneity of disparate orders, to be completed in the same short time span, which creates the extreme pressure for timely coordination experienced in these kitchens. Chefs become mere functional links in a chain. Lack of cooperation or efficiency by any individual worker in this context would stop the whole line, and, in this particular respect has some resemblance to industrial work on the assembly line.

However, this division of labour does not result in a fragmentation of the product into minute parts where the worker executes completely standardized detail work and loses sight of the final product. Most preparation still is by hand and requires manual dexterity, as well as a sense of taste and of the aesthetic. Also the relatively small size of kitchens leaves the final product visible to all who have contributed to it. It still enables the development of a craft satisfaction and pride in a perfect product. Nevertheless, introduction of a division of labour and the demand for measurable efficiency have inserted an important element of 'the industrial order of worth' into the craft paradigm. This has considerable consequences for the quality of work organization as experienced by line chefs.

However, in one British kitchen—that of the *River Café*—the strong division of labour—'the regimented French style'—has been abandoned in favour of job rotation.[10] This is a kitchen in which 50 per cent of chefs have a degree. It looks as if, with raised educational standards, chefs no longer regard a strict and regimented division of labour as 'fair and appropriate behaviour'.

It is this amalgam of a (craft-related) demand for product quality, coupled with highly traditional authority relations, and allied to an industry-style division of labour and a demand for speed and efficient coordination between chefs, which often produces an explosive mix in its effect on interpersonal relations. The fast and demanding pace of work, particularly during lunch and dinner 'rush hours', coupled with the relentless pressure to maintain excellence, are experienced while working long hours in a confined space, at often high temperature. All this produces high levels of pressure and leads to psychological stress and frayed tempers. It occasions the constant use of swear words, often verbal abuse of line workers and, more rarely now, physical violence against the latter by *chefs de cuisine*.

An interview by Simon Wright with Gordon Ramsay on his career trajectory during the 1990s details incidences of physical violence experienced by Ramsay for slight disregards of the *chef de cuisine*'s orders in both the kitchens of Marco Pierre White's *Harvey's* and, less routinely, at *Le Gavroche* under Albert Roux.[11] When Ramsay subsequently became head chef of the restaurant *Aubergine*, his kitchen was referred to as 'Vietnam', likening work in it to being a war zone.[12] Another story circulating in the British industry is of a high-ranking *chef de cuisine* burning the hand of a lower-level chef on the stove because he decorated the plate with four rather than three raspberries. German two-star chef Tim Raue explains:

> This rough manner which occasionally goes substantially below the belt, has something liberating, almost like catharsis. You abuse each other, without taking it too personally. Because you simply need a vent to get rid of this frenzied pressure.[13]

Another German chef mentions frequent abusive references to customers who spring vegetarian and food allergy requirements on the kitchen as 'food cripples who would do well to frequent other shitty restaurants'.[14] Shrinking violets who cannot take the constant, if often jocular, abuse thus are unsuited to this occupation.

Serious violence appears to be rare nowadays, but shouting and verbal abuse continue, though by no means in all kitchens: 'I shout if I have to, if I have told people the same thing for the third time. It happens once per service' (British two-star chef); 'Yes, I shout. There is a little bit of abuse' (British two-star chef); 'I do shout occasionally if I have said something before and before that' (German three-star chef).

German chefs also have spoken of various kitchen utensils being hurled across the room and about the often deafening noise from pots and pans and various machines used.[15] A former German chef, referring to his apprenticeship in the early 2000s, sums it up like this: 'There can hardly be another work place which is shaped to a comparable degree by the use of faecal language and aggression.'[16]

However, several *chefs de cuisine* in both countries also volunteer that they are actively trying to abandon the abuse they themselves had experienced during their years of training. Thus a German two-star chef comments in a newspaper interview:

> I now scream less than in the past. I was screamed at as an apprentice, and I try not to become too loud, but I do not always manage it. Sometimes I do lose it, but I would like to emphasize that I do not throw pots and dishes about.

During our interview, he added that: 'I screamed until about five to six years ago. Now I just leave the kitchen.'

But such behaviour is not ubiquitous. Several chefs tell me that they would not tolerate shouting abuse in their kitchens. Two German chefs unwittingly evoke the human qualification of the civic order of worth. They point out that shouting abuse at employees no longer fits the current social climate. It violates workers' dignity, and employees will no longer tolerate it: 'You can no longer shout at them. We are no longer an island. They now don't stand for it. There has occurred a strong re-thinking.'

> The times have changed...I must admit that sometimes I would like to be as emotional as Eckart Witzigmann or Lothar Eiermann. Yet today you have to take a stronger grip on yourself as people have become much more sensitive and take criticism quickly very personally. The relationship to commis chefs was much rougher in those times than it is today.[17]

Some chefs in both countries, indeed, insist on silence during service, except for the calling out of orders, to heighten concentration. In the words of German one-star chef Mario Gamba: 'I am very calm and concentrated. Calmness is very important.' Other examples of this attitude are German chefs Harald Wohlfahrt, Eric Menchon, and Joachim Wissler, as well as British chefs Michel Roux and Martin Wishart, who all demand absolute concentration on the job at hand. Three-star Harald Wohlfahrt, who achieves compliance through calm authority, will have influenced a whole generation of younger German chefs in their management style.

Yet a third (albeit small) group of chefs do not demand deep concentration, nor do they try to ensure compliance by authoritarian command. Instead they try to elicit commitment by running a relaxed kitchen in which some entertainment lightens up the long working times: 'The kitchen is a bit like an artist's atelier; there is no shouting, we even have TV in the kitchen' (German two-star chef); 'We always have Sky Sports on. I don't like concentrated silence. It is relaxed to an extent but you have to find a balance—it has to be professional' (British two-star chef).

All in all, however, it is believed that to become a top chef you need not only to learn what excites the palate but you additionally have to know how to survive in a kitchen. The account of work in the kitchen conveyed so far, including the relationship between the *chefs de cuisine* and their brigades, departs in significant aspects from the rosy picture provided by French business scholar Balazs.[18] Whereas she presents (French) *chefs de cuisine* exclusively as charismatic leaders who envision, empower, and energize employees, I have dwelt also on some of the dysfunctional and stressful elements of kitchen organization and of relations in the kitchen hierarchy.

The Work Environment

Trying organizational arrangements are aggravated by an often poor work environment. Two-star chef Raymond Blanc vividly depicts the negative organizational and physical features of work in fine-dining kitchens, where space is at a premium or where there may be no daylight:

> then there is the extreme sauna-like heat of the kitchen which batters your senses, along with the movement all around you. Then there is the noise and the swearing…the professional kitchen brings out savage characteristics. The environment is so unyielding it will extract the worst out of anyone. At the end of the service you are sweating like a pig, you are burnt out and you are pale, turned white by the sheer intensity of the heat and the pressure.[19]

A German ex-chef describes the situation in similar terms:

> It is hot in the kitchen, very hot; there is hardly any natural light, and pots and pans are crashing about…All the time, one has to speed up and speed up some more.[20]

Some positive developments have occurred also in the work environment. In some restaurants, underground kitchens have given way to lighter kitchens, sometimes integrated into the restaurant, as, for example, in the British *River Café* or the German *Söl'ring Hof*. Or take the very bright kitchen of *La Vision*, situated on the thirteenth floor of the Hotel Wasserturm in Cologne and enjoying a beautiful view over the city. However, underground kitchens with only artificial light still exist, particularly in London's tall and narrow buildings. Heat and steam, as well as frequent small injuries, such as cuts and burns, continue to make for an unpleasant work environment.

These taxing working conditions are by no means compensated for by good working hours. On the contrary, hours are long and often anti-social. As unionization is very low in these predominantly small enterprises contractual limitations of working hours usually are disregarded.[21] A report on working time in London restaurants describes working hours as follows:

> Most chefs are employed to do seven shifts. They will start at seven in the morning, take a break from four to five pm and may finish as late as twelve o'clock. That's a double shift and you do two a week. Then there are shorter early and late shifts. They do a minimum of forty-eight hours but it can be as much as eighty.

It is very hard work, and the drop-out rate is high, with many ex-chefs becoming cabbies.[22]

In both countries, chefs often work up to sixty hours per week. (For greater detail on working hours, see Chapter 4.) The afternoon break often is not kept, particularly by chef proprietors.

Despite the long hours, pay is widely viewed as low by *chefs de cuisine* and lower chefs alike, particularly until you have reached the position and much increased responsibility of a *sous* or head chef. Even this low level of pay is considered hard to recoup by my head chef interviewees, given the generally high levels of staffing and low levels of profit in the fine-dining industry. A German one-star chef tells me with regret: 'But the low wages are the last thing! But there is no money for it.' Moreover, for most chefs advancement up the hierarchy is slow, and many never reach the top, i.e. the better-paid positions of *sous* and head chef.

How are young chefs able to bear this high-pressure atmosphere, poor physical working environment, relatively low degree of discretion, and low financial reward? It is made bearable if the head chef's inspirational qualities convey to them a passion for producing good food and/or the craft pride in the quality of the product which gives high levels of satisfaction to diners. The deep satisfaction gained at the end of successful service is well conveyed by Raymond Blanc:

> But at the end of each service, successfully completed, you know that you have achieved something close to perfection. You get a few seconds of bliss a couple of times a day.[23]

When appointing a new chef, *chefs de cuisine* therefore seek out individuals who, they believe, show a passion for the job and are able to give dedication and total commitment. Thus a British one-star chef says: 'Above all, I look for a passion for food. They should positively want to do the job. I look for very basic skills and techniques. They could be self-taught.'

Equally, if not more important to sustain line chefs' motivation is a firm belief that they, too, may one day reach the exalted status of a Michelin-starred chef and/or of a restaurant proprietor. Also the close team work necessitated by lateral coordination creates camaraderie similar to that experienced by soldiers. It forges close relationships, transcending individual kitchens. (These will later be called upon in close professional networks, even across national borders—the so-called brotherhood of chefs.) However, there also is fierce competition between chefs, partly generated by the many ranking systems they are subject to. Those chefs who are not sustained by the experience of intrinsic rewards and fail to feel compensated for the relentless pressure, shortage of personal time, and relatively low pay, either leave the occupation early or succumb to alcohol and substance abuse.[24] Thus, during recent decades, around 50 per cent of those doing the German apprenticeship to become a chef terminated their contract before completion or could not fulfil requirements.[25] The following replies from British one-star chefs to my question of *How long, on average, do kitchen staff stay with you?* also indicate a retention problem:

> A year. I have to start all over again after a year. It is the hardest and most deflating part. It's easier if they do stay longer. (One-star chef Colin Kelly)

> No other industry thinks it is acceptable that a key player in a business stays with it, maybe for a year…and yet they are our biggest assets. (One-star chef Alan Murchison)

This carries obvious negative consequences for continuity and a wasteful training effort on the part of head and *sous* chefs.

There is, indeed, a high labour turnover in many kitchens and, in Britain (and particularly in London), a huge shortage of chefs. High labour turnover is produced by both high dissatisfaction with the above extreme demands of the work and, in the early career stages, also by the enduring craft feature of a journeymanship, albeit now pursued in an informal manner. This involves seeking a succession of short placements or internships in highly reputed kitchens (the so-called *stages*). Young chefs seek *stages* to further perfect their skills and to derive professional value from the national and sometimes international renown of the restaurant's *chef de cuisine*. Hence high labour turnover, particularly at the lower level of *commis* chef and *chef de partie*, is common in both my British and my German samples.

Nevertheless, labour turnover appears to be more pronounced in Britain. This is likely to be connected with the considerably higher proportion of foreign chefs British kitchens have to rely on. These chefs often return to their home country after a few years. Thus the average length of stay in the job of chefs in Britain is two to three years and the proportion of foreign chefs employed amounts to 59 per cent. (Chefs stay longer in the provinces than in London.) In German kitchens, by contrast, only 15 per cent of employed chefs are foreign, and this proportion includes quite a few Austrians in the south. While the length of employment is very variable in German kitchens, many more interviewees speak of 'a long time' of tenure.

The very international composition of British kitchen staff is striking. A British one-star chef from a smaller town reports: 'Only 50 per cent of kitchen staff are British. The other 50 per cent are from all over the world. I have one from Nepal and one from Japan at the moment.' Or a London chef: '30 per cent are British, and the others come from South Africa, Australia, Italy and Ireland.'

Another London chef mainly recruits his staff from Commonwealth countries and explicitly rules out employing chefs from France:

> [They come] from Australia, India and New Zealand—I get few applications from Europe. I do not want to employ French chefs—they do not put in the work any more—it's the impact of French legislation.

Even in a rural Cumbrian hotel restaurant, the 40 per cent of foreign kitchen staff come from Russia, Poland, India, and France. In a one-star restaurant in a remote village in Wales, the proportion of foreign chefs even rises to 75 per cent, including a Czech, Lithuanian, and Philippine chef.

While this international composition of the British brigade makes the kitchen an interesting place of work which may generate new insights for the *chef de cuisine*, it also carries some risks. As a one-star chef sees it: 'Foreigners still predominate in British restaurants. If the Polish and Lithuanians were to go home, the industry would collapse.' The current difficulty in Britain for non-EU chefs to get a visa has already dangerously has reduced the pool of chefs from former Commonwealth countries. In German kitchens foreign chefs are relatively rare and are mostly from neighbouring countries. The predominantly German composition of brigades poses no problems of labour supply in years to come.

To sum up this section, it has been shown that, in both countries, the combination of two seemingly incompatible organizational principles and associated modes of evaluation—the craft and the industrial—causes tensions in both hierarchical and lateral work relations. These are further aggravated by a trying work environment and a low quality of working time. Given the relatively low level of compensation in terms of pay and conditions, many young chefs cannot cope, causing considerable labour turnover, as well as personal pathology. My account has emphasized that the process of empowering and energizing brigade members, noted by Balazs,[26] often is unsuccessful and that only the hardier and more resourceful young chefs are sufficiently energized to imbibe the vision of their leader.

However, those who feel passionate about producing good food find that the opportunity of developing a perfect product and experiencing craft pride serve to compensate for the hardship of the kitchen labour process. For some young chefs the dream of future celebrity makes them hold on to the job. Several chefs also tell me that they love the job because they know that the results of their hard work make guests/customers happy. They enjoy an immediate positive feedback no longer afforded by many manual jobs.

I additionally suggested that the differences between Britain and Germany in skill training systems—the apprenticeship versus NVQs—provide German *chefs de cuisine* with a more assured supply of skilled young staff. I suggest that this makes it more likely that high product quality is achieved *on a consistent basis*—one important demand of Michelin inspectors. It is therefore one of my explanations of the higher performance achieved by German chefs in the Michelin system competition. However, fine-dining restaurants do not only provide food of the highest quality, but also an exceptional and often inspiring dining experience.

The World of 'Inspired' Worth

Although most chefs see themselves primarily as good craftspersons or artisans, a significant minority also have artistic aspirations. To rise to the apex of the profession, that is, gaining two or more Michelin stars, something additional to craftsmanship is required. This additional ingredient is the *inspiration* to produce something out of the ordinary, something original, which is aesthetically perfect and provides the diner with a truly exceptional taste experience. Many of the chefs I interviewed emphasize that giving high satisfaction to customers and, indeed, providing them with an outstanding and unique experience, is one of their main motivators. The chef has a vision of the food his or her kitchen will produce.

The dishes produced have to diverge from and surpass mainstream *haute cuisine* dishes, i.e. the restaurant's cuisine has to show individuality and distinctiveness and be the expression of creativity. Exceptional chefs have to move beyond being a mere craftsperson who works according to a traditional set of rules. They have to depart from the canon of classical French cuisine, think of new ways of preparing the food and/or broaden the taste spectrum or the range and combination of food textures. They will display fantasy and imagination. Like artists, they will strive for presentational beauty and, even more so, develop new taste sensations which reach beyond the ordinary.

Alternatively, the exceptional chef will become more radically innovative, often with the use of scientific knowledge. Such chefs start from the premise that foods are mixtures of different chemicals and that, if we understand the chemical properties of food, we can manipulate them and combine them into molecules to create different and surprising aromas, tastes, and textures— hence the use of the term molecular cuisine. Chefs can transform our very conceptions of given foods, presenting them in a new form and with different textures, with more intense flavours or in unexpected combinations. (For more detail on molecular cuisine, see Chapter 6.) Whether the *chef de cuisine* is inspired by art or by science, or a combination of the two, successful chefs usually are passionate and often driven about their work.

Three chefs in Germany and four in Britain view themselves first and foremost as artists. A further ten German chefs view themselves as artisans with artistic inclinations. In the words of a three-star chef: '[Being a chef is] a precise craft with artistic elements.'

Only four British chefs opt for this identification, with the remaining either ruling out any artistic quality—'people who think they are artists are mad' (one-star chef Shaun Hill)—or giving second preference to the notion of being an entrepreneur.

Artists' claims to originality, the American sociologist Richard Sennett points out, are claims for individuality and stand in tension with the craftsperson's more collective orientation.[27] It is also widely assumed in the literature on creativity that this kind of inspired activity can only flourish in an environment which fosters creativeness. How can the inspired world of worth exist in an environment ruled by the demand for technical precision and industrial efficiency? And how can creativity develop in a hierarchical command structure which requires obedience, discipline, and suppression of individuality for the sake of team spirit? In other words, how can the inspired order of worth be reconciled with the simultaneously operative craft and industrial principles of production and the managerial demands they entail? Are these different worlds of worth perhaps less incompatible than the theoretical approach of Boltanski and Thévenot implies?[28] Or do there exist bridging and/or adjustment procedures that make the integration of the various orders of worth less problematic than it appears at first glance?

First, craft principles of work and creativeness do not necessarily compete but may also enhance one another. Craft skill, several chefs tell me, does not stifle creativity but is its necessary basis. Craft discipline forms an indispensable precondition for creativity and innovation. Thus a German one-star chef: 'An artist will only be able to develop on the basis of know-how/expertise. He must first have a craft basis, just as an opera singer', and a one-star British chef: 'if you are methodical it allows for creativity'.

Furthermore, hierarchy and obedience to the master craftsperson, a second component of craft, as well as an industrial-style of coordination and team work, do not impede creativity. This is so because, for many chefs, particularly in Britain, the fount of all inspiration is the *chef de cuisine*. For these chefs, creativity seems to be the prerogative of the *chef de cuisine* alone, while the brigade merely turns into reality the visions developed by the head chef—the only figure embodying true 'inspired' worth. Such chefs thus speak as artists rather than craftsmen, and they certainly do not seek to empower their lower-level employees, as envisioned by Balazs.[29] Thus a British two-star chef: 'Only senior people are the creative ones'; or a British one-star chef: 'Creativity comes from the top. I don't want any under me to be creative. They have to be able to do the work'; or 'When you work in a team, employees bring ideas, but I take the conceptual lead' (British one-star chef).

Although lower-level staff have to share the head chef's commitment to consistent excellence they mostly are not expected to provide impulses for innovation. A related strategy is to employ some staff only for their disciplined execution and others for their creative promise. The manager of a London one-star restaurant informs me: 'You need people who do as they are told, plus the creatives.' Or, more colourfully, from a former three-star chef: 'You need a few donkeys and the odd thoroughbred.'

Sometimes, lower-level chefs are encouraged to implement their creative ideas in the production of *Amuses Gueules* or, in Germany, *Grüsse aus der Küche*—the tasty little titbits served before the dishes from the formal menu— though never on items from the menu itself. Thus a German three-star chef voices what several of his colleagues suggest: 'There are creative starts, but unfortunately they remain only starts. I give employees some space [for crea- tivity] in the area of Amuses Gueules.'

However, several chefs take a less elitist and more inclusive approach: 'I also brainstorm with the whole team, we taste everything together' (British one-star chef Phil Thompson). In his kitchen, employees are encouraged to come up with new ideas for dishes.

Harald Wohlfahrt, too, is known to be a motivator of his young staff who strongly promotes able chefs and does not have to stand at the centre of things himself.[30] Wohlfahrt, my interview establishes, sees himself primar- ily as a craftsperson and only secondarily as an artist. Some of the *chefs de cuisine* thus try to motivate and empower their employees in the terms laid out by Balazs, but this does not seem to be the most typical pattern of leadership.

Even the *chef de cuisine* does not enjoy ideal conditions for developing ideas and unfolding creativity. In other creative industries, there is role specializa- tion for professional innovators, such as designers or makers of television programmes. *Chefs de cuisine*, in contrast, have to develop creativity on top of their many other and more prosaic tasks, such as staff recruitment, manage- ment, and purchasing, which will be described in Chapters 4 and 8. It is the relentless pressure to be innovative which may be the hardest demand two- and especially three-star chefs have to cope with. One of the most famous chefs, French Auguste Escoffier, already expressed his weariness about this pressure at the turn of the nineteenth century:

> Personally, I have ceased counting the nights spent in the attempt to discover new combinations, when, completely broken with the fatigue of the heavy day, my body ought to have been at rest.[31]

Hence, the head chef is not the esoteric visionary found, for example, in reli- gious movements, but mostly has to seek inspiration in the midst of a hectic daily working round:

> Menus change every six weeks which means you constantly have to innovate in your head. The daily business, however, does not afford sufficient calm. The big

problem with creativity is to create space for oneself. I find it when I am running and also at home. (German two-star chef)

Or: 'One gets the best ideas when one holds the head free but it is difficult to hold your head free' (German three-star chef).

Going for a run to overcome various tensions and to gain space for thought is, indeed, a strategy employed by several of the interviewed chefs. Additionally, the *chef de cuisine* takes time out from the kitchen and engages in gourmandizing travel, to seek inspiration from the example of his or her peers—a practice adhered to by nearly all the chefs I interviewed. A British one-star chef enthuses:

> [I am inspired] by other leading chefs. I quite regularly eat out, mostly in Britain. During our annual holiday in France, we choose the places to stay with starred restaurants in mind.

Once the *chef de cuisine* is well established and the restaurant has acquired a solid reputation, other ways to gain creative space become possible. A second, more hands-on head chef may be employed as is the case in several of the restaurants I visited. The chef proprietor/patron may gain time to think and experiment by creating an experimental or development kitchen (as, for example, Heston Blumenthal, Sat Bains, and Simon Rogan have done).

It has been shown that the kitchen of a fine-dining restaurant is subject to a type of work organization in which industrial and craft types of organizational norms are interwoven with a distinctive individual and usually very creative working style. Chefs react to the contradictory demands emanating from different orders of worth in a number of ways, ranging from stoical acceptance, via attempts to compartmentalize, to experience of stressful cross-pressures from conflicting guiding principles. The strain it may cause is expressed by this German two-star chef: 'The free space for creativity is becoming successively more narrow...Sometimes you are really driven.'

On the whole, however, it is thought that demands from these seemingly contradictory orders of worth can be reconciled and any resulting pressures can be managed. A British one-star chef just accepts the pressures: 'You just create the best you can in the limits set for you by circumstances.' Put more positively, it is clear that those chefs who last the course show incredible dedication and craft pride and often express spontaneous joy about their chosen professional activity.

However, the inspired order of worth is found to be harder to combine with another mode of evaluation and its associated metrics of performance and organizational logic—the market order of worth.

Cultural or Capitalist Enterprises?

Fine-dining restaurants do not merely produce cultural experiences where goods depend on a strong input of both craft skill and artistic imagination. They additionally are business enterprises competing in a market and compelled to make a profit. According to Boltanski and Thévenot, 'inspiration can unfold only if the market world can be set aside'.[32] Yet to disregard the market world is not an option in top-level restaurants, as even an employed chef cannot ignore their managerial and purchasing role as head of a kitchen. At most, some of the chefs employed in luxury hotels may be more or less cushioned from market pressures. Hence a chef solely devoted to producing inspired food who does not invest time and effort in some of the bread-and-butter issues, like the wage bill or the relation between the high cost of produce and the prices on the menu, would not last long in the position of commander-in-chief. *Chefs de cuisine* therefore constantly have to juggle the allegedly incompatible orders of market and inspired worth. In their own words:

> Pressure does not make creativity bubble up. One has to accept the tension and set priorities, but I do find it stressful. (German two-star chef)

> You do notice the pressure. It affects creativity in the short run. (German one-star restaurateur)

> No, they [economic pressures] never have affected me. I can make something out of nothing. It does not have to be truffle. (British one-star chef)

Chefs have to find a way to manage these contradictions and sometimes even turn them to their advantage. Before expanding on the different ways of juggling the competing logics of the inspired and the market order of worth, it is important to set out the challenges involved in turning a fine-dining restaurant into a highly profitable enterprise.

It is hard to make the craft features of the business—small scale, handicraft production, and pursuit of high quality and excellence in both food and service—compatible with achieving a good profit. Despite the high prices charged by top-end restaurants, making a decent profit often is a real struggle. Concerning the scale of operation, in both Britain and Germany—in contrast to equivalent US restaurants—it is small, with an average of sixty-five covers in Britain and forty-one in Germany, each in at most two services (in Germany often only one service) on five to six days per week. Yet the costs to be covered nevertheless are very high. A fine-dining restaurant demands high levels of investment in staff, produce, and wine. Produce used in the kitchen has to be the best the market offers, and the commitment to serving only the freshest produce often results in waste. According to the writer and former restaurateur Nicholas Lander, 'the gross profit is inversely proportional to the quality of the food served'.[33]

The biggest outgoings in up-market restaurants, integral to the concept of a fine-dining restaurant, are for staff. Several of my respondents estimate them at around 30 per cent of all costs. In the kitchen, the labour-intensive preparation of high-quality and inspirational food demands a high ratio of chefs to diners, with an average ratio of one chef per six covers in the British and one chef for every three covers in the German sample. In the front-of-house, the necessity for attentive and individual service poses a similar imperative for investment in staff, with a high number of waiting staff per guest. These ratios assume a full house which, particularly at lunch time, is far from guaranteed in many of the restaurants I visited. Several chefs see getting a high occupancy rate as one of their chief worries. Thus for a London two-star chef one of the main psychological pressures is: 'to retain the loyalty of customers. There is so much choice nowadays.' This sentiment is echoed by a German two-star chef who identifies the biggest economic pressure, namely 'if you do not get a sufficient number of guests'.

Although wages are relatively low for both kitchen and restaurant employees (with the exception of the head chef's salary), employees in the kitchen are as a rule full-time and permanent. In the restaurant, there is some part-time employment in Britain (twelve out of twenty have some part-time employment), whereas nineteen out of twenty German restaurants have only full-time employees. Hence the opportunities for saving on staff outgoings are circumscribed. Savings can be made, on the one side, if the restaurateur and his or her family remain prominently involved, adopting the role of restaurant manager and/or sommelier. But this is a situation now no longer typically found. I have only three cases among my German and none among my British restaurants. However, this form of organization still is more prevalent in German rural inns (*Landgasthöfe*), and, as shown in Chapter 2, a few examples may also be found in Britain. At the other extreme, staff costs can be managed by increasing the scale of operations, i.e. the number of covers and/or sittings per service. This is not yet considered acceptable in most British and German fine-dining restaurants, but is more common in the USA.

The cost of produce is close to that of staff—between 25 and 30 per cent of all costs, according to my respondents. (The price of food generally is subsidized by that of wine.) While head chefs aesthetic inclinations may push them to buy the best available product in the market, their business sense sometimes reins them in and makes them choose a cheaper, though never a cheap, product, particularly for set-price lunches. It is emphasized by several interviewees that the quality of produce would always be the uppermost consideration. Thus two-star German chef Niels Henkel says: 'You must have a healthy mix between cost saving and guarding quality which must remain excellent.' And one-star British chef Shaun Hill states: 'I wish I was an entrepreneur—I would make more money. I would much rather buy a better piece of ingredient.'

The cost of produce is, of course, influenced by the proportion of luxury foods the restaurant puts on its menu, such as lobster, truffles, foie gras, and now also certain kinds of line-caught fish or specially reared beef—a topic to be discussed in Chapter 6. In such situations, the chef experiences particularly acutely the dilemma presented by the different performance criteria of the inspired and the market order of worth.

Last there is the cost of buying a prime property and fitting out the kitchen with modern equipment. Prices of estate or even of renting are much higher in urban than rural areas, particularly in prime urban areas. The costs of renting and buying are particularly high in London. In central London, the cost of purchase is £70 per square metre, and the rent commanded for a restaurant may be £500,000 per annum.[34] Even renting a property can be extremely costly as the expense of renovating and outfitting the restaurant and kitchen still is borne by the chef. Lander estimates the start-up costs in London (for a rented property) to be £1 million.[35] A British two-star chef outside London comments: 'It cost thirty grand to set it [the restaurant] up, and the reinvestment was about a million.' German prices for real estate, in general, tend to be significantly lower, but they are higher in Hamburg and Munich than in the capital Berlin.

A British outfitter of restaurant kitchens puts the cost of a middle-range kitchen at £2,500 per cover—a staggering cost of £125,000 for the average size restaurant.[36] A German two-star chef trumps even this high amount for his custom-fitted kitchen in a circular building: 'The 70 square metre large kitchen was made to measure in the best stainless steel and cost 7,142 euros per square metre—nearly 500,000 euros.'

Many chefs tell me that they aim for state-of-the-art (and expensive) equipment and my visits to kitchens have shown that gleaming modern stainless kitchens are, indeed, common. Additional economic pressures reported by my interviewees include high energy costs (German one-star chef), the high rate of VAT (British two-star chef), and rising food costs (two British chefs).

How then, given the generally high costs and the low scale in the fine-dining industry, do chefs deal with the simultaneous demands of the inspired and the market orders of worth? Five different outcomes in reaction to their seemingly contradictory logics have emerged from my fieldwork. (Many chefs fall into more than one group.) First, a significant proportion of chefs are unable to fight on both fronts simultaneously and become bankrupt or just leave the profession. Second, they struggle on with 'no profits' from the restaurant and instead seek to subsidize the restaurant with income from supplementary activities. A third group of chefs seeks out an employment contract where they serve mainly as the inspirational figure head, and the search for profit becomes a secondary, though not a negligent consideration. The fourth and most typical group of chef proprietors accepts the fact that running a fine-dining restaurant does not present them with an opportunity to get rich quickly. Chefs in this group place equal or more importance on creating excellent and imaginative products. They settle for making only a moderate or sufficient (for survival) profit. Lastly, a fifth group of chef proprietors actually relishes the financial challenge and show themselves to be as creative in the field of business management as in the aesthetic and cultural fields of their activity.

The first outcome, which stems from the inability to juggle the demands of excellence and creativity with that of making a profit, is particularly marked among one-star chefs. Three of the German chefs report no profits and are operating on the edge of viability, while one British chef does not earn a sufficient profit to pay himself a salary. One German former two-star chef who struggled for many years to break-even by running his kitchen by himself claims: 'There are only a few chefs in Germany who manage to live from the restaurant alone.' A British one-star chef is equally explicit: 'It is almost impossible to survive just on the [one Michelin-starred] restaurant. You have got to do other things.'

As I interviewed mainly current Michelin-starred chefs, I did not include all those defeated by these combined pressures. Stories of burn-out or flight into drug-taking abound. The examples of Simon Hopkinson in Britain and of Eckart Witzigmann in Germany are only the most high-profile and therefore best-known ones. While such coping strategies are difficult to probe in interviews, they are believed to be quite common in the industry. Thus the British trade magazine *Restaurant* devoted a large part of one issue to the problem of drug abuse.[37]

Historically, instability is indicated by the significant turnover rate of restaurants in the one-star category (either because of loss of star or because of closure), particularly in Britain. While in the UK, 45.5 per cent of one-star restaurants listed in 2002 had disappeared by 2009, the corresponding proportion for Germany was 26.0 per cent.[38] In 2012, however, the proportion of one-star restaurants losing their star—through either closure or the withdrawal of the star by Michelin—was only 7 per cent in the UK and 5 per cent in Germany.[39]

The second group—which is relatively large—does not make a sufficient profit from the restaurant but supplements income with earnings from one or more supplementary activities. A small number of interviewees in both countries—six in Britain and three in Germany—rely on earnings from their usually small hotels to keep themselves financially afloat. Another activity which subsidizes or may even provide their main income is running one or more non-starred restaurants. Eleven out of twenty of the British chefs, though only one of the German chefs, run one or more other restaurants, such as gastro pubs and bistros. Further activities to subsidize their income include offering outside catering; consulting for food-producing companies or for restaurant/hotel groups; and running a cookery school. Writing cookery books, doing a regular journalistic column, and appearing on television shows are further means of enlarging chefs' incomes. It is, indeed, very common among my respondents to be engaged in three or more such activities.

However, only attaching rooms to their Michelin restaurant—the so-called restaurant with rooms—and running a second restaurant are said to provide significant supplementary income. Even when they spend a considerable proportion of their time on it, only a few chefs state that they derive a substantial share of their income from the other supplementary activities. An exceptional British one-star chef, however, derives all his personal income (after covering costs) from one outside activity, namely consulting for other restaurants and a large food store. This result must be influenced by the fact that my sample contains no chefs with either regular television work or large consultancy contracts who proved to be unavailable for interview. It was pointed out to me that (other) chefs may gain a considerable amount of income from consultancy services to airlines, cruise ships, and larger restaurant companies. Albert Roux tells me that, in the past, he provided consultancy services to Marks & Spencer on their range of ready-cooked meals which must have generated a handsome supplement to his restaurant income.

Most of my interviewees claim that they engage in their supplementary activities either for marketing purposes or, particularly in cases of writing cookery books or appearing on television, to develop themselves and gain intrinsic satisfaction. Tom Kerridge, who recently gained a second star for his gastro pub, tells me:

> Some external jobs are massively enriching. Without the BBC show our business would not have taken off as it has. Also I thoroughly enjoy doing these things—to get some experience of how different industries work.

A similar sentiment is expressed by a British one-star chef: 'I see [these activities] as enjoyable. It is about building the brand and the business.'

Some of the British respondents thus are not, in principle, averse to making a handsome profit, they simply find it difficult or undesirable to make it from running a Michelin-starred restaurant. (For further details on this, see Chapter 11.) The fine-dining restaurant, for them, is a labour of love, which they subsidize, if necessary, with outside earnings.

A third strategy of chefs is to avoid the potential conflict between an inspired and a profit orientation by becoming employees in a luxury hotel or by finding a wealthy sponsor who looks beyond accounts and profits. In top hotels, the restaurant often is viewed by owners as the beacon for the hotel, exerting a strong or even the main attraction for potential hotel guests. Accordingly, the restaurant may be subsidized by the income from hotel lettings. This type of subsidized restaurant is found mainly in Germany (nine interviewees are employed in such hotels) and only rarely in Britain. (Of the nine German three-star chefs, all but two work in such hotels.) The *Gault Millau Deutschland* mockingly refers to these chefs 'as docked in the safe harbour of a large hotel'.

Thus the Director of Catering at the hotel Frankfurter Hof (part of the Steigenberger Group) says about its one-star restaurant:

> The *Français* is not self-supporting. Profit is made up in other areas of the hotel. The business side is more neglected... You can cook more freely in a luxury hotel and are able to be very 'deep'.

Another prominent example of the restaurant luring clients to the hotel is Harald Wohlfahrt's three-star *Schwarzwaldstube*, situated in the relatively remote Black Forest village of Baiersbronn. According to Wohlfahrt: 'The owner regards the restaurant only in a limited way as a business and would tolerate an occasional loss.' Such an indulgent financial attitude also is reported by two-star Dirk Luther of *Meierei*, Glücksburg, as well as by two-star Christian Lohse of *Fischer's Fritz*, in the Berlin Regent Hotel. (Both Wohlfahrt and Lohse pride themselves nevertheless on making a good profit.)

A willingness to tolerate an occasional loss is found in a more attenuated form in the German luxury hotels managed by the Althoff Group. Its employed chefs (they are managerial employees, equal to the hotel director), such as three-star Joachim Wissler (*Restaurant Vendôme*), two-star chefs Niels Henkel (*Restaurant Schloss Lerbach*), and Christian Jürgens (*Überfahrt*), mainly are required to recoup their costs: 'A healthy Nought is sufficient' or 'Mr Althoff shows a mixture of forbearance and of a profit orientation.'

But these three chefs emphasize that they are given a budget and cannot completely disregard financial demands. They have to engage in careful sourcing and skilful husbanding of produce, as well as use staff in the most efficient manner, as long as the demands for excellent food and service are taken account of. They are therefore still affected by economic pressure, as expressed by Christian Jürgens: 'One has to accept the tension [between demands from the two different orders of worth] and set priorities, but I do find it stressful'.

Last, three-star Sven Elverfeld reports that his employer, the Ritz Carlton, tolerated losses during the first three years of his tenure, allowing for the building of his reputation in an unpromising location—the small industrial town of Wolfsburg where the outlook from the restaurant is directly on to the VW works:

> There was no profit in the early years but our aim is profit, that we are self-sufficient. We do not have to make a high profit but we must break even. It was very difficult to build up this restaurant.

As even subsidized chefs cannot shed managerial responsibility and cost control, they still may find the cross-pressures hard to bear, especially if they have highly developed artistic ambitions, as is the case for this German one-star chef:

> [I experience it as a strong pressure] that everything is oriented towards making a profit; it is counter to quality. Culture becomes an enterprise which needs subsidy. The capital of man lies in his creativity…It [the cross-pressure] absolutely has an effect—it leads to strong depression. As an artist, I suffer like a dog from this.

It is not surprising that most of these subsidized chefs have no strong entrepreneurial inclinations. They either have no plans to open their own restaurant or, if they do, their realization depends on the emergence of the right circumstances—which I take to be the appearance of a financial backer. Thus, when asked whether they plan to open their own restaurant, two German two-star chefs reply: 'Not at the moment, it will depend on the opportunity' and 'This is a wish I have at the back of my mind.' A one-star German chef says: 'Every chef has plans but these have a utopian character at the moment.'

A fifth (less cushioned) German one-star chef openly rejects the responsibility that comes with ownership: 'I would rather not [open my own restaurant]. Being self-employed means you are permanently engaged, and there are days when you would like to chuck everything.'

In Britain, in contrast, not many chefs I interviewed work in luxury hotels. Where they do, I do not find cross-subsidization by the hotel. Thus while two-star chef Marcus Wareing must undoubtedly act as a beacon for the London Berkeley Hotel, he has to pay the hotel a market rent and has to function as a normal for-profit enterprise. The employed chefs of the St James Hotel, London, and of Holbeck Ghyll in Cumbria, too, are each expected to make a good and a sufficient profit. A one-star executive chef, looking after both the starred restaurant and overseeing catering for other operations of the organization, views the more business-like behaviour of the complex—it forms part of a bigger company—very negatively:

> Profit does not have to be as high as for the golf course, but there are targets to achieve. If I don't achieve them, the chairman and/or the general manager would see me and ask why did you not hit the targets and why did you not hit the covers…There are a lot of people behind desks trying to tell you what to do and who don't understand the kitchen. That's why I would like to do my own thing.

Alternatively, wealthy sponsors or business partners have the same effects for chefs. In both countries, business partners rarely are commercial partners. They are either friends or customers, or they are entrepreneurs from within the restaurant industry, with industry knowledge and with realistic expectations about the gains to be made in fine-dining restaurants. They may also be patrons of the culinary arts who do not expect to make a profit and/or merely seek to recover the costs. This latter phenomenon is particularly notable in Germany. A prominent example of the latter is the building contractor Fritz Eichbauer (he now has delegated operational control to his son Felix) who set up and financed the Munich restaurants *Tantris* and *Terrine*. He has pumped money into them since 1971. The one-star chef of *Terrine* tells me:

> It is not the purpose to make a profit but just to cover costs...I have nothing against gain but it is utopian to regard such an enterprise as a channel for gain. I only want to create cover.

Another sponsor of this kind is Jürgen Grossmann, owner of the *Georgsmarienhütte Holding* who finances Thomas Bühner's *La Vie* in Osnabrück. Such 'patrons of the culinary arts' may wish to inject culinary excitement into a region otherwise not well served by top-level restaurants. Or they simply wish to create their very own house restaurant and thereby improve the image of their business or increase their prestige, just like the aristocratic rulers of old. That they are not an exceptional phenomenon in Germany is confirmed by the journalist and editor of the *Gault Millau Deutschland*, Patricia Bröhm.[40]

In the British industry such patrons of the culinary arts do not exist. However, business partners who know the industry and are aware that a starred restaurant does not yield very high returns are more common in Britain. A British one-star chef tells me:

> [I only aim for] sufficient profit. My investors understand the restaurant's goals. It suffices if I get a good return because maximum profit would mean squeezing the whole place down.

A British employed one-star chef who is thinking of setting up on his own is looking for just such a tolerant partner with deep pockets:

> My next step is to own one [a restaurant]. You need a partner you can trust, the banks are not lending. It has to be a partner who likes the fun and the show-off.

The greater availability of supportive hotel owners and wealthy sponsors must give German chefs an advantage over their British colleagues. They enjoy a better staffing situation and are generally freer from financial pressure. In theory, they can devote more energy to the creative aspects of their work. However, if American sociologist David Stark's insights about 'resourceful dissonance' are taken seriously,[41] British chefs—who are forced to devote more attention to the financial aspects of the restaurant—should be spurred to higher creativity by the dissonance they constantly experience. Which of these two interpretations is closer to the truth is impossible to decide with the existing data.

The biggest group of chef-restaurateurs in both countries—74 per cent of the British and 95 per cent of the German chefs—is the fourth group mentioned earlier. It consists of those who have resigned themselves to the fact that you cannot, or even should not, aim to make a large profit in a fine-dining restaurant. They either run their restaurant primarily as a vehicle which enables them to unfold their creativity, or they place an equally high weight on the entrepreneurial and the inspired role. Thus a London two-star chef, running a highly successful restaurant, professes a lack of concern with profit:

> This enterprise is not based on monetary gain…we don't even talk about it, just get on with the cooking. We think about standards and how we will get there. We do not work in a profit-oriented way.

Two German one-star chefs express a similar feeling in ethical terms: 'As I am an aesthete, maximization of profit does not fit'; 'Profit is always low. I do not see this as commerce, but as an ethical thing—I delight in people, in the work and I have respect for it.'

Other chef owners in both countries express the view that an expectation for *high* profit is not compatible with maintaining high standards in all areas of their business. Such chef proprietors only aim for *sufficient* profit to cover costs, invest in the restaurant, and make a reasonable living. The following quotes illustrate this tendency and expresses chefs' professional motivations:

> Maximum profit is an accountant's world, not mine…We are not driven by attaining maximum profit. Other business goals [we pursue] are that we 'aim to please' and 'to develop the staff and myself'. (British one-star chef)

> I am content with little and do not want to get rich quickly. (German two-star chef)

> I am satisfied with 65–68% of gross profit—below the industry rate. I have reinvested most of it in the last seven years, and only this year for the first time have made a net profit. (British two-star chef)

> I do not aim for profit pure and simple but for sufficient profit to put the enterprise on a secure basis. We must have sufficient reserves so that we can always pay the staff. (German one-star chef)

This lack of a developed market orientation also comes to the fore when I ask chefs about whether they consider their competitors when setting prices. Sixteen chefs (eleven German and five British chefs) think that they need not fix their prices in relation to comparable restaurants in the market. This is because they either believe themselves uniquely talented—'I know my worth' (British one-star chef)—or because they have no close competitors such as in the case of some of the more remote German restaurants. In view of these priorities, it is not surprising that only four chefs in each sample identify themselves first and foremost as entrepreneurs/business people.

It has to be borne in mind that many of these chefs, particularly in Britain, have received little or no preparation for the business side of being a chef proprietor/patron but often had the role of business person thrust upon them. This is well brought out by Wright's in-depth interviews with Marcus Wareing and Heston Blumenthal.[42] Wareing, having been asked quite suddenly by Gordon Ramsay to become chef patron at *L'Oranger*, comments as follows:

> I had no understanding of how a restaurant should be run. I hadn't a clue how to run a kitchen, hadn't a clue how to talk to people...didn't even know how to write a menu properly.[43]

The situation was even more challenging for Heston Blumenthal who had no financial backing and no kitchen experience of note. Blumenthal remembers: 'It was chaos, it was absolutely chaos. [There was] shambolic organization and a crippling lack of experience.' Indeed, Blumenthal regularly had to go to the supermarket down the road to get the necessary produce.[44]

Phil Howard, who has proven himself both as a top chef and as a restaurateur, nevertheless also finds the conflicting demands a challenge. In a 2012 interview with the *Fine-Dining guide* in June 2012 he says:

> I've always found the notion of chef/patron a puzzling one—how a chef can deal with the coal face of a kitchen and front of house day to day while managing to run a business has appeared the impossible challenge.[45]

Paradoxically, German chefs, who by and large feel market pressure less acutely, have often received some accountancy training as part of both their apprenticeship training and, more extensive business knowledge, as part of the course for the *Meister* qualification.

Chefs in this fourth group generally do not perceive much tension between the demands of the inspired and the market order of worth: 'You take it in your stride, you just deal with it' (British two-star chef); 'Yes, I can combine it all with my life in general in an optimal manner. For me this occupation is a delight, not work' (German two-star chef). A very small group of chefs even know how to turn this constant financial pressure to their advantage—they react to it in accordance with Stark's 'resourceful dissonance':[46]

> You have to become even more creative to handle the situation. (British one-star chef)
>
> Economic pressure makes you more creative. You have to work more intelligently. (British one-star chef)
>
> Economic pressure does not affect creativity negatively, it rather acts as a challenge. (German two-star chef)

> The pressure has risen, the guests have higher expectations. One has to learn to transform the pressure into positive waves, as motivation. (German three-star chef)

But several chefs also point out that, although they had not entered this profession/craft to head a small business, their current position makes inevitable a life with feet in both the entrepreneurial and the artistic/creative camp. Thus:

> I am not an entrepreneur—I am a chef—. . . [after a pause] but you have to become a bit business-savvy nevertheless. (British one-star chef)

> My passion is the food and the restaurant, but if you do not understand the business you are in trouble. (British two-star chef)

> To set up the restaurant, I had to have also entrepreneurial drive but my roots are in craft. (British one-star chef)

The fifth and last group comprises chefs for whom business considerations and pursuit of profit come top in the hierarchy of the two orders of worth and in the priorities they set. These often are chefs who started out in their professional career primarily motivated by their passion for good food but over time have experienced a shift in value orientations:

> First and foremost, it is a business. It is not a vehicle for me as a chef. Fifteen years ago I only cared about food. Now it matters that the business is performing. (London two-star chef Phil Howard)

However, Howard is still present in the kitchen of *The Square* and continues to deeply care about the food his restaurant serves. Others go much further and change from being a chef to becoming primarily a business person. These are usually older chefs who can no longer stand the exhausting pace of kitchen work on a permanent basis or who no longer wish to confine themselves for long hours in the kitchen. High-level chefs, like Marco Pierre White and Gordon Ramsay, have largely abandoned the stove for the sake of business interests on a wide front. (For further details, see Chapter 11.) They and other longer-serving chefs appear to have tired of the constant high pressure of running a Michelin-starred kitchen. A one-star British chef, who now spends 50 per cent of his time outside the kitchen, speaks for other older chefs when he says: 'I am fifty now. I do not want to get burned and stressed out for the rest of my life.'

One-star British chefs Antona, Blackiston, and Haworth, too, now largely take a back-seat role in the kitchens, which are efficiently run by their head chefs. Among the German chefs interviewed, only three-star Juan Amador falls into this 'entrepreneurial' category, spending half to two thirds of his time on supplementary activities.

To sum up this section, even if chefs derive no or little profit from the Michelin-starred restaurant, they may—with a few notable exceptions—nevertheless attain a good income overall if the profit from either hotel rooms, consulting, or second restaurants is taken into consideration. However, without supplementary earnings it is only possible to run an independently owned restaurant with a high degree of self-exploitation, if at all.

By and large, *chefs de cuisine* have worked out more or less stable compromises between the performance criteria of the two competing orders of worth. Many maintain that they have developed appropriate psychological coping strategies: 'You just cannot let this pressure get you down'; 'No, it does not affect my creativity. It can be contained; a rational person can handle it.' Moreover, many chefs have reduced the pressure by lowering their expectations of profit, effectively putting primary emphasis on the inspired order of worth.

Conclusions

A multiplicity of orders of worth may be seen as a defining feature of fine-dining kitchens, necessitating the bridging of both different normative worlds and modes of organization. Additionally, the persistence of aspects of craft organization, including its small scale, comparatively archaic features of work organization, and unusually taxing work demands and conditions, make the fine-dining restaurant a peculiarly outmoded business organization in an economy shaped by large corporate entities. Yet these unusual organizational features and seemingly disparate orders of worth are reconciled with more or less interpersonal friction and individual stress. Moreover, they even result in an excellent final product—a high quality and delicious meal, together with unusually attentive customer service. The experience this affords guests, as will be shown in Chapter 9, is highly valued by a small, but growing group of customers as an oasis of good taste and individual style in an otherwise highly routinized world of consumption. Furthermore, it is not only guests who profit from the distinctive ethos and organization of fine-dining kitchens. Such kitchens also manage to inspire and thereby transform young people, whose earlier lives have been devoid of any inspiration and aspiration, to become chefs. Some of these *chefs de cuisine* do, indeed, become charismatic leaders, but many other young people fail to find this type of work organization and environment either energizing or empowering.

My interview data have shown both basic commonalities in the way the industry is organized in Britain and Germany, as well as a few notable divergences in the degree of importance bestowed on different orders of worth. The latter are due to both cultural and institutional differences, understood as objectifications of historical compromises between different orders of worth. The first is a stronger embrace by German chefs of the craft principle and the notion of skill. There prevails a smooth integration in Germany, but not in Britain, between the craft and the industrial order and the mechanisms for skill creation associated with each. Whereas the German industry has adopted a formal apprenticeship system guaranteeing an assured supply of employees with a homogeneous set of basic skills and aspirations for quality production, the formal British system functions only imperfectly. Consequently, a supply of skilled young chefs is less assured. This has resulted in both a high level of informal training and in the employment of an unusually high proportion of foreign chefs. More seriously, this less assured supply of skilled labour makes it harder to generate consistent quality, the *sine qua non* for gaining and retaining Michelin stars. In sum, it is suggested that the relentless pursuit of quality is more reliably fostered in the type of craft organization common in Germany, than in the more diverse and haphazard setting of British fine-dining kitchens. The latter is put forward as one explanation for the lower number of Michelin stars awarded in comparison with Germany.

The second divergent feature between the two national fine-dining industries is the much stronger embrace by British than German chefs of the market order of worth. This is manifested in the divergent ownership structures—the much higher incidence in Britain of self-employed chefs—and in the different attitudes to risk held by chefs. Whereas nine of the twenty German chefs interviewed are employed by luxury hotels and are sheltered from full exposure to market pressure, in Britain none of my interviewees is in this category. These employed German chefs are in no hurry to embrace risk and become self-employed. British chefs additionally are more entrepreneurial and more profit-minded in their widespread setting up of one or more additional high-end restaurants.

An explanation of why the market order of worth is more fully embraced by British chefs must invoke the contrasts between a British liberal market economy (LME) and a German coordinated market economy (CME), developed by social scientists Hall and Soskice.[47] The divergent features of these two types—particularly in the system of financing and the values this has bred and institutionalized—have penetrated even this culturally impregnated service industry. British chefs certainly have embraced entrepreneurialism more avidly than their German counterparts. While this may be partly a response to the greater lack of generous backers than in Germany, it also clearly points to a better fit with British entrepreneurial values and the more pronounced financialization of business activity in the wider economy.

Notes

1. L. Boltanski and L. Thévenot, 'The Sociology of Critical Capacity', *European Journal of Social Theory* 2.3 (1999): 359–77; L. Boltanski and L. Thévenot, *On Justification: Economies of Worth* (Princeton: Princeton University Press, 2006) (translation from the French of *De la Justification: Les Economies de la Grandeur*).
2. Boltanski and Thévenot 1999.
3. V. Klink, *Sitting Küchenbull. Gepfefferte Erinnerungen eines Kochs* (Hamburg: Rowohlt Verlag, 2009), 100.
4. M. P. White, *White Heat* (London: Pyramid Books, 1990), 12.
5. *Verordnung über die Berufsausbildung zum Koch/zur Köchin* (February 1998), available at <http://www.Bundesgesetzblatt.de>.
6. *Yes Chef! Magazine* 22 (2012): 74–5 and 23 (2012): 64–5.
7. *Yes Chef! Magazine* 12 (2010): 54–5.
8. Information from former two-star chef Niels Potthass.
9. S. Wright, *Tough Cookies: Tales of Obsession, Toil and Tenacity from Britain's Culinary Heavyweights* (London: Profile Books, 2006), 12.
10. Information from Joseph Trivilli, one of the *River Café* head chefs.
11. Wright 2006: 24f.
12. *The Guardian*, G2 (14 February 2012): 8.
13. T. Raue, *Ich weiss was Hunger ist. Von der Strassengang in die Sterneküche* (Munich and Zürich: Piper Verlag, 2012), 83.
14. G. Weber, *Kochen ist Krieg* (Munich: Piper, 2009), 11.
15. *Süddeutsche Zeitung* (24–26 December 2011): V2/3.
16. Weber 2009: 11.
17. Interview with a two-star chef by M. Eckhardt, *Kochköpfe. Dreizehn Köche hinter den Kulissen* (Bremen: H. M. Hauschild GmbH, 2002), 49.
18. K. Balazs, 'Take One Entrepreneur: The Recipe for Success of France's Great Chefs', *European Management Journal* 20.3 (2002): 247–59.
19. R. Blanc, *A Taste of My Life: One Man's Hunger for Perfection* (London: Transworld Publishers, 2008), 204–5.
20. Weber 2009: 18.
21. *Süddeutsche Zeitung* (24–26 December 2011): V2/3.
22. *The Guardian* (7 June 2008).
23. Blanc 2008: 205.
24. Weber 2009: 13 and Raue 2012: 174, on German chefs.
25. *Süddeutsche Zeitung* (24–26 December 2011): V2/3.
26. Balazs 2002.
27. R. Sennett, *The Craftsman* (London: Penguin, 2008), 66.
28. Boltanski and Thévenot 2006.
29. Balazs 2002.
30. *Süddeutsche Zeitung* 86 (13 April 2012): 9.
31. Cited by S. Mennell, *All Manners of Food: Eating and Taste in England and France from the Middle Ages to the Present* (Oxford: Basil Blackwell, 1985), 161.
32. Boltanski and Thévenot 2006: 239.

33. N. Lander, *The Art of the Restaurateur* (London: Phaidon, 2012), 329.
34. *Financial Times*, Life and Arts (19 July 2008): 4.
35. Lander 2012: 152.
36. *Financial Times Magazine* (27/28 August 2011): 43.
37. *Restaurant* (August 2011).
38. For further detail, see C. Lane, 'The Michelin-Starred Restaurant Sector as a Cultural Industry: A Cross-National Comparison of Restaurants in the UK and Germany', *Food, Culture and Society* 13.4 (2010): 493–519.
39. All calculations based on figures provided by *Michelin Deutschland* and *Michelin Great Britain* for the corresponding years.
40. P. Bröhm, 'Schlemmer in Spendierhosen', *Der Feinschmecker* 11 (2010): 106–11.
41. D. Stark, 'Heterarchy: The Organization of Dissonance', in D. Stark, *The Sense of Dissonance* (Princeton: Princeton University Press, 2009), 1–34.
42. Wright 2006.
43. Wright 2006: 184.
44. Wright 2006: 73–4.
45. <http://www.fine-dining-guide.com/interview-phil-howard-and-rebecca-mascarenhas>.
46. Stark 2009.
47. P. A. Hall and D. Soskice, 'An Introduction to Varieties of Capitalism', in P. A. Hall and D. Soskice (eds.), *Varieties of Capitalism: The Institutional Foundations of Comparative Advantage* (Oxford: Oxford University Press, 2001), 1–70.

4

Fine-Dining Chefs: Iconic Figures or Work-Horses?

Top chefs already have been introduced in Chapter 3 where they were placed at the centre of restaurant organizations, as craftspersons/industrial managers, inspirational leaders, and as those crucial to the business side of the enterprise. In this chapter I examine additional aspects of both their professional identities and their attitudes to the star(s) they have been awarded. After tracing their career progression I will enquire what it means to chefs to be awarded, retain, and/or lose Michelin stars. I then will examine how 'inspirational' worth—chefs' creativity and even innovativeness—is often converted into the value of 'renown' or fame, thereby setting up another set of potentially incompatible normative principles and logics of action. Last, I will make clear that before becoming cultural iconic figures and charismatic leaders of younger chefs, *chefs de cuisine* have to spend long periods where they might well feel like and be regarded as overburdened work-horses.

Who are the Chefs? Social Origins, Gender, and Education and Training

Social Origins, Education, and Vocational Training

Traditionally, chefs have come from working-class or farming backgrounds and have had low educational qualifications. In both countries, several of my interviewees have come from a deprived background. Quite a few chefs thus have managed the transition from 'obscurity to celebrity' within their working lives. At the very least, becoming a chef has meant becoming a skilled craftsperson and at best, becoming a chef proprietor, i.e. the owner of their own small business (in Britain) or a managerial employee (in Germany). In recent decades, becoming a Michelin-starred chef has even propelled many of them into minor or even major stardom. It is thus one of the few working-class occupations offering a potential avenue of considerable upward social mobility. Moreover, it is an occupation which, despite its many drawbacks, fills young men and women with passion and elicits extremely high levels of dedication.

In Britain, the entry into the occupation in the recent past has been widely viewed as 'the last resort' option.[1] A supplier to top restaurants in the north-west of the country comments:

> Often it is touch and go whether they gain respect from being a member of a gang or from becoming a good chef. They have been close to a gang culture, and the brigade becomes the new gang.

Marco Pierre White and Gordon Ramsay are cited as Wright's main examples of chefs with such a background. These and other older chefs usually have come from backgrounds where there has been a lack of alternatives and where fine food was not even known before embarking on a chef's career. In 1990, according to White himself: 'The catering world in Britain [was still] like the French Legion; it's the last resort of the inadequate. Anyone who falls out of school falls into it.'[2]

White did not particularly want to become a chef but, at the age of sixteen, merely wanted the freedom that comes with leaving home. A comparable example from Germany is Berlin two-star chef Tim Raue. He has written extensively about his years of violent inter-gang warfare as a member of the Kreuzberg gang '36 Boys' (Kreuzberg was a very deprived area but is now becoming a newly trendy district of Berlin).[3] He even regards his time with the gang as a good preparation for his work as a chef, 'for in the kitchen, you fight a battle on the highest level twice a day'.[4]

From among my British interviewees, Alan Murchison, Sat Bains, Glynn Purnell, Andreas Antona, and Martin Wishart—all chef proprietors who are highly respected among their colleagues and run economically viable businesses—had received little encouragement to achieve academically or were simply not interested. Antona's observation—'I just was not interested in school'—sums up what others feel as well. In Germany, three-star chefs Harald Wohlfahrt and Joachim Wissler, as well as two-star Johannes King and Eric Menchon, have had a similar trajectory from humble social origins and/or low levels of general education to national, and in some cases, international fame. Chefs tell me about their low level of general education with some pride as it makes their attainment of the position of chef proprietor/ patron of some renown even more remarkable.

However, in Germany there has always been a sizeable group of chef proprietors whose parents already owned a restaurant, usually a modest rural inn (*Landgasthof*). They thus have come from lower middle-class property-owning families. Among them are Hamburg chefs Martin Herrmann of *Le Pavillion* and Steffen Henssler of *Henssler & Henssler* and Douce Steiner of *Zum Hirschen*, Sulzburg, as well as three-star chef HelmutThieltges of *Waldhotel Sonnora* and two-star chef Hans-Stefan Steinheuer, of *Zur Alten Post*. The hotel restaurant *Adler* (Eagle) in the Black Forest is particularly remarkable in this context. It has been owned by the Zumkeller family for six generations and has held a Michelin star in continuity since 1966. This phenomenon distinguishes German from British chefs and has been fostered by a long-standing policy of support for the so-called *Mittelstand*, the owners of small and medium-sized enterprises. Even in Britain we now have the phenomenon of the 'second generation' Michelin chefs in the two French Roux families.

While the general picture of chefs' modest social origins still applies to many chefs today, there now exists a significant proportion—more than half in my sample—with higher educational qualifications. They have achieved, at least, a solid middle-level education and, at best, educational qualifications beyond this. Moreover, of chefs now *starting* an apprenticeship in Germany, the majority are said to have *Abitur* (A-levels).[5] As Munich chef Jacob Stüttgen observes: 'the profession of a chef has become tremendously attractive in Germany'.

In Britain, the head chef of the *River Café*, himself a graduate, tells me that 50 per cent of his chefs have degrees. While the latter is likely to be an exceptionally high proportion, it nevertheless shows that even graduates now see cheffing as a desirable career. Shaun Hill of the Walnut Tree Inn, who has seen the industry develop from the late 1960s onwards, also notes a strong improvement in the young people now applying for jobs with him: 'They are much brighter, more motivated. The change came in the early 1980s.'

One indicator of the newly acquired popularity of the job of a fine-dining chef, revealed by my interviews in both countries, is that *chefs de cuisine* do not have to advertise when they seek to employ a new chef. Young people apply to them for jobs in large numbers. Whether these young people are attracted by the possibility of devoting their working life to the pursuit of excellence and perfection no longer available in many other middle-level careers, or whether they simply hanker after (the often illusory) celebrity must remain an open question.

Table 4.1 shows the highest general educational qualification of my respondents. For German chefs, I have distinguished between *Hauptschulabschluss* (roughly equivalent to the old British Secondary Modern certificate or to a small number of lower-level GCSEs) and *Mittlere Reife* (roughly comparable to a good spread of GCSEs in Britain). Where chefs were educated in another country, I asked for the closest British/German equivalent level. The proportion with higher general educational qualifications would have been higher

Table 4.1. Highest general educational qualifications of *chefs de cuisine*

	Tertiary academic	Tertiary hospitality	A-level/ *Abitur*	Several GCSEs/ *Mittlere Reife*	1–2 GCSEs/ *Hauptschul-Abschluss*	Total
British chefs	3	2	2	8	5	20
German chefs	1	1	2	9	7	20

if younger chefs below the level of *chef de cuisine* had been included. In both countries, the majority of my respondents are more than forty years old.

As the equivalency of the British and German educational qualifications is only a good approximation, their comparison cannot go beyond suggesting the rough comparability of educational achievement in the two national samples. (The slightly higher number of British chefs with tertiary educational qualifications reflects the number of self-taught, career-changing chefs among them.) The data provide modest support for the popular perceptions in both countries that educational advancement has raised the reputation of the occupation of chef and that chefs increasingly supplement their intuitive approach to cooking with intelligent analysis.

These general educational qualifications are usually augmented by vocational qualifications. In Germany, it is extremely rare among fine-dining chefs not to have completed an apprenticeship (there was no one among my interviewees). Even in the larger group of forty-six chefs with two or three Michelin stars, I found only two with no record of an apprenticeship—André Köther and Christian Grünwald. In Britain, in contrast, the situation is more diverse. While most of the older chefs hold a City & Guilds apprenticeship qualification, several of the younger chefs possess NVQs (New Vocational Qualifications), awarded after one or two years of mainly college-based study. But, given the low regard for this qualification among *chefs de cuisine*, possession of such a qualification is not made a condition for employment. Also in Britain, we still find a significant number of top chefs who are self-taught career-changers—a continuation of a historical trend starting before the Second World War. Among the latter are several well-known chefs, such as Heston Blumenthal of *The Fat Duck* and Raymond Blanc of *Manoir aux Quat'Saisons*. In my sample, Frances Atkins, Galton Blackiston, Shaun Hill, Phil Howard, Alan Murchison, and Ruth Rogers fall into this group. Even the doyen of British *haute cuisine* and trainer of a large number of subsequent chefs, Albert Roux, did not undertake a general chef's training, but did an apprenticeship in a *patisserie*.

Table 4.2. Vocational educational qualifications of *chefs de cuisine*

	Apprenticeship/ City & Guilds	NVQs	Master Chef (German *Meister*)	Hospitality College/ *Hotelfachschule*	No training
British chefs	9	3	0	2	6
German chefs	19	0	6	1	0

Table 4.2 provides details of vocational qualifications. It shows that a significant proportion of German chefs have invested also in becoming a *Meister* (master craftsperson). While it is not clear what influence this may have on culinary excellence, it has other organizational implications. The syllabus includes both basic financial training, as well providing knowledge of how to manage employees. The lack of vocational training or the provision of only very basic training in Britain hence may have very deleterious impact on the possession of business knowledge and financial skills. This is vividly illustrated by Wright in his portraits of Marcus Wareing and, more so, Heston Blumenthal who, in his early years at *The Fat Duck*, often came close to financial disaster.[6]

Equally, or often more important, for chefs' subsequent careers, however, are the (often unpaid) internships (*stages*) in high-end kitchens they manage to do after the completion of the basic vocational training. These will be reviewed below.

Gender

Head chefs in the top restaurants of both countries are fairly solidly male. The low representation of women historically started in early nineteenth-century France where women were assigned to domestic kitchens and men to professional ones. While three female French chefs—Marie Bourgeois, Marguerite Bise, and Eugenie Brazier (referred to as "the Lyon Grandmothers")—each gained three stars during the middle of the twentieth century, there then followed a gap of more than fifty years. Only in 2007 did Anne Marie Pic of *Maison Pic* in Valence, daughter and granddaughter of famous three-star chefs, make it to the top of the culinary hierarchy.

The nineteenth-century stereotype about gender roles now is no longer accepted in Europe. However, women's low presentation at the top levels of the profession in Britain and Germany has changed only very slowly, to assume some slight acceleration during the last decade. Women's under-representation may be explained by the following circumstances. First, the long and exhausting working schedule and the unsocial hours are completely incompatible with child-rearing—a task still mainly reserved for women. This is confirmed by three-star chef Elverfeld: 'Women must decide whether they want to follow the profession or a family. The long and late hours are not compatible with having a family.' Second, the very charged atmosphere in kitchens, where swearing abounds and physical violence is not unknown, has not been attractive to women. Additionally, more or less disguised sexism has been rife. Third, as in other male-dominated professions, there has been a lack of mentors and female role models.

Even if active discrimination against women no longer is widespread, women are not exactly welcomed in high-end kitchens. Often, they are greeted with the prediction that they will not last a week. However, during the last decade or so a number of positive changes have occurred, and a few *chefs de cuisine* now actively prefer to employ women. Both the physical and social environments of kitchens have improved. Television programmes and, even more so, kitchens open to the restaurant, have put them under more intense external scrutiny. In Britain, female and highly visible chefs like Ruth Rogers and Rose Gray of the *River Café*, opened in 1987, have acted as pioneers, and their culinary and business success has served as an example to other women. In Germany, Hamburg one-star chef proprietors Anna Sgroi and Cornelia Poletto may be seen as such role models. (Poletto, however, gave up her starred restaurant in 2012.)

In both Britain and Germany, the number of starred female head chefs has increased, though it still remains low in proportional terms and leaves women under-represented in restaurants with multiple stars. As one British chef points out: 'I have three girls [sic] in the kitchen—it is slightly exceptional.'

In Germany, in 2013, there were eight female Michelin-starred head chefs/ chef proprietors which amounts to a mere 3.5 per cent of all such chefs and is significantly lower than the proportion in Britain. Moreover, nearly all are at one-star level, with the sole exception of two-star Douce Steiner, a second generation chef patron in the restaurant *Zum Hirschen*, Sulzburg. Among the female *chefs de cuisine* are: Caroline Baum (*Restaurant Amador*, Mannheim); Erika Bergheim (*Nero*, Essen); Ulrike Stöber (*Landhaus Mühlenberg*, Daufenberg); Anna Sgroi (*Restaurant Sgroi*, Hamburg); and Alexandra Seeliger (*Aquarello*, Munich). In Britain, there were ten Michelin-starred female head chefs in 2012, i.e. a proportion of 17.3 per cent. Besides Ruth Rogers, they include: Frances Atkins (*The Yorkshire Arms*, Ramsgill); Angela Hartnett (*Murano*, London); Hélène Darroze (*Connaught Hotel*, London); Tessa Bramley (*Old Vicarage*, Sheffield); Lisa Allen (*Northcote*, Langho); and Anna Hansen of London's *Modern Pantry*. Most notable are Rachel Humphrey (head chef of *Le Gavroche*, London) and Clare Smyth (head chef of *Gordon Ramsay*, London). Rachel Humphrey, who started at *Le Gavroche* as an apprentice in 1996, became head chef in 2001. She heads a brigade of eighteen chefs, and one of her *sous* chefs also is female. Clare Smyth was made a partner in restaurant *Gordon Ramsay* in 2013.

Only three years after Gordon Ramsay famously asserted that women 'can't cook to save their lives' he volunteered that 'women learn much quicker and bring a far greater level of patience and tolerance to a kitchen than any male chef I have met'.[7] In the same article, female chefs express their own opinions. Clare Smyth suggests that the presence of women has reduced bullying behaviour by men. Angela Hartnett, however, warns that the culture change is not as great as some *sous* chefs might hope. She admits that she, too, can be aggressive in certain situations. In the kitchen of Jacob Stüttgen's Munich restaurant *Terrine*, women are even in the majority. Stüttgen believes that 'it is easier to work with women—they are less argumentative'. Tom Kerridge of *Hand & Flowers*, too, expresses a preference for women chefs: 'They bring calmness and the organizational ability male chefs lack—the latter have more ego. The girls [sic] break up the male testosterone.'

However, serious obstacles remain for women who want to become top chefs. The profession has a work culture which assumes full availability of its members in kitchens. My interviews show that all but one restaurant only employ full-time chefs. (One German restaurant permits a female chef to work mornings only.) As most chefs work twelve hours or more per day, working time quality is incompatible with bringing up children. Those few women chefs who made it to the top of their profession are either young and/or childless, or, particularly in Germany, work in traditional family-owned and run restaurants where husbands and/or parents help with childcare.

The Road to Michelin Status

Only a small minority of all chefs succeeds in attaining a Michelin star and an even smaller number—twenty-four in Britain and forty-six in Germany (in 2013)—manage to advance to two- or three-star status. Although not all chefs aim for the award of stars, the majority consider it the ultimate accolade and yearn to have one or more stars. (For more details, see Chapter 10.) They are prepared to put themselves through a lot of hardship to reach this goal. As in the pursuit of all sought-after awards, you have to have talent, ambition, discipline, and perseverance to reach your goal. But for the great majority of top-level chefs neither talent, nor hard graft suffices. I suggest that, additionally, they have to develop their career strategically and collect the social capital which will smooth their way to the top. Acquiring social capital refers to gaining social connections in the field on both a national and, increasingly, international level. It involves seeking out and working with the most highly reputed chefs in the field. The latter are sought after not only to learn about their technical prowess, but also to experience their vision and absorb their attitudes, including their leadership style. However, another tacit objective for young chefs is to gain reflected glory—to increase their own worth by becoming the disciple of a great 'master'.

Regarding social capital, German two-star chef Johannes King comments on his early employment, in the Berlin restaurant of Frenchman Henri Levy (now no longer in business): 'Henri Levy had contact with all of the grand kitchens in Europe. I was able to establish networks—terrifically important!'

An article about three-star Harald Wohlfahrt points out that:

> the young chefs [in his kitchen] who today give their all will be able to pick their place of work tomorrow. Nothing looks as good in your curriculum vitae like having spent a year or two with Harald Wohlfahrt.[8]

In a similar vein, British chefs, such as Marco Pierre White, Gordon Ramsay, and Marcus Wareing, trained by Albert Roux, greatly benefited from his connections to chefs in France. They secured placements in high-level French restaurants they would never have gained access to by themselves (none understood French at the time).

In this context, it is worth citing the views of three chefs who nominate the most influential employers for their subsequent careers. Mario Gamba of Munich's *Aquarello* states that: 'Winkler [of restaurant *Aschau*] has shaped my life. I have taken on many of his attitudes—techniques you can learn by yourself.' Birmingham one-star chef Andreas Antona says: 'Mosimann was a great influence. He made me realize that you have to have an element beyond craft. A new perspective was gained.' And Gordon Ramsay said of first entering the kitchen of Marco Pierre White: 'The guy was awesome and vibrant and wild...He taught me how to taste.'[9] According to Wright, Ramsay had seen 'the levels of intensity needed, the unyielding commitment to quality, the relentless rhythmic consistency, the refusal to accept the slightest flaw, the intolerance of imperfection'.[10]

A German chef comments in a similar vein on his time as *commis* chef (the most junior chef in the brigade) under Eckart Witzigmann—the doyen of German *haute cuisine*, with a reputation for being almost as temperamental as Marco Pierre White: '[I was struck by] his attitude of extremely high expectations which greatly raised the pressure. Such a burdening was as extreme as the man himself.'[11]

All these quotes demonstrate that what is primarily learnt by younger chefs from the greats of the profession is the relentless pursuit of excellence and/or a general outlook on food and cooking, rather than any detailed techniques or recipes.

Having worked in the kitchen of a Michelin-starred chef—particularly one with multiple stars—greatly increases subsequent career opportunities for young chefs. To receive training from a two- or three-star chef almost is a prerequisite for subsequent stardom. If these masters practise their artistic craft in France, Spain, Copenhagen, or the US metropolises (New York, Chicago, and San Francisco/Bay Area), then the social capital accumulated is even greater. The value of these *stages* to young chefs—the modern equivalent of the journeyman ship—is reflected in the fact that they are often unpaid. Employers sometimes offer only board and lodgings and occasionally no remuneration at all. However, many chefs also take paid jobs abroad during the early stages of their career. London one-star chef Jason Atherton well sums up the benefits of foreign *stages*:

> I really believe travelling makes you grow and transforms you into a mature chef because you start to learn new cuisines, new cultures and new management styles you won't have come across in the UK. You also get to meet new people that will become friends for life and may help in your career.[12]

Drawing on both my interview data and on my data archive on all two- and three-star chefs, I investigate chefs' career paths in this light. Of the twenty-four British chefs with multiple stars, I use the career data for sixteen chefs, leaving out some chefs mainly trained in France where star level is not always stated. It is notable that, for fourteen of the sixteen chefs, my hypothesis about the importance of social capital is confirmed. However, two chefs—Heston Blumenthal and Raymond Blanc—became three- and two-star chefs respectively without the benefit of the social capital conferred by having been disciples of multiple-starred Michelin chefs. They instead acquired their skills and vision in a lone, lengthy, arduous, and sometimes nearly fatal learning process.[13] The other fourteen have worked in the kitchen of at least one, but more often of two or three chefs with multiple stars. (The two French-born chefs Claude Bosi and Hélène Darroze completed most or all their *stages*/post-apprenticeship training with high-level chefs in France.) For the remaining twelve British two- and three-star chefs, the social capital derived from their association with multiple-starred chefs was further enhanced for all but three by a period of work with a high-level chef in France, often facilitated directly or indirectly (Roux scholarships) by the Roux brothers.

The data for Germany's multiple-starred chefs provide a less fragmented picture, lending overwhelming support to my claim about the beneficial effect on career development of social capital. Of Germany's forty-six multiple-starred chefs, two—Andrée Köther and Christian Grünwald—are eliminated because their biographies provide no data on post-apprenticeship jobs, and for a third chef—Frank Rosin—only unidentifiable foreign ones are listed. Of the remaining forty-three, close to 100 per cent have worked with one or more (up to four) multiple-starred Michelin chefs. Among the latter, three-star chefs Eckart Witzigmann (for the older chefs) and Heinz Winkler, Dieter Müller, and particularly Harald Wohlfahrt (for chefs now in their early forties) stand out. Most of these chefs did not do their apprenticeship with a multiple-starred chef but only acquired the knowledge and competency to network *during* their apprenticeship years. The two exceptions not confirming my hypothesis are French-born chef Eric Menchon, who has been trained by and worked only with French non-starred chefs, and Martin Herrmann who only worked in the restaurant owned by his family.

Although I was able to find data on foreign *stages* only for twenty-four of the forty-six chefs, these are sufficient to show that German chefs are less focused on France than their British counterparts. They network also in neighbouring Austria and Switzerland, in other European countries (Spain, Italy, Britain, Greece, and Ireland), as well as in more far-flung locations, such as Dubai, New York, and Hong Kong. Already during the 1960s, the doyen of German chefs, Eckart Witzigmann, had worked not only in France but also in Britain (*Café Royal*), Switzerland, Belgium, Sweden, and the United States.

For the younger and often better-educated chefs, both connections and opportunities abound. This opportunity to travel to, and hold jobs in, foreign countries has become an additional attraction of the profession for young people, without the financial resources and social competence necessary for non-packaged travel.

Once chefs' minds have been opened to great cooking, inspiration also may come from reading the cookery book of an outstanding and innovative chef. Thus British two-star chef Sat Bains was greatly influenced by Marco Pierre White's book *White Heat*—'a book that rocked the industry'—when it appeared in 1990, just as in the 1970s, many chefs had been bowled over by the books of French chef Paul Bocuse.

Chefs can further augment their social capital by networking at national and international industry events and by informally visiting esteemed colleagues to personally sample their meals. Both kinds of networking are exceedingly common. The practice of paying informal visits to great chefs to examine their dishes is almost universally indulged in by my respondents. Thus Nottingham chef Sat Bains says: 'The most influential chef for me was Ferran Adria. I never worked there but I went to eat there once. It proved a catalytic experience.' In a similar vein, Blumenthal became hooked on *haute cuisine* after a youthful visit to the French three-star restaurant *L'Oustau de Beaumanière*.

These visits thus go beyond sampling the food cooked by great chefs but also are devoted to seeking aesthetic and culinary inspiration. German three-star chef Harald Wohlfahrt comments: 'You have to look into the pots of your colleagues. I travel to Hong Kong, Tokyo and New York.' Berlin chef Tim Raue agrees:

> Just as art students in Florence wander from museum to museum, we dragged ourselves from gourmet temple to gourmet temple. The experiences we had there were our university seminars. There we educated our palates.[14]

Sometimes the models are nearer home, as they are for one-star London chef Colin McLoughlin: 'All our (my wife and myself) spare money goes into eating out in London. It excites you, for instance going to The Square.'

Networking confirms the metaphor of 'the brotherhood of chefs'. According to one-star chef Alan Murchison: 'Most of my friends are chefs. We have a similar humour and mentality. Chefs are like a brotherhood. Chefs in the UK are fiercely competitive but also very friendly.' Networking is equally common among British and German chefs: fifteen chefs from each country speak about a high or medium high degree of networking. Those who maintain a low degree of networking, almost invariably are constrained by lack of time (particularly among employed chefs) or greater geographical isolation. Bonds between chefs often have been forged through common suffering and the resulting camaraderie in earlier years of training, although competition between chefs also is intense.

The extent to which such networks are national or international provides interesting information about the varying degrees of cosmopolitanism chefs now have in their outlook and how far-flung their search for inspiration is. In this respect, an important difference between British and German chefs is revealed. While more than two thirds of German respondents interested in networking extend their networks across national borders, only half of the British chefs respond in this manner. Chefs who spent some of their early careers abroad tend to maintain much wider networks. Thus Birmingham chef Andreas Antona who had worked in Germany and Switzerland says: 'I network both locally, nationally and abroad, particularly in France, Germany and Switzerland.' It is notable that to reduce the transaction costs of such foreign travel, British chefs frequently travel in groups, particularly to Asia. Thus Edinburgh chef Martin Wishart: '[I network] a fair amount. We go in groups to Singapore and New York.'

To sum up, the section on career development has shown that nearly all chefs who gained two or three stars benefited immensely from having worked in the kitchens of one or more Michelin-starred chefs. In addition to acquiring from them all 'the tricks of the trade', they often gained a vision and an impetus to succeed. Their teachers not only smoothed their subsequent career path, but their masters' renown also endowed them with reflected glory.

These practices are equally developed among British and German chefs. The main differences between them are that British chefs, both in their choice of post-training placements/jobs and in their professional networking are very narrowly focused on French chefs in Britain and in France. German chefs, in contrast, work most frequently with the greats among German or German-speaking Austrian chefs. But with respect to both their foreign *stages/jobs* and their networking contacts, they choose chefs from a larger group of countries, that is they appear to be more cosmopolitan in their choice of career contacts. While language and geography explain the greater involvement with Switzerland and Austria, this does not apply to all their choices. Finally, it is astonishing that only one chef from each country has worked in the other.

Chefs as Work-Horses

Before gaining Michelin stars and subsequently reaching national or international renown, chefs have to commit themselves to sustained physical hardship and social isolation and, in some cases, extreme psychological pressure. I have already made repeated references to both and will now describe in more detail the daily grind which is part of the life of both aspiring and actual Michelin-starred chefs. Many chefs believe that the balance in the kitchen is tilted more towards hard grind than towards exercising one's talent and engaging in inspired activity, at least during the early years of their career. Wright expresses this well when he says: 'Kitchens may no longer be the workhouses they once were but you still don't get anywhere without putting yourself through some real pain.'[15]

Why, the reader may ask, are chefs destined to endure such physical hardship? It is partly because of the speed and precision required during service and partly because of the deleterious physical environment of heat, noise, and the danger of cuts and burns. Additionally, the unsocial hours exert a damaging influence. For the *chef de cuisine* there is the added pressure that he or she is facing, at one and the same time, towards the brigade, suppliers, customers, financiers, and the gastronomic critics/guides, while still remaining the inspirational head for the brigade. Thus the activities chefs engage in range from constant innovation and redesign of the menu, monitoring and inspiring the staff, to sourcing the food and balancing the books. They additionally face customers and engage in a spot of marketing through writing cookery books and appearing on television. Added to this may be activities like calculations about the produce–price equation; reservation arrangements; and writing references for members of their brigade. As a consequence, chefs work very long hours, often during unsocial times, and they feel constant cross-pressure from the demands of these various activities. Although a good *sous* chef, or better still, another head chef, can take on some of these activities, the buck nevertheless stops with the *chef de cuisine*.

The demands and pressures on ambitious lower-level chefs, that is, chefs who aspire to the position of head chef/*chef de cuisine* and covet a Michelin star, are immense. Wright captures the hardship suffered very well. He describes the early years of Gordon Ramsay, Heston Blumenthal, Marcus Wareing, and Shaun Hill, based on in-depth interviews, in very expressive terms. Ramsay comments on the physical and social hardship experienced:

> It was a claustrophobic, isolated life, largely lived in the confines of the kitchen box. Fatigue became a constant companion, a permanent shadow to be coped with but rarely shaken off.[16]

The exhausting schedule this required is confirmed by Wareing who was employed in Ramsay's then restaurant *Aubergine*: 'Gordon was in the kitchen every day at eight o'clock and left every morning at two o'clock.'[17]

Blumenthal's early years in *The Fat Duck* were characterized by chronic sleep deprivation:

> You'd get so delirious you would be trying to light the blowtorch by holding it under the tap...I remember one day looking down at a piece of cod...[which] I'd cut in to strips and triangles—I'd just fallen asleep with the knife in my hand but kept going.[18]

In comments on Marcus Wareing during his apprenticeship years, Wright remarks:

> He marked himself out through sheer hard work, and the absence of any social life outside work meant that there was little to interfere with his dedication to the job.[19]

Even for chefs who have made it—my Michelin chefs—long hours and physical exhaustion endure. In both countries, chefs speak of a working time of between eleven and sixteen hours per day (one British employed chef works nineteen hours at the week-end). They typically put in these hours five days a week, but often six and sometimes seven. Theoretically, there is a break in the middle of the day, but more often than not it is not taken. Thus a young British one-star chef: 'It is very long hours and days off are spent recuperating instead of on recreation.' Or an older, female British one-star chef:

> It's so stressful and so hard. It's like labouring—you just burn yourself out. You get to the point where the ideas aren't coming. It's like writer's block, and sometimes I think, pack it in now, the story's over. But you rest, and then you get back into it.

When you are relatively young—in your twenties and thirties—you still feel sufficiently passionate about the job to shrug off the long hours, as does this two-star British chef proprietor, who works fourteen hours per day: 'The hours worked are massive. But I like working hard. When you are most tired you are most driven.' Another young self-employed British two-star chef, who works sixteen hours per day, looked pale and tired on the day of the interview. When I asked him what makes him keep such long hours, he replied: 'Job satisfaction, things I want to achieve. I enjoy pushing myself.'

Clare Smyth, head chef and partner of three-star *Gordon Ramsay* restaurant indicates what sustains chefs to work such long hours:

> I find it easier to do something that I'm passionate about. It would be harder to work eight hours a day in a job that I didn't enjoy than 18 hours a day doing something that I love.[20]

But as you begin to age you realize that these long hours cannot be sustained for ever:

> The number of hours I work are very difficult to maintain and are very strenuous—you always have to maintain the highest possible effort. It will become more difficult as you age. But at the moment I work only twelve hours per day which is a comparatively moderate number of hours. (German employed two-star chef)

Of the twenty German chefs, thirteen work five days per week, four work six days, one four days, one five to six, and one seven days. However, the chef with the highest weekly hours works only during the spring and summer months, and several of those working six days per week only do an evening service. Of the twenty British chefs, three work seven days per week, two six, eight work five days, three five to six days, two four days, and two older chefs 'not so many days now' (see Table 4.3). In British restaurants two services per day—lunch and dinner—are much more common.

The fact that, at both extremes, British chefs work both more and less hours must be due to the fact that many more are self-employed. However, the chef with the longest hours—nineteen at week-ends—is employed. He tells me: '[I work] seven days a week at the moment and there is no overtime payment.' That such exploitative conditions are counter-productive is underlined by the fact that this particular chef has lost his star since the time of our interview.

Table 4.3. Days per week worked by chefs

	Not so many days	**4** days	**5** days	5–6 days	**6** days	**7** days
British chefs	2	2	8	3	2	3
German chefs	0	1	13	1	4	1

At the early stage of their career, chefs work extremely long hours, but as they become older and well established, they scale down their hours of kitchen duty. They recognize that they have lost some of the commitment to hard work and that continuance of a punishing work regime risks burn-out and even premature death. If they have found alternative sources of engagement and income, they pass on the reins around the age of fifty.

To conclude this section, becoming a Michelin chef and achieving fame often come at a heavy cost. Chefs cannot become culturally iconic figures without first enduring several decades when they are simply work-horses. Although their passion and drive often inclines them to make 'light work' of the downsides of being a Michelin chef, the experience of real drudgery should not be overlooked. It is as well that young people entering the profession with high and sometimes overblown expectations take full cognizance of this circumstance.

The Meaning of Michelin Stars: Receiving and Retaining the Stars

There is almost 100 per cent unanimity among German and British chefs that being awarded the first Michelin star was a source of great joy and pride for them as persons, as well as increasing the number of their customers and therefore their income to a significant extent. Although my question to chefs about the psychological impact of Michelin stars invites both positive and negative responses, the majority first offer a positive reaction. Chefs greatly respect the Michelin organization and repeatedly affirm inspectors' exceptional degree of professionalism. (For more details on chefs' views on the Michelin organization, see Chapter 10.)

The following citations illustrate chefs' reactions to the award. One-star chef Alan Murchison tells me: 'The sense of achievement is overwhelming. I can tell you where I was when the phone call came. You know the day.' For German two-star chef Hans Horberth: 'it was an affirmation of my person—really great!' And two-star Phil Howard reacted in a similar way: 'We all need a bit of recognition. It gives you more confidence...The stars give you affirmation.' One-star Phil Thompson speaks of the reward of having become a member of a small and illustrious group, an even closer brotherhood: 'I joined this tight-knit community, am now part of a gang.'

Only one British one-star chef does not share this pleasure: 'I would love to have not chosen a star—it is a phoney concept.' A second British one-star chef speaks about merely 'gaining satisfaction' from being awarded a star and later tells me that he would not mind if he lost it.

The situation often is more complex when it comes to the second or third star. The second and the third star bring both new and bigger rewards and greater pressures. The second star, for example, gives you entry into the prestigious *Relais and Chateaux* guide. Although Michelin no longer require it, many chefs have made extra investment into the décor and the staff, and the loss of the second star would bring both reputational and financial damage. Two-star London chef Marcus Wareing expresses both the satisfaction of gaining the second star and hints at the fear of losing it: 'It was my personal and private ambition [to receive a second star]; you have to learn to live with success and failure.'

British two-star chef Brett Graham notes the increased customer expectations: 'There is a bit more pressure [since I received the second star]. People come with higher expectations.' A British one-star chef opines: 'There is a change from a one-star to a two-star restaurant: the guests change—they are arseholes.'

The third star makes the chef part of a small and highly select band, providing visibility not only at the national but also at the international level. German three-star chef Juan Amador puts it in these words: 'One is somebody at the international level. One realizes that one is playing in a certain champion's league competition.'

A three-star restaurant attracts international gourmet tourists whose often inflated expectations and constant (mostly critical) comparisons across restaurants and national borders do not always render them the most welcome guests. (For further details on gourmet tourists, see Chapter 9.)

Not all of my chefs aspire to multiple stars. Even when they do, they do not necessarily have a strategy to advance to a higher level. Seven of the British chefs and nine of the German chefs say that they do nothing at all to get an additional star or to retain existing stars. For some, it is simply that, as they do not know Michelin's precise criteria for advancement, there is nothing they can reasonably do to fulfil them. A German two-star chef responds: '[I am doing] nothing, I cannot influence this. I just continue to cook in my way.' A British one-star chef agrees: 'I am doing nothing to achieve the second star. Two stars will come by default. I am not going to chase it.'

A significant proportion of chefs in both countries insist that their cooking is not oriented towards the expectations of Michelin inspectors but to those of their customers/guests. Two German one-star chefs articulate this position: 'I cook for guests, not for inspectors'; '[I am doing] nothing whatsoever. I remain authentic. I cook for my guests and not for the guides.'

Even the doyen of British starred cuisine, Albert Roux, holder of three stars while chef proprietor at *Le Gavroche*, was not primarily oriented towards getting and keeping stars:

> The stars never were the most important thing for me. I had three ambitions: to do well for and focus on my staff; my repeat customers; and my business…The repeat customer is the ambassador for my restaurant.

He even counsels against a strong focus on achieving stars as this can lead to neglect of the prime business goals:

> Young chefs do not always understand that takings are not profit, and their business then gets into trouble. This has something to do with the high turnover among one-star chefs.

A few chefs, however, genuinely do not want a second or third star. They either find the prospect of multiple stars too constraining of what they want to do in their restaurants, or they believe that their type of restaurant would not be eligible for an additional star. Thus a German two-star chef:

> [I am doing] nothing [to achieve the third star]. It is not our goal. We desire the greatest possible number of repeat guests. We seek a stylish and relaxed atmosphere. It must not be too strained. With the third star, you are truly under pressure.

Another German two-star chef explains:

> [I am doing] nothing at all. We'll leave that one. Two stars already are a great surprise and pride. Bistros surely would not be considered for a third star by the *Michelin Guide*.

And a British one-star chef professes: 'I don't want the second [star]. The place does not need it, nor deserve it.'

Only a small number of chefs are comfortable with expressing their ambition for gaining one or two more stars (or for keeping the existing star(s)) and reveal that they actively work towards this goal. Among the older British chefs, Gordon Ramsay is known for his burning ambition to gain the third star. Simon Wright well sums up this obsession:

> A trio of asterisks in a little red book represented the culmination of more than a decade of toil and extraordinary dedication and, to him [Gordon Ramsay], it felt like nothing ever had or ever will.[21]

Ambition is equally fierce among some one-star chefs. British chef Alan Murchison tells me: 'I am obsessed by what we do. I have made a conscious decision to be the best.' German chef Tim Raue even made public his burning ambition in his recent book (he was awarded his second star in 2013):

> I waited year after year for the publication of the Michelin results, and each time put aside the list with disappointment when our name was not on it. When it eventually was awarded it was a great event…Today I live for the second star.[22]

Other chefs anxious to advance to the next level tell me what they think it takes to achieve it. Three British one-star chefs obviously know the Michelin criteria for advancement: '[We must] make our food more exciting. Quality and skill are there. To get a second star, staffing levels are not important, but sustaining the surprising and excellent element is important.' Another says: 'We are just upping the innovation levels and always striving to improve.' A third British one-star chef lists a mixture of measures which, in his view, might make a second star likely: 'We are refurbishing and upgrading the restaurant; are refining the service; and we are adding more intrigue to the dishes.'

A German and a British two-star chef both believe they already are on the right track and just have to keep at it: 'Receiving three stars is only a long-run goal, one has to give one's best every day. I am working hard, but it is really up to them' (German two-star chef); 'We try to keep up the standards and improve every day.' Finally, long-time German three-star chef Harald Wohlfahrt reveals what he does to keep up the constant high level of performance: 'I fight every day. He who fights can lose, but he who does not fight has already lost.'

In sum, chefs vary in their attitudes towards receiving stars. They do not always actively work towards receiving a star, particularly when it comes to the second star. Other goals pursued by chefs are to simply produce good food and keep their customers satisfied. All except one of my respondents, however, are happy to be the holder of one or more Michelin stars. Their value in promoting their restaurants, but also in giving personal satisfaction and affirmation, for them, is second to no other honour.

Are Michelin Stars a Poisoned Chalice?

The view that chefs generally are extremely proud of and pleased with their stars, however, is sometimes contradicted. There is a quite widespread opinion, mainly communicated by the press, that there is a darker side to the award of stars. It is even claimed that a star can turn into a curse for its holder. While none of my respondents hold such a view, several nevertheless indicate that the receipt of stars (and stardom) does not harmonize with their own concept of restaurant food and ambience. Thus a German two-star chef: 'It affected my pride but I am not going to lose the connection to the soil/locality (*Bodenhaftigkeit*). Stars are not what drives me.' The only British one-star chef cited as hostile to the Michelin organization believes that stars prevent you from developing a casual style of dining and instead oblige you to have table cloths and fancy cutlery.

Furthermore, some of my respondents admit that the pressure to maintain their Michelin-starred status causes them stress and anxiety, though in no case is this seen as acute. A British one-star chef speaks for many when he indicates that the biggest psychological pressure of the job is: 'making sure that it is consistent every single night—the stress levels have increased'. A British and a German two-star chef add:

> The business is very constantly judged. We are constantly rated. This is different to other art forms: every human being feels entitled to judge what you do and express their opinion.

> You always work under a certain degree of pressure. You always have to achieve 100 per cent, even when you don't feel like it.

A British one-star (employed) chef tells me: 'It [the star] has had an impact, but only because I take it on this way. I would hate to lose it and fight every day to keep it. I do lots of overtime.'

Yet there are many chefs who manage the pressure well and who point out that you have to keep a sense of perspective. Thus, a German three-star chef says he does nothing to keep his stars: 'One must not hurt oneself with this stress, the fear of losing a star. We just do it with love and dedication.' A German one-star and a two-star chef express similar sentiments: 'We carry the star with pride and responsibility but I do not want to get involved in the competitive Olympiad of the stars'; 'It is often very stressful but one should not make oneself ill—there are more important things in life.' Similarly, two British one-star chefs say:

> I used to put in more hours of work because of the star, but not any longer. A Michelin star should not be the over-riding issue.

> I never worked for the first star. If Michelin give me a second I shall feel honoured but I am not losing any sleep over it. I am not actively trying to get a second star but am progressing naturally. I don't want to force it. It is not a test you have to pass.

Asked what he does to retain his third star, German chef Elverfeld replies: 'I am focused on development and the product—this is the best way to keep the quality, and I am not focused on Michelin.'

A few chefs even relish the pressure. Two British, as well as a German one-star chef, claim: 'It did not increase levels of anxiety. I do not do stress', 'I love pressure', and 'A little bit of stress is healthy.'

However, the chefs I interviewed are in one sense a biased sample—they all held Michelin stars at the time of my interviews. It is often suggested in the press that holding one or more Michelin stars subjects you to unbearable pressure and that many chefs have 'given back' their stars when they could no longer bear the strain. The British example most frequently cited is that of

Marco Pierre White. In 1999, White gave up his three-star restaurant, *Marco Pierre White* at the Hyde Park Hotel, to embark on other ventures in the restaurant industry. His comments at the time are reported to have been:

> I was being judged by people who had less knowledge than me, so what was it truly worth? I gave Michelin inspectors too much respect, and I belittled myself. I had three options: I could be a prisoner of my world and continue to work six days a week, I could live a lie and charge high prices and not be behind the stove...[23]

A careful reading of this quotation reveals that, although he had some complaints about the Michelin organization, another circumstance probably triggered his decision. He faced the choice between either staying six days in the kitchen or taking a back seat in his kitchen and thus receiving the stars without putting in the work to deserve them. But this conundrum is not as compelling as presented by White and is not necessarily viewed as such by other chefs. White has been described as a bit of a control freak and probably would not have been able to surrender control to another head chef to gain himself more time away from his kitchen. It is also noteworthy that White engaged in many supplementary activities and therefore had increased his workload far beyond what was required to maintain his three stars.

Among those who gave up their starred restaurant during 2011/12 in Germany were Cornelia Poletto, Andreas Gerlach, Holger Stromberg, and Christian Rach. Poletto cites the tremendous physical and mental stress, combined with the precarious profit, as well as the constraints on her exercised by the Michelin system, as reasons for withdrawing from 'the race'.[24] Poletto thus puts her finger on an additional point, namely the precarious financial reward for an all-engrossing involvement in terms of time and energy. Gerlach has found this both physically and mentally exhausting and suffered a kind of burn-out which told him to call a halt. Stromberg suffered physical exhaustion, and Rach is simply wary of a statistic circulating in the industry that chefs, on average, die prematurely, at the age of 56. However, these chefs, too, have taken on extra restaurants (Stromberg and Rach) and/or have taken on regular television work (Poletto and Rach).[25] Whether it is therefore running a Michelin-starred restaurant or the overload of supplementary engagements which has driven them to close their starred restaurant is far from clear.

What stands out from this examination is that the hard work imposed by the holding of multiple stars, if not carefully managed by either delegation or avoidance of supplementary activities, can, indeed, lead to a chef's burn-out, resulting in flight or nervous breakdown. It would be an exaggeration to say that Michelin stars invariably or even frequently turn out to be 'a poisoned chalice'. However, every year, there is a small number of chefs who feel that the stars have become a burden and who give up their starred restaurant.

In Britain, the departure of Skye Gyngell from one-star *Petersham Nurseries Café* in Richmond, in February 2012, throws light on a different way in which a Michelin star can come to be perceived as a yoke around one's neck. In this case, Michelin's fairly recent practice of awarding stars also to establishments located in an extremely simple physical environment (the café is situated in an annexe to a garden centre, has 'rickety tables and haphazard service' and 'loos in a shed') seems to have misjudged customers' expectations. Customers have come to associate a star also with a comfortable environment, particularly if the cost of the meal is well above the industry average. At *Petersham Nurseries*, they found their expectations disappointed and presented Skye Gyngell's staff with frequent criticisms. This, together with a very large number of diners—up to 120 in a sitting—in the end made Gyngell perceive the Michelin star very negatively. In her own words:

> It's been a curse. That probably sounds very ungrateful. Since we got the star we've been rammed every day, which is really hard for such a tiny restaurant. And we have had lots more complaints.[26]

Tom Kerridge has been equally inundated with customers since receiving a second star for his relatively simple gastro pub in 2012: 'It [the impact of the second star] has been massive. The first star usually helps business, but the effect of the second was almost uncontrollable.' But unlike Gyngell, he is generally delighted about the extra publicity his second star has given him. He regards the phenomenal growth as a challenge, rather than as a curse.

For British chef Marc Wilkinson of *Fraiche*, in the Wirral, the only way to cope with the pressure placed on him by the receipt of one star has been to remove all evidence of this and other awards from both his website and his restaurant: 'I removed them from me. I just woke up one morning and removed them. I hoped that it would encourage people not to have a preconceived notion of what the restaurant would be.'[27]

To sum up this section, the award of Michelin stars enhances both chefs' reputation and turnover but also places considerable psychological pressure and physical demands on them. The majority of chefs are delighted about their raised reputation in the profession and the greater exposure the stars have provided among the dining public. They have found ways to cope with, or even relish the accompanying pressures. However, a few chefs every year buckle under the pressure and, in the end, regard their star(s) as a 'poisoned chalice'. The receipt of the second and third star in particular introduces further pressures for a minority of chefs. However, they also confirm the chef's inspirational worth and thereby open the door not only to a much enhanced business volume, but also to personal renown. Such fame reaches beyond their circle of customers and makes them visible to a much larger circle of people—they become a celebrity.

The Rise of the 'Celebrity' Chef: In Front of the Television Camera or at the Stove?

Whereas in the 1970s and 1980s, the job of chef often was for those who could not find anything better to do, today it has become surrounded with glamour. Some chefs have become superstars, in many aspects—though not in terms of earnings—comparable to first division footballers and pop stars. In this section I explore how renown or fame, i.e. public marks of recognition, is achieved. I consider what effects celebrity has, not only on the chef concerned, but also on the industry, as well as on the public's relation to food and dining. It is additionally of interest whether and how *renown* may be converted into worth in the market.

The phenomenon of celebrity chefs again raises the question of chefs' considerations of what has value or what counts in their professional activity, that is, of competing orders of worth. I will explore how another order of worth—that of *opinion*—has come to define the activities and image of many Michelin-starred chefs. I address the question of how the values and guides for action entailed may be combined, or stand in conflict with, the guiding principles of the *inspired* order of worth. The latter is marked by a passion for excellence and by a high degree of creativity, usually developed as part of the chef's work in the kitchen and/or in relative solitude. Are Boltanski and Thévenot overly dramatic to suggest that 'once individuals...attach importance to external signs of success, i.e. fame, they become unworthy in the world of inspiration' and even that the 'temptation of fame is one of the chief causes of a fall'?[28]

'In the polity of fame', according to Boltanski and Thévenot, 'worth depends solely on the number of people who award their esteem. Worth is measured by visibility, the degree to which a person is available to the gaze of others.'[29] How then do chefs emerge from behind the stove and become visible? Is this availability to the gaze of others a new phenomenon in the lives of professional chefs? The notion of a celebrity chef, highly visible not only in his or her own country but also abroad, arose soon after restaurants were first founded in late eighteenth-century France. Restaurant critics brought top chefs, i.e. chefs who enjoyed inspired worth, to the attention of the dining public through the medium of print: through reviews of their culinary art in both the general press and specialized magazines. Once a chef had become well known to the upper and upper middle-classes in France, he could exploit this still fairly limited fame to address an even wider section of the public with his own cookery books. If these sold well and appeared in many editions, fame was assured. The resulting public exposure eventually transcended national borders, reaching an educated public also in many other developed societies.

Thus Carême in the early nineteenth century and Escoffier in the early twentieth century probably were the first international celebrity chefs. But celebrity chefs were found not only in France. According to Clarissa Dickson Wright,[30] Britain saw the beginning of the rise of the celebrity chef—she considers it 'the curse of the modern age'—during the Stuart era, i.e. in the second half of the seventeenth century. She particularly singles out Patrick May, a professional cook born in 1588. He cooked for the minor aristocracy and, in 1660, published one of the first cookery books written by a professional chef, *The Accomplisht Cook*. A little less than two centuries later, another chef acquired widespread fame in Britain—the Frenchman Alexis Soyer—who became *chef de cuisine* of the Reform Club in 1837. In his case, it was not merely his cooking and cookery books which gained him public esteem. He probably was the first ethically engaged chef when he took an active interest in the bodily welfare of British soldiers, fighting the Turks at Gallipoli. However, all these chefs remained isolated examples.

The real basis for the rise of the celebrity chef was laid only in the late 1960s by the rise of *nouvelle cuisine*. By elevating the chef's importance—the person who offered design on a plate—this development removed the chef from the obscurity of the kitchen and ushered in the age of the chef proprietor/patron. This followed closely on the heels of an important socio-technical innovation—the widespread availability of television.

While historically a chef's fame was limited both by the print medium's reach and by the fact that reading books was confined mainly to the middle-classes, the arrival of television has transformed the situation. It eventually became the prime medium to make visible top chefs to the viewing nation as a whole. Since then, chefs have been able to acquire a large public, interested in culinary matters and in the persona of the chef who presents them. Among the first famous British television chefs was Fanny Craddock who, together with her husband Johnny, entertained the nation with her Escoffier-inspired cooking and her theatrical and faintly ridiculous style, between the early 1950s and mid-1970s. She was followed by Keith Floyd, the flamboyant chef who held the nation in thrall between 1985 and 2000, always with a glass of wine in hand. Both were entertainers, and neither of them was a professional chef, let alone a Michelin-starred one. The first professional television chef was the Frenchman Boulestin who had cooked in London from the 1930s onwards and whose cookery books first made French cuisine accessible to the British public.[31] Another professional chef who transformed himself into a national celebrity through television was Swiss-born Anton Mosimann, executive chef at London's Dorchester from 1975 to 1985 and the first *chef de cuisine* in a hotel restaurant to gain two Michelin stars.[32]

The provision of televised mass entertainment, together with the exponential growth of interest in lifestyle programmes and particularly in food, has provided Michelin chefs with the opportunity to gain recognition from a vast audience. Gaining fame is not solely related to the chef's capability in the kitchen or even his or her inspired worth. It additionally is due to the chef's overall personality and the extent to which he or she succeeds in forging a connection with the viewing public.

The format of cookery and food programmes varies, but for many, entertainment value has been the first priority. The majority of the audience is not primarily concerned to learn to cook. As pointed out by Clarissa Dickson Wright: 'with the ever-diminishing desire to cook has come an ever-growing desire to watch cookery programmes on television'.[33]

Other critics are more scathing and talk about the development of "gastro porn", that is, a performance around food which is fantasized over rather than acted upon. Even the long-time television chef Keith Floyd came to regret what became of some cookery programmes when, in 2001, he grumbled:

> We have become a nation of voyeurs. We don't cook anymore, we just watch TV programmes about cookery…Nobody takes cooking seriously now, it's just cheap entertainment…a series of game shows.[34]

The picture is similar in Germany. The first television chef who could not even cook was Clemens Wilmenrod, an actor, who was a huge success in the 1950s. Many others followed, and today television chefs abound. Names like Johann Lafer, Sarah Wiener, Tim Mälzer, Alfred Biolek, Christian Rach, Alfons Schuhbeck, and a long list of others are German household names. Rach, in some eyes, appears to be Germany's answer to a combination of Jamie Oliver and Gordon Ramsay in that he has taken up social causes, such as offering deprived young people the opportunity of a chef's training. More of the television chefs now are professional chefs who have their own restaurant. However, none of the Michelin-starred chefs, except for one-star Schuhbeck, Lafer, and Rach, appear regularly on television. (Rach now has given up his one-star restaurant to devote himself solely to television work.) As in Britain, their cookery shows provide predominantly entertainment.

However, it would be wrong to leave the evaluation of television chefs at that. Some programmes also aim to educate and convey knowledge about food and cooking, and a food programme such as, for example, the *Hairy Bikers*, can be entertaining and instructive at the same time. Other programmes, such as *Master Chef* or the *Great British Menu* try to instruct and inspire. They retain their entertainment value, however, by running competitions where viewers come to identify with contestants and enjoy the nail-biting suspense of finding out whether they have backed the 'right horse'. These programmes do not trivialize food. They have the effect—whether intended or not—to inspire young people with or without a prior interest in food to become chefs, or to make existing chefs aspire to higher levels of achievement. It is obvious that contestants on *Master Chef* revere Michel Roux, one of the judges in 2013, and very much regard him as a role model. It would not be too far-fetched to say that a few television chefs on the more educational programmes become charismatic leaders who acquire a dedicated following. Among their followers there are always some young people, without other avenues of upward mobility, who become truly inspired to gain the same craft skills and inspired worth as the famous television personality. Several of the winners of the *Master Chef* competition have, indeed, gone on to open their own restaurants.

However, even this type of programme attracts criticism, particularly from chefs. They object that it does not portray the reality of the kitchen as all the preparation has been done beforehand: 'It is not real-world cooking.'[35] Instead, the programmes present a chef's work in an idealized way.

Some food programmes have the additional merit of making consumers aware of both the value of good food and of the many damaging practices which endanger our food supply. Their presenting chefs are serious about the need for more nutritious home cooking. They have managed to plug in to the current fascination with food and particularly with the theatre provided by *haute cuisine*. British chefs like Rick Stein, Raymond Blanc, and Michel Roux and German ones like Tim Mälzer and Alfred Biolek have struck a chord with a large section of the viewing public and have gained wide public recognition. Mälzer's cookery show is said to have attracted more than a million viewers on weekdays and is viewed as a reflection of the upward tendency which cooking and food now enjoy in Germany.[36] One German representative survey, undertaken by a television programme magazine, established that two thirds of their audience were inspired by the programme to try out a recipe in their own kitchens.[37]

In general, however, neither in Britain nor in Germany is the popularity of cook shows indicative of a new-found love for cooking. It is rather interpreted as a vicarious enjoyment of a virtuosity at the stove few viewers themselves possess, let alone aspire to replicate. Nevertheless, as a consequence of such frequent and widely viewed programmes, chefs have emerged as iconic cultural figures or as charismatic leaders who inspire a following among some young people who themselves become chefs.

It does not matter that the majority of chefs do not participate in these programmes. Furthermore, they often judge those who do as prioritizing entertainment above instruction, or worse, as making themselves vulnerable to derision from their colleagues. Critics fear that such programmes divert from the true value of good food or that exaggerated fame may backfire. Once a chef has appeared regularly on one or more television programmes, he or she has become a household name, as well as a brand which can be bought by food companies to raise their profile and sales.[38]

Being a celebrity chef has obvious advantages for chefs. Without a marketing budget, doing a TV programme is a means to put one's restaurant on the map. It additionally provides marketing for chefs' cookery books and may turn their cookery courses into places of pilgrimage for hobby cooks. In terms of return, appearing in a cookery show is more influential than getting a good review or having a cookery book out. Celebrity has enhanced chefs' market worth and ensured them a much more substantial income than could ever be derived from their restaurants alone.[39] But, at the same time, the embrace of market worth, together with the often 'entertainment' character of the television programmes, may seriously threaten a chef's inspired worth. The chef is in danger of becoming more identified with a television persona than being recognized as a serious and creative chef. In any case, new substantial demands on a chef's time make it difficult to sustain the 'inspired' aspect of the profession.

Whereas celebrity inevitably entails recognition by a large number of people, the development of inspired worth demands private space and a certain degree of seclusion from the 'public gaze.' The two orders of worth thus appear to be intrinsically incompatible, just as feared by Boltanski and Thévenot.[40] Moreover, the worth of fame is inconstant. The chef who has endangered his or her professional status for the sake of becoming a television celebrity in the longer run may well end up with nothing. Also a chef's public identification with a particular restaurant subsequently makes it more likely that viewers expect him or her to be present when they visit the restaurant. Paradoxically, the chef has re-established the 'ties to the stove' that external involvement was supposed to loosen. This is noted by one perceptive British chef: 'If you go on television, then guests want to see you [in the restaurant].'

This negative development, however, is not inevitable, and a sense of proportion is necessary. It obviously depends on the balance a chef maintains between dedication to the restaurant and appearances on television. It additionally matters, whether chefs become 'mere' entertainers, or whether they extend their role in the kitchen—as instructor of a younger generation of chefs—also to the television screen.

Many of my respondents have appeared on one or more television programmes, but for most it does not occupy a substantial part of their time. (Those more heavily involved with television, such as Blanc, Ramsay, Michel Roux Jnr., and Eckart Witzigmann, declined to participate in my research.) A few chefs express their enjoyment of periodic involvement in television programmes. Thus two-star Johannes King says: 'I appear on television—6 to 8 times in the year on ZDF (national channel) and about 30 times on regional television. It is fun for me—it is possible to combine it with the business.' Having visited his restaurant, the evidence backs up his claim. Despite relatively frequent television appearances, he still is able to produce inspired food. The same applies to British two-star chef Tom Kerridge. He, too, derives enjoyment from his television work but also remains dedicated to his Marlow pub-restaurant, *The Hand & Flowers.*

Other chefs recognize and value the marketing effect of appearing on television. One-star chef Phil Thompson tells me: 'I have done bits of TV work as a judge on *Master Chef.* It is good for networking and advertises the place.' London two-star chef Marcus Wareing sees the marketing potential of television appearances, without losing sight of its often negative features:

I am available for the media, but much of the television is too boring and unrealistic…On the one hand, the media work raises the importance of fine-dining restaurants and of good food, but on the other side there are a lot of gimmicky food shows.

But more chefs in both countries volunteer comments which show that they are aware of the double-edged nature of extensive participation. They do not exactly present themselves as artist-monks, permanently tied to their stoves. But these chefs nevertheless reject the image of a public entertainer or object to the artificiality of the television process of cooking. They either feel ambiguous about television appearances or reject them outright.

One-star German chef Mario Gamba tells me:

I mostly decline to appear on television—I do only one programme during the January–March period which is a focused thing. In television, they are not concerned with quality—they are only concerned with laughter, and I am no clown.

Three-star Sven Elverfeld says: 'I will not do television simply as a show but if it is a documentary about us then that is fine.' British one-star chef Shaun Hill is more emphatic: 'TV—not if I can help it. I don't enjoy it. It is very time-consuming, and you are at the mercy of their cameras.' Three German chefs are outright hostile:

I refused all of that. It is a mere 'Punch and Judy' show. I do not have the need to go public.

Regarding television, people like Schuhbeck [German one-star television chef] and Ramsay are an embarrassment for the guild. These people destroy more.. .

It is more important for me to get a perfect dish onto the plate than to pull jokes in a cook show…there is nothing worse for me than to watch how four outstanding chefs mutate into a group of idiots on television and do each other down with some kinds of evaluations.[41]

Even such an international superstar as French chef Alain Ducasse surprisingly does not endorse stardom: 'A chef has to stay an artisan, not become a star.'[42] German two-star chef King realizes that restaurant guests also feel ambiguous about chefs' television appearances. Whereas some recognize that television appearances can be demeaning, others enjoy the reflected glory of a celebrity chef: 'Some guests tell me: "But King, there is no need for you to do this", whereas others like it.'

When we enquire about the impact of celebrity chefs on the wider society, answers again express ambiguity. On the one side, despite the often 'mere entertainment' character of cookery programmes, many positive consequences may be discerned. These include raised awareness of the importance of high-quality, fresh, and local food and of the necessity to protect and even resurrect rare animal and plant breeds. Food programmes have incited a greater questioning of supermarkets about the provenance of their food. This wider social impact has been particularly pronounced when a television chef also adopts ethical issues and engages in a campaign against damaging attitudes and practices around food. An example here is Jamie Oliver. He now is an international celebrity and generally is viewed positively among my respondents in both countries. But Oliver is not and probably does not aspire to become Michelin-starred.

On the other side, it is well known that the emergence of the celebrity chef for many viewers has remained 'mere' entertainment. While it has increased the knowledge of top-level chefs and their food it has not significantly changed the relation to food of a large part of the population. Domestic consumption of unhealthy food and use of fast-food restaurants have not markedly declined, nor has there been an increase in cooking at home, particularly in Britain. In Britain, a fifth of our food still comes out of plastic containers and the microwave. During the last ten years, the British have become the fattest nation in Europe.

The picture is not dissimilar in Germany. However, the 'healthy food' lobby is more engaged and active there, and food degradation and unhealthy eating have not assumed quite the same high levels. Food provenance recently has become a major issue. In sum, there definitely has been some positive impact of making Michelin-starred chefs highly visible and accessible to a much enlarged public, but it is difficult to judge how far it has ousted or moderated unhealthy food consumption habits.

Reservations about celebrity chefs are less marked, when their impact on the fine-dining restaurant industry is considered. There has been one highly positive consequence: celebrity has raised the industry's reputation among young people. This has eased recruitment and also has attracted better educated applicants for jobs. The career choice of chef is no longer made for want of anything better to do. For *chefs de cuisine* this is largely positive. However, many young chefs now join the profession with celebrity chefs as their main role models. They have only a dim awareness of the fact that a large number of chefs fall by the wayside. Hence *chefs de cuisine* now face the task of getting young chefs to scale back their expectations. They have to make them understand that dedication and hard grind have to be invested before the possibility of fame arises.

During recent decades, a number of celebrity chefs have acquired international fame and have become known even to people generally not interested in *haute cuisine*. French chef Bocuse, American chefs Alice Waters and Thomas Keller, Spanish Ferran Adria, and, most lately, Danish René Redzepi, all have acquired international reputations and visibility. In each case this has occurred primarily because of the inspired character of their food and/or because of their highly innovative cuisine. Ferran Adria even has had a very successful film made to create better understanding of his molecular or, as he prefers to call it, techno-emotional cuisine. Although Gordon Ramsay also has acquired international fame, his renown primarily is based on his television performance skills, among which the use of foul language is not insignificant. Whereas it is probably correct to say that none of the former chefs has lost his or her inspired worth because of fame, it is more difficult to assert this with any conviction about Gordon Ramsay. Thus, it is not necessarily fame itself which destroys inspired worth. It matters how fame is handled and whether top chefs allow themselves to be turned into 'mere entertainers' or instead use their visibility and iconic status with discernment. Finally, it must be remembered that fame does not come easily, nor is it bestowed on every chef.

Summary and Comparison

I have shown how fine-dining chefs develop from relatively modest or even disadvantaged social beginnings to highly respected and sometimes even famous *chefs de cuisine*. My study of the road travelled highlights both this astonishing career mobility and the tremendous sacrifices made to reach this relatively exalted end state. Both psychological stress and physical toil are encountered along the road and require resilience, adaptability, and physical robustness from chefs, but above all passion and dedication, to last the track. To evaluate their identifications and attitudes, I again used the lens of competing guiding principles and scenarios for action Michelin chefs have to work with. They seek to accommodate the conflicting normative demands and operational imperatives of the inspired order of worth and that of renown or fame, and they achieve it with more or less success.

The most hazardous complementary activity, that is, the one which most interferes with chefs' inspired worth, is regular television work, in order to seek celebrity status. This not only increases the workload but, more seriously, draws the chef away from the kitchen and from the search for new inspirational dishes. The claims made by Boltanski and Thévenot,[43] however, exaggerate the inherent incompatibility between the two underlying orders of worth. For many chefs it simply remains a valuable marketing opportunity which puts their restaurant on the map. However, when television work becomes a second career and chefs become dependent on their television earnings, the chef's inspired status becomes endangered. When chefs buy-in to the values of 'light entertainment' television and allow themselves to be turned into entertainers, their inspired worth becomes seriously jeopardized.

Notes

1. S. Wright, *Tough Cookies: Tales of Obsession, Toil and Tenacity from Britain's Culinary Heavyweights* (London: Profile Books, 2006), 61.
2. M. P. White, *White Heat* (London: Pyramid Books, 1990).
3. T. Raue, *Ich weiss was Hunger ist. Von der Strassengang in die Sterneküche* (Munich and Zürich: Piper Verlag, 2012).
4. Raue 2012: 58.
5. G. Weber, *Kochen ist Krieg* (Munich: Piper, 2009), 13, 298.
6. Wright 2006.
7. <http://www.telegraph.co.uk/news/uknews/1576029/Gordon-Ramsay-eats-his-own-words.html>.
8. *Süddeutsche Zeitung* 86 (13 April 2012): 9.
9. Cited by Wright 2006: 14, 15.
10. Wright 2006: 42.
11. Interview by M. Eckardt, *Kochköpfe. Dreizehn Köche hinter den Kulissn* (Bremen: Verlag H. M Hauschild, 2002), 45.
12. *Yes Chef! Magazine* 25 (2012): 23.
13. For a glimpse of Blumenthal's early career, see Wright 2006: 57–90.
14. Raue 2012: 109.
15. Wright 2006: 116.
16. Wright 2006: 18.
17. Wright 2006: 179.
18. Wright 2006: 74.
19. Wright 2006: 153. For comparable, but less penetrating and comprehensive coverage on the work of German chefs, see Eckardt 2002; Weber 2009; and V. Klink, *Sitting Küchenbull. Gepfefferte Erinnerungen eines Kochs* (Hamburg: Rowohlt Verlag, 2009).
20. *Restaurant* (April 2013): 8.
21. Wright 2006: 49.
22. Raue 2012: 286, 192.
23. <http://en.wikipedia.org/wiki/Marco_Pierre_White>, accessed 27 December 2009.
24. <http://www.karriere.de/beruf/sternekoeche-auf-abwegen-10362/>.

25. <http://www.karriere.de/beruf/sternekoeche-auf-abwegen-10362/>.
26. <http://www.telegraph.co.uk/foodanddrink/foodanddrinknews/9094386/Skye-Gyngell-curse-of-the-Michelin-star-has-driven-me-out-of-the-kitchen.html>.
27. <http://www.thestaffcanteen.com/the-staff-canteen-meets/marc-wilkinson-chef-patron-restaurant-fraiche-oxton-the-wirral>.
28. L. Boltanski and L. Thévenot, *On Justification: Economies of Worth* (Princeton: Princeton University Press, 2006) (translation from the French of *De la Justification: Les Economies de la Grandeur*), 163, 238.
29. Boltanski and Thévenot 2006: 99.
30. C. Dickson Wright, *A History of English Food* (London: Random House Books, 2011), 188.
31. J. Burnett, *England Eats Out: A Social History of Eating Out in England from 1830 to the Present* (Harlow: Longman, 2004), 198.
32. <http://www.caterersearch.com/Articles/30/05/2002/43041/From-rationing-to-Ramsay>.
33. Dickson Wright 2011: 42.
34. Obituary for Keith Floyd, *The Telegraph* (15 September 2009).
35. *Yes Chef! Magazine* 8 (Winter 2009): 17.
36. *Spiegel Online* 44 (2006): 1.
37. *Spiegel Online* 44 (2006): 1.
38. For an extended treatment of this topic regarding American chefs, see M. Ruhlman, *The Reach of a Chef* (New York: Penguin, 2007).
39. *Yes Chef! Magazine* 8 (Winter 2009): 17.
40. Boltanski and Thévenot 2006.
41. Raue 2012: 223.
42. Ducasse, cited in *Observer Food Monthly* (18 September 2011).
43. Boltanski and Thévenot 2006.

5

Distinctiveness, Homogeneity, and Innovation in *Haute Cuisine*

High-end chefs enjoy a tremendous influence over what is consumed in restaurants more generally and, via the media, also shape the repertoire of both food retailers and, to a lesser extent, of households. Fine-dining chefs therefore moderate contemporary tastes; that is, they act as taste makers. It is widely assumed that, because Michelin stars are awarded to them, their food is highly creative and even innovative. While this is certainly the case for a minority of chefs, particularly in comparison with lower-level restaurants, a significant degree of copying and of following trends, instead of leading them, also prevails. There also is a tension between developing a distinctive style and the imperative of continuous innovation. This chapter will show both chefs' leadership in the fine-dining scene and the originality and individuality often distinguishing their creations, as well as the following of fashions and the homogeneity this engenders.

In Chapter 4, I wrote about chefs' identity and how both their values of craftsmanship and of art are invoked and stand in complex tension in chefs' self-image. Chefs as artists lay claim to individuality, originality, and to a continual breaking of the accepted mould, i.e. to being innovative. In contrast, chefs as craftspersons are more tradition-bound and follow a canon acquired during an early period of their career, usually during the period of training: 'Craftspersons...accept the constraints of practical usefulness of the objects, and place less weight on uniqueness and formal innovation.'[1]

These competing evaluations of what has worth resurface again when we closely examine the dishes chefs actually prepare and the culinary style they profess to adhere to.

Creativity and Innovation in *Haute Cuisine*

The high-end restaurant sector now is widely regarded as a creative industry where creativity and innovation have an important role to play. Whereas innovation in many manufacturing industries implies the creation of a new functionality for a product, in the fine-dining industry—as in other creative industries—innovation entails the evolution of new aesthetic product features (including new taste sensations) and, less typically, new intellectual ones. The creativity of *chefs de cuisine* is about the generation of new ideas, while innovation—the generation of new products and/or processes—involves the acceptance of these new ideas as valid or fruitful by the industry's market participants, such as gatekeepers and customers.[2]

A widely accepted definition of innovation is that it occurs when artistically inspired individuals identify new problems and, at the same time, offer compelling solutions to these problems.[3] While valuable, such a definition does not help us to assess the very broad spectrum of innovatory activity encountered in high-end cuisine. Hence I favour the adoption of an *additional* conceptual lens current in other industry contexts, namely a distinction between 'radical' and 'incremental' innovation. This roughly corresponds to Cave's distinction between 'normal' creative work that serves an extant market and 'innovative effort to break open an avant garde frontier'.[4] Whereas radical innovation changes the whole architecture of *haute cuisine*, incremental innovation affects only selective aspects which are changed in a more gradual manner. In the case of incremental innovation, creative solutions remain discrete and leave many traditional elements of *haute cuisine* untouched. Finally, successful innovators usually become champions of a new fashion in gastronomy, as their ideas diffuse through the industry within and across national borders. Fashion leaders then become *haute cuisine*'s taste makers.

The demand for creativity and innovation in the restaurant kitchen, particularly among two- and three-star restaurants, challenges chefs to develop an individual and highly original culinary style. Chefs are expected to develop new taste sensations and presentational innovations. They are challenged to generate new spectacular moments where dishes excite, astonish, and even shock diners. Paradoxically, this creative imperative is imposed in an industry context where scope for a wholesale change of the architecture of culinary output (radical innovation) is extremely challenging. The challenge arises from formidable barriers to both product and process innovation. One such barrier is the finite nature of product components (ingredients). Another challenge derives from the craft nature of culinary creation where the process of production makes relatively low use of technology and affords limited scope to process innovation.

The demand for constant innovation has not always been a feature of European *haute cuisine*. Throughout the nineteenth century and for the first six decades of the twentieth century, the tradition of French classical cuisine laid down accepted ingredients, combinations of ingredients, dishes and techniques of preparation. (Spectacle and theatre, however, were not unknown even during the classical period, with sensational table centre-pieces—often sculpted from sugar, marzipan, or pork fat—already common during the periods of Carême and Escoffier.) Up to 1970, according to Pitte,[5] there had occurred little change in the menus of French restaurants; no more than one or two new dishes per year were added. What, then, has brought about the requirement of constant innovation which now is an integral component of high-level chefs' working life? The watershed for change occurred in France, from the late 1960s onwards, when concentration on classical cuisine alone came to be partially replaced by the far-reaching innovations which constituted *nouvelle cuisine*. (For details, see Chapter 1.) One of the ten commandments, publicized by *Gault Millau* in 1973, was 'to be creative and even innovative'.[6] Further impulses for innovation came from the internationalization, if not globalization, of product markets and the development of global media, introducing both new ingredients and new techniques. But an even more decisive impulse for innovation has been provided by gastronomic guides and competitions which make elevation to high rank dependent on the originality and individuality of a chef's cuisine. The *Michelin Guide* uses the criteria of individuality of style and of trend-setting capability to award two and particularly three stars: 'In the three-star area, individuality and trend-setting becomes important' (interview with the editor of *Michelin Germany*).

In contrast, more radical innovation—as present in molecular cuisine—receives low emphasis by the Michelin organization. However, other guides and competitions are more inclined to reward innovation per se. The *Gault Millau* guide and the British Pellegrino Awards are more focused on innovation; that is, they reward chefs who offer new and compelling solutions to the substantial problems of originality of taste and visual presentation in the dishes they produce. (For further details, see Chapter 10.) Mere adherence to the classical tradition, even at a high level of quality and consistency, is no longer sufficient to merit this promotion. As the number of Michelin-starred chefs steadily increased in both Britain and Germany, greatly intensified competition between them has provided yet another spur for chefs to distinguish themselves through creative and original food. Finally, a small but vocal segment of customers—the gourmet tourists, frequenting highly starred restaurants all over the world and airing their criticisms and recommendations on social media sites—have come to demand constant innovation.

It is very difficult to determine what counts as innovation or even originality in British and German *haute cuisine*. It is broadly accepted that only molecular or techno-emotional cuisine—which originated with Spanish Ferran Adria—merits the label of avant-garde cuisine. It offers new solutions to the problem of over-familiar flavours, textures, and consistencies, together with new forms and visual presentations of foodstuffs. This is particularly the case when extensive reliance on molecular methods occurs, as is the case in British Heston Blumenthal's cuisine. (A detailed consideration of molecular cuisine in Britain and Germany will be offered below.)

Incremental innovation, in turn, is often difficult to distinguish from mere fashion. I have erred on the generous side and consider chefs as engaged in incremental innovation if they have adopted more than one of the following incremental innovations: (a) using new ingredients (including new body parts of animals, wild and foraged ingredients, or extremely rare and usually exotic ones)—sometimes this strategy is connected to the adoption of a distinctive philosophy, such as an emphasis on seasonality or extreme localism; (b) devising new dishes and/or taste sensations through unusual combinations of ingredients, textures, and temperatures; (c) developing new modes of presenting food which surprise, excite, or intrigue the diner, i.e. introducing some theatre into dining; and (d) deconstructing traditional national/regional dishes and reinventing them in a new form. Although some new techniques of cooking also have been introduced, such as *sous vide* preparation—precisely controlled long and slow cooking—and thickening of liquid foods with a Pacojet, these have been adopted too widely by high-level chefs to bestow innovative advantage. It is against this background that I evaluate chefs' own perceptions of the intensity and kind of innovation they practise

How far has innovation been embraced by British and German chefs, that is, how many believe themselves to be innovative? Alternatively, to what extent do chefs reject an innovative style in favour of a more craft-oriented one? And how do chefs define what counts as innovation? Last, how innovative is British and German *haute cuisine* in general from the standpoint of its more detached observers or relatively independent industry critics?

Of the twenty British chefs I interviewed, thirteen consider themselves to be innovative (one of whom qualifies it with 'probably') and a fourteenth opts for 'creative, not innovative'. There is no clear relationship between a positive response and the possession of multiple stars. Of the six chefs who make no claim for an innovative style, four view it as incompatible with their culinary philosophy/style. One of them is two-star British chef Tom Kerridge:

> No, it [my food] is well thought-out and considered but not necessarily creative and least of all innovative...The majority of what I do is 'proper cooking'.

British one-star chef Kelly of the bistro *Wild Honey* says:

It [innovation] is not the style of the restaurant...But we always look for something new—it is important to keep us exciting. We don't want to be just a normal restaurant.

One-star Shaun Hill declares himself bound by tradition because 'it filters out the stupidity in innovation', and two-star London chef Phil Howard puts the same feeling more politely:

We don't do that [innovation]. Most top chefs are avant-garde, they are challenging but not what I would want to eat. They are necessary for innovation but get too much recognition. They do not give consistent pleasure and delicious food.

It is notable that one of the four British three-star chefs, Alain Roux, explicitly rejects the descriptor 'innovative' for his cooking. Moreover, he casts a fundamental doubt on the possibility of innovation in *haute cuisine*:

There's no invention in my cooking. No chef can claim to have invented any dish from scratch, with the possible exception of Blumenthal...here at the *Waterside* the menu evolves gently.[7]

This doubt also is shared by two-star London chef Brett Graham who recognizes the low scope for innovation in *haute cuisine*: 'No, [I do not consider my cuisine innovative]. There are very few innovative people in this trade– only one or two in this country.'

Among the twenty German chefs, seventeen consider themselves to be innovative, one opts for 'only creative', and two do not aspire to innovativeness. All four German three-star chefs I interviewed think of themselves as innovative—after all the gastronomic guides have given them licence to do so. Yet the two chefs who reject the attribute of 'innovative' are two-, rather than one-star chefs. Two-star Johannes King is more intent on craftsmanship:

We are situated between the traditional and good craftsmanship. We are not specialists in producing the most innovative things. What you cook must make sense and not just be a fashion. I do not want to innovate for the sake of innovation.

His two-star colleague Eric Menchon also indicates that constant innovation somehow warps the profession: 'No, [I do not consider my cuisine as innovative]. It is more important to express one's heart.'

The responses of these self-aware British and German chefs who are not afraid to disavow a striving for innovation also find an echo in the responses of some diners, detailed in Chapter 9. For some chefs and diners, perfection in preparation and taste is more valuable than constant innovation which easily descends into mere fashion. Nevertheless, to satisfy the *Michelin Guide*'s criteria for the award of three stars, perfection has to be allied to distinctiveness of cuisine, stopping short of constant innovation.

When I asked chefs what their innovativeness consists of I received a diverse range of responses. They range from only marginal changes introduced to their dishes to constant changes in the dishes themselves. Some of the changes they put forward would not normally be considered as innovation, such as: 'we try to be seasonal in our produce use, as for example, with wild herbs' or '[Being innovative, means] above all, putting things on the plate that enthuse people.' Yet others have trouble finding a convincing description of their innovative approach, offering only a very general definition: '[It consists of] presentation; cooking techniques and ultimately taste'; 'Innovation lies in the way they plate the food.'

But many more chefs are able to describe constant incremental innovation in motivational and substantive terms and, moreover, combine several of the types listed above. They are passionately dedicated to innovation as lower-level problem-solving. Two-star German chef Luther says: 'We always try to develop ourselves further and to always introduce new dishes.' British one-star chef Glynn Purnell claims: 'I am trying to evolve and look at new dishes all the time.' German three-star chef Wissler reports: 'I work on the basis of curiosity; I constantly want to discover something new.' Two-star British chef Marcus Wareing says: 'I always think "out of the box"—try something a little different; introduce new flavours. Innovation is continually ongoing.' One-star Indian chef Atul Kochhar reports that: 'We go into uncharted territory, in terms of both flavour and texture combinations. An example is our innovation on vindaloo. We do a pork vindaloo with crackling.' Finally, one-star German chef Markus Nagy says: '[Innovation means] giving a new interpretation to current products, to cook and/or prepare them in a different way and to create a different dish.'

All the above, except Dirk Luther and Markus Nagy, also see themselves primarily as artists. When asked about the sources of inspiration for their innovative activity, several of these chefs point to inner motivation—the idealized inner necessity for artistic creation—rather than to just external stimuli:

> My own nature [inspires me to be innovative], I am an artist. (British one-star chef Glynn Purnell)
>
> I myself [am the source of innovation]. I love art and architecture, design and fashion. It makes you think in a questioning/challenging way. (British one-star chef Sriram Aylur)
>
> I myself [am the inspiration]. Things are always occurring to me which surprise. (German one-star restaurateur Brzinsky)
>
> I myself am the source [of inspiration]. I am never content with what I am doing. (German one-star chef Ali Güngörmüs)

Those chefs who reject the label 'innovative', in contrast, are more liable to see themselves as good craftspersons who bear in mind the functionality of their product, i.e. whether the customers will enjoy the tastes their dishes convey.

Furthermore, while a handful of chefs reject submitting their dishes to the judgement of customers, most do not lose sight of market values. They recognize that the value of their innovative solutions has to be negotiated and that customers are among those who judge the success of the innovation. Others, in contrast, behave like artists who will not be diverted from their innovative course by anyone. When asked the question *If you have a dish on the menu you personally consider really great but it is infrequently ordered, do you take it off the menu?* most chefs say they would work out a compromise or even remove the dish: 'We change the dish. Also if a lot comes back on the plate, we change it' (British one-star chef); 'I try and please customers 90 per cent of the time, rather than realizing my own vision' (British one-star chef); 'I am not a self-promoter. I feel myself to be the host. The guest is in the foreground' (German two-star chef). Another German chef answers diplomatically: 'The guest is not always right but he has to gain the impression that one takes him seriously.'

However, some chefs with a strong 'artistic' element in their identity want their own vision to prevail. Thus one British chef answers with a categorical 'no [I do not take customers' tastes into consideration]—taste is very subjective', and another replies: 'I am always pleasing customers, but it does not compromise my vision. You cannot please everyone.'

A German one-star chef is even more emphatic in upholding his own artistic vision: 'I want to present my restaurant to the guests. I do not need creative guests, I am creative myself.' A German two-star and a one-star chef, too, both believe first and foremost in their own vision or capabilities: 'I always say that "the bait must please the angler and not the fish". We must be satisfied with what we produce here'; 'I do what is in my capabilities, my knowledge. I do not attempt to please anybody. It's love me or leave me.'

I also asked chefs whether they bear in mind the expectations of Michelin inspectors when they develop new dishes. Not surprisingly, few chefs admit to such a practice which might be seen to compromise their originality. They are even less likely to heed the expectations of other guides and critics who are generally much less well regarded than Michelin inspectors. (For further detail, see Chapter 10.) Yet the general requirement to be distinctive, original, or even innovative is widely embraced.

Many of the self-proclaimed innovators in Britain and Germany, however, feel the need to keep a balance between innovation and tradition and between change and continuity. When asked whether their style is characterized by tradition or innovation, even the avowed innovators are aware that you need a basis in tradition, in order to be able to innovate:

We never lose the basis, the proven (*das Bewährte*) when we innovate. (Three-star chef Wohlfahrt)

You have your roots but are open to innovation. You need not follow every fad. (One-star Birmingham chef Andreas Antona)

It is innovation in small steps because experience is important when you want to try something new. (Three-star German chef Joachim Wissler)

My style is constant but is constantly optimized. (Two-star German chef Hans Horberth)

Innovation means to re-examine and not to change things too quickly. (German one-star chef Gamba)

I believe in gradual innovation because consistency is very important to me. (One-star chef Nigel Haworth)

The art is to take tradition into account and then adjust the composition to contemporary ways, adjust it to people's life-style. (One-star chef Jacob Stüttgen)

Chefs thus are still beholden to the craft basis of their work but, at the same time, judge that they have added an artistic element to their craft. By and large, they view the two identities and accompanying guiding principles as compatible. However, this does not mean that they find it easy to constantly innovate, without forfeiting their own distinctive style.

Chefs also are well aware that what counts as innovation in some circles may be regarded as a gimmick in others. Several chefs suggest that a risk of gimmickry emanates from molecular cuisine. Its less-skilled practitioners are often viewed as devising unusual tastes just to intrigue or even shock diners, rather than to please them. Thus British two-star chef Brett Graham states: '*The Ledbury* is more about instinct, flavour, and seasonality than technical wizardry and research—the kitchen is bold and original without resorting to avant garde posturing.' One-star British chef Sriram Aylur says that what is important is 'lateral [gradual and evolutionary] innovation, not shock or innovation for the sake of it'. German Johannes King tells me that 'Tensions and seeking staginess play no role with me.' Three-star German chef Sven Elverfeld comments: 'I tried all the new [molecular] techniques five years ago but then decided what is good for this restaurant. Taste has to remain at the forefront.' Two-star chef British Phil Howard shares this sentiment: 'I am not out to impress, but to please people: we serve delicious food in beautiful surroundings with great hospitality. I don't try to challenge customers in any way.'

Two-star British chef Marcus Wareing resisted the influence of Danish *Noma*'s innovative quality when a new head chef who previously had worked at *Noma* 'had to be pulled back' and soon after that left his employment. More generally, when questioned about their taste preferences, a large majority of both British and German chefs are neither interested in producing 'unusual flavours' nor do they aim to shock guests when giving them taste experiences—both among the aims of some techno-emotional chefs. These chefs do not believe in innovation for innovation's sake but rather keep in mind that they also have to please customers. Their attitudes veer more towards the ethos of crafts-persons, rather than being those of self-assured artists.

Overall then, neither British nor German chefs are radically innovative (with Blumenthal the one exception in Britain). They do not break through an avant-garde frontier or subvert the whole architecture of contemporary *haute cuisine*. Nor are they perceived as such by internationally comparative rating systems, such as the Pellegrino Awards, when establishing their rank-ing. Both a British and a German chef explicitly share this evaluation. Thus, three-star Harald Wohlfahrt concedes: 'There is, as yet, no innovator [in Germany] like Adria or Redzepi.' And Britain's Brett Graham agrees: 'There are very few innovative people in this trade—only one or two in this country.'

Critics from outside the industry are more negative, such as the German food philosopher Jürgen Dollase, who decries what he regards as the uniform-ity of German *haute cuisine*:

> From the island of Sylt in the north of Germany to the Alps in the South, you get the same, internationally purchased and the stylistically copied, rather than individually developed dishes.[8]

Dollase implicitly ascribes this uniformity in part to the influence of the German training system:

> Training is concentrated on learning the craft in a thorough manner. Creativity has no room in this process—there is a defined list of classical techniques which have to be learnt. Even if a chef goes on to do his *Meister* (Master) there is not much about culinary problems and possibilities in the narrower sense to be thought about.[9]

Whether he is right to single out the incompatibility between a craft-based and an inspired approach to cooking is another matter. The *Michelin Guide*, having awarded a third star to ten German chefs, clearly does not share Dollase's view. It finds plenty of originality, though not necessarily radical innovativeness. Nor do my own investigations bear out the charge of 'uni-formity'. (See my discussion of this aspect below.)

Conversely, some analysts of the creativity of Heston Blumenthal con-nect his innovatory approach with the fact that he is a self-trained chef. In trying to understand the properties of food and of various cooking pro-cesses he simultaneously has acquired opportunities for his own explo-ration. He has gained the chance to do things differently from the way taught in conventional training courses. In other words, teaching yourself creates openings for innovation which may be blocked by the constraints of professional convention. However, it is clear that Blumenthal's qualities of curiosity, coupled with dogged persistence, are exceptional. There are many other self-trained chefs in Britain who have not reached the same height. It therefore would be perilous to assume that lack of training invariably has this effect, and it would be equally unwarranted to assume that professional training necessarily stifles creativity.

To sum up this section, a large proportion of both British and German chefs, responding to various pressures, feel compelled to stress the innovativeness of their food. Chefs are vitally concerned about the display of originality. More German than British chefs consider that they are innovative. This probably is connected with the fact that, in the British sample, there are far fewer multiple-starred chefs—five as against eleven in Germany (due to many more refusals in Britain of interviews by that group of chefs). On the whole, multiple-starred chefs are more confident and, due to recognition from Michelin, have developed higher aspirations. But it is noteworthy that many British one-star chefs regard themselves as innovative. Their self-perception thus disregards the industry conventions of who displays an original style or expresses individuality in their work, as defined by the *Michelin Guide*. Some of these chefs may simply adhere to what Becker calls 'a romantic myth' of having special gifts.[10] However, the high industry pressure, combined with the wish to progress within the industry, also play their part in shaping their identity as innovators.

Yet very few of them present themselves self-consciously as avant-garde artists. While they are, indeed, continually striving to introduce new dishes and taste sensations most of them only practise incremental innovation at best—though sometimes at a medium- to high-level—and at worst display routine creativity. Despite an overemphasis on innovativeness among them, particularly in Germany, they do not jettison their craft values and practices. There is a healthy recognition among chefs that tradition needs to remain an important basis of their cooking. A few chefs in both countries do not succumb to pressure for innovation at all and are more concerned to produce 'real' or simply 'delicious' food.

Finally, the imperative for innovation emanating from gastronomic arbiters and the intense competition in the high-end restaurant sector also results in a widespread *following* of trends, rather than initiating them. It is notable that this pronounced quest for the new more often leads to imitation of what already is out there and to the following of fashions or, sometimes, even fads.

Fashions in Food

According to the German sociologist Georg Simmel,[11] fashion is based on two human proclivities—imitation of the group and individual differentiation.

Fashion is dynamic: acceptance of a fashion will be followed by some deviation from it—some change in the fashion. Once the fashion has too many followers and no longer permits the expression of individuality or distinction, it will be abandoned, and a new norm becomes established. There thus occurs a dialectical process of success and diffusion and eventual abandonment and failure. At this point a fashion turns into a fad, that is, widespread uncritical acceptance of what once entailed some originality.

Fashion-following is widely acknowledged in high-end restaurants—chefs refer to it as looking into the pans of their fellow chefs. They are, however, aware that they have to tread a careful path between adapting a fashion with a new creative twist, merely copying it, and, worst of all, still following it when it has become a fad emulated by chefs in lower-level restaurants. Once the combination of scallops with black pudding, for example, is served in pubs, fine-dining chefs have to move on. A one-star chef shares this feeling, albeit about chocolate fondants:

> We stopped doing Chocolate Fondants a couple of years back, they just became too mainstream and started popping up in pubs which is at the point we went 'No, we are stopping them'.[12]

In practice, however, it is difficult to distinguish the adoption and reworking of a fashion from offering a moderately innovative solution. Hence my review below of current culinary fashions envisages more of a continuum between incremental innovation and an adaptation of a fashionable trend, rather than making a hard and fast distinction. For high-end chefs, adoption of a fashion occurs because they face the consistent conundrum that the diversity of ingredients for use in their dishes is finite, yet they are expected to be original in the dishes they design. Consequently, the resulting search for novel ingredients and novel combinations of foods is relentless and has led to what one critic calls a 'neurotically accelerated' speed, in order to remain cutting edge.[13] It fuels the adoption and adaptation of the following fashionable trends.

Ennobling Humble Ingredients

Michelin-starred restaurants are often attacked as opulent temples of gastronomy, serving expensive luxury foods. A very common counter-trend partly invalidating this claim is the practice of ennobling simple and cheaper products. While 'head-to-tail' cooking of meats, first introduced by British chef Fergus Henderson, is not widespread in either Britain or Germany, the use of cheaper cuts of meat has increased markedly. New methods of preparation—such as vacuum cooking—make such cheaper cuts more tender and tasty. At the same time, this shift also has entailed a move from expensive beef—a traditional *haute cuisine* meat—to the utilization of pork, which is cheaper. Doing imaginative things with pork, German three-star chef Wissler tells me, has been considered as quite daring and risky in Germany where pork is held to be a common and low-prestige meat. But he and other chefs, also in Britain, consider new forms of utilization, such as paper-thin slices incorporating the essence of pork tails, or crisped-up pigs' ears, as innovative or, by now, fashionable. The resurrection of humble vegetables has to be viewed in the same light. But the disproportionate homing in on some vegetables—such as, for example, beetroot, sprout leaves, or kohlrabi—is in danger of becoming faddist.

How then do my respondents view the use of luxury ingredients, as opposed to more humble ones? Of the British chefs, six prioritize luxury in their choice of ingredients, nine economy, and four like to keep the two in balance. (One feels unable to answer the question.) Among German chefs, three prioritize luxury, six economy, and ten attempt to achieve a balance between the two (see Table 5.1). The proportion of luxury ingredients a customer *actually* gets varies quite significantly between restaurants and does not always neatly correspond to the above answers. Among British chefs the proportion ranges from 5 to 20 per cent of all ingredients (eleven chefs) to 40–50 per cent (four chefs) and, in one case, 60–70 per cent. Eight German chefs name a proportion of 5 to 20 per cent of luxury ingredients, seven opt for 40–50 per cent, and one claims 100 per cent of ingredients used fall into the luxury class. (Four avoid a precise answer.) The proportion of luxury ingredients is neither consistently related to the number of stars chefs hold, nor to the price charged for a meal. It therefore more often reflects the personal inclination of the chef, as well as the pressure emanating from the kind of restaurant he or she cooks for.

Whereas the figures on attitudes towards luxury and economy do not show a marked difference between British and German chefs, those on actual

Table 5.1. The growing importance of economy in chefs' selection of produce

	Number of chefs prioritizing	Number of chefs prioritizing	Number favouring	Prop. of luxury produce used	Prop. of luxury produce used	Prop. of luxury produce used
	Economy	Luxury	A balance	5–20%	40–50%	>50%
British chefs	9	6	4	11	4	1
German chefs	6	3	10	8	7	1

practices reveal that German chefs favour the use of luxury ingredients more than their British counterparts. This probably is connected with the fact that more German restaurants are situated in luxury hotels.

However, in both countries the majority of chefs use luxury ingredients both sparingly and strategically as when they use a shaving of truffle, a dot of caviar, or a single scallop to lift a dish based on a fairly ordinary fish to a higher level. A very small proportion of chefs *mainly* use the cheaper cuts of meat and inexpensive fish. They have made it their business philosophy to offer bistro-type food cooked at a very high level of competence at affordable prices. This is the case, for example, in the British and German bistro restaurants *Wild Honey* and *Le Moissonnier*, respectively, as well as in Tom Kerridge's gastro pub and in the German *Osteria Enoteca*. In all four cases, luxury ingredients do not exceed 10 per cent. Two-star chef Eric Menchon of the bistro *Le Moissonier* reveals: 'I have a problem with luxury products, partly because of the price. Simple products are more fun to prepare.' And one-star German restaurateur Brzinsky says: 'I prefer not to work with luxury products. You have to be able to conjure luxury from a simple product. It has to be surprising.'

A minority of chefs—four in each country—unashamedly offer a high proportion of luxury ingredients (50 per cent or more), arguing that the 'customer expects this' or that it is in keeping with a top-level restaurant. The kitchen director of the German top hotel Frankfurter Hof, with its one-star restaurant *Le Français*, for example, states: 'We only have select products. We use a lot of truffles. This is what the guests demand, and it is also in our style of cooking.' Harald Wohlfahrt, the three-star German chef of an up-market hotel restaurant agrees: 'We must not save to the death. This concerns the independence of a three-star chef. I do opulence on the plate. The whole cuisine is a form of luxury.'

Another German three-star chef, however, Juan Amador, who runs an independent restaurant, has a very different attitude:

> I use luxury produce relatively seldom. I use such produce only if the creation of a dish requires it, to get a perfect composition. It is never luxury for its own sake.

Most chefs, however, take great pride in turning humble vegetables or cuts of meat into 'luxurious' dishes which, they claim, are every bit as delicious and more original than dishes based on luxury ingredients, such as lobster, truffles, turbot, and fillet steak. British two-star chefs Claude Bosi and Sat Bains explain: '"Economy" for me means not buying prime cuts [of meat]. It's what you do with it that matters'; 'My choice is to go for humble ingredients and turn them into an extravagance.' One-star British chefs Phil Thompson and Alan Murchison concur: 'I prefer cheaper cuts of meat that have more flavour. I use head of pig. I get a whole animal in'; 'You can get amazing flavour from humble products if cooked the right way. Oxtail has more flavour than fillet steak.' German two-star chef Henkel makes a similar case: 'A fresh herring can be as luxurious as a turbot.'

Chefs thus view a product as luxurious if a relatively humble ingredient like rabbit or pork belly has been prepared in such a way as to lend it both tenderness and an unusual depth of taste. This redefinition of luxury lifts a menu item out of the ordinary and into the realm of *haute cuisine*. Crucially, this practice of ennobling humble ingredients also reduces the cost of ingredients to keep meal prices in bounds. It chimes with a new democratic current among customers and with efforts to use mainly foods that are sustainable. Chefs additionally appear to welcome it as a challenge to their professional ingenuity, and, for some, less luxurious ingredients are more in tune with their own class background and personal taste. Thus three-star German chef Thomas Bühner:

> It must not always be sole, trout is good as well…I was not born with a golden spoon in my mouth. There are no products that do not taste good, but only products that have not been prepared in the right way.[14]

However, chefs realize that customers who pay a lot of money for a meal in an up-market restaurant expect *some* luxury, and most take pains to evolve a proper balance between economy and luxury on their menus. If the practice of using cheaper animals, cuts of animals, and vegetables is used judiciously and chefs maintain a balance between 'cheapness' and good taste, this practice has a lot of value. In view of the economic downturn and the financial pressures on chefs, it probably will become a stable component of even fine-dining restaurants' menus. It thus should not be regarded as a fad although it is now too widespread to still be fashionable, let alone lend distinction.

Even if main dishes have become more puritanically reduced, luxury may still creep in by the back door. It comes in the guise of sometimes three *amuse-bouches*; of offering three to four different sorts of home-baked bread with different varieties of butter, oils, and salts. Finally, when you think that you have finished the meal, out come the chocolate, jellies, and little cakes. Some of the *amuse-bouches*, in particular, are very inventive and, according to German chefs Wissler and Horberth, provide opportunities for lower-level chefs to display their originality. Starting the meal with delicious bread, too, is one of the pleasures of attending a starred restaurant. Yet all these extras together greatly add to the cost of the meal, and some slimming down of overall offers would not come amiss. Chefs may think themselves to be exceptionally generous. However, such a surfeit of extras defeats their economy measures in other parts of the menu and will only serve to fuel criticisms of decadent opulence.

Seasonality and Locavorism

If it is hard to find a sufficient number of humble meats and vegetables to ennoble, then an emphasis on seasonality of fruits, vegetables, and meats is viewed as another way to distinguish oneself from other chefs. As with the first strategy, this one, too, serves multiple purposes, being novel and cost-saving, as well as enhancing taste. German one-star chef Rainer-Maria Halbedel explains that vegetables and fruits in season are cheaper than imported out-of-season vegetables, and their superior taste is an added bonus: 'If you serve a product only during its season it is at the peak of its taste—and this is akin to luxury—but it is also at its lowest price.'

It is, however, not a very new strategy but merely one chefs periodically rediscover. In Britain, seasonality was already the battle cry of Elizabeth David in the 1950s and Jane Grigson in the 1960s.[15] Alice Waters, of Californian *Chez Panisse*, influenced by Elizabeth David, also made seasonality a central part of her culinary strategy in the early 1970s.

Among my respondents, British Brett Graham defines his general culinary style by reference to seasonality. His London colleague Marcus Wareing entitles one of his menus 'Seasons of Britain', and German two-star chef Niels Henkel calls his menu 'Pure Nature'. Many other chefs emphasize seasonality when they talk about the inspiration for composing a new menu. Thus two-star Phil Howard's explanation stands for many others:

> I change the menu five times per year: one season is January to March; then April to September which is divided into three sub-seasons, taking account of produce available [in the warmer/most productive months]; and October to December where game and mushrooms star.

This strategy thus characterizes a win-win situation, that is, it qualifies as a fruitful or value-enhancing solution to a problem, rather than a faddist one. But the pursuit of seasonality has become a bit of a mantra, and suspicion about consistent adherence to this approach is expressed:

> A lot of people play the game [of pretending to do seasonal cooking] but don't actually do it. I am very disciplined and purist about it—I would not use green beans flown in from Kenya. Ninety-five per cent of our produce is local. (Two-star British chef Phil Howard)

Fergus Henderson expresses a similar sentiment:

> There was a time when everything by necessity was local and seasonal. But now it has become a mantra which we use to reassure ourselves with, without ever really doing it.[16]

Being seasonal therefore has become a very common fashion which, by itself, is unlikely to confer distinction and competitive advantage. It has to be given another twist or two by allying it with localism, including the extreme localism of foraging for locally growing wild herbs and vegetables.

The strategy of local sourcing—what the French refer to as *terroir* cooking—also is widely embraced by my chefs. Local sourcing, too, is hardly new—it was already one of the ten commandments of the *nouvelle cuisine* manifesto published by *Gault Millau* in 1973, and even before that Brillat-Savarin had called for 'La nature', that is, for respect for freshness, for cuisine of the season and of the market.[17] Localism turned this practice into a culinary or political ideal that values eating what has been locally produced and is seasonal. Referred to as *locavorism*,[18] it assumed some novelty value. There is no agreement on what counts as local. Most chefs take it to be the local region/county. However, quite a few British, especially London chefs, define as 'local' what has been produced in Britain.

Yet localism, in the narrower of the two above definitions, is not an easy route to take when you seek to distinguish yourself from other chefs. It is challenging because the modern system of both food production and distribution has moved away from having a local character, that is, from processing or distributing the produce where it originates. Most of the suppliers to fine-dining restaurants are now commercial organizations distributing from a central hub. Thus even in a fish-rich coastal county like Norfolk there remain few local fishermen, and distributors have to go to Billingsgate for their supplies. To attain genuinely local produce, a chef has to invest considerable resources into finding small independent local producers. (For further details on local sourcing, see Chapter 8.) Chefs who are deeply committed to seasonality and localism have made this strategy more viable by establishing their own gardens—as, for example, did British chefs Nigel Haworth and Raymond Blanc, as well as German chefs Rainer-Maria Halbedel, Johannes King, Sören Anders, and Michael Hoffmann.

Hence, as one British chef points out to me, genuinely local sourcing is quite rare. Far fewer chefs than claim to support locavorism actually do engage in comprehensive local sourcing. Most of the chefs who declare a strong local orientation nevertheless have a mixed sourcing strategy. Chefs plausibly point out that the local product is not always the best one and that they prioritize quality before local origin. Thus, for example, chickens, pigeons, and lobsters are believed to be better in France. Two-star London chef Brett Graham says: 'Everything comes from within three hours from London. Only squab pigeons and some vegetables come from Paris.' And German two-star chef Niels Henkel states:

> You purchase regionally in the first place, then in Germany. But Germany is not that good where poultry is concerned; there we have to buy in France. In the last instance, quality counts first.

Chefs thus rarely are ideological about locavorism but practise their localism flexibly and pragmatically. Localism is rarely viewed as a political or ethical ideal but more as a strategy to enhance freshness and therefore taste, as well as procuring ingredients when—because of their seasonality—they are at their cheapest. Many British chefs do not even attempt local sourcing but are content if most of their produce is grown or raised within Britain. Fostering locavorism thus is not an easy fashion to adopt. It needs a lot of effort and commitment. Only if it is done consistently does it lend distinction to a chef's culinary style.

Foraging

A further step towards localism is foraging for wild plants and herbs, a fairly recent fashion copied from the current superstar of European chefs—Danish René Redzepi. Redzepi combines extreme localism—foraging from sea-shores and hedgerows—with molecular techniques of preparation. The rise of foraging is prompted by a desire to seek out undiscovered ingredients, as well as reviving forgotten ones; it emphasizes *terroir*. In short, foraging holds out the promise of finding rare or even previously unknown produce. As several chefs point out, a certain amount of local foraging—particularly for mushrooms and herbs—has long been practised and makes eminent sense: 'We did this [foraging for wild herbs] well before *Noma* came onto the scene' (three-star German chef Harald Wohlfahrt).

However, until recently foraging has not been a central component of sourcing and of inspiration for dishes. Danish chefs—the current champions of this fashion—live in a predominantly agricultural country consisting of several islands. Access to wild foods of land and sea is less challenging than it is in Britain or Germany. Moreover, notoriously busy chefs hardly have the time to spend the day foraging in areas which, for London chefs, may take two hours to reach. Groups of chefs therefore occasionally go out with an expert forager who is familiar with local herbs and roots. Thus, a trip to the sea-shores of Kent—heralded as a natural *terroir* for London—yields a multitude of finds. For most people, they sound 'weird and wonderful', such as hairy bitter cress, bristly ox tongue, sea celery, and sea purslane.[19] However, for most chefs the effort/yield equation does not make sense and has given rise to the commercialization of what started out as quintessentially individual food adventurism. In both Britain and Germany companies now exist supplying 'foraged' produce—*The Forager* and *Essbare Landschaft* (Edible Landscape) respectively. This serves to accentuate the odd and faddish aspects of this phenomenon.

But this has not stopped chefs from adopting foraging, though mostly on a minor scale. Eight British and ten German chefs employ or, more often, source from a forager (sometimes only for mushrooms). Nigel Haworth's menu even features a 'Forager's Soup'. For only one chef—British Sat Bains— is this an important source of ingredients in that he especially employs a forager to keep him supplied. He does a dish called 'NG7', which uses wild ingredients from his immediate (postal) area (chickweed, Jack-by-the hedge, wild chervil, and goutweed amongst others).

The fashion for foraging is retrogressive and, in many parts of Britain and Germany, quite unrealistic. Birmingham one-star chef Glynn Purnell recognizes its absurdity in a highly urban environment when he says:

> It's no good me putting foraged stuff on there [the menu], I am slap-bang in the middle of the most industrial city in the country ... If I go foraging in Birmingham I would find dog shit and crisp wrappers.[20]

Without Danish top-listed René Redzepi as champion of this practice, it would never have caught on. It is destined to become a fad, rather than a solution to the problem of increasing the variety of ingredients. However, like all fashions, it has drawn attention to some good elements destined to stay— tasty and relatively easily obtainable wild herbs and roots, like samphire and wild garlic (which you can now buy in German markets).

Vegetable (Vegetal) Cuisine

Yet another current culinary fashion that strongly emphasizes seasonality is one which elevates vegetables to gourmet status. This trend makes vegetables equal to fish or meat as the main component of a plate or dish. This is sometimes referred to as 'vegetal cuisine' to distinguish it from vegetarian cooking (see Box 5.1). Again, a worship of vegetables has been around for

---

Box 5.1 MICHAEL HOFFMANN: AN ARDENT CHAMPION OF VEGETAL CUISINE

The current star of vegetal cuisine in Germany is Berlin one-star chef Michael Hoffmann who is concerned with both taste and sustainability, as well as with avoidance of cruelty to animals. Hoffmann's customers can order either from a purely vegetal menu or select a vegetable course from the ordinary menu, as well as enjoy dishes in which vegetables assume a central place. To sustain this focus, Hoffmann grows both unusual and rare varieties of vegetables and herbs in his large garden outside Berlin. He takes great pains to cook his vegetables in a way that lifts them to gourmet status. A dish on his menu may consist of a puree of sweet potatoes, served with an assortment of braised garden root vegetables, such as leek, fennel, chard, and small Teltow beets (a local Brandenburg speciality). As far as Hoffmann's customers are concerned, those committed to vegetal dishes remain a minority of around 30 per cent.[a]

[a] *Süddeutsche Zeitung* 48 (3 December 2010).

a much longer time among a small number of chefs. Thus the 1981 British *Good Food Guide* identified twenty-eight restaurants that cooked vegetables in an interesting and taste-enhancing way, while cooking vegetables well was a central concern of Eckardt Witzigmann—the chef behind the German revival of *haute cuisine* in the 1970s. But it is the French three-star chef Alain Passard who, since 2001, has become recognized as its main champion and who further pushed the boundaries of vegetable cooking. Passard prides himself on offering rich, naturally tasting and organic produce, grown by an army of gardeners in three gardens in different regions and soils of France. More recently, René Redzepi's cooking has provided a further lift to the status of vegetable cuisine among chefs.

German chefs have shown themselves particularly receptive to the new vegetal trend. Nürnberg two-star chef André Köthe has been championing vegetal cuisine almost as long as Passard. For him, it is the quality of preparation and of taste alone which count. An example of his repertoire is 'Beetroot with Caramelized Caraway Seed' where pieces of beetroot, sautéed with herbs and spices, are served with a beetroot essence and placed on a cream of Roquefort cheese, garnished with caramelized caraway seed and a small assortment of herbs. He conserves and pickles a large variety of unusual flower buds and herbs.

While Michael Hoffmann is just the best-known of Germany's chefs who elevate vegetables, salad greens, and herbs to pride of place on the plate, there are numerous others who are inspired by vegetables. Among the German chefs I interviewed, Johannes King has become wedded to a more healthy vegetable-oriented cuisine, while Niels Henkel offers a purely vegetable-oriented menu: 'We offer a purely vegetable menu. This is a future trend—a very creative field. It is well accepted by both men and women.' Two-star Christian Jürgens, too, offers a plate called 'Garden Celebration' with fourteen different vegetable miniatures.

It is notable that this trend towards a vegetal cuisine is most developed in ecology-minded, green Germany. In Britain, in contrast, the vegetable has moved into the limelight among only a few chefs, such as London chefs Alyn Williams and Brett Graham, Lancashire's Nigel Haworth, and Cumbria's Simon Rogan. In both countries, we are dealing with a trend currently agreeable to only a minority of diners but which can add value also to more mainstream menus. It both enhances the attention given to the taste of vegetables and satisfies those diners committed to more ethical and/or healthy dining. It is a fashion destined to solve one of the central problems of *haute cuisine*, as well as those of the world's food supply and the current obesity crisis.

Exoticism and the Influence of the Global

A strategy diametrically opposed to localism to increase and diversify the ingredients chefs can draw on is global sourcing, that is sourcing from countries around the world, with different climates and seasons. This enables chefs to introduce into their cuisine not only greater diversity, but also some exoticism. Additionally, if a global outlook is paired with attentiveness to local/national ingredients and dishes it is now rewarded by German gastronomic guides. In their 2013 awards of stars, the Michelin organization justified a third star for Kevin Fehling on the grounds that he combines an approach 'open to the world' with an emphasis on national dishes. *Gault Millau* Germany has taken the same approach.

Such reliance on foreign and exotic elements has grown in response to both economic and media globalization. These have made access easier not only to traded goods but also to foreign cultures and networks of chefs. The latter, in turn, have tempted chefs to look into many more foreign pots and pans, thus experiencing more temptation to take up a new fashion. This development has generated some derogatory and satirical comments from industry critics, ranging from accusations of creating a 'global mish-mash' to 'opportunist conquest of the latest culinary foreign outpost'. Raymond Blanc, for example, claims 'that we are witnessing…a complete meltdown of cultures…we have become a global village where everything is fair game'.[21] Wolf Thieme, in the German monthly food magazine *Der Feinschmecker*, quips:

> You haven't yet been in the Whampoa Club in Shanghai or at Gaton Acurio in Lima? Then off into an airbus, perhaps with a detour via Bangkok (Supanut Khanarak) or Melbourne (Greg Malouf), even if your taste buds are still paralysed by the board menu.[22]

While the keenness of chefs to push geographical and cultural boundaries is unmistakable, efforts in this direction among starred chefs have neither been as indiscriminate, nor as far-reaching as some critics infer. Although most of my interviewees tell me that the flow of *ideas* now is global, their actual *practices* do not necessarily correspond to this supposed openness to global influences and exoticism. For some chefs global borrowing only has minor importance because 'our guests still have national tastes. I do not like English mint sauce' (Kitchen Director Wannhof of the hotel Frankfurter Hof).

A few chefs, however, are more inclined to borrow from other cuisines and culinary cultures. German chef Christian Jürgens declares himself a globally oriented magpie: 'One acts globally—because of the internet. When I see a really good idea I take it and adapt it to my own cuisine.' However, such borrowing by the chefs I interviewed is principally of discrete produce or spices. Chefs use exotic ingredients (mainly from Asian cuisines) relatively sparingly to place accents and to introduce contrasts or variety to essentially European, and often French-inspired dishes. An awareness that the indiscriminate use of exotic ingredients undermines authenticity is expressed by one-star British chef Andreas Antona: 'Using lemon grass or star aniseed too often can turn you into a Chinese restaurant.' However, chefs mainly use individual ingredients, sauces, or spices and rarely borrow a whole dish.

Thus of the British chefs, the great majority—fifteen chefs—use exotic ingredients only occasionally or very occasionally, two never use them, and only in two cases are exotic ingredients a frequent component of chefs' dishes. Several chefs make a point of buying most of their produce in their own country: 'I use no exotic produce, even langoustines are from Scotland' (London two-star chef Howard).

Exotic spices, not surprisingly, are used a little more extensively but even here the majority of British chefs—thirteen—only make occasional use of them. German chefs are a little more drawn to both exotic ingredients and, more so, spices. Yet even among German chefs only four use exotic ingredients frequently, though for exotic spices the number rises to ten. One of the four, Markus Nagy, says: 'If the product is right it can come from anywhere in the world.'

For a few chefs, however, borrowing from Asia goes beyond merely using its ingredients. Two British and one German chef emphasize Asian flavouring technique: '[I am influenced by] Asian flavour, i.e. aromatic flavour, not just spices. But it is all about balance' (one-star chef Alan Murchison); 'I like Asian food—it is very rustic but also very flavoursome' (one-star chef Phil Thompson); 'My way of flavouring has Indian and Arabian origins' (three-star German chef Harald Wohlfahrt).

German three-star chef Joachim Wissler has different reasons for adopting elements of Asian cuisine: 'I am impressed by Asian traditions and products. I integrate them where I find they fit. They are incredibly healthy and digestible.' Two German three-star chefs, Amador and Elverfeld, single out the aesthetics of Japanese cuisine as inspiration, particularly its comparatively spare style of presentation: 'Yes, the Japanese model has influenced me in my plate arrangements—the clean lines and the minimalist way' (Sven Elverfeld).

Berlin two-star chef Tim Raue goes further on the route towards appropriating Asian cuisine. He is seeking distinction by offering primarily interpretations of Asian (mainly Chinese) dishes. In the 2013 Michelin awards of stars, his Dim Sum were judged by Michelin's international director, Michael Ellis, as 'the best I have ever tasted anywhere between Hong Kong and Berlin'.[23]

In both countries, it is mainly Italian chefs who are not at all drawn to exotic ingredients and spices and are more concerned with the authenticity of the food they prepare. Thus German one-star chef Mario Gamba says: 'My guests want Italian cuisine. It is important to keep the balance with your own culture and not to become too playful.' One-star German chef Brzinzky says that: 'Despite innovation, one must be able to recognize dishes as Italian. One must be able to detect the soul of Italy.' And British one-star chef Ruth Rogers reports: '[We use] no exotic ingredients ever, and no exotic spices.'

The adoption of international/global influences, it may be surmised, is connected to the exposure chefs have had to foreign countries during their 'journeyman travels'. Although in both countries, a majority have worked for a shorter or longer period in another European country (mainly France and Switzerland), in this generation of chefs—most are in their forties—few have done *stages* which took them beyond Europe. Only one German chef among the interviewees has worked in Dubai and Japan. Familiarity with the exotic thus mainly comes from travel and the media.

Another way to gauge the attraction of the exotic comes from answers to the following interview question: *In which restaurants would you very much like to eat or have recently eaten?* In both countries, chefs mainly name other restaurants in their own country or in other European countries. No restaurants in Asia are mentioned, and the most distant ones mentioned are three Australian ones. The question of whether they consider themselves as cosmopolitan chefs or as British (German) chefs also elicits answers which show them much more connected to their national environment than to any global or international sphere. Only three British and eight German chefs consider themselves to be cosmopolitans. Another British chef mentions an identification with both Britain and his country of origin (in this case, India). Altogether then, and contrary to much journalistic and academic perception, British and German chefs do not have a very highly developed global orientation. Although they profess themselves open to global ideas, non-European cuisines have only had a marginal impact on their culinary styles. Both British and German chefs are far from producing a 'homogenous global mish-mash'. However, the borrowing of flavours goes well across national boundaries. It cannot be coincidental, for example, that both British Brett Graham and German chefs Wissler and Elverfeld are very taken with the aroma of pine needles and try to incorporate it into their dishes, though by different means.

It would therefore be an exaggeration to claim that there now exists, among Michelin-starred chefs, an 'imperialist food adventurism'.[24] The exotic Other hardly exerts a *strong* lure for chefs in either country—with only a very small number of exceptions, somewhat influenced by Japanese technique. Nor are high-end chefs strongly drawn to the styles of ethnic cuisines in their own country. As already indicated in Chapter 2, few ethnic restaurants have managed to acquire Michelin status. In both Britain and Germany, ethnic cuisines exist largely separately from *haute cuisine*.

Borrowing from, say, Indian or Chinese cooking thus is not at all common, with German two-star chef Raue being quite exceptional in his adoption/adaptation of Chinese dishes. Yet one cannot deny that there exists a much more pronounced awareness of what is happening in other countries' and other chefs' cuisines.

Given the long influence in Britain of colonialism one would expect British starred chefs to be more shaped by global influences, but it is actually German chefs who appear slightly more tempted by exoticism than British ones. But the difference between them is not striking.

Unusual Food Combinations

If chefs can no longer surprise diners by presenting them with new ingredients or new ways of preparing familiar ones, there still remains the route of replacing classical food combinations with new and unusual pairings. As German one-star restaurateur Brzinsky explains: 'I permanently innovate. I combine things which do not belong together and are meant to evoke surprise.'

Sometimes a chef discovers a new complementarity in taste between ingredients hitherto not combined, and at other times a new pairing simply serves to startle and shock. If a chef should feel deserted by culinary imagination he or she now can use a new commercially offered service. A Belgian firm offers a software application, called the *Foodpairing Tree*, which will suggest novel pairings for a chef's suggested base ingredient, such as, for example, 'Crème brûleé of tomato with coffee'.

My analysis of menus reveals that neither the British, nor the German chefs of the restaurants I visited make a habit of a strategy of novel and/or shocking combinations, and some do not adopt such pairings at all. The (for me) intuitively strange pairings listed below usually are the odd-ones-out in a given chef's repertoire. Examples are: turbot in peanut jus or rabbit with octopus (Munich chef Stüttgen); scallops with pig's ears (Glücksburg's Dirk Luther); frogs' legs with sauerkraut (Berlin chef Christian Lohse); parsley foam with mackerel, lemon, and tandoori (Sören Anders, Karlsruhe); scallop–pear–chicory–liquorice (Nottingham chef Sat Bains); veal, miso, aubergine, and peanut butter caviar (London chef Claude Bosi); lamb, goats curd, sea beat, broccoli, and almond (Welwyn's Phil Thompson); poached egg yolk–smoked haddock milk foam–cornflakes–curry oil (Birmingham's Glynn Purnell); and foie gras, blackberry, cobnuts, hyssop, milk, and walnut bread (Marcus Wareing at *The Berkeley*).

My data show that serving unusual combinations of foods is not a pronounced practice among chefs of either country. However, the British king of unusual combinations, such as egg-and-bacon ice-cream, Heston Blumenthal, is not among my respondents.

Playing Games: Deconstructing and Reconstructing Traditional Dishes

This is a highly individual fashion where the appearance of a dish disguises a set of very familiar taste sensations. It thus constitutes a *trompe l'oeil* technique where the eye signals something different from what the palate eventually perceives. These taste sensations are said to evoke memories of popular national and/or regional dishes or of landscapes. This approach is inspired by molecular cuisine's tendency to deconstruct, that is, to divide a dish into its elements, analyse them, and then reassemble the parts in a new form, consistency, or temperature. It is mostly practised by German chefs who transform traditional hearty bourgeois or peasant dishes into *haute cuisine*. It constitutes an elaborate intellectual game designed to both surprise guests and, by evoking memories, delight them. Inducing nostalgia in diners is believed to engage them at the emotional level (see Box 5.2).

This approach of deconstruction and reconstruction is utilized by a few higher-level chefs. Kevin Fehling of *Belle Epoque*, the latest (2013) German recipient of a third star, has introduced hearty German dishes such as 'Eisbein mit Sauerkraut' (salted pork knuckle with pickled cabbage) to his menus in an imaginative manner.

Such a fashion for deconstruction and reconstruction of traditional national dishes is not very common in Britain. This probably is due to the simplicity of most national dishes—how do you deconstruct roast beef and Yorkshire pudding? It is no accident that this approach is more common in Germany. First, there is more of a national cuisine to draw on, and second and equally important, such deconstruction and reconstruction involves a highly complex and skill-intensive procedure. However, one very prominent British example of this fashion is Heston Blumenthal's culinary repertoire (Box 5.3).

Box 5.2 SVEN ELVERFELD: AN ENTHUSIAST OF THE TECHNIQUE OF DECONSTRUCTION/RECONSTRUCTION

A very prominent representative of this approach is German three-star Sven Elverfeld for whom it constitutes a very significant part of his culinary repertoire: '30 to 40 per cent of my dishes are based on memories and traditional dishes are transformed.'

Elverfeld has reconstructed both popular regional dishes, such as a Hessian cheese dish called 'Handkäse mit Musik' and a Berlin dish of 'Calves Liver with Onions', and national favourites, such as 'Sauerfleisch', a dish of jellied sweet and sour pork. Elverfeld explains how he transforms the latter—a really hearty peasant dish:

In this dish the knuckle of pork is made into a kind of rillette round, covered with a thin layer of jellied sauerkraut. All the pickles—of carrot, radish and turnip—are individually prepared and the pâté of knuckle is surrounded by pork sauce and thin rounds of cucumber and beetroot jelly.

Elverfeld engages his guests both at the emotional and the cognitive level.

Box 5.3 HESTON BLUMENTHAL'S PRACTICE OF DECONSTRUCTION AND RECONSTRUCTION

Heston Blumenthal's rediscovery of more complex historical dishes has led him to a comparable deconstruction and reconstruction, such as the introduction of his 'Meat Fruit'—a chicken parfait constructed to resemble a mandarin orange—in his new restaurant in the Mandarin Oriental Hotel, *Dinner*. At the *Fat Duck*, Blumenthal uses his molecular techniques in a slightly different manner. His practice of serving *trompe l'oeil* dishes offers not only great theatre but also make diners think about processes which transform food in unexpected ways. While he does not transform traditional British dishes he offers many allusions to British culture, such as his staging of the Mad Hatter's Tea Party or serving egg-and-bacon ice-cream.

German *trompe l'oeil* dishes, however, are less theatrical and not the mainstay of menus in the way they are for Blumenthal at the *Fat Duck*. Another German chef—one-star Jacob Stüttgen—comes closer to Blumenthal when he uses deconstruction and reconstruction to appeal to his customers at the intellectual level. In doing so, he imposes high demands which not all diners would rise to:

> The guest has to experience that something that he knows is being presented to him from a new perspective. I want to create the ability in guests to think abstractly. Blasé gourmets are uninteresting.

Inventive Methods of Preparation

Chefs—unless they use molecular techniques—now find it difficult to distinguish themselves by their method of preparation and cooking. Use of technology in the fine-dining kitchen has accelerated in recent years, partly as a spillover from molecular cuisine, e.g. the nitrous gun to make very light foams of fairly solid matter. Other new technical devices, such as *sous-vide* preparation and the use of the Pacojet, quickly diffuse to all high-end and even lesser kitchens. Use of a wood-fired oven (Sven Elverfeld at *Aqua*) or a smoking oven (Mecklenburg's *Haus am See*) allows chefs to vary the tastes of their meats and fish and acquire a small degree of distinctiveness. But the only way preparation now bestows an innovative advantage—albeit only a temporary one before becoming fashionable—is to employ certain flavour-enhancing materials. A British chef, keen on such techniques, is two-star London chef Brett Graham. He bakes root vegetables in clay; skewers scallops or pigeon on liquorice sticks; and cooks venison on Douglas fir. His earlier cooking of deer on hay now has become so widely copied that it has become a fad.

Conclusions

The above review of moderately innovative/fashionable culinary practices has tried to show that chefs in both countries constantly strive to distinguish themselves from other chefs. However, this occasionally results in a certain degree of homogeneity. As homogeneity of cuisine is something a starred chef, particularly a two- or three-star chef, cannot get away with for long, the pace of fashion has greatly accelerated. It is another aspect of the contemporary chef's work which exerts considerable strain and, as will be shown in Chapter 6, may even cause problems of identity.

As in previous chapters, I have compared and contrasted British and German chefs. Regarding innovativeness, the number of chefs who regard themselves as innovative is slightly higher in Germany, that is, seventeen as opposed to thirteen in Britain. However, once one takes account of the fact that there are far fewer chefs with multiple stars in my British sample (chefs judged to be original by Michelin)—that is five as against ten in the German sample—the proportion of British chefs who regard themselves as innovative is astonishingly high.

Aiming to be innovative—which often descends into being merely fashionable—is part-and-parcel of chefs' 'inspired' orientation. However, it is mostly held in check by their identity as craftspersons. Hence culinary fashions rarely are outrageous. This is partly due to the fact that, in addition to observing the values of the inspired order of worth, most chefs do not lose sight of market values. They realize that the great majority of diners will not tolerate unusual and/or shocking tastes or modes of presentation. Although a bit of theatre at the table is not unwelcome, this cannot, for most diners, occur at the expense of taste. (For further details on diners, see Chapter 9.) Most of the fashions reviewed make good sense, in that they provide viable solutions to the problem endemic in contemporary *haute cuisine*—there is a finite range of ingredients for the construction of dishes. They not only increase diversity and surprise for diners but also enhance the eating experience. Once a fashion has run its course a residue—a valuable nucleus of a fashionable style or practice—remains and becomes absorbed into culinary canons.

Most innovative and/or fashionable approaches are equally common among both British and German chefs. Two slight exceptions have emerged in the analysis of chefs' deconstruction and reconstruction techniques and of vegetal cuisine. Their greater adoption by German chefs, I have suggested, are due to specificities of German food traditions, skill training for chefs, and a more pronounced societal 'green orientation'. Another difference is the use of larger proportions of luxury ingredients in Germany. This must be due to the larger number of chefs in my sample—eight—who work in and are partly subsidized by luxury hotels. A last divergence—a slightly higher use by German than British chefs of exotic spices—is a counter-intuitive finding. Their more sparing use by British chefs may be explained by the fact that, in the face of a stronger and highly popular ethnic restaurant sector, starred chefs may be more anxious to differentiate themselves from lower-level chefs.

Notes

1. R. E. Caves, *Cultural Industries: Contracts between Art and Commerce* (Cambridge, MA: Harvard University Press, 2000), 25.
2. Caves 2000.
3. Caves 2000: 22.
4. Caves 2000: 204.
5. J.-R. Pitte, *Gastronomie française. Histoire et géographie d'une passion* (Paris: Fayard, 1991), 203.
6. C. Fischler, *L'Homnivore. Le gout, la cuisine, le corps* (Paris: Editions Odile Jacob, 1993), 249f.
7. *Yes Chef! Magazine* 23 (2012): 13.
8. J. Dollase, *Kulinarische Intelligenz* (Wiesbaden: Tre Torri Verlag, 2006), 29.
9. Dollase 2006: 26.
10. H. Becker, *Art Worlds* (Berkeley, CA: University of California Press, 1982), 14.
11. G. Simmel, *The Sociology of Georg Simmel* (New York: Free Press, 1950).
12. Marc Wilkinson interview by *Staff Canteen*, <http://www.thestaffcanteen.com./the-staff-canteen-meets/marc-wilkinson-chef-patron-restaurant-fraiche-oxton-the-wirral/>.
13. S. Poole, *You Aren't What You Eat* (London: Union Books, 2012), 68.
14. Interview with Bühner in *Der Feinschmecker* 12 (2012): 59.
15. K. Colquhoun, *Taste: The Story of Britain through its Cooking* (London: Bloomsbury, 2008), 346, 362.
16. Interview with *Observer Food Monthly* (15 May 2011): 29–36.
17. Pitte 1991: 198; Fischler 1993: 247f.
18. J. Johnston and S. Baumann, *Foodies: Democracy and Distinction in the Gourmet Foodscape* (New York and London: Routledge, 2010), 20.
19. *Financial Times Magazine* (26/27 March 2011): 44–5.
20. Interview by *Big Hospitality*, <http://www.bighospitality.co.uk/People/Glynn-Purnell-on-London- restaurant-offers-The-Asquith-rebrand-and-foraging-in-Birmingham>, accessed 23 January 2013.
21. R. Blanc, *A Taste of My Life: One Man's Hunger for Perfection* (London: Transworld Publishers, 2008), 394–5.
22. *Der Feinschmecker* 9 (2011): 10
23. <http://www.guardin.co.uk/lifeandstyle/2012/nov/08michelin-guide-dishes-stars-germany>.
24. Johnston and Bauman 2010: 105.

6

Chefs' Culinary Styles

A Diversity of Culinary Styles

Not so many decades ago—during the 1980s and 1990s—it was relatively easy to define a chef's culinary identity or style as most top chefs subscribed to classical and/or modern French cuisine. At the beginning of a new decade of a new century, the situation has become much more complex because of a far greater diversity of styles *among* chefs, as well as a greatly increased complexity *within* individual styles. Even Ralf Flinkenflügel, the editor-in-chief of *Michelin Germany*, when asked about the culinary identity of a group of German chefs, agrees that 'It is very difficult to define a style,'

The French model of cuisine is still the most important among both my British and German respondents, but it appears to be no longer dominant. A number of chefs in both countries no longer want to define their identity primarily through adherence to French cuisine, even if their actual dishes quite clearly are French-inspired and gastronomic guides list them as doing French cuisine. British Heston Blumenthal comments:

> Chefs are now thinking that they don't have to cook French food. They are using their own style with these [molecular] techniques and local ingredients and cooking something that sings the praises of their own country.[1]

German two-star chef Christian Lohse agrees: 'Now there are new chefs who are less dependent on French style.' The remark of one German one-star chef is quite exceptional in its certainty about the continuing superiority of the French model: 'My kitchen is French, and I am proud of it.'

However, few chefs have totally discarded the French model and still view it as the basis to which are added their own stylistic inventions. The attitude expressed by German three-star chef Sven Elverfeld is representative of what many other chefs, in both countries, feel: 'Classical cuisine is my foundation stone, and on it I build with both traditional and modern elements.'

Chefs who have described themselves as French in the recent past now claim to have evolved a new identity. If chefs do call their cuisine 'French', it rarely now is the *only* culinary style they mention. There are a number of reasons for a partial loss of salience among chefs of the model of French *haute cuisine*. First, we are dealing with second-generation Michelin chefs who have acquired sufficient confidence in their own talent so as not to admit *any* strong external shaping influences on their culinary taste or style. This is particularly evident at two- and three-star level and hence is more common among my German interview partners. Three-star German chef Sven Elverfeld explains:

> I have had twelve years of development and have travelled a lot. After three to five years, one has gained the security and the will to attempt to develop one's own independent style, to recognize 'Elverfeld'.

His three-star colleague Joachim Wissler agrees: 'You reach the stage where you try to free yourself from influences, but there were some. One does not let oneself be led very strongly.'

Two-star chef Johannes King from the north German island of Sylt also has departed from purely French cuisine and has found his own personal style:

> It would be difficult to say what is now French...I have the conviction that I have found my own identity and have the courage to expand it further. It is the sea and what is around it—Schleswig Holstein.

German two-star chef Christian Lohse rejects any national label for his cuisine and wants to emphasize a personal style, even though his food bears a very strong French imprint:

> I only have a personal identity. I do a new kind of Berlin cuisine...It is 'Berlin' because I work with other Berlin chefs; I source produce from around Berlin; and I have guests from Berlin.

However, he names French classical cuisine and *nouvelle cuisine* as second influences on his cooking.

Only one British two-star chef, Marcus Wareing, expresses a comparable self-confidence:

> My cuisine has a French basis acquired while training, but it is cosmopolitan and fundamentally British (in the ingredients used). My cuisine is about me—about innovative and creative thinking.

Second, the constant pressure for originality and an individual signature exerted by both gastronomic arbiters and, less so, a small group of customers has forced chefs to continually reinvent themselves. Consequently some of them are no longer very sure of their own identity. A few profess to have difficulty in defining their style or philosophy. Quite a number of chefs are influenced by several traditions, and a few are what can only be called eclectic—a label not willingly accepted by chefs themselves. This sense of continuous evolution of culinary style is well illustrated by the case of British two-star chef Brett Graham. In a 2010 interview with Simon Carter of the *Fine-Dining Guide*, Graham still defined his cuisine 'as modern French, cooked with classical technique'.[2] However, in our 2011 interview, he no longer wishes to foreground his French credentials. After a lot of hesitation, Graham responds to my question about culinary identity with: 'It is seasonal cuisine, slightly modern, but with classical roots. I use as many British ingredients as possible.' Yet quite a few culinary terms on his menus still are described in French language, betraying the fundamental French basis of his cooking. Gastronomic guides and critics, too, find his cuisine difficult to define and refer to his cooking variously as Modern French or Modern British. This may be due to the fact that, as a highly original chef, he is constantly evolving, and this individuality no longer can be captured with existing labels. In a similar way, German one-star chef Stüttgen has been listed in the *Michelin Guide* as 'French-Mediterranean'. However, he feels that this no longer properly defines his culinary identity which has become exceedingly complex, if not totally eclectic:

> I don't know it [my identity] myself. I have learnt the French way. Today, it is difficult to orient your style to regions—I am more oriented towards the world....Spanish simplicity, Mediterranean influences and also some German ones. I also have been travelling in the USA and have adopted Creole influences. Also some Asian ones.

British two-star chef Sat Bains is similarly perplexed about how to define his culinary identity as it has continuously evolved in recent years:

> It is very difficult to categorize yourself. It has been an evolution. Modern British, because the ingredients make it so...Other cultural heritages are classical French and Punjabi. The latter helps me to understand spices better.

What then are the culinary identities as viewed by British and German chefs who have a clear concept? Among British chefs, seven define their primary culinary identity as French and seven opt for British. When pressed about what constitutes the British element, most only refer to the use of British produce. One of the older and more relaxed chefs—Shaun Hill—seems to be aware of the slight absurdity of this label. He comments with obvious irony: 'It [the identity of my cuisine] is British. Such a meaningful thing—it covers almost anything! I would use any idea—I tend to be a magpie.'

However, a very small number of chefs claiming a British identity also introduce actual British national or regional dishes while continuing on the basis of French technique. Lancashire chef Nigel Haworth, for example, tells me: 'I try to convey to diners a sense of Englishness... You now can get all the ingredients.' Although he mainly has in mind the 'provenance of ingredients', his kitchen also prepares a few Lancashire dishes. London-based Indian chef Atul Kochhar, who views his cuisine as Indian in the first place, also introduces elements of a British culinary repertoire into his cooking:

> The way I prepare food, it is a mixture of Indian style and Britishness. I switch to a British style particularly when making puddings, such as bread-and-butter pudding. I also do an Indian version of roast leg of lamb, for example, or pork with crackling.

It is well to remember that the attempt to (re-)establish a British cuisine is not new. Already in 1987, an editorial to the *Good Food Guide*, entitled 'The British Revival', declared: 'For the first time since the end of rationing, British cooks are producing British dishes that bear comparison to the major cuisines.'[3] Unfortunately, this claim was not borne out by developments in the following decades. In 2007, only ten restaurants, less than one twentieth of those listed for London, were characterized as doing 'British' cuisine.[4]

Two British chefs see their style as Modern European, one as Italian, one as seasonal, one as pan-Indian, and another as regional Indian. All but three of the twenty chefs name the influence of a second culinary style, and five chefs additionally refer to a third influence. Those who see themselves as Modern British usually give French as the second influence and vice versa. Additionally, the Swiss, Swiss-German, Italian, and Spanish models, as well as multicultural/cosmopolitan and Asian styles, are viewed as second culinary reference points. (Two British chefs did a long *stage* in Switzerland and/or Germany.) The third influence in most cases is not viewed as strong. (For details, see Table 6.1.)

Among German chefs, a majority of thirteen claim a French culinary identity. This comparatively greater loyalty to the French model exists even though there are far fewer French-born or French-trained chefs in Germany than in Britain. The more persistent influence must be due to the geographical proximity to France in south-western Germany. It may also have been perpetuated by the ubiquitous apprenticeship training. One chef names Italian cuisine as the main influence, another German regional cuisine, and five name a variety of other influences. German national or regional cuisine is named by five chefs as a second influence, but Asian cuisine is chosen as a second influence by seven chefs. Among the nine chefs who name a third influence, Asian is given four mentions and German national/regional cuisine is mentioned twice. All but the one chef committed solely to an Italian culinary model name a second influence on their cuisine, and nine cite a third tradition which inspires their cooking. In many cases, these additional influences

Table 6.1. Culinary models shaping chefs' styles: chefs' responses in absolute numbers

		French	British	German	Italian	Modern/ other European	Asian	Cosmopolitan/ multicultural/ international	Other	None/ no answer
British chefs	Main influence	7	7	–	1	2	2	–	–	–
	Second influence	4	2	–	1	2	3	2	2	–
	Third influence	–	1	–	–	1	3	–	–	–
German chefs	Main influence	13	–	1	1	–	–	–	5	–
	Second influence	–	–	5	1	–	7	1	2	2
	Third influence	–	–	2	–	–	4	–	3	7

Source: Author's calculations from interview data.

are secondary. But it is notable that German chefs name more culinary influences and that these are more varied than is the case for their British counterparts. The comparatively large number of mentions of Asian cuisine as either a second or a third influence also stands out. This finding chimes with an earlier observation that German chefs are greater users of exotic spices and, much less so, exotic ingredients. (For details, see Chapter 5.)

After this general overview of contemporary culinary identities of chefs interviewed, let me now turn to specific styles of cooking mentioned by chefs, such as *Neue Deutsche Küche* (New German Cuisine), Modern British, molecular or techno-emotional cuisine, and regionalism or commitment to *terroir*.

Neue Deutsche Küche

A small number of highly placed German chefs, who have been dissatisfied with the relatively low profile German high-level gastronomy enjoys abroad, have tried to provide more focus to what goes on in German fine-dining restaurants. They have created a new label for marketing what they are doing, namely *Neue Deutsche Küche (NDK)*. These chefs have organized themselves around the somewhat intellectual magazine *Chefsache*, and, in September 2011, presented *NDK* to some of their continental European colleagues by holding a symposium. On this occasion, they launched the following manifesto (author's translation):

> The first generation of the great German chefs oriented their activities towards French haute cuisine. Only with the change of generations did the German top cuisine find its own identity. A typically German, modern and progressive style

increasingly established itself. It is truly shaped by German virtues. If one draws comparisons with figurative art, the German chef artist does not fill the canvas with expressive brush strokes or explosions of colour. He first makes a sketch, constructs and builds up his work in a planned manner, where each brush stroke is placed with great care. Just like German design or German engineering art, the New German School stands for honesty, perfection, industry and ordered creativity.[5]

At the symposium four of the most important representatives of this new culinary approach—three-star chefs Bau, Henkel (now two-star), Elverfeld, and Bühner—did some show-cooking to demonstrate 'that the German art of cooking belongs to the best to be found in the world today'. A fifth and very prominent representative is three-star Joachim Wissler. The chef awarded a third star in 2013, Kevin Fehling, also falls into this camp, as do two-star chefs Hans Horberth (Cologne) and Daniel Achilles (Berlin). A cultural historian comments on 'the new upwards trend and the new self confidence in *Neue Deutsche Küche* in the last few years'.[6]

It is notable that the description of *NDK* names only the industrial virtues these chefs are supposed to hold in common, and issues of substance or technique are avoided. This is not accidental as each of the member chefs wants to *both* guard his own originality *and* belong to a larger group which is better marketed abroad. *Michelin Germany* comments: 'This is just the style of the successful young chefs—they do not work with copied ideas.' Chefs therefore are not averse to 'riding the wave' of the high reputation abroad of German manufacturing industry which they very much envy and covet.

My interview with one of the leading chefs—Niels Henkel (at the time still three-star) elicits more detail about *NDK*, as practised by him. For him *NDK* means two things:

First, products from the region. You purchase regionally in the first place, then in Germany…Second, you do classical German combinations, such as Pears, Beans and Smoked Ham (Birnen, Bohnen und Speck); or mackerel with mushrooms and apricots. A river fish called Brook Char (*Bachsaibling*) is cooked with capers and served with a vinaigrette prepared with rape oil. There is an inner logic to follow. Around 50 per cent of my dishes are *Neue Deutsche Küche*.

When I ask him how *NDK* had been received by guests he replies: 'It is well received by the guests, especially by the foreign guests.'

Three-star chef, Joachim Wissler, who views himself as the most important representative of *NDK*—'I am the person who personifies it, it is said'—provides another description:

NDK is a cuisine which has a lot of potential but the heartiness of German food has led to it being scorned. One has concerned oneself with what is its essence and has newly integrated this into top cuisine. I was the first [in Germany] who has occupied himself with pork, all kinds of things from the pig. You now can get good varieties of pigs in Germany. It is easier with freshwater fish, because of the cleaned up rivers in Germany—as a consequence of the ecological policy. I do not adopt such a strict regime as Redzepi—we do not have the same environment. I do order lobster from Brittany.. .

Is *NDK* becoming recognized abroad and lending German high-end gastronomy a stronger profile? It is perhaps a little early to judge, but at the time of my interviews in 2011 dissatisfaction among chefs with the lack of a reputation abroad still was stronger than any awareness of greater recognition. Although the marketing attempt, at one level, is very clever, at another, the lack of common substance or technique in the cooking of the member chefs cannot excite the imagination. *NDK* probably will not become a European, let alone a global concept. A recent article on three-star Thomas Bühner in the magazine *Der Feinschmecker* comments: 'With colleagues he [Bühner] once proclaimed the *Neue Deutsche Küche*—it has died away.'[7] Nevertheless, as I will argue below, the concept of *NDK* does provide clues about some aspects of the specific character of German top chefs, as compared with their British colleagues.

Modern British Cooking

The widely professed turn to Modern British cuisine is much harder to grasp as there is no overarching concept which comprises dishes, ways of preparation, and/or aesthetic approaches. The restaurant critic Jay Rayner fittingly referred to 'that hazy thing called modern British'.[8]

The first and foremost way in which it manifests itself is in using British products. This now is much more widely practised as the availability of excellent British produce has increased. A commitment to sourcing British produce is quite widely embraced: 'Everything comes from within three hours from London. Only squab pigeons and some vegetables come from Paris' (two-star London chef Brett Graham); 'Local sourcing is very important to me. Local, for me, means southern England but also UK suppliers' (London two-star chef Phil Howard).

Even French-born chef Claude Bosi, committed to French cuisine, sources mainly in Britain. His main courses feature meats from Norfolk, Yorkshire, and the Welsh Elwy valley, while his fish and seafood come from Scotland and Cornwall. Head chef of Lancashire *Northcote Manor*, Lisa Allen, puts on 'Lisa's Great British Menu'. It is not only based on produce sourced in Britain but also features a few British dishes, such as 'Wild Rabbit & Leek Turnover, Piccalilli'. But there is no chef among my respondents who mainly or even frequently cooks British dishes, in whatever form.

Second, a claim to provide British cuisine has manifested itself in a turn to history, but this is still a very exceptional phenomenon. One example is Marcus Wareing's concept for the bistro-restaurant in *The Gilbert Scott* at the Renaissance Hotel at St Pancras station, a magnificent renovation of a nineteenth-century railway hotel, opened in 2011. The other is Heston Blumenthal's concept for *Dinner*, the restaurant run by his old head chef at *The Fat Duck*, Ashley Palmer Watts, in the London Mandarin Oriental hotel. Wareing and his head chef have looked mainly towards the period around the year in which the hotel was opened (1874) and have scoured old cookbooks, like Isabella Beeton's. Thus Marcus Wareing says: 'Isabella Beeton did not just write for housewives but she also had recipes for "royal" food.'

Blumenthal, in contrast, has searched more indiscriminately for inspiration from British history. He has selected and, with modern techniques, ingeniously adapted whatever excellent recipes he could find, ranging from the fourteenth to the eighteenth centuries. Dishes such as 'spiced pigeon with artichokes and ale sauce; tipsy pudding (from 1810), featuring grilled pineapple with a grilled brioche soaked in sweet wine and brandy; a "ragoo of pig's ear" from 1750', have received high praise.[9]

Third, there are attempts to deconstruct and reconstruct traditional British dishes, but such attempts have been very infrequent and have remained isolated items on menus, rather than significantly shaping the chef's general style.

Molecular Cuisine

Molecular cuisine uses knowledge of science, particularly of chemistry and physics, to understand the molecular composition of a food, to deconstruct it and then assemble it in new forms. It is about applying new techniques and using chemicals, such as xanthan, nitrogen, alginate and lactat, to achieve emulsions, foam, and warm jellies; spherification (where you create balls with a liquid filling); it concentrates flavours or turns liquids into cream-like consistencies. Experiments in physics work out optimal cooking times, as well as determining what alternative processes of transformation (e.g. freezing) obtain the best results in terms of tenderness or the least loss of taste.

It was Professor Nicholas Kurti, an Oxford scientist, who, in the early 1980s coined the phrase molecular gastronomy when he founded the discipline that examines the science behind the food. Another important scientific promoter is Brian McGee who, in 1984, published *On Food and Cooking*. The book was to become a bible for some chefs—amongst others for British Heston Blumenthal. In 1992, there occurred the first molecular gastronomy workshop in the Sicilian town of Erice, convened by Professor Kurti.[10] It was also in the early 1990s that the molecular method made the transition to a professional *haute cuisine* kitchen. At that time, chef Ferran Adria began to develop it at his Catalan restaurant *El Bulli*. *El Bulli* soon gained the attention of the wider fraternity of chefs for whom Adria's restaurant became a veritable site of pilgrimage. Adria does not like the term 'molecular' but prefers the label 'techno-emotional cuisine' to indicate that his work is more than simply using chemical techniques. Adria, who closed his restaurant in 2012, wants you 'to think and feel food, to orchestrate your mood, mess with your idea of what it could and should be'.[11] His food is as much about theatre—providing surprise, perplexity, shock, and delight—as it is about taste. His dishes—blackberry risotto with game meat sauce or steamed shrimp with tea, for example—must appear bizarre to many mainstream diners, but they were received with tremendous enthusiasm by many chefs.

Visiting chefs and a steady stream of (unpaid) *stageurs* took some of Adria's ideas back to their own kitchens and further developed them. European chefs Andoni Luis Aduriz, Paco Roncero, Massimo Bottura, Heston Blumenthal, and even Chicago-based Grant Achatz have taken the approach to new heights, recognized and rewarded by high ranking by the international Pellegrino Awards. (For details, consult Chapter 10.) Many other chefs have tried Adria's cuisine but have felt that its use of chemicals and/or its 'shock and awe' tactics' are not compatible with their own approach to cooking and dining. Thus Raymond Blanc, who for a while worked closely with Kurti, in the end decided that he wanted 'to be in an environment that is utterly comfortable, rather than one where you feel you are being told to observe little tricks'.[12]

Some German opponents of molecular cuisine feel that 'it takes away the cook's skill' or 'it creates dishes which they [guests] have no need for, such as warm jellies'.[13]

It is now widely suggested that molecular cuisine has become too 'fashionable', having entered too many mainstream kitchens where lack of skill often made a mockery of the initial intent behind the approach. During the second decade of the twenty-first century, it has become a cuisine which journalists declare to have outlived its usefulness:

> Yet molecular cuisine also has suffered from an image crisis during its meteoric rise. In 2006–2009, dissenting voices were crying out that things had gone too far.[14]

Writer and journalist John Lanchester also makes the point that 'molecular-inspired cuisine is now on the way out: people who went for it in a big way, now have largely abandoned it.'[15]

Journalists now love to make fun of this cuisine, when, for example, they refer to 'lab-coated cook-ringmasters'.[16] Journalist Tim Hayward probably speaks for many diners when, after a visit to Bristol's *Casamia*, he urges a return to 'delighting the palate':

> Quite a lot of thought—and liquid nitrogen—had gone into this to turn the sheep's curd into an ice cream-like grit, laid over cold peas...my neighbour whispered: 'cheesy peas'....Don't we need something else besides interesting texture and flavour? Should it not delight the palate?[17]

Among some of my chefs, too, molecular cuisine is seen to be on the way out. A German chef, with a lot of sympathy for Adria's work, recognizes both its initial (radically) innovative nature and its current loss of influence:

> During the 1990s, *El Bulli* was a very interesting form. Adria dissolved old structures....Over time it became misinterpreted and spoilt. People clung to techniques, and his basic idea was lost. The trend is collapsing. But we still are grateful for the various techniques—the binding agents. (German one-star chef Jacob Stüttgen)

Some molecular techniques—such as thickening liquids, determination of 'done' time, and concentrating taste—have been widely adopted and are being selectively used in less avant-garde cooking. Also the approach behind molecular cuisine—knowing the chemical and physical properties of food—has been of considerable benefit to chefs, giving them more control over what happens to food when it is being transformed by heat. A research unit of the Max-Planck-Institute in Mainz, led by the physicist Thomas Vilgis, specializes in just such experiments about the physical properties of food and their optimal transformation, the results of which are made available to chefs.[18]

In both Britain and Germany molecular techniques have entered the kitchens of Michelin-starred chefs to a greater or lesser extent. Among my British respondents, no one defines him/herself by reference to techno-emotional cuisine, but Sat Bains, Glynn Purnell, and Phil Thompson use molecular techniques selectively. Bains's British colleagues probably would endorse his own estimation of his innovativeness: 'The kitchen it is a creative hotpot. I allow the chefs to be innovative. We also have built a Development Kitchen across the way.' Bains's development kitchen—which is equipped with a lot of new technological devices—serves to try out every new dish devised before it enters the restaurant.

Another innovative chef with his own development kitchen is Simon Rogan. Jason Atherton, of *Pollen Street Social*, was the first British chef to work in Adria's kitchen, and, not surprisingly, it has left a strong influence on his culinary style.

It is only in Britain that one chef—Heston Blumenthal—still adheres to techno-emotional cuisine in an integral form, honouring not only the techniques but also the ideas of theatre and thought-provocation around food.

Blumenthal has been described in the following terms by the British *Good Food Guide*:

> He is a showman, scientist, experimentalist and food historian....He is a provider of fun, fantasy and wide-eyed wonder. His food is an astute amalgam of meticulous research, culinary know-how, daredevil wizardry and whiz-bang surprises, such as egg-and-bacon ice-cream or nitrogen-poached green tea-and-lime mousse, salmon poached in liquorice gel with asparagus.[19]

The alleged demise of techno-emotional cuisine is partly reflected in Blumenthal's considerable descent in the Pellegrino list of the World's 50 Best Restaurants from 13th place in 2012 to 33rd place in 2013. At the same time, it remains very difficult to get a table in his restaurant. However, Blumenthal's low intensity of innovation—some dishes stay on his menu for years—makes you wonder whether he or the continually incrementally innovative chefs contribute more to the vibrancy of contemporary British *haute* gastronomy.

In Germany, there is no one identifying wholeheartedly with techno-emotional cuisine. German three-star chef Juan Amador, previously closely associated with it, had become much less enamoured by the time of our interview: 'But at the current time, we are getting a bit more classical, much calmer. One just has one's epochs.'

Yet molecular cuisine is still accorded some influence in Germany in terms of the occasional recourse to molecular techniques by six of my chefs. Two-star Niels Henkel's remark may be considered representative of the other five chefs' stance: 'Yes, I use them [molecular techniques] if they make sense. It must fit in terms of taste, and I don't choose them because of the effect.'

Indeed, the deconstruction and reconstruction of traditional German dishes, which form a feature of the *NDK*, could not have taken place without the use of molecular techniques. Among those using molecular techniques, three-star chef Joachim Wissler is said to be the most avant-garde.

In sum, while techno-emotional cuisine as a style of cuisine may now have developed beyond its peak, molecular techniques are still widely used and continue to inspire innovative culinary creations.

The Return to 'Nature'

There has occurred a pendulum swing back to a more 'natural' cuisine and to *terroir* which, for some chefs, curiously has become fused with molecular cuisine. One-star chef Phil Thompson explains:

> I think the market has gone full circle. There was a period when you would go out to eat and the entire menu would be jellies, foams and an array of chemical products. I think there is a general move back towards stripping the food back to bring out the most of the ingredients without too much of the technology of food.[20]

Both Danish René Redzepi and Spanish Joan Roca and Andoni Luis Aduriz—currently highly-ranked chefs in international ratings—combine molecular techniques with a return to *terroir* gastronomy. In Britain, Sat Bains and Simon Rogan have become associated with this approach although Bains rejects the label 'molecular' as outdated.

German Niels Henkel even has a whole menu entitled 'Pure Nature' and claims this as one of the elements of his culinary style. Among my less avant-garde Michelin-starred chefs, this 'return to nature' often takes the form of trying to make the 'ingredients shine' in an unadulterated way. 'Bringing out the taste of the main ingredient on the plate' is, indeed, one of the items chefs highlight most strongly when they talk to me about their stance on taste. Among British chefs, thirteen give 'bringing out the taste of the main ingredient' high priority, and among German chefs eight do the same. Three-star German Sven Elverfeld emphasizes what others also feel: 'The intrinsic taste of the produce has to shine through.' One-star chef Rainer-Maria Halbedel further elaborates on this approach:

> I emphasize the product's own taste. For example, Red Bream has an iodine taste of the sea (when it is very fresh) which can be enhanced with oil and herbs. I do not envelope things with pastry which stifles own taste, even if it looks good.

Regionalism or the Cuisine of 'Terroir'

The turn to the locality, as already mentioned above, also is well developed, though it is rarely a turn to the region in a full sense—to its native produce, as well as its culinary heritage and culture. Mostly, it is not comparable to the French notion of *terroir*. In Britain, regional food traditions appear to have been mostly obliterated, due to early industrialization and urbanization and the highly centralized food supply system that accompanied these socio-demographic changes. Hence it is not surprising that only three or four of the chefs I interviewed see any meaning in regionalism. (Additionally, one of the London Indian chefs practises regional Indian cuisine, and for him 'region' means 'tradition and context'.) Among British chefs, the embrace of a regional focus is discernible principally among northern chefs, and even here it consists mainly of local sourcing. For the many chefs in and around London, however, regionalism does not make much sense:

> For me the whole of Britain is a region. There isn't much of actual regional cuisine. (Marlow-based chef Tom Kerridge)

> We are close to London. In this country, 'regional' means northern. (Phil Thompson of Welwyn Garden City)

> Sourcing locally is quite difficult in this urban home county region. (Berkshire-based chef Alan Murchison)

Last, Welsh chef Shaun Hill bluntly denies the existence of a regional cuisine:

> There is nostalgia about regional food, but it is a fantasy. There is no regional cuisine at all.

One example of a northern chef committed to local sourcing is Lancashire-based Nigel Haworth for whom 'regional' means above all 'provenance of ingredients'. He also occasionally prepares Lancashire dishes, such as 'Black Pudding and Pink Trout', as well as tripe which he prepares in a non-traditional British way. It is significant that Haworth, who worked for a while in Switzerland, ascribes his orientation to the region to the experience he gained there. Yorkshire chef Frances Atkins, too, sources distinctive local foods, such as the deer on her doorstep: 'Regional, for me, means using fresh local produce, with a Yorkshire accent.'

Additionally, Norfolk-based chef Galton Blackiston emphasizes local sourcing, in the sense of maintaining a local supply network. Scottish Martin Wishart, too, sources most of his fish and shellfish in the region. However, not even all chefs in the provinces view regionalism as a viable strategy. South Wales-based Shaun Hill, ever the realist, comments: 'Regional cuisine [in Wales] is minuscule. The Welsh aesthetic heritage is in singing but there is no joy in food.'

In Germany, by contrast, regionalism was very pronounced until the end of the Second World War, and, unlike in Britain, a heritage of regional diversity has not been obliterated. Historical differences and likes and dislikes in food consumption have been particularly pronounced between south-west Germany and the other regions. The latter, in turn, differ from each other in complex ways. However, a basic, widely noted dividing line has long been a love of pasta (*Teigwaren*) in the south-western states and of potatoes in the more northern and north-eastern states. Regionalism in food and cooking has remained particularly strong in Baden, Franconia and, somewhat less so, in the rest of Bavaria.

Regionalism has been kept alive in Germany much longer than in Britain by a number of influences: the relatively late emergence of the German state and of a German national capital in 1871; the greater political and cultural decentralization, both before and after unification in 1871; the later onset of industrialization and urbanization; and also the periodic return to regional roots during times of severe economic hardship. When food provision became increasingly difficult there occurred a return to traditional patterns of eating which still had its effects many years later.[21] Historically, such economic crises had both a longer and deeper impact in Germany than in Britain.

Overall, regional traditions have remained sufficiently distinctive and accessible to provide an impetus and a basis for the development of fine food, from the late 1970s onwards. One author even likens the richness of regional products to that found in France. He finds the main difference between the two as being that German products often do not transcend regional boundaries.[22] This trend to regionalism also is reflected in the huge quantity of regional cookbooks on the market since the beginning of the 1970s.

However, even in the German context, an embrace of *terroir* in *haute cuisine* has proved challenging, though less so than in Britain. One reason for this is that in luxury hotels (where eight of my German chefs work), the Michelin-starred restaurant usually is only one of two to four restaurants, and one of the additional restaurants usually offers regional cuisine. The smaller hotels of, for example, two-star chefs Alexander Herrmann in Franconia and of Hans Stefan Steinheuer in Rhineland Palatinate, have both a Michelin-starred restaurant and more modest rural inns serving only regional cuisine.

The turn to regionalism—where it occurs—takes a variety of forms. First, there are chefs who try to maintain both exclusivity and a regional character on one menu and therefore constantly execute the difficult division between fine food and *Bodenständigkeit* (the German equivalent of *terroir*), such as, for example Michael Fell of *Egener Höfe*, Rottach-Egern. Many other restaurants, such as *Zum Storchen* in the village of Schmidhofen, Baden, Markus Nagy's Baden restaurant *Zum Löwen*, and Daniel Achilles's Berlin *Reinstoff* express their dual identity in two separate menus. A second way of combining these divergent culinary styles is the imaginative deconstruction and reconstruction of regional dishes by some two- and three-star chefs, such as Wissler, Henkel, Elverfeld, Fehling, and Achilles. Using experimental techniques of preparation, these are attempts to turn robust German regional and national dishes into *haute cuisine*. A third route is to give a dish a local reference. Two-star chef Christian Jürgens, for example, whose restaurant is situated on the Bavarian lake Tegernsee, serves many dishes with local references. At the time of my visit, he offered a dessert covered with small autumn leaves (made from different colours of chocolate) from the iconical mountain around the lake, as well as pebbles from the lakeshore, made of cottage cheese and potato. Two-star Daniel Achilles, Berlin, bordering on the *Land* (regional state) of Brandenburg, mixes this *trompe l'oeil* approach with the extensive use of regional dishes and produce, lifting regionalism to an entirely new level. His menu, entitled 'Very Close By', contains dishes like 'Snails in a Brandenburg field' or 'Gatow [a Brandenburg town] little beets with eel from the Müritz [local river]'. All such dishes retain the familiar flavours that awaken memories but present them in a more refined and often witty manner. Whether they appeal to real regionalists or mainly delight because of their playfulness and culinary virtuosity must remain contentious.

The fourth and most frequent expression of regionalism is the use of regional produce. As Niels Henkel suggests: 'You purchase regionally in the first place.' Given the much more pronounced regional dispersion of starred restaurants in Germany, as compared with Britain, regional sourcing also is a more common approach—half of the chefs interviewed believe in regional sourcing. For Johannes King, for example, all but one of the forty suppliers to his restaurant on the west coast island of Sylt are local, that is, they reside in the local state of Schleswig Holstein. He points out that a strictly regional supply network cannot be divorced from the local culture. For King:

> Everything north of Hamburg counts as local. All fish that comes from the south have disappeared from my menu. I use few Mediterranean elements—I now use rape seed oil and fewer vinegars from the south.

Baden chef Markus Nagy also maintains a regional focus, but it is less exclusive than that of King: 'My focus is both Baden regional and Mediterranean.' However, for Nagy 'regional' still means local dishes and traditions, rather than just local sourcing. His Baden colleague Sören Anders, too, maintains a two-fold and somewhat incongruous focus—he is both inspired by regional traditions and is internationally oriented. But regional sourcing sometimes has a purpose other than identifying with the local food heritage, as this Munich-based chef makes clear:

> I am, of course, also oriented to region and use the products of Bavaria, Northern Italy, and Austria. But I am consciously trying to distinguish myself from Bavarian cuisine. (Jacob Stüttgen)

The overview so far of contemporary culinary styles or tastes of British and German chefs shows significant diversity of styles within countries and even by individual chefs. Both of these characteristics make it difficult to make a general comparison of the two national cuisines. Such a comparison becomes only possible by moving to a higher level of generality and examining the degree of complexity of either preparation and/or plate arrangement.

Simplicity versus Complexity

Simplicity of conception of a dish is not recognized as a major trend in contemporary cuisine. However, a closer examination of the above antinomy allows a more general comparison of the culinary styles of British and German chefs, despite a bewildering multiplicity of concepts and styles both within and between countries. In both countries, when asked to choose between simplicity and complexity of style, a majority of chefs opt for 'simplicity'—fifteen in Britain and twelve in Germany. However, my own experience of eating in both countries has convinced me that complexity of style is both more pronounced and more common among German chefs than the mere numerical difference of three suggests.

The propensity to select one main ingredient and then surround it with a multitude of accompanying decorative, contrasting, or often aroma-enhancing additional ingredients, purées, jellies, and juices is far more notable among German, than among British chefs. While German chefs, as claimed by *NDK*, do, indeed, have some of the virtues of German manufacturing industry—after all, they all draw on the same dual training system—they also share one of its vices. I am referring to an obsession with detail—in this case the detail on every plate—'where each brush stroke is placed with great care' (from the manifesto of *NDK*). This frequently leads to an over-engineered product, or—in *haute cuisine*—to a plate with a surfeit of enhancements of the main product. This is well demonstrated by an analysis of three-star Thomas Bühner's dishes, following a visit-cum-interview to his restaurant *La Vie* by the magazine *Der Feinschmecker*.[23] Thus his dish of 'Lobster, Sea-Urchins, Mussels, Mandarin, and Olives' contains thirteen ingredients. A Christmas dish of 'Filet of Venison in a Reduction of Christmassy Spices' has the venison surrounded by the following multitude of accompaniments: black pudding prepared three ways (in the form of a muffin, croquette, and cream); smoked beef marrow; dots of lemon-thyme jelly; a deep-fried artichoke chip; polenta with smoked butter; a blossom stuffed with cream of thyme; dots of potato mousseline; beetroot; a scattering of sprout leaves; and an artful dusting of five-spice powder. While the finished plate looks stunning and shows an imaginative matching of flavours, such a plate also suffers from over-complexity and must take an awfully long time to assemble. One wonders whether a less elaborate arrangement might not have provided the diner with a sufficient range of flavours to savour in one session. Thomas Bühner is not the only chef to have gone this way of turning out slightly over-engineered plates. His colleagues Sven Elverfeld, Hans Horberth, Niels Henkel, Dirk Luther, and Christian Jürgens have comparable tendencies. Henkel informs me: 'I am more likely to use many elements, and the diversity is in the execution rather than in the products.' Such elaborate plate arrangements, requiring high technical proficiency, are noted also by a recent article in the daily newspaper *Frankfurter Allgemeine*, based on interviews with a number of chefs. According to the author, 'it counts as good taste to play with the most diverse jus, dips, essences and espumas...The optical appearance alone is proof of the now much higher technical and artistic effort.'[24]

While British top chefs also care passionately about every detail on the plate, they generally show more economy in plate arrangements. Given that over-engineered products also abound in other German industries, the evidence points to the influence of the German training system. It both induces perfectionism and invites a use of high skills to go slightly over the top in design and execution of products. Yet it is also a German chef who extols simplicity in his cuisine and thereby underlines diversity *within* countries and the danger of over-generalization. Three-star chef Juan Amador describes his aesthetic conception as: 'to reduce things to their essential. Also one needs a central point [in the composition] and one must not be too playful.'

Central Preoccupations of Chefs: Taste and Texture

One of, if not *the* most important asset a top chef commands is to have a trained and highly sensitive palate and to be able to discriminate between, as well as produce, subtle differences in taste. Chefs must know how to develop clear tastes and to achieve subtle variations in and successions of taste even within the same dish. They additionally must think up exciting combinations of different tastes. *Michelin Germany* states the following expectations regarding 'taste':

> The dish has to taste of the main/basic ingredient; there has to be a harmonious combination of the tastes; the contrasts in taste made have to be helpful to the dish…The more tastes are introduced, the more difficult it is to do it successfully, but great chefs can do it. (Interview with the editor of *Michelin Germany*, 1 February 2012)

Of all the chefs I interviewed, Harald Wohlfahrt, the Old Master of German gastronomy, is most eloquent in answering my questions about taste:

> You have to create excitement in the mouth. One has to feel the art of cooking in one's own body and the flavours in the mouth. I want to communicate my own taste sensations and the ways I have developed taste.

But *de gustibus non disputandum*. While German chef Joachim Wissler is concerned to preserve an ingredient's delicate taste by the appropriate method of preparation, British Brett Graham takes the opposite approach: 'Things need to have flavour and punch—I do not do airy, delicate flavours.'

The vast majority of the forty chefs I interviewed rate taste as more important than the aesthetically pleasing arrangement of food on the plate, and a few chefs seek a good balance between the two: 'We never compromise flavour for anything but there is a way in which both can be achieved' (two-star Phil Howard).

In addition to taste, texture and temperature of food—which sometimes can enhance taste—also have high saliency for top chefs. German chef Niels Henkel, for example, 'like[s] to play with temperatures and use[s] frozen, cold, warm and hot [foods] in different combinations', and Joachim Wissler observes:

> Taste is communicated by different consistencies of food. Thus, if you can serve something in a crumbly form, the taste remains for a long time in your mouth.

Developing contrasts in textures of food is thought to be important by a large minority of both British and German chefs.

Finally, to illustrate how flavours and textures are cleverly combined and contrasted, I provide a description of a starter, served to me by German one-star chef Rainer-Maria Halbedel:

> A savoury crème brûlée contains a very finely chopped tartar of smoked salmon and is surrounded by a lovage foam with a deep herby flavour which beautifully complements the crème in both taste and colour. The lovage flavour also appears in the accompanying sorbet which counter-poses a more grainy texture to the smooth crème brûlée. For me, this creation—as well as some of Halbedel's other dishes—is more consonant with the 18 points awarded by *GM* than the mere one star given by *Michelin*.

Showcasing Chefs' Taste: Menu Making and Presentation

Menus are a minor literary form and, as such, convey something about the *Zeitgeist*—about its concerns and taboos, as well as its fashions. Menus additionally convey information to the guest about the restaurant and the *chef de cuisine*. A good menu not only imparts relevant information but also seeks to create excitement and anticipatory pleasure. The seductive power of menus is underlined in these comments: 'A menu should be able to give wings to your imagination';[25] 'as a literary artefact the menu is powerful indeed, a psychic amuse-gueule'.[26]

The moment the waiter distributes the menus a very important phase in the customer's dining experience begins. He or she tries to take in and sometimes understand what is on offer, how much choice is available, and, if the menu is of the 'à la carte' type, whether it enables them to put together a coherent and varied sequence of dishes, with a variety of taste sensations. Although this may be a slightly stressful exercise for some diners, for others it evokes considerable anticipatory pleasure. The menu therefore has to be carefully thought out, both in terms of the capabilities of the kitchen and of meeting customers' expectations. Both its optical qualities and its language have to appeal and may be considered as part of the restaurant's ambience, as well as reflecting its general aspirations.

Restaurant menus provide further insights into British and German chefs' tastes or culinary styles and what aspects of these they want to communicate to customers. The menus I collected from the restaurants visited—I concentrate on those for dinner and omit an analysis of the wine list—generally reflect the values and preoccupations of our time. They avoid being too ostentatious while still conveying a degree of distinction. They are visually appealing, as well as being physically manageable for the diner, and like other restaurant furniture, they are sufficiently sober so as not to distract from the food.

Most restaurants have both an 'à la carte' and a tasting or chef's menu, often offering choices as to the number of courses to select from the latter. The spread in popularity of tasting menus in both countries has occurred in response to both customers' preference for smaller and more varied dishes (a tapas-style approach), as well as to chefs' desire to showcase the wide range of their art/craft. It enables chefs to insert some highly innovative dishes into the long sequence of offerings. Moreover, a fixed tasting menu is easier to manage for the kitchen in organizational terms. However, a few of the smaller restaurants simply have one set menu, sometimes with a choice of main course.

Most of the menus are inside folders or have a fold-out format made of cream or white card (there were two exceptions to the colour cream in Britain and one in Germany). They have the restaurant's name on the front in a contrasting colour or type. The type used for the actual menu is functional rather than elaborate, and the information provided does not patronize the guest. The menus do, however, differ in size. The largest menu—that of Wohlfahrt's *Schwarzwaldstube*—has the dimensions of 40 × 26 cm, while the smallest— that of Edinburgh's *Martin Wishart*—is only 15 × 11 cm. In Germany, in particular, the polarization between hotel restaurants and small independent ones often is evident also in their menus. The most modest menu is issued by one of the smallest (in terms of staff employed) German independent restaurants, consisting of only a folded ordinary A4 sheet of paper. A second German small independent establishment issues no menu at all for its set dinner. Instead the chef explains each dish as he brings it to the table.

Up to the early 1980s, menus in most high-end restaurants were in French. This indicated both the hegemony of the French model of cuisine and a conception, at the time, of what lent distinction. This has radically changed in both countries. The change mirrors not only the attempt to turn away from the French model of cuisine but additionally tries to replace elitist hauteur with a more relaxed and democratic ambience. (For a fuller discussion of ambience, see Chapter 7.) Most of the forty menus are written in the native language. Although French has not totally disappeared from all menus, for the majority of menus it has now only a marginal status. In Britain, even French-born Claude Bosi offers a menu in English language.

In keeping with German chefs' greater adherence to the French paradigm of cuisine, a slightly greater persistence of the use of French language on menus is found. Four chefs use it extensively, though none do so exclusively. Both French-born chef Eric Menchon and Berlin chef Christian Lohse offer an 'à la carte' menu in French, with a German translation below each item. Two other chefs, Harald Wohlfahrt (*Schwarzwaldstube*) and Patrick Bittner (*Le Français*), still retain French language for the different headings of the 'à la carte' menu, though they have dropped it for the tasting menu. None of these practices are adhered to in Britain. However, even in British restaurants French has not totally disappeared but sometimes enters by the back door. In six British restaurants (*Restaurant Martin Wishart, Wild Honey, Simpsons, The Ledbury, The Hand & Flowers*, and *Hibiscus*), descriptions of dishes occasionally contain French culinary terms, such as *parfait* of duck, *terrine, millefeuille, soufflé, clafoutis, galette, jus, sauce épiceé, fondant, chantilly* of oysters, *velouté, confit, Etuvé* of Beef, *Pommes Boulangère*, and *Bérigoule* Mushroom. This reflects the fact that ways of preparing certain dishes remain based in French classical cuisine and that often no suitable English term exists. Thus even the chefs who claim that they no longer practise French cuisine evidently have been unable to escape the influence of French cuisine altogether.

The Italian restaurants in both countries, highly committed to authenticity, all give the names of dishes in Italian. Two of the three then explain them in English/German: 'Vitello Tonnato—finely sliced roasted veal with tuna mayonnaise, capers, Swiss chard, anchovies & parsley' (*River Café*). In Munich's *Acquarello* the more elaborate dish of 'Bocconcini di fileto Fassone ripieni con fegt d'oca, riso e lenticchie, nuvolo di Balsamico' is translated as 'Bocconcini vom Fassone Rinderfilet, gefüllt mit Gänseleber auf Linsenrisotto und Balsamicowolke'.

However, the third restaurant—Frankfurt's *Osteria Enoteca*—makes no concessions to the diner and provides the names of the dishes mainly in Italian, though the menu has some dishes incongruously interspersed with German words: 'Zuppa inglese, Schokolade, Tutti Frutti' or 'Rotbarbe (Red Mullet), Pomodori, insalata'.

The two British Indian restaurants in my sample, *Benares* and *Quilon*, have contrasting approaches to menu language. While Atul Kochhar retains the Indian names of his dishes, followed by a description in English, Sriram Aylur's menu is in English.

Language used is restrained, rather than florid. British one-star chef Andreas Antona understands the importance of language when he says: 'The menu is the message to our customers, it must never be flowery, but convey our selling points.'

The format of introducing menu items is fairly uniform within and between countries. Contrary to the claim by the 2013 *Gault Millau Deutschland*, only a few of these chefs now offer a purist staccato of 'Scallop, cucumber, grape pineapple weed' (Marcus Wareing). In Germany, three-star chef Joachim Wissler still practises this style, adding only two descriptive terms to his main ingredient: 'RASCASSE [green tomato juice: black quinoa]'. British Sat Bains, too, provides minimal information about ingredients and none about mode of preparation. However, alone among the British chefs, he informs the customer in what proportions the five different tastes are represented in the dish by way of dots in different sizes and colours. Our table certainly was intrigued by the latter, and we made a game of spotting the different taste sensations in the dishes put before us, particularly the (for us) novel fifth taste of *umami* (a term borrowed from the Japanese and meaning 'savoury'). Most chefs, however, realize that a minimalist description is unlikely to seduce the customer. Instead, they offer a slightly more extended description which adds also the methods of preparation and/or some of the more minor accompaniments.

Most chefs try to describe dishes by mentioning the main ingredient in larger type and three to four of its accompanying ingredients underneath in smaller type. The following descriptions still are on the brief side but provide sufficient information for the customer to gain a mental picture of what is being offered and/or how it has been prepared:

> Quail
> Roast Breast, English Asparagus & Toasted Hazelnuts (*Auberge du Lac*)

or

> Artichoke salad
> Our own cured bacon, Hens [sic] Yolk (*Morston Hall*)

Other chefs are slightly more forthcoming:

> Roast English rosé veal, caramelized onion and anchovy (*Wild Honey*)
> Breast of duck rolled in liquorice charcoal—quinoa—pea terrine—pea salad-tamarind (*Purnell's*)

or

> Roasted Fish in plantain leaf
> Marinaded tilapia fillet wrapped in banana leaves and roasted (*Quilon*)

However, a few chefs go in for a longer and/or more complex description. In Britain, Claude Bosi, Nigel Haworth, and Andreas Antona stand out:

> Glenarm Organic Salmon slow cooked in Olive Oil, roast globe Artichokes, Button Mushrooms & Onion Toast, Barigoule Sauce, Eucalyptus (Claude Bosi)
>
> Cockerham Goat Butter Puff Pastry Wrapped Fillet, Chargrilled Cutlet, Scottish Girolles, Goats [sic] Cheese and Garden Epicure Potato Gratin (Nigel Haworth)
>
> Slow-cooked belly of suckling pig, potato gnocchi, espelette pepper, artichokes, chorizo, rocket, baby squid (Andreas Antona)

In Germany, Hans Horberth has some elaborate dish descriptions:

> Bircher Müsli in the Evening
> Oat flakes ice cream, topaz—apple fried in two salted butters, two types of banana, marinaded raisins and lemon yoghurt

The affectation of naming the origins of produce, right down to the name of the farm where the animal was born and killed, no longer exists. However, in keeping with more regional sourcing, we do get the name of the locality from which produce has been sourced: thus Martin Wishart, among other dishes, offers 'Loch Ryan Oysters and North Berwick Lobster', as well as 'Ayrshire Hare'. Although he offers mostly produce of regional provenance, he slips in the occasional more exotic dish, such as 'Coconut Parfait with pineapple compote, passion fruit cream and warm doughnut'. Frances Atkins's menu, too, reflects her Yorkshire regional focus. It features, amongst other dishes, the following regional delights: 'Yorkshire Potted Beef'; 'Whitby Crab'; 'Fillet of Yorkshire Beef'; 'Loin of Nidderdale Lamb'. The same applies to Nigel Haworth's menu which lists 'Bowland Beef Tartar'; 'Native Muncaster Lobster'; 'Cockerham Goat'; and 'Hesketh Bank Strawberries', but also contains many dishes from other parts of Britain or the world.

Other chefs, with a determinedly national British focus in sourcing inform us that the rabbit came from Yorkshire, the salmon from Glenarm (*Hibiscus*); the mackerel from Cornwall and the langoustines from Scotland (Phil Howard); Orkney scallop, Cornish seabass, and Dorset snails (Marcus Wareing); Cornish skate, Lancashire beef, and Cotswold venison (Tom Kerridge). In Germany, Markus Nagy's regional/German national 'à la carte' menu offers not merely German produce but features exclusively German dishes. (At the same time, his second 'à la carte' menu offers international cuisine with ingredients from various parts of Europe and beyond.) Sven Elverfeld and Niels Henkel make a point of listing both the German and the foreign origins of their main ingredient in cases where these are distinctive, such as 'Venison from the German Altmark' and 'Snails from the Odenwald' regions, as well as 'Lamb from the French Limousin'.

A yet third group of mainly German chefs—but also British Brett Graham—inform you of country of origin, even when it is not the home country: 'Iberian Ham', 'Perigord Truffles', 'Pyrenean Lamb' (Brett Graham), 'Alsace Pigeon', 'Bresse-Poularde', and 'Milk Lamb from the Pyrenees' (Harald Wohlfahrt), or 'Iberian Belota Pig' and 'Nebraska Beef' (Markus Nagy).

To ascertain how chefs view their menu-making activity I asked two questions: 1. *What considerations come into play when making your menu?* and 2. *What do you try to convey to diners when making your menu?* An analysis of their answers shows, first, that a reference to seasonality of ingredients is exceedingly frequent—it is put top of the list by eleven British and seven German chefs in their answers to question 1.

Second, some chefs are very much concerned with the practicalities of food availability, staffing levels, and safe and timely delivery. One-star Galton Blackiston is concerned with the following: 'Time of year; what fish is landed on the day.' Two-star chef Tom Kerridge has several practical concerns: 'What would I like to eat? Will it sell? Where is the idea for the dish coming from? What do we do with a traditional dish? What works together?' Shaun Hill is equally concerned with practicalities and prioritizes: 'Availability; cost; cooking possibilities.' London one-star chef Atul Kochhar expresses concern with 'demographics, for example, when many Arabs are expected in town we do not put too much pork on the menu.' Two-star London chef Brett Graham mentions another very important practical consideration: 'Also consistency—can we do it to a high standard for a full restaurant?'

A third factor of menu making is some chefs' focus on evoking excitement and enjoyment. Three-star Harald Wohlfahrt, for example, would like 'to seduce the guest with a few hours of pleasure (*Genuss*). My stove is my instrument, [I use it] just as [one would] a piano.' Two-star Eric Menchon is genuinely customer-focused:

> I try to surprise people. One can get a lot of delight out of dining, it makes people very happy. It can be an exceptional experience which pushes away the monotony of every day.

Christian Jürgens has a similar goal: 'I am no missionary but I want to convey to our guests something of the joy we experience when preparing the food.'

German chefs Hans Horberth and Rainer-Maria Halbedel respond in an almost identical manner: 'I want to evoke the zest for enjoyment (*Lust zum Geniessen*)'; 'I try to inspire in the guest a genuine zest for enjoyment' (*pure Lust am Genuss*).' Four British chefs also seek to evoke excitement and/or surprise but wax less lyrically about it.

Delighting and exciting guests is, of course, like all seduction, not totally altruistic. A fourth factor of menu making, then, is that it is an inducement to spend lavishly—market evaluations enter the interaction, though they are never at the forefront. Financial considerations are mentioned by five British chefs, of whom two tell me that cost calculations would not enter at the early stage of menu making, and one informs me that 'it's quality first and price second' (one-star chef Martin Wishart).

None of the German chefs mention cost calculations. However, one British and one German chef each is concerned that their menu is perceived as offering 'value for money': 'I aim for an enhancement in terms of both value (*Wertigkeit*) and taste of items on the menu' (Hans Horberth of Cologne *Vision*). Marcus Wareing, too, wants to convey 'quality and value for money'. When I asked whether this objective had been prompted by the recession, Wareing replies: 'We have always done it, but it has become intensified by the recession.'

Fifth, a surprisingly small number of chefs—given their Michelin status—try to convey an image of the restaurant and of themselves as chefs. British two-star chef Brett Graham is somewhat exceptional in wanting to demonstrate 'that *The Ledbury* is a little different to other restaurants'. Alan Murchison wants to put across 'personality and quality'. Shaun Hill is concerned to convey 'that money has gone mainly on what is on the plate. There has to be integrity—no menu creep—I don't like it.'

Sixth, chefs express concern with the structure of the whole menu and with balance and, mostly in Germany, harmony between the various sections: 'To achieve an enhancement of taste from course to course; no repetition; [I] aim to create a big arc of excitement (*Spannungsboden*)' (three-star Harald Wohlfahrt); or three-star Joachim Wissler: 'A menu has to demonstrate a spectrum. You can combine lightness [of taste] with a very intensive taste.'

Three-star Juan Amador has similar concerns, but expresses them more like the artist he views himself to be:

> Regarding tastes, one must not start in a very loud fashion. A menu is like a piece of music. One has quiet and loud passages. A menu is like a journey, it has several dimensions.

Two-star British Sat Bains wants to 'emphasize balance...I try and start off with a powerful hit of flavour and then perhaps follow with a soup "to tease the palate".' Two-star chef Phil Howard thinks of the various needs that customers have:

> We try to apply repertoires of styles of cooking—we have both rich and light dishes. Women are more concerned with issues of nutrition and health. We therefore always have a number of dishes in each section that appeal to different wants. We try to have, for example, at least one salad.

Finally, one-star chef Colin McLoughlin (*Wild Honey*) aims for 'Balance of taste and textures'.

A seventh objective of chefs is to achieve good communication with diners and their favourable reception of the menu: 'I also want guests to be comfortable and not intimidate them. I don't use strange French terms' (one-star chef Alan Murchison). Martin Wishart, in contrast, deliberately inserts a few French terms:

> I keep it simple so that guests can tell the main ingredient and technique...I do not over-elaborate the dish. I put in French classical terms. It should also sound beautiful.

Two-star Tom Kerridge—a very customer-oriented chef—also is concerned with 'accessibility': 'I serve them ingredients they know but give them the best version they have ever had.' But Kerridge does use some French terms and optimistically thinks that 'people now know French terms'.

Simplicity is also valued by one-star chef Andreas Antona: 'I make it small and precise. It has become simpler over time.' Simplicity/accessibility of the menu is, indeed, mentioned by four British, but by no German chefs.

Eighth, two British Indian chefs also hope their menus tell customers about their concern with the sustainability of food:

> I try and create a role model in terms of sustainability of sourcing. I am concerned about the ocean. It is an ongoing education. We have bought Pollock and Coulee instead of cod. (Atul Kochhar)
>
> I...show them that I am environmentally concerned and the ethos of the local land; I am concerned what species of fish I serve and only use a certified fishmonger; do not use anything from an endangered species or area, even where eggs are concerned. (Sriram Aylur)

However, not all chefs think primarily or solely of diners when making the menu. Two German one-star chefs freely express their opinion:

> We are not one hundred per cent oriented to the guest. But the guest is part of the equation. The cook also must feel good about it in the kitchen. We determine jointly what happens. (Jacob Stüttgen)
>
> [I try to convey] my own philosophy of enjoyment. It is difficult to consider the bulk of the guests. (Kitchen Director Wannhof)

I also gleaned some ideas about the different organizational approaches chefs have to menu making. For some, it is a very systematic activity. Thus, one-star Sören Anders has a very structured approach: 'I am a "head" person when designing the menu. I do sketches.' He then describes to me with a sketch the development process [for dishes] as having seven stages. All these sketches are kept on file. For others, in contrast, the menu is changed when ideas for new dishes suggest themselves: 'One works on new dishes besides all the other work, and the card is changed when new dishes are ready' (German three-star chef Elverfeld).

All this makes evident that menu-making is both a very important and a difficult and time-consuming task. Chefs have to make time for it amidst their many other tasks. It requires a sensibility which is not necessarily their strength, given their sometimes relatively low level of general education. Moreover, the rewriting of menus involves costs. Any changes have to be effectively communicated to all the staff, including the front-of-house staff. Perhaps more important, frequent menu change means that the attainment of consistency and perfection has to be pursued anew each time and holds obvious risks for chefs. Customers, it is said, on the whole like menu changes, if they are properly explained to them. However, chefs have to be wary of deleting signature dishes which differentiate them from other chefs in the market and have become part of the brand.[27]

It is therefore all the more remarkable that menus get changed very frequently. Of the British chefs, eight change the menu three to five times per year, coinciding roughly with the seasons. For a further nine it is an ongoing process—new dishes constantly are added to the menu. For one chef, menu change occurs every two weeks. (One chef did not respond to this question.) The odd-one-out among British chefs is two-star gastro pub proprietor Tom Kerridge who says: '[The menu is changed] not very often. I cook dishes until they are absolutely right and they then stay on. People come back for the same dish.' Sat Bains, in contrast, believes that young chefs thrive on menu change which enables them to learn constantly new things.

Of German chefs, nine change the menu with the seasons, variously defined. Five redo the menu every four to eight weeks, two every one to two weeks, one every day (a hotel restaurant), two irregularly, and only two do it constantly. Thus menu change with the seasons is the most frequently mentioned approach in both countries, confirming chefs' professed emphasis on seasonality. More German than British chefs name a definite period for menu change, leaving the more informal and flexible (British) method of 'constant change' less widely embraced (see Table 6.2).

To sum up this section, although there are differences in menu length and style *within* countries, commonalities between countries are more striking. Menus convey information about the chef's culinary style but also about the status claimed for the restaurant. Not only the content of the menu but also its formal appearance, its structure, style of communication, and the language used are indicative of the chef's intentions and aspirations. Beyond this, menus are documents expressing the *Zeitgeist* of contemporary *haute* gastronomy. They generally are not ostentatious (excepting the huge menu of one German restaurant) and are no longer written in a florid and over-the-top style. Most have distanced themselves to a greater or lesser degree from the French paradigm and communicate in the native language, even if—in the cases of a few German chefs—they now render it underneath the French menu description. Chefs do not set out to intimidate diners although some diners nevertheless will be overawed. Even many names of dishes/ingredients in the native language often will be unfamiliar to all but the seasoned

Table 6.2. Frequency of menu change by chefs (in absolute numbers)

	Change with seasons	More frequent change also within seasons	Constantly	Hardly ever/ irregularly	No response
British chefs	8	1	9	1	1
German chefs	9	7	2	2	0

diner. But a certain degree of mystery about what will be forthcoming may also intrigue the adventurous diner, and dishes are usually explained when actually served.

Menus mean to address the diner at several levels: to inform about what is on offer, about the range of the chef's repertoire, and the national or regional origins of the produce used. But menus are also designed to excite the diner about what will be forthcoming and seduce him or her into spending lavishly. In sum, menus seek to indicate the chef's culinary style or taste but they are also—mostly covertly—a selling device. Chefs' *inspired* and *market* guiding principles become inextricably intertwined.

The differences between British and German menus are mainly about language of communication and accessibility. More British than German chefs mention simplicity and accessibility of the menu. Whether this is due to the nature of the German sample—more high-level chefs and more restaurants in luxury hotels, or whether it indicates that German restaurants are more formal—is impossible to say. Keeping it simple and accessible, for British chefs, means also keeping French to a minimum on the menu or abandoning it altogether. Most German chefs adopt the same attitude, but a few still use French, though never without translation. German chefs are more expansive about the enjoyment and pleasure a menu should stimulate. British chefs appear more preoccupied with all the practicalities of menu making, with the famous British pragmatism coming to the fore.

Conclusions

I have made evident the great diversity in culinary styles both between chefs and within the productions of individual chefs. This is a consequence of the fact that the paradigm of French *haute cuisine* is no longer hegemonic and a variety of other styles jostle to take its place. However, few chefs have freed themselves entirely from the French model—it still provides the technical basis for most. Additionally they are subject to conflicting global, national, and regional influences, and chefs have absorbed and often combined these in different ways. But an attempt to reassert the national—in building new identities, in sourcing practices, and, less so, in actual dishes—appears to be gaining ground. An orientation to the region also is discernible, but regionalism is often problematic for chefs, and it has been shown that the problems differ for British and German chefs.

Conversely, while chefs simultaneously show a greater openness to global influences, this has not yet penetrated actual practices to a high, let alone a dominating degree. German chefs have gone slightly further along the road of absorbing global influences than their British colleagues. In this respect,

British high-end restaurants may be actively trying to differentiate themselves from lower-level and cheaper restaurants, particularly from the ubiquitous ethnic restaurants. In neither the British nor the German case can one speak of the adoption of a 'global mish-mash', as suggested by Dollase.[28] While 'exotic' ingredients and spices are utilized, they neither dominate nor displace European-style dishes.

In the area of culinary identity and style, as in many aspects of chefs' professional activity, divergent guiding principles or orders of worth channel their actions and interactions. The tension between inspired (artistic) and craft principles becomes evident in the way chefs conceive, execute, and present their dishes to customers. Additionally, market evaluations intrude, though usually in a very discreet manner. While a minority of chefs present themselves solely as craftspersons, for most the integration of the craft and more artistic elements of their job is an ongoing issue. The tension between the two orders of worth, however, is not usually at the surface and may no longer be perceived as such by chefs. Market values have to be ever present in chefs' culinary endeavours. Yet their responses to my questions make clear that market values are not necessarily at the forefront of their planning.

The analysis in this chapter also reveals a number of smaller differences in actual culinary style or cuisine between the two nationalities. Although the French model of cuisine now holds a weaker sway among chefs in both countries, more British than German chefs no longer regard themselves as wedded to French *haute cuisine*. This effort to build an alternative culinary identity—which is not always reflected in actual practice—also reveals itself in British chefs' menu making. This result is somewhat counter-intuitive, given the relatively large number of French-born chefs in Britain and their historical influence on the revival of *haute cuisine* in Britain. It may well be the case that an assertion of Britishness (not Englishness) represents an attempt to gloss over against this disproportionate presence of French chefs in British high-end kitchens. The continued residual influence of the French model in Germany has to be explained in a different way. Close geographical proximity to France in the states of both Baden-Württemberg and the Saarland, as well as a lingering presence of French practices in the national training system, are more likely explanations.

Notes

1. *Restaurant* (May 2012): 56.
2. <http://www.fine-dining-guide-com.brett_graham_ledbury_chef_interview_2010>, accessed 27 November 2012.

3. A. Warde, 'Imagining British Cuisine: Representations of Culinary Identity in the Good Food Guide, 1951–2007', *Culture, Food and Society* 12.2 (2009): 151–71 (159).
4. Warde 2009: 163.
5. Introductory text of the Prospectus for *Chefsache* 2011, the forum for ambitious chefs and those who want to become such.
6. *Süddeutsche Zeitung* 141 (21 June 2011).
7. *Der Feinschmecker* 12 (2012): 59.
8. *The Observer Magazine* (7 July 2013): 33.
9. *The Guardian Weekend* (12 March 2011): 75; *Observer Food Monthly* (16 October 2011): 46–49.
10. R. Blanc, *A Taste of My Life: One Man's Hunger for Perfection* (London: Transworld Publishers, 2008), 321–6.
11. *Observer Food Monthly* (19 June 2011).
12. Blanc 2008: 331.
13. *Der Feinschmecker* 3 (2010): 98–101.
14. *Observer Food Monthly* (19 June 2011).
15. *Guardian Weekend* (17 July 2012).
16. S. Poole, *You Aren't What You Eat* (London: Union Books, 2012), 134.
17. *Financial Times Magazine* (2/3 June 2012): 43.
18. *Süddeutsche Zeitung* 219 (21 September 2012).
19. *Good Food Guide 2010*: 175–6.
20. <http://www.fine-dining-guide.com/chef-interview-phil-thompson-auberge-du-lac-welwyn>.
21. U. Spiekermann, 'Regionale Verzehrsunterschiede als Problem der Wirtschafts- und Sozialgeschichte. Räume und Strukturen im Deutschen Reich 1900–1940', in H.-J. Teuteburg, G. Neumann, and A. Wierlacher (eds.), *Essen und kulturelle Identität. Europäische Perspektiven* (Berlin: Akademie Verlag, 1997), 248–82 (278).
22. F. Thiedig, 'Das schmeckt irgendwie nach mir selbst, oder: vom regionalen Geschmack zum Terroir', in T. Hauer (ed.), *Das Geheimnis des Geschmacks*. Werkbund-Archiv 29 (Frankfurt am Main: Anabas Verlag, 2005), 164–75.
23. *Der Feinschmecker* 12 (2012): 56–67.
24. M. M. Schwarz in *Frankfurter Allgemeine* (15 July 2013). <http://www.faz.net/aktuell/lebensstil/essen-trinken/sternegastronomie-es-kann-nicht-immer-kaviar-sein-12281679.html>.
25. *Süddeutsche Zeitung* (25 November 2011).
26. Poole 2012: 52.
27. *Yes Chef! Magazine* 12 (2010): 44–5.
28. J. Dollase, *Kulinarische Intelligenz* (Wiesbaden: Tre Torri Verlag, 2006).

7

Front-of-House Staff: Hosts, Sales Persons, or Communicators of Expert Knowledge?

When diners book a table in a top restaurant they hope to receive much more than merely excellent food. They additionally expect to be served by attentive and highly professional service staff who will attend to their wants and needs in both a friendly and an expert or professional manner. Diners desire that staff will do everything to make their evening a very pleasant and memorable experience. Many chef proprietors/patrons tell me that service staff should be able to anticipate a customer's wants before the latter has had a chance to express them. It would not be an exaggeration to say that diners can look forward to being cosseted and indulged. The gourmets among them additionally desire that their knowledge of food and understanding of cooking will be widened and deepened. In other words, diners expect service staff to be both the perfect hosts and food and wine professionals. The chef proprietors/patrons place the same expectations on service staff. However, they additionally will demand that, in attending to customers, service staff also bear the financial requirements of the restaurant in mind and effectively market what it has to offer. The vital importance of excellent service staff is grasped by this German one-star chef: 'We cannot afford incompetent service, even if the food is good, whereas a highly competent service can compensate for mistakes made in the kitchen.'

These various demands on service staff present these not necessarily well-educated employees with a formidable challenge. They simultaneously face the requirements of disparate and even incompatible moral philosophies, namely those of the domestic order of worth, broadly interpreted, and those of the market order of worth. The first views the restaurant as a place similar to a home in which customers are welcomed as if they were personal guests, while the evaluations of the second view the restaurant as a business like any other. The fundamental conflict in the role understanding of service staff arising from these contradictory demands is perceptively commented upon by one of the German chef patrons, Jacob Stüttgen:

> It [restaurant service] is a very demanding occupation. It is an occupation with mixed objectives—they have to be sales person and host. This is a contradiction which you have to master by doing the splits.

The additional requirement on service staff for professional competence, though not necessarily incompatible with the values/evaluations and human qualifications of the two discussed orders of worth, nevertheless necessitates a careful and judicious balancing act when service staff enact their various roles. It also requires both formal and informal training, if it is to meet the expectations of largely sophisticated customers who pay a considerable sum for a meal in a top-level restaurant.

An additional contradictory set of experiences confronting personal service employees and one that makes their recruitment highly problematic nowadays is that in democratic societies like Britain and Germany, the civic principle of equality is well established. It conflicts with the necessity for front-of-house staff to render personal *service* to customers and, in the process, show them a degree of deference. The latter is widely believed to be incompatible with enjoying equal status. In the words of sociologists Mars and Nicod:

> However much the barrier between servant and master seems to have been lifted in our society generally, we find in reality that those providing a service are still not expected to enter freely into transactions.[1]

What distinguishes the rendering of personal services in fine-dining restaurants from most other service provision is the requirement for staff always to invest positive and other-directed emotions into relationships with customers and to never allow themselves to give vent to any frustration that arises from this job demand.

Before investigating how far these various normative principles are orienting the behaviour of restaurant service staff and what difficulties clashes between them present both for the staff themselves and for restaurant owners/managers, a more basic introduction to the occupations concerned with restaurant service is in order.

Front-of-House Staff: A General Profile

Staff organizing the proceedings at the front-of-house may be divided into three basic categories, namely: general waiting staff; the wine waiter or *sommelier*; and the restaurant manager, sometimes also referred to as the *Maître de*. Waiting staff, in turn, are hierarchically differentiated into first head waiter, station head waiter, *chef de rang* and *demi-chef de rang* and *commis* waiter. These French titles, partially mirroring those of kitchen staff, are still widely used although the number of ranks may be reduced in smaller establishments. The higher ranks have more customer-facing tasks, enjoy more discretion, and do fewer or none of the more strenuous or dirtier tasks, like carrying trays and clearing tables. Distinctions of rank sometimes are indicated by differences in uniform.

Waiting staff lay the tables, take the orders for food, and answer any customer queries about the menu. They serve the food in the right sequence and to the right members of the dining party. Waiters explain what ingredients constitute a given dish. Finally, service staff clear the tables, present the bill, and accept payment, as well as making sure, together with the restaurant manager, that every customer receives a farewell.

The *sommelier*—there may be a head and one or more assistant *sommeliers*—also has a broad spectrum of tasks but a deeper knowledge base. He or she possesses a thorough and inspired knowledge about the matching of wine and food, as well as being responsible for buying, storing, and pricing wine. The high investment costs of buying wine and the impact of the available wine selection on the restaurant's reputation make the wine waiter a crucial member of staff. The *sommelier*'s role is not always as well understood as that of waiting staff, and he or she has a more demanding task when first approaching customers about ordering drinks. *Sommeliers* not only have to match the wine with the food but also with what they think the customer will countenance in terms of costs.

The restaurant manager has the most onerous job. Not only is he or she responsible for all the waiters. The manager additionally is the person who intervenes if communication between customers and waiting staff enters a crisis. Any complaints and unpleasant incidents are resolved by the manager. Additionally, the manager liaises with the chef to avoid/smooth friction between the kitchen and the waiting staff. Managers are the first point of contact for customers, that is, they 'meet and greet' customers although some restaurants designate a specific person for this function. It is widely agreed that customers' impression of the restaurant is strongly influenced by how they are met and greeted.

Besides executing these physical and mental tasks, waiters and managers have to make an emotional commitment to do these tasks with a smile, as well as displaying empathy to discern customers' less routine wishes. They do what sociologist Arlie Hochschild calls 'emotional labour':

> This labour requires one to induce or to suppress feeling in order to sustain the outward countenance that produces the proper state of mind in others—in this case the sense of being cared for in a convivial and safe place.[2]

In other words, service staff have to smile even when they do not feel like smiling, and to care for the customer, even if they feel no affinity with him or her. In the eyes of Hochschild, they are compelled to insincerely act out a role and thereby suppress their own individuality. More recent writing on inter-active service work has gone beyond Hochschild's fous only on emotions. Sociologists of employment Chris Warhurst, Dennis Nixon, and Christine Williams additionally posit the mobilization of embodied dispositions, inter-nalized during a middle-class childhood. Among these, 'looking good and sounding right' are held to be particularly important in what they term 'aes-thetic labour'. [3]

All these attributes and tasks are detailed by precise rules of behaviour. These specify the manner of greeting, seating, offering drinks, handing out menus, taking orders, replenishing drinks, removing finished table wear, tak-ing payment, and finally saying goodbye. During this process waiting staff have to constantly liaise with kitchen and bar staff to facilitate the effective-ness of processing orders. (Nicolas Lander's book on restaurateurs reproduces these rules, as specified by restaurateur Russel Norman.)[4] It is very likely that most of the starred restaurants apply such a canon of detailed rules.

Additionally, there are general rules about appearance, attitude, comport-ment, and amount and nature of conversation with customers that approxi-mate the dispositions, Warhurst and Nixon have in mind.[5] However, many of these rules have to be inculcated during training as their embodiment during a process of childhood socialization cannot be relied upon among waiters from often modest social origins.

These various service tasks and deployment of desired genteel dispositions require both formal and informal on-the-job training, and different training structures exist in the two countries. As for kitchen staff, the training system for service staff is more formal, structured, and systematic in Germany than in Britain. This divergence results not only in a different quantity but also quality of supply of service staff. The effects of these differences are evident in what kind of persons chef patrons recruit as service staff, what they specify as necessary aptitudes and attitudes, and how they conceptualize their tasks.

The Training of Service Staff

Whereas in Germany, there exists a systematic, publicly provided system of training for all three categories of service staff, in Britain systematic formal training for waiters and restaurant managers hardly exists.[6] For *sommeliers*, it is commercially provided and is said to be insufficiently clearly structured and unsystematic. In both countries, waiting staff in smaller restaurants mostly are informally trained on the job. In Germany, however, nearly all two- and three-star restaurants have formally qualified staff, whereas in Britain this is more hit-and-miss, and where a full complement of qualified staff exists, they mainly have been trained in Europe.

In Germany, two routes into restaurant service occupations exist: either the three-year apprenticeship training in restaurants, or the tertiary route of a *Hotelfachschule* (Hospitality College), offering specialization in all the hospitality functions. For both future restaurant managers and *sommeliers* there then follow several years of experience in top-level establishments. To become a certified *sommelier* you then add on a six-month, part-time, day-release course, covering the theory and practice of wine waiting, provided and examined by the local Chambers of Commerce found all over Germany. This course has become very popular with women who now constitute almost 50 per cent of trainees. But there are still problems in recruiting sommeliers: 'Good *sommeliers* are very difficult to recruit as they are the "new stars". We don't like stars. We don't want staff giving long monologues to customers' (Berlin two-star chef Lohse). They also may find better rewarded employment in the wine trade.

Restaurant managers in Germany possess several years of experience in top waiting positions. They are recruited either externally or internally and are predominantly German nationals. An informal interview of the *Maître de* at the two-star *Überfahrt* in Bavaria establishes that both the *sommelier* and the *Maître de* have been trained in *Hotelfachschulen* and consider themselves career service staff in the industry. The service I received at the restaurant was highly professional, but at the same time relaxed and very friendly. Other managers in restaurants with multiple stars possess a similar training background, as well as a systematic progression through the ranks of waiting. For instance the *Maître de* of two-star *Falco*, after his formal training, had progressed from *commis sommelier*, to Head Waiter and then *Maître* in a one-star restaurant to his current position.[7] The *Maître de* of one-star *L'Atelier*, in the Munich hotel Bayrischer Hof, served an even longer and less linear 'journeymanship' of seven years in six different starred restaurants.[8]

In Britain, there are no apprenticeships for waiters/waitresses, and where training exists, it is considered inadequate (interview with Birmingham one-star chef Purnell). A large proportion of the waiting staff has been trained informally or has been recruited from France and Germany. Restaurant managers, too, are sometimes recruited from abroad. For instance, the Welwyn *Auberge du Lac* had quite a young female German manageress. Alternatively, and more frequently, managers are trained internally, selecting them from the best waiting staff. The manager of the London *River Café* speaks for many British chefs:

> It is very difficult to get a good restaurant manager and *sommelier*, but we side-step this by appointing from within. This is widely encountered among British restaurants.

For *sommeliers* there now exist a number of commercially operated training courses, provided by organizations like the Court of Master Sommeliers and the UK Sommelier Association. They all offer different course contents and qualifications, and the available training is viewed by some people in the hospitality industry as offering 'sporadic and messy training routes'.[9] The profession does not yet enjoy any prestige in the UK and is poorly visible to school leavers. For waiters with few or no qualifications, the profession is considered difficult to master. Some *sommeliers* in smaller establishments possess only informal training. According to a British one-star chef:

> It is a long and hard training. The candidates are usually not sufficiently intelligent for it. John [not his proper name], the *sommelier*, has learnt by experience, courses are too technical for him. I sit down with him.

There are, however, shortages of good service staff in *both* countries.

> Whereas chefs go from strength to strength service staff are still lagging.... and the top restaurants have a hard job getting new young staff.[10]

> It is generally not simple to get well-trained skilled staff (*Fachpersonal*). They probably are not trained in sufficient number. (Two-star German chef Luther who, despite this comment, has both a German *Maître de* and *sommelier*)

Shortages in the two countries, however, have to be interpreted within a wider perspective. Whereas German chef patrons bemoan the shortage of *formally qualified* service staff, British chef patrons/restaurateurs are concerned about a chronic shortage of people of *any* calibre. Many of those eventually recruited in Britain accept the job because it is the only one they can get (particularly migrants), or they just fill in time between jobs (information from British two-star chef). In Britain, the majority of service staff, from the bottom to the top levels of *sommelier* and *Maître de*, are foreign, posing an even worse problem than in the kitchen for continuity and hence quality. Thus two-star London chef Claude Bosi defines his main problem with service staff as: 'They do not stay long enough. The French come only for short spells.' Nigel Haworth of *Northcote Manor* comments: 'The German waitresses only stay for a year'; and Frances Atkins of the *York Arms* states: 'I use foreign students who stay for a year.'

However, just as among chefs, there also is a small group of middle- or even upper middle-class people among British waiting staff, such as British and foreign students waiting for a job or resting actors/actresses who already have all the 'social graces' and are quick to learn the additional rules.

In addition to problems of constant labour turnover, the 'curse of Babel', that is, an inadequate ability to communicate in English, can be an additional issue. While Driver diagnosed its existence already in the 1980s,[11] Chris Cooper, *sommelier* at the Savoy Hotel, notes it for the current time:

> The grasp of the English language from service staff in the UK can be an issue...I feel there's about to be an increasing number of diners demanding clear and confidently-spoken English.[12]

One of my interviewees, however, considered communication 'not such a big issue', as long as there is a nice smile: 'I want them to be polite and look nice. Communication is not so important.' His Indian *commis* waiter does, indeed, have an inadequate grasp of English. If one agrees with Driver that an excellent experience in a top-level restaurant can be achieved only by mutual understanding between the kitchen, the waiting staff, and the customer, then the 'curse of Babel' can seriously undermine the achievement of British starred restaurants.

Confronted with this situation of a chronic shortage of properly trained staff, British chef proprietors/patrons employ three main coping strategies to circumvent institutional constraints. First, they may expect only the minimum from waiting staff and refer problems upwards to the *Maître de*. Thus a British one-star chef:

> I do not require professionalism from new [waiting] staff but give them training. But the presence of my highly professional restaurant manager and *sommelier* ensures that the rest of the 'small' staff work effectively.

Second, patrons or managers may regulate their conduct with a multitude of precise rules, to overcome lack of knowledge and experience.[13] Third, they look abroad to recruit trained staff, using, for example, the German recruitment agency ZIHOGA (which arranges exchanges for foreign students/workers to gain work experience in the hospitality sector) (Birmingham chef proprietor Andreas Antona), or equivalent French agencies.

The difficulty for both British and German restaurateurs in attracting good service staff does not merely lie in the insufficient availability of trained people. Even people who have undergone the general training for working in German hotels—which includes training as a waiter—often do not wish to take the restaurant waiting route. One big problem is that there exists no meaningful career structure which is partly a function of the small size of most restaurants. Although a *commis* waiter may eventually become a restaurant manager, very few of these top positions become available. Very occasionally, a restaurant manager makes it to the position of restaurateur, particularly in Britain. A British one-star chef proprietor regrets that 'there are limited opportunities to move up the ladder', and a London two-star chef concurs: 'Finding good staff is a big issue. The young people nowadays also want to climb the ladder fast.' Two German chefs agree:

> Skilled restaurant worker is not as popular as skilled hotel worker because it is seen to have less career prospects. We rarely appoint anyone without a vocational training.

> It is very difficult [to get a good *Maître de*]. Our restaurant is too small to provide sufficient learning opportunities for future promotion. (Two-star chef of a restaurant with around forty covers)

A second and very fundamental problem in both countries is that many young people do not like jobs in which they are required to serve others. (This aspect will be explored further below.) According to a German chef:

> It is becoming more and more difficult [to find a good restaurant manager]. Fewer people choose this occupation. Nobody wants to be in service.

Third, pay and conditions do not compensate for the other two problems. The working hours are longer than average and usually unsocial. (The Conditions of Employment statement of a London two-star restaurant, for example, requires a minimum of 48 hours per week and split shift working.) Although remuneration is not high, a German chef points out that it is close to that of kitchen staff and, given several add-ons like food and tips, he believes it to be satisfactory. In Britain, the level of pay for service staff is said to be below that of kitchen staff and is held to be poor. A one-star chef opines: 'It is very hard to get what I am looking for. The pay is shocking.' Whereas his *sous* chef earns £28,000 per annum, plus two staff meals a day, his restaurant manager receives less. A *commis* waiter at a London two-star restaurant can expect a starting salary of £1,355 gross per month (from the same Conditions of Employment statement). However, pay is said to be above that in the lower-level restaurant industry, and in some fine-dining restaurants it is well above the industry average. A good restaurant manager can earn between £30,000 per annum and a six-figure sum.[14] A consideration of the reward package must take into account also the food provided at either cost price or free of charge, as well as tips (where staff receive them). In several (particularly the more remote) places, subsidized accommodation is additionally provided. However, overall, the business model of fine-dining restaurants—small scale and no multiple sittings—does not yield a sufficiently high income to pay good wages.

There also are job characteristics which may be viewed as attractive, as one restaurant manager points out: 'What is a plus of the job is the meeting of many interesting people and the ample learning about wine and culinary matters.'[15] A former (middle-class and temporary) waitress in one of Britain's famous early post-war fine-dining restaurants tells me that she and her friend learnt so much during their work that one could almost regard the restaurant as an equivalent of a finishing school in its effect on them.

Service Staff Employed

In order to provide the high quality of service expected in fine-dining restaurants, the number of staff employed per cover is relatively high. Table 7.1 shows the relation between the two in Britain and Germany. The table reveals that the number of service staff in the two countries differs, being much lower in Germany, but, despite this difference, the average number of staff per cover—four—is exactly the same in the two countries. The only notable difference is that, in Germany, in three cases the owner and/or spouse are included in an already low number of service staff. In one restaurant in a remote location in Mecklenburg, service is provided exclusively by the owner and her husband.

A much more marked difference between restaurants in the two countries is in the proportion of foreign service staff employed, with a contrast of 53 per cent in Britain versus 10 per cent in Germany. There is only one provincial British restaurant that employs no foreigners: there are seven establishments with between 80 and 100 per cent foreign service employees, and in six restaurants between 50 and 65 per cent of staff are foreign. In contrast, in Germany, only two restaurants employ between 40 and 50 per cent foreign staff (one is in Berlin and the other is an Italian restaurant in Munich). Nine have no foreign staff and the rest have only between 2 and 20 per cent of foreigners in service positions. In Germany, the foreigners are mainly French and, in Bavaria, Austrian. They usually are young people doing a year abroad as part of their training.

The composition of British foreign service staff, in contrast, sometimes is described to me as consisting of a multitude of different nationalities. The chef patron of the London Indian one-star restaurant *Quilon* describes it like this: 'It is almost a United Nations—thirteen different nationalities, both Indian and European.' Atul Kochhar of London restaurant *Benares* says of his staff: 'They are a multinational crew. Currently, I have a couple of

Table 7.1. Number and national origin of service staff

Country	Average no. of covers	Average no. of service staff	Covers per member of staff	Proportion of foreign staff
Britain	64	17	4	53%
Germany	41	10	4	10%

Scandinavians, South African, Polish, Italian, French, German, Algerian, and Filipino staff. I have had Japanese.'

Staff in these and other restaurants include quite a few economic migrants from Eastern Europe who presumably cannot get any higher-status jobs. These young people not only have to be given the normal training but additionally require teaching in language and culture. Some British chef patrons favour migrants from Australia and New Zealand who at least share the language and many aspects of culture. It is notable that several British restaurants have well-trained German, Swiss, and Austrian staff on their year abroad. In one case, the *Maître de* told me that the Germanic quota is to be increased as the company management would like to go for 'that second star'. Several British chefs deliberately refrain from recruiting too many French staff who are viewed as either not wanting to work the necessary hours or as simply 'too arrogant':

> The French have changed their work attitudes in recent decades. Their legislation on maximum working hours made them less employable. They have become more English than the English. (Birmingham one-star chef Antona)

A London two-star chef agrees: 'To recruit a good *sommelier* is difficult if you do not want arrogant Frenchmen.'

Having service staff from various national backgrounds may also be seen as an advantage, as, for example by this London one-star chef: 'We consciously hire people with multilingual skills so that there is no language barrier.' Service staff thus are highly diverse not only in terms of national origin, but also in social origin. Relying on embodied dispositions, as suggested by Warhurst and Nixon, would therefore be a hazardous strategy. Informal training, particularly in Britain, is a *sine qua non*.[16]

My interview schedule does not contain specific questions on employment policy. Hence I am unable to judge whether measures exist which overcome some of the difficulties chef patrons experience in this area. There is, however, one restaurant—the *River Café*—where I was able to conduct an interview also with the restaurant manager, and hence was able to get a more detailed view (Box 7.1).

The case of the *River Café* demonstrates that, even without a good public training system to draw on, the problem of staff recruitment and retention can be managed successfully, provided sufficient resources are invested into it. My impression is that the *River Café* is somewhat exceptional in its staffing policy and manages to attract young people who 'look good and sound right'.[17]

Service Staff as Hosts

In the introduction to this chapter, I pointed out that service staff are required to orient their activity to contradictory guiding principles and develop qualities

Box 7.1 EMPLOYMENT POLICY OF THE *RIVER CAFÉ*

The *River Café* stands out for its excellent employment policy. They pay above the going rate, provide a lot of staff training, and cultivate a very democratic ethos. The restaurant manager outlines the caring atmosphere they cultivate:

> There is more care shown to staff—there is a kind of family feeling. We help employees also with a private problem. They enjoy the same food as the guests, every day, and we have special parties. They also can build staff accounts where they gather points to entertain also their family members. Pay by and large is above the going rate.

Staff wear their own clothes, helping them to express their own individual style. The proprietor, Ruth Rogers, and her managers have succeeded in creating an atmosphere where serving customers is seen as fun. Consequently, the *River Café* does not experience the same staffing problems reported elsewhere in the industry, and vacant positions usually are filled by word of mouth. According to the manager: 'We have a very low turnover of serving staff. Waiters get to know the ethos of the *River Café* and the guests.'

that are not easily reconciled. Their behaviour is governed both by the domestic order of worth, that is, they receive diners as hosts, and by the market order of worth—they are expected to act as sales staff. The contradiction between these two orders of worth is further complicated by the need to present themselves as experts or professionals in the field of food and drink. A visit to a top-end restaurant certainly involves a commercial transaction, and the solicitude of staff for diners has an ulterior motive. In the words of Hochschild, 'worked-up warmth becomes an instrument of service work'.[18] Mars and Nicod, too, point out that waiters meet the expectations of their customers

> by offering an idealized view of their situation, which involves concealing or underplaying activities...and motives which are incompatible with the impression they are attempting to put over.[19]

In other words, waiting staff are said to be play-acting and pretending warmth and empathy they do not feel, and both the latter authors and Hochschild claim that service staff have to suppress their personality.[20]

It is integral to the nature of service in a high-end restaurant that the role of host or the management of emotions on the part of service staff is at the forefront of considerations for both the restaurateur and the service staff. Front-of-house staff present themselves above all as welcoming hosts, and chef patrons select and train their staff with this role primarily in mind. The *Maître de* of two-star German *Falco* sums it up: 'One has to be a wholehearted host, just as if at home. One learns to divine people's needs.'[21] Two-star German chef Niels Henkel concurs: 'The [service staff] must treat diners almost like private guests', as does German two-star chef King: 'They have to know that they are hosts—every one of them.' And two-star Berlin chef Tim

Raue shares this view: 'Our service staff...immediately convey the feeling to a person of being a guest at a friend's house.'[22]

Chef patrons are very much concerned that the gap between sincere and simulated warmth becomes almost imperceptible and that the smile of service staff does not come across as 'stuck-on'. They select staff very much on the basis of the 'right personal characteristics' so that suppression of 'real personality' does not become too pronounced. Thus the restaurant manager of the British *River Café* says that: 'I look for personal ability by which I mean enjoyment of people, passion, attractiveness in both appearance and manners.'

In Germany, the role of host is made very explicit by referring to diners as 'guests'. In Britain, the use of the word 'customer' does not gloss over the market aspect of the relationship, but the role of pleasant host nevertheless is equally in the foreground of interactions. Whereas in Germany expertise is given equal value to pleasantness and good appearance, in Britain 'a pleasant personality' receives the prime emphasis. Thus German two-star chef Jürgens: 'We are the host. One meets guests with reserve and *competence*.' One-star chef Nagel, too, requires 'warmth, friendliness, and professional *competence*'. In contrast British chefs Kerridge and Blackiston say that: 'Personal characteristics come first. They have to be smiley. We can do the rest'; and 'A smile is massively important.' The answers of these latter two British chef proprietors are representative of a large number of my respondents who all rate a pleasant disposition as the top requirement for this job.

Hochschild suggests that, because service staff (flight attendants in her study) do not really feel the emotions they have to express, there is the danger that they suppress any personality and come across as 'behaving like automatons'. German three-star chef Elverfeld wishes that 'they show honest, not artificial friendliness'. However, an article in the German daily *Süddeutche Zeitung* suggests that the problem is difficult to manage:

> Often there is nothing more than soulless intoning of learnt rhetorical flourishes. Chef patrons I interviewed fear nothing more than 'soulless intoning'.[23]

Restaurateurs have tried to overcome this problem of false friendliness by recruiting service staff 'with personality'. Service staff are no longer required to behave according to a set etiquette but are encouraged to interact with customers in their own individual manner. This emphasis on personality probably is most pronounced at the British *River Café* where the young attractive staff are not even required to wear uniform. Thus the restaurant manager, who explicitly disavows the US style of serving, informs me: 'We look for people with a certain style. We look for non-robotic, professional waiters who understand what customers want.'

While most other chef patrons still retain the uniform for serving staff, they share, in both countries, this manager's explicit welcome of the expression of individuality or personality: 'Service staff must retain their human profile and not become marionettes' (German two-star chef).

A British one-star chef wants his service staff to have 'personality and a quirky character'. To illustrate this he points to the 'striking beauty of the female restaurant manager and the modern hairstyle of the *sommelier*'. Two German chefs express a similar sentiment:

> Service staff have to preserve their individual qualities and not go on auto pilot [*etwas runterspulen*]. The guest...notices whether the employee does something out of his/her own initiative. They have to behave naturally.

> They have to develop their own personalities—have to find an individual form to meet the guest with friendliness and communicativeness.

Chef patrons and their restaurant managers support the development of emotional authenticity and do not necessarily wish to prescribe the details of staff's emotional presentation. These attitudes express the changed conception of the modern top-level restaurant, the rejection of the stiff and formal style that has been part and parcel of the traditional French service tradition. This impression is further strengthened by the fact that most chef patrons want their staff to be relaxed, rather than stiff: 'They have to be able to use discretion, be warm, relaxed and not too stiff' (three-star German chef). And a British one-star chef: 'It is very important for staff to be relaxed and enjoy their work.' Some chef patrons, however, explicitly balance the term 'relaxed' with that of 'professional'.

Returning to the concepts of emotional and aesthetic labour and the ideas of Hochschild and Mars and Nicod,[24] this expression of personality is, of course, only very partial. A set of precise rules still has to be observed. Furthermore, it remains a requirement that negative sentiments and impolite remarks are never expressed. Mars and Nicod correctly point out that an assumption of the role of serene and obliging host is much easier for service staff in fine-dining, than in lower-level restaurants. This is because frictions, arising from poor organization and problematic food, largely have been eliminated in this type of restaurant. Additionally, guests come mainly for an enjoyable experience and a relaxed and even drawn-out evening and are much less likely to create unpleasantness.

Smiling agreeably, however, is not enough to be a good host. Additional qualities and behaviours are expected from front-of-house staff. Service staff have to put guests at ease, particularly when they first arrive. In his or her dealings with customers, Mars and Nicod point out, 'it is imperative that the restaurant manager should relieve any anxieties or allay any suspicion that are felt in the preliminary stages'.[25] According to a German three-star chef:

> the guest must remain in the centre; staff must be able to recognize the needs of the guest and must help them to overcome his or her inhibition. We help the guest to overcome it.

Customers who are seemingly ill at ease in an up-market restaurant may be given particular consideration. Staff have to anticipate what guests would like: 'The art is to discover quickly what the guest wants' (German three-star chef). Staff have to develop an understanding of people and to develop an ability to read the cues or signals customers are sending out so that they can develop an appropriate set of responses.

Empathy is, indeed, a quality highly prized in service staff by all employers. They must bring items like bread to the table or refill glasses, before guests have had to ask for them. Wine waiters also must divine quickly in which price category customers want to move when choosing wine and avoid embarrassing diners.

Two rather different experiences I had in the restaurants I visited illustrate this ability to anticipate the guest's wishes. In one London restaurant my coffee had been served while I had left the table to make a phone call. When the waitress saw me returning she removed the coffee and brought a new and still hot cup of coffee. In a German restaurant, the waitress must have observed me running my hand over the unusual wall covering by the side of my chair. When she came next to the table she explained unasked that the wall had been covered with deer hide from animals hunted in a nearby wood. One British chef proprietor—Brett Graham of *The Ledbury*, Notting Hill, London—particularly impressed me with his pronounced customer orientation which I sensed both as an interviewer and as a subsequent (anonymous) diner in the restaurant (Box 7.2).

When I asked chef patrons to select from my list qualities they held to be important when employing new service staff, some personal qualities, surprisingly to me, were not welcomed by all restaurateurs. Thus, while some chef patrons expect their staff to be good communicators, others place lower or no value on a good facility with language: 'Being well spoken [one of my categories to choose from] is not so necessary' according to the manager of a one-star London restaurant who mainly looks for 'attractiveness in both appearance and manners'.

A few chefs volunteer that the local—not very refined accent—is quite acceptable, and two British provincial chefs specify that they prefer staff with local accents. This finding partially contradicts the stipulation of 'sounding right' in a middle-class kind of way, emphasized by Williams and Connell.[26]

Box 7.2 THE CUSTOMER FOCUS AT *THE LEDBURY*

In an interview with *Fine-dining Guide* in 2010, *The Ledbury*'s chef proprietor Brett Graham defined his proudest achievement in the following terms:

> Having the satisfaction of looking at the customer sheet every day and seeing how many are returning guests and how far in advance we are booked! Two years ago we knew it was going to be a tough market so we set out to look after our customers as best as possible and look to build up loyalty from a customer base.

An exceptional orientation to customers was evident also when I interviewed Graham in 2011. Even when my questions were not specifically about customers, his answers, on four separate occasions, came back to customers.

On a subsequent evening visit to the restaurant, together with my husband, I was able to experience this customer focus in practice. Staff were highly attentive from beginning to end, and, better still, they were very friendly, without being intrusive. Although Mr Graham did not do the round of the restaurant, he received me very cordially in the kitchen, taking the time out during the still frantic dinner service to say a few friendly and informative words.

Finally, are female staff expected to use their sexuality or beauty to charm guests into compliance (or extra spending), as suggested by Hochschild?[27] It requires more extended observation to give a definitive answer. A couple of chefs point with approving pleasure to some 'strikingly beautiful' service staff they have managed to recruit. However, there are several indications that, in the main, femininity is not an overt part of the sales bargain. First, when my respondents indicate 'attractiveness' as a quality they desire in their staff, this usually refers to both male and female waiters and often indicates personality, as well as looks. Second, I have been struck by the fact that quite a few of the waitresses are exceptionally plain and appear very unsophisticated, although they always are friendly and courteous. British one-star chef proprietor Shaun Hill has deliberately retained, from the previous owner, some middle-aged female staff 'because they were connected to the locality'. 'Looking good' may be welcome, but it is not a necessary requirement for employment.

Altogether, from my own experience of dining in a number of the restaurants whose chefs I had interviewed, I felt that hospitality was being taken very seriously and was rendered in a style which significantly enhanced my overall dining experience. To give one example, I was impressed when, in a German restaurant on the first floor of a small hotel, the restaurant manager wished us a cordial farewell not merely at the restaurant door but accompanied us all the way down the stairs to the front door of the hotel—a gesture very reminiscent of a more personal host–guest relationship. In this same restaurant we had asked to take our coffee in the separate lounge where we were the only guests. The waitress nevertheless stayed with us for at least twenty minutes, just in case that we had any other wish or requirement.

Finally, it is only in Germany that *chefs de cuisine* actively consider themselves as hosts who, for at least a short time, form part of the front-of-house team. Chefs' training includes, amongst others, a module on how to associate with guests: they have 'to assume the function of host'.[28] The overwhelming majority of the German chefs I interviewed routinely do the round of the restaurant to talk to guests while very few chefs in Britain do so. German chefs receive vital feedback from customers, and the latter, as will be shown in Chapter 9, greatly enjoy meeting the chef. British chefs, in contrast, more rarely emerge from the kitchen as active hosts and have to gain their feedback by other and usually indirect means, such as looking at the returned plates or perusing the list of complaints.

Service Staff as Sales Persons

Does my overall strong endorsement of the fact that service staff mainly treat customers as guests mean that market values have no relevancy? Or, to put it into Hochschild's more critical language, have 'dollar bills intervened between the smiler and the smiled upon' and rendered 'spontaneous warmth' less credible?[29] The answer is, of course, that the market relationship between customer and service staff has not been and cannot be suspended. At the very least, the customer wakes up with a bump to the commercial character of the interaction when the bill is presented. It is because the bill in top-level restaurants is comparatively high, that commercialism can be confined mostly to this last moment, and the 'sales' component can be kept fairly unobtrusive for most of the evening/lunch-time. It is essentially by paying a comparatively large sum for a meal in a fine-dining restaurant that the customer buys the illusion of being a much-indulged guest for an evening.

However, none of the forty chefs mention the ability to sell when asked what qualities they look for when appointing service staff. Indeed, some chef patrons are very concerned that any 'pushy selling', particularly of wine, should be avoided. Thus, a London one-star chef tells me that service staff

> must be conscious of what customers want, namely knowing what their experience is and what their means are. They must not push anything onto the customers.

Another British one-star chef concurs: 'I don't want over-officious people on wine.' My own experience as a diner consistently confirmed the fact that 'pushy selling' is not a practice employed in top restaurants. The market relationship, although present in transactions, is kept well hidden in order not to undermine staff's primary role as host. This absence of a 'hard sell' is found in both British and German restaurants, despite the generally more developed business orientation of British chefs. In sum, given this underemphasis of the 'market' character of the interaction in fine-dining restaurants, service staff do not experience a very strong tension between the values associated with being a host and those characteristic of being a sales person.

Service Staff as Experts

A third requirement of service staff is that they possess and apply professional knowledge (*Fachwissen*), that is, that they are fully informed about the food and the wine on the menu and can explain matters to customers if called upon. It is significant that this third requirement on staff is mainly posed by German chef patrons. It is clearly another consequence of the fact that German service staff have undergone superior training, which has imparted the professional knowledge and what do with it, that expertise is highly valued by their employers. To some of them, it is equally or even more important than a pleasant disposition and/or appearance. Thus two-star chef Christian Jürgens comments: 'First comes competency. Overall appearance comes second.' A three-star German colleague places the same emphasis on a 'high professional (*fachlich*) competency; they must offer correct but relaxed service; the *sommelier* must have a high degree of competency but must not be stiff.' Another German three-star chef adds: 'They have to know the dishes. Service staff try all the new dishes.'

What is more, German service staff have been taught, as part of their apprenticeship, to advise guests in a foreign language, at a basic level. Such an aptitude becomes particularly important for staff in a three-star restaurant that regularly attracts a certain number of travelling gourmets.

Being informed about the food additionally makes possible the appreciation by service staff of what chefs produce. It thereby enhances mutual understanding between kitchen and service staff which is rewarding for both chefs and for diners. One-star Munich chef Gamba sees it this way: 'They [service staff] are, in a small way, ambassadors of the kitchen. They have to pass on information and knowledge.' His two-star colleague, Johannes King, orders his priorities differently:

> For service, the human dimension is more important than the qualification. The first impression [a person makes] is terrifically important. You cannot have any ruffians in the service team while you might accommodate them in the kitchen.

This mutual understanding between kitchen and service staff, based on knowledge and expertise on the part of the latter, is sometimes felt to be lacking in British restaurants. One chef patron remarks:

> [I would like the service staff] to share my outlook on the product. Most of them are just doing it for the money and don't share the same passion as the kitchen.

A London two-star chef concurs: 'It is very hard to find a good restaurant manager, i.e. someone who understands what you do.'

But the best British restaurants, particularly if they are in London, manage to get staff who, given internal training, can develop an understanding of the essence of what the kitchen achieves:

> They have to be knowledgeable and informed but also friendly. They must be confident. There always occurs a briefing before lunch service where they go through the menu and talk about any new dishes. (London two-star chef Phil Howard)

The same is true at two-star *The Ledbury*, a highly customer-focused restaurant. Senior kitchen staff and front-of-house staff regularly meet before a service to discuss changes in the menu, special options, and which regulars are booked in that day. Additionally, every second Monday is a training day for service staff.

While most diners, as I will show in Chapter 9, welcome learning about the often unusual food and/or food combinations and textures that are put before them, waiters tread a narrow path between providing a knowledgeable introduction to the dishes and intruding on customers' conversations, especially if the latter have ordered, say, from an eight-course gastronomic menu. Chef patrons are aware of the double-edged nature of staff's explanatory role. If anything, serving staff now err on the side of introducing dishes in an exceedingly brief and even hurried manner, presumably for fear of being accused of 'stalking' the customers, rather than advising them.

Service in a Democratic Society

Personal service occupations stand very low in the social hierarchy of advanced societies like Britain and Germany. They are placed below many manual workers because their functions are felt to be more dependent and more at the mercy of others.[30] The democratic political ideology, particularly the notion that all citizens are equal and can expect to be treated as such, has become deeply ingrained in these societies. To serve others and thereby forfeit one's equality and dignity therefore is a deeply problematic component of personal service occupations, such as waiting. Christopher Driver, a former editor of the British *Good Food Guide*, expresses this in his usual trenchant manner when he writes about waiting staff in Britain in two historical periods: 'Then [1880] and now [1980] the British urban lower middle-classes as a whole lacked taste, talent, or training for serving in restaurants.'[31]

Two contemporary British one-star chefs concur: 'This is a dying trade. The country does not support serving occupations'; 'The culture of service is not highly respected in the UK, and the job of restaurant manager is not highly developed.' A German chef patron sees it in the same way:

> 'Service' is not yet valued in Germany, and serving staff do not have the high reputation they have in France. There are some guests who still believe we are servants.

However, despite the cultural endorsement service staff are believed to receive in French society, this alleged high reputation often still goes hand-in-hand with a degree of pomposity and *hauteur* towards guests—a feature most British and German diners interviewed object to in very strong terms.

Chef patrons, on the one hand, believe that 'the guest is king' and has to be treated as such, but, on the other, they realize that deference and servility are outmoded in contemporary society. They take great pains to square the circle, that is, to reconcile the guiding principles of the civic order of worth with a top restaurant's code of service implying deference to the guest:

> The first thing is to do everything for the guest—the customer is king. Staff must recognize guests' wishes, the guest always comes first. But they must communicate as equals, and they should expect respect. (German two-star chef)

With two exceptions in each country, chefs do not advocate deference towards guests. Most are at pains to emphasize that rendering service must never become servility. The following quotes are representative of what most other chefs expressed:

> They have to serve but not be subservient. (German three-star chef)
>
> Staff are not servants, they are equals. (British one-star chef)
>
> They are there to serve, without being servile. (German one-star chef)
>
> They show deference but it should be clear that they provide a service and are not servants. (London two-star chef)

One exception in Britain is the chef patron of a London Indian one-star restaurant who explains that deference to diners is part of Indian culture: 'They [service staff] show deference. It comes from the Hindi background where the guest is god.'

However, a few of the German chefs rejected any show of deference outright: 'Deference is outmoded' (German owner of a one-star restaurant). Or a very influential German three-star chef:

> We live in a democratic society; there has occurred an unprecedented rapprochement [between the social strata]. One must not be subordinate, and one must not stand for any nonsense.

Several of the German, but only one of the British chefs, additionally point to staff's qualified/professional status which they view as endowing them with a shield of authority against customers demanding servility.

> One meets guests with reserve and competency. One doesn't kow-tow. One does not have to make oneself look smaller than one is. (German two-star chef)

> Yes, they [service staff] have to adapt and be respectful, but, at the same time, they are professional people who also have to receive recognition. (German one-star chef)

In Britain only one interviewee, the restaurant manager of the *River Café*—it has a well-developed internal training system—suggests that professionalism can engender the authority to counteract any tendencies towards subservience: 'Staff have to show both a degree of deference and show pride in their profession. They have to serve, without being subservient.'

The fact that chefs frequently come from the same social background as waiters also makes them feel social solidarity with service staff. Moreover, as employers, they want to protect them from demeaning treatment by customers. In both countries, chef patrons set clear limits to what service staff have to tolerate. Several chef patrons have an explicit house rule that offensive behaviour towards service staff will not be tolerated. In difficult situations, the restaurant manager steps in to deal with any unpleasantness:

> If guests get unpleasant, as, for example, it is experienced with arrogant grouse shooters, the girls call the manager to intervene. They themselves must not become confrontational. (British one-star chef)

Or a London two-star chef:

> If they are treated badly by a client, i.e. if there is any rudeness, the restaurant manager will step in to deal with it, but such things are rare.

A London one-star chef holds a similar view:

> The customer is always right—even if he is wrong. I only step in when people behave obnoxiously. I want the service staff to be polite, disciplined and eager to serve.

This intervention by restaurant managers, of course, has the dual purpose of protecting less experienced and authoritative staff *and* preventing an unpleasant public scene by helping the offending customer to save face. As the following quote illustrates, complaints mostly are not received in a confrontational manner, and the customer is treated just as a domestic guest or even as 'king':

They [customers] are largely happy. If they are not happy, we make sure they become happy. For example, if someone complains about a dish, we never query their judgement. We just replace it and do not charge for that dish.

Unpleasantness is avoided at all cost.

But if customers become very offensive—and several chefs emphasize that this is a rare occurrence—they will be asked to leave or may even be forcibly evicted. Thus a one-star British employed chef reports: 'Customers make waiters feel inferior. There are some terrible customers. I have in the past asked a whole table to leave.'

Chef Raymond Blanc, in his 2008 book *A Taste of My Life*,[32] relates an amusing incident where a group of 'well-built' chefs entered the restaurant to deal with some rowdy and offensive Oxford student diners. This is a rare acknowledgement that, very occasionally, diners exploit their elite status to cause embarrassment to service staff.

The most typical area in which friction between customers and service staff may arise is the handling of customer complaints about food and, just as frequently, about seating. Most chefs answer my question about complaints by saying that customer complaints are relatively rare. This is the case because, on the one side, food quality generally is at a high level and gives little cause for complaint. On the other, most diners do not possess the knowledge and expertise to challenge a starred chef about his food. Some chefs indicate that the most demanding customers are the 'travelling gourmets' who seek out all three-star restaurants in Europe or even further afield and tend to find fault. As experienced diners, they have the confidence in their own knowledge of food and in their taste to lodge complaints. A German three-star chef comments: 'The guests have become much more independent (*mündig*), and they have many more possibilities to compare.'

Restaurant Ambience: Are Fine-Dining Restaurants Pompous and Stuffy?

I have implied that front-of-house staff make a large contribution to a restaurant's ambience. However, they are only a part of what constitutes the mystery of the 'right ambience'. Furnishings, lighting, décor, spacing of tables, staff uniforms, as well as requirements or not for a dress code for guests are all among the elements that contribute to creating an ambience.

As sociologist Joanne Finkelstein observes, the restaurant, as part of the entertainment industry, 'is much concerned with the marketing of emotions, desires, moods and states of mind',[33] and ambience is a crucial means in achieving these effects. Chef patrons are aware of the fact that 'ambience' is a very important component of the 'package' offered to draw in customers and most have very definite views on this topic. 'Ambience' has also become one of the weapons with which some academic and journalistic critics try to denigrate Michelin-starred restaurants which they decry as 'over formal and stuffy French-style restaurants'. Instead they praise a bistro-type style as more appropriate to current sensibilities. Chefs' own views implicitly try to meet and deflect such criticisms when, with few exceptions, they strongly come out in favour of a 'relaxed style', lack of pomp and 'faffing around', as well as a low level of formality.

Many of today's chef patrons have come from a working-class background. They often feel uncomfortable with a luxurious style of furnishings and with a stiff and formal atmosphere which is the result of a large set of rigid rules and conventions, as well as of décor. Thus two-star chef proprietor Sat Bains:

> [I aim for] elegance and sophistication. Yes, but I do not want it to be something that it isn't. It has to be very honest. I am a working class guy from Derby...I am fed-up with French pomp.

When given a list of eight characteristics to choose from that might define their restaurant's ambience (see appended Interview Schedule), all chefs list a 'relaxed style' among their three most important preferences, and for several it is the only choice. 'Relaxed style' is viewed as the counterpoint to stiffness—with hands behind your back and bowing to madam—as well as to formality, which are both widely abhorred. Other popular choices regarding ambience are 'elegance' and 'sophistication'. Conversely, no chef patron chooses 'luxury' as a defining characteristic, and several chefs explicitly single it out for rejection. However, despite chefs' own wishes and perceptions, some of the hotel restaurants in Germany do appear luxurious.

The following references to 'relaxed style' are representative of what is felt by the majority of chefs. Thus one-star Birmingham chef Antona states: 'Our restaurant is very, very informal. I hate formality! No rules. I am a very laid back person.' German two-star chef Niels Henkel says: 'The service staff must create an atmosphere of well-being. The guest should be able to relax—no dress constraints.' British one-star chef Martin Wishart asserts: 'We are calm and relaxed; not formal or stuffy.' And British one-star chef Shaun Hill tells me: 'I want it to be informal, friendly and that money has gone mainly on what is on the plate.'

Even *chefs de cuisine* of restaurants located in elegant manor house or other luxury hotels, such as Henkel's in Schloss Lerbach, Wissler's in Schloss Bensberg, and Elverfeld's in the Wolfsburg Ritz Carlton hotel, aim for 'a relaxed style'. Thus Henkel likes to 'to have it relaxed, not too stiff'; Wissler's goal is 'to obtain unforced/relaxed perfection'; and Elverfeld aims for fun: 'The whole [thing] has to be fun, service and wine are part of it. It must not be stiff, the guest has to feel comfortable.'

Additionally, as has been shown in Chapter 6, a relaxed style also extends to the composition of the menu. Menus written solely in French no longer exist. Only a very small number of German restaurants describe dishes in both French and German, and a handful of British ones sprinkle the menu with occasional French terms. Social exclusivity is no longer cultivated.

The notion of 'formality' to describe the conduct of service staff is ambiguous. It may simply mean the adherence to some basic rules of etiquette, such as when to approach the diner and when to leave him or her alone or when to clear the table. Alternatively, it may refer to the tone of staff–customer interaction where formality is equated with a degree of pomposity. Most chefs understand it in the latter sense, but a few in each country interpret it in the former sense and equate formality with professionalism. Most chefs eschew a high degree of formality in terms of the tone of interaction. Among the British chef patrons five view their restaurant as formal, and for three of these—Phil Howard, Sat Bains, and Galton Blackiston—formality is equated with professionalism: 'We are formal only in the sense of being professional' (Sat Bains); 'We are pretty formal but I call it professional' (Galton Blackiston). Among German chefs, three see their restaurants as having a medium-high degree of formality, but in all of them constraining rules of etiquette are eschewed.

Chef patrons/restaurateurs impose few formal rules to regulate the conduct and appearance of customers—the only exceptions being 'no smoking', 'no rudeness to staff', as well as some very minimal rules on dress. Where a dress code exists it is with a very light touch. Objections are directed mainly against the wearing of shorts, flip-flops, sweatshirts, and walking gear, and no chef states a tie requirement. Only two British chefs specify a 'smart casual' dress code. Together, these various changes in ambience indicate and reflect changes in the style of sociality, and fine-dining restaurants have conformed to the *Zeitgeist*.

A small number of chefs appear to regard their restaurant as 'a temple of gastronomy', defined by writer and food journalist John Lanchester as 'restaurants with muted colours and lacking any striking design so that attention is not diverted from the food'.[34] Other commentators add to this list of characteristics 'a hushed atmosphere, that is temple-like quietness'. As far as general décor is concerned, most chefs favour timeless elegance with fairly neutral colours—usually beige, and any over-the-top gimmickry or extravagant design features are rejected. (These latter features are more common among non-Michelin, upper-middle level restaurants which attract diners through quirky or striking design features, as much as through the food they serve.) Thus two-star London chef proprietor Phil Howard states:

> We…are understated and not fashionable. We consider ours a mature grounded restaurant. The restaurant appeals to business customers. We are understated and reliable.

German two-star chef patron Christian Jürgens describes the décor of his restaurant as follows: 'Straight modern spirit, with cream-coloured upholstery and few other colours.'

This does not necessarily result in dullness because of the use of varied textures and of a small number of more idiosyncratic decorative features. Thus in the middle of the ceiling a striking lamp-like construction of concentric circles of different colours of metal—a modern interpretation of a chandelier—adds style and character to the room, as do large black-and-white photos of the lake, on the banks of which the restaurant is situated. Three German chefs explicitly exclude having art on display. Three-star German chef proprietor Juan Amador suggests that: 'too much art diverts attention'. Three-star chef Wohlfahrt, too, thinks art superfluous: 'the art is already present in the cooking'. One German one-star chef even goes as far as favouring neither flowers nor candles on tables.

In Britain, Lanchester includes Marcus Wareing at the *Berkeley* among his temples of gastronomy. Wareing himself describes it as 'very business-like, very grown up—this is defined by our client base'. Wareing therefore aims less at creating a 'temple of gastronomy' than trying to develop a style which appeals to business guests who form a sizeable proportion of his client base. In sum, in both countries, there exists a small number of 'temples of gastronomy' in the sense that interior decoration does not distract attention from the food. However, there are no luxurious and stiff and formal restaurants, nor do the restaurants I experienced generally have a 'hushed atmosphere' or 'temple-like silence'.

What about the use of either national or regional décor? Not many chef patrons are keen on either a traditional or a regional/national style. The two Indian restaurants in London deliberately refrain from traditional design features of Indian restaurants, such a flocked wallpaper. They instead include more subtle references to the country of their own origin and that of their food. Atul Kochhar of the London restaurant *Benares* describes it as follows:

> When I had this restaurant designed I wanted clean lines and a modern approach but I also wanted to be an architect of Benares [an important town on the Ganges] and represent air, water and earth.

There is a fountain at the entrance to the restaurant and on one side of it the diner looks out onto a garden which represents earth. The sculptured white walls in the dining room represent the water of the Ganges. The intricate screens are typical of Indian decoration. The décor thus has Indian elements, without in any way calling to mind the décor associated with cheap high street Indian restaurants. When I asked Sriram Aylur whether he aimed for an Indian style, he replied: 'Kind of, but not in an "in your face" mode.'

One German restaurateur, who is a second-generation owner, has taken pains to preserve all the traditional features of his pub-like restaurant, such as distinctive panelling and an ornate tiled stove. One-star chef proprietor Markus Nagy, too, preserves some of the traditional features in his *Landgasthof* (rural inn), dating from 1827, such as wood-panelled walls and a painted ceiling. Three further German restaurants display some discreet references to their region, such as incorporating local wood or stone into the décor. In one case—the *Söl'ringhof* on the island of Sylt—décor alludes to the restaurant's location by the sea by the use of the colour blue and a beautiful ceiling lamp representing water bubbles. But these latter three restaurants cultivate an ambience that is a far cry from traditional German *Gemütlichkeit*. The one notable exception is Harald Wohlfahrt's three-star *Schwarzwaldstube* in the hotel Traube in Tonbach, Black Forest, which has many features of the regional Black Forest style. According to Wohlfahrt: 'We are very bound by tradition and have a lot of pine and fir wood in the restaurant.' However, the décor has been chosen by the owner, rather than by Wohlfahrt himself.

In Britain, the Lancashire restaurant *Northcote Manor* uses local artefacts and material to identify with the region, while Sat Bains displays some artwork from local artists to connect with the region of Nottinghamshire.

Yet, despite the widespread favouring by chef patrons of a relaxed style and a rejection of formality, such as a stringent dress code and arrogant service staff, Michelin-starred restaurants are continually criticized as exhibiting 'gratuitous faffing, poncery, grovelling *Maîtres de* and arrogant sommeliers'.[35] Preference is given by such critics to gastro pubs and bistros which are viewed as more relaxed and as putting the food more at the centre of their endeavour. While most gastro pubs and bistros are, indeed, more relaxed than three-star restaurants, the differences in the above respects are becoming less striking. Several Michelin-starred restaurants are very close to gastro pubs or bistros, and the differences between the types of restaurants are gradually eroding. Yes, most fine-dining restaurants do still favour starched table cloths and napkins, and most diners greatly value this feature (see discussion in Chapter 9). Also staff uniforms, although creating a degree of formality, help customers to distinguish service staff from fellow guests. Moreover, many bistros possess also negative features, not found in Michelin-starred restaurants, such as having little space between tables and even being cramped, as well as having several sittings per service in order to increase revenue. Whether the food is more at the centre of things in bistros and gastro pubs than in Michelin-starred restaurants is, at the very least, debatable. However, this is not to deny that there still is some unnecessary poncery in starred restaurants, such as placing the napkin on the customer's lap or providing a little footstool for ladies' handbags, but these practices, in the restaurants I visited, now are rare. Hence, overall, rather outdated images of restaurant ambience are still promoted by critics. They may make good copy but, on the basis of my evidence, no longer accurately portray the reality of most Michelin-starred restaurants.

Conclusions

Chef patrons, this chapter has shown, face just as many problems with front-of-house staff as they do with kitchen staff. Their biggest problem, particularly in Britain, is a chronic and severe shortage of service staff with adequate experience or training at all three levels of service. This makes it much harder to obtain continuity and to achieve the very high level of all-round competence expected from service staff in fine-dining restaurants. This is not to suggest that service in British restaurants generally is of a poor quality but that achieving an adequate service quality takes a lot more effort on the part of chef patrons and restaurateurs. In both societies, recruitment is hampered by the fact that personal service, which requires a degree of deference to customers, now is held by many young people to be incompatible with the guiding principle of equality in the civic order of worth. In both countries, being a good host achieves unambiguous priority. It renders a visit to a fine-dining restaurant a rare and pleasurable experience in a society where personal service is cut to the bone in many other service industries.

The greatest challenge facing service staff is to serve customers without becoming servile or submissive, repressing their own feelings and impulses in the process. Today's chef patrons are very much aware of all these challenges and have adopted a more open-minded and relaxed approach to what degree of formal rule-following they impose on staff conduct and how much conformity or, alternatively, expression of personality they expect or even encourage. Nevertheless, even in this more relaxed environment, if the customer remains king, the waiting staff and restaurant manager, by definition, are put into a subordinate position.

Service staff, I have pointed out, make a big contribution to the creation of a good restaurant ambience. Many critics of fine-dining restaurants with Michelin stars focus on restaurant ambience as a core element of their critique. They claim that stiff and formal service, as well as superfluous poncery, remain characteristics of Michelin restaurants and that they are upheld, in an undefined way, by the *Michelin Guide*. I have tried to show in this chapter that such a characterization of Michelin-starred restaurants now is a caricature and no longer applicable to the majority of British and German restaurants. A relaxed ambience is close to the heart of most chef patrons and, where a degree of formality is still desired, it is usually viewed as synonymous with professionalism.

Many starred restaurants, particularly at the two- and three-star level, still have features commonly associated with 'temples of gastronomy'. By this I mean that décor is relatively subdued and sober and that quirky or striking design, including works of art, does not distract diners from an appreciation of the food. It is true that these restaurants forgo the most fashionable and trendy new design features and that they unashamedly put high-quality and creative food at the centre of the restaurant experience. Whether this is a cause for decrying them as not being part of contemporary taste is, at the very least, debatable.

Most of the features of and problems around service staff and ambience I have introduced in this chapter are common to both British and German restaurants and must be considered inherent to fine-dining restaurants. The main difference established between British and German restaurants again derives from the different training systems. Although German chef patrons, too, have problems of staff recruitment these are not as severe as in Britain. As with kitchen employees, restaurant service staff are better trained, particularly in two- and three-star restaurants. This divergence leads to a second distinction between the two countries' restaurants, namely that German respondents give more weight to possession of knowledge and expertise by staff. They consequently envisage that expertise will lend service staff professional status which, in turn, may shield them from condescending or rude behaviour from customers.

The costs that restaurateurs or chef proprietors have to incur—and hence the competing modes of evaluation they have to juggle—also differ according to the number of stars held or aspired to. It is claimed that Michelin inspectors make the award of stars dependent on the opulence of the restaurant itself and on the number of serving staff employed, with a *sommelier* an absolutely must. Two-star chefs who aim to move up to the higher category, it is further asserted, have to find a large amount of investment capital, to transform their restaurant to the required three-star level of splendour. Such investment, it is further claimed, cause chef patrons considerable anxiety if the loss of a star destroys the expectation for a higher level of profit. These requirements, however, are unambiguously rejected by the Michelin organization.

Misconceptions about what Michelin inspectors expect also may be found among academic commentators and even among some chef patrons themselves. First, both the British and German representatives of Michelin Publishing that I interviewed confirm in very definite terms that the *Guide* awards stars *only* on the basis of the persistent quality and, at higher levels, the creativity of the food and *not* on ambience (which is indicated by the knives and forks) or quality of service. Second, the degree of luxury is inconsistently allied to the number of stars. Thus, I have visited a few luxurious one-star restaurants, but I also know of several two-star and even two three-star restaurants where the perfectly pleasant surroundings lack any sign of opulence. The latter applies both to the three-star *Fat Duck* in Britain and to Amador's three-star restaurant (then still) in Langen. However, whether inspectors totally disregard the quality of service must remain contentious, and a certain level of quality of service probably is taken for granted.

Notes

1. G. Mars and M. Nicod, *The World of Waiters* (London: Allen & Unwin, 1984), 101.
2. A. Hochschild, *The Managed Heart: Commercialization of Human Feelings* [1985] (Berkeley and Los Angeles: University of California Press, 2003), 7.
3. C. Warhurst and D. Nixon, 'A New Labour Aristocracy? Aesthetic Labour and Routine Interactive Services', *Work, Employment and Society* 21.4 (2007): 785–98; C. L. Williams and C. Connell, '"Looking Good and Sounding Right": Aesthetic Labor and Social Inequality in the Retail Industry', *Work and Occupations* 37.3 (2010): 349–77.
4. N. Lander, *The Art of the Restaurateur* (London: Phaidon, 2012), 201.
5. Warhurst and Nixon 2007.
6. However, Hannah Skeggs's article on '100 Years of Culinary Expertise', *Yes Chef! Magazine* 23 (2012): 64–5, reports on new courses at Westminster Kingsway College's School of Hospitality that cover industry-accredited qualifications for front-of-house, including the 'art of service', restaurant manager, and the Institute of Hospitality Diploma.
7. Interview in *Der Feinschmecker* 9 (2009): 70–1.
8. <http://www.bayerischerhof.de/resources/_docs/de/Vita%20Team%20Atelier.pdf>.
9. Editorial to *Imbibe Magazine* (March–April 2012). <hhtp://imbibe.com/article/sommelier-training-could-do better>, accessed 3 September 2012.
10. *Süddeutsche Zeitung* (17 November 2009).
11. C. Driver, *The British at Table, 1940–80* (London: Chatto & Windus, 1983), 154.
12. <http://imbibe.com/article/sommelier-training-could-do better>, accessed 3 September 2012.
13. See the reference to detailed rules above, as communicated by Lander 2012.
14. *The Guardian* (13 June 2013): 10.
15. *Der Feinschmecker* 9 (2009): 70–1.

16. Warhurst and Nixon 2007.
17. Williams and Connell 2010.
18. Hochschild 2003 [1985]: 89.
19. Mars and Nicod 1984: 35.
20. Hochschild 2003 [1985].
21. Interview in *Der Feinschmecker* 9 (2009): 70–1.
22. T. Raue, *Ich weiss was Hunger ist. Von der Strassengang in die Sterneküche* (Munich and Zürich: Piper Verlag, 2012), 259.
23. *Süddeutche Zeitung* (17 November 2009).
24. Hochschild 2003 [1985] and Mars and Nicod 1984.
25. Mars and Nicod 1984.
26. Williams and Connell 2010.
27. Hochschild 2003 [1985].
28. *Verordnungg über die Berufsausbildung* (February 1998), available at <http://www.Bundesgesetzblatt.de>, 367.
29. Hochschild 2003 [1985]: 5.
30. This is emphasized also in the book by Richard Sennett and Jonathan Cobb, *The Hidden Injuries of Class* (Cambridge: Cambridge University Press, 1977), though in a different context.
31. Driver 1983: 148.
32. R. Blanc, *A Taste of My Life: One Man's Hunger for Perfection* (London: Transworld Publishers, 2008), 427–8.
33. J. Finkelstein, *Dining Out: A Sociology of Modern Manners* (Cambridge: Polity Press, 1989), 20.
34. *Guardian Weekend* (17 March 2012).
35. John Lanchester, 'Restaurants', *Guardian Weekend* (26 February 2011): 59.

8

Supplier Relations: Quality, Price, and Trust

The vital importance of suppliers of produce to fine-dining chefs cannot be overemphasized. A good chef treats his or her ingredients with respect and lets them shine. Ingredients cannot shine if they are not excellent, and for good raw materials you need good suppliers. Suppliers, in some cases, may be viewed almost as part of the restaurant or, at least, as strongly interdependent with chefs. One-star Alan Murchison emphasizes: 'This relationship [with suppliers] is critical. I have twenty-odd suppliers, and I have personal relations with all of them.' One-star British chef Phil Thompson feels the same way:

> The most important thing is to have long-standing positive relationships with suppliers...In all cases the relationships are strong, and in certain cases they have become friends, even to the point of dining in the restaurant here with their families.

German one-star chef Rainer Maria Halbedel of Bad Godesberg agrees: 'Suppliers are very important, and I try to cultivate these relations. I demand first-class quality, but my suppliers are paid well and on time.'

Yet even in this generally close and trusting relationship chefs may have to wrestle with contending conceptions of what has value, i.e. they have to decide which mix of normative principles or orders of worth should rule their relationship with suppliers. Can the relationship be mainly a very personal relationship of trust (domestic order of worth) or must it be concerned chiefly with market rationality? Related to this, chefs, in many instances, have to judge whether market values can be cast aside so that they may indulge their creativity, called forth by the inspirational quality of some types of produce. How often and when should chefs allow their passion for exceptional, but expensive produce to override the market values that they are also bound to consider?

Before answering the above questions, I consider who are the suppliers to starred restaurants, as well as explain why the relationship possesses such importance for chefs. In a third step, I examine how chefs try to manage their supplier relations. This leads me also to revisit the topic of localism in sourcing, including the currently fashionable notion of foraging. I conclude the chapter with some thoughts on the wider importance chefs' purchasing practices have had for the greater availability of higher quality and more diverse foodstuffs in recent decades.

Who are the Suppliers to the High-End Restaurant Sector?

The availability of a wide range of suppliers of high-quality foods should not be taken for granted. As Chapter 1 made clear, the development of a Michelin-starred restaurant sector from the 1960s to 1980s was impeded by the lack of availability of a good supply base, and some of the early starred chefs were compelled personally to import the produce they needed from France. One chef who worked in France during the 1960s, Shaun Hill, points out to me that France then had a much superior supply base, as compared with Britain.

> It was interesting to see the French supply chain. The level of back-up was tremendous, particularly from the traiteur. The chef could buy things which, in England, did not exist.

According to a German food scholar,

> In 1977, 80 per cent of materials were still imported from France. But from the end of the 1980s, restaurateurs had advanced to selecting food from farmers in their immediate environment who are prepared to raise free-range animals and ecologically grown vegetables.[1]

The memoirs of British chefs, such as Michel Roux and Raymond Blanc, also attest that the situation was similar in Britain.[2]

Today problems of supply largely have been resolved, and a wide and diverse range of high-quality suppliers is available, even if they do not equal the French situation in all respects. Two-star chef Niels Henkel points out: 'During the last ten years though, product quality in Germany has greatly improved. There now is lamb from the (German) Eiffel mountains.' Even today, however, some products, like chicken and shellfish, are still believed to be better in France.

As in earlier decades, the quality and, more so, the distinctiveness of the supply base still rise and fall with the prevalence of suppliers who are themselves producers of an artisan nature, such as butchers and bakers, or practising self-taught skills such as cheese making and line-fishing. Suppliers thus may be either large commercial firms or small specialist suppliers. Concerning specialist suppliers of fish, Sylt chef Johannes King tells me: 'Some are very specialist, e.g. for caviar from European fishes.'

The smaller suppliers, in turn, may be independent artisans or small farmers, such as butchers and fruit growers, or even individual fishermen or foragers of wild herbs and mushrooms. German chef Gamba illustrates this search for specialist produce: 'One example [of my specialist suppliers] is a small butcher who only has 10–20 calves' and he is proud of having 'got to know a butcher in Paris who sells wild quails', while three-star chef Wohlfahrt swears by the marbled beef from Pomerania. A Scottish chef, Martin Wishart, has 'a farmer who brings lamb from Shetland twice a year'.

These highly specialist craft-type suppliers are usually referred to as producers, i.e. they themselves generate a product that is relatively rare and/or distinctive. German two-star chef Johannes King well describes the difference between suppliers and producers:

> With mere suppliers, one can ask them to substitute one product for another if one of them is not satisfactory. I know what is available and can ask for it. With producers, you have to talk to them and ask what is available, what can he offer you. He brings the new products. If you have an open and interested producer, he is very valuable. Both sides can bring their specialized (*Fach*) knowledge to the relationship.

Moreover, as the product goes into chefs' kitchens by the shortest route, cutting out the intermediate firms that the larger commercial firms utilize, it is also distinguished by superior freshness. The best of these producers are highly sought after by chefs, and they are able to select the chefs they wish to supply. Examples in Germany are the Manor of Polting, supplier of game, poultry, and freshwater fish, and a Franconian grower of old varieties of vegetables.[3]

Suppliers may be local (in the region), national, or located abroad. Despite the much improved supply base in both countries, most chefs are still importing some French (and other foreign) produce, usually supplied by Rungis Express—a firm founded by a German entrepreneur in 1978—which supplies produce from Paris's Rungis wholesale market in order to deliver to restaurants in Germany. Gradually, deliveries also came to be made all over Europe, including Britain. Today, Rungis Express not only supplies French produce—both prepared (pâtés and terrines) and fresh—but also products from all over the world.

Chefs in my sample have supplier networks carefully built up and nurtured over time. The number of core suppliers that they have is highly variable—ranging from three to 130. Although larger networks are usually maintained by larger restaurants, such a correspondence is not invariably found. A few chefs have a very large network because they either cultivate a sizeable number of very specialist suppliers/producers or because they engage in dual sourcing, i.e. they hedge against risk by maintaining more than one supplier for a given product. Thus British one-star chef Murchison, similar to many other chefs, informs me that he has some suppliers for only one product:

> I buy my smoked haddock from a guy in Scotland whose grandparents already catered for restaurants. I also have one person I buy my crab from—he is located in Devon.

The largest network—130 suppliers—is maintained by German two-star chef Christian Lohse whose restaurant also has the largest number of covers (ninety). Nearly all the other German chefs have only between three and ten suppliers, and only three-star chef Elverfeld and two-star chef King have forty-five and forty suppliers respectively. In both cases, this large number of suppliers corresponds to their selection of many small specialist suppliers and producers. King, for example, has eight suppliers just for fish, in addition to catching his own. The recent criticism by *Gault Millau Deutschland* that a lot of chefs buy mainly from generalist commercial suppliers and therefore all use the same uniform produce is not borne out by my research.

Most of the British chefs have between six and twenty suppliers—reflecting their larger number of covers. Four British chefs stand out by buying from a network of 80–90, 100 plus, 110, or 'too many to count' suppliers—namely, Indian chef Sriram Aylur, Claude Bosi, Sat Bains, and Joseph Trivilli of the *River Café*, respectively. The *River Café* is exceptional also for the large number of its covers—up to 150. Its head chef, Joseph Trivilli, certainly engages in multiple sourcing: 'We have four suppliers for fish alone, three main ones for vegetables, and three for cheeses.'

The other three establishments are only of medium size, and their large number of suppliers seems to indicate that they have many specialist suppliers and producers. Sat Bains subsequently has confirmed this:

> Over the years, I have found some really small, artisan producers that specialize in only one thing, be it salt, butter, chocolate, pork and game, and I have decided to use them continually even though the cost over the year is higher.

Price, Quality, and Distinction: The Nature of Supplier Relations

The quality of a chef's supplier network closely influences the quality of the meals he or she serves. Nearly all the chefs emphasize that they only buy high-quality products, even if they cost above average, and that they try to get the freshest foodstuffs possible. There is a great emphasis on buying only seasonal and, therefore, fresh produce. Two-star London chef Phil Howard makes this clear: 'But I do not rely on vegetables and fruit that are out of season and have to be flown in from afar. I get fish delivered every day.' German three-star chef Wohlfahrt trumps the latter when he says: 'I get fish delivered twice a day.'

However, both the notions of 'quality' and 'freshness' are flexible. Quality does not always mean the best cuts of meat, but is instead 'added' in the cooking process. This happens when what are widely perceived as inferior cuts, such as pork cheeks rather than loin, are subjected to long and slow cooking, to yield the maximum tenderness and flavour. Likewise, the humble cauliflower, available all the year round, can be transformed into something special—smoked cauliflower custard—with the help of a Thermomix. That these practices also have to do with cost-saving, particularly for the cheaper lunch-time menus, is no secret. With widespread rises in food prices, using cheaper cuts of meat is one way to accommodate price rises in produce without raising menu prices. Similarly, some of the products are advertised as coming from fairly local, sometimes named, farms and thus convey the impression of utmost freshness. It is, however, usually not made clear that the meat may have travelled across the country to an abattoir, before it is dispatched elsewhere for wrapping and only then reaches the final link in the chain—the restaurant. Likewise, fish may be caught in Peterhead, only to be sent on to the harbour of Lowestoft where it is then passed off as local supply.[4]

In both Britain (excepting Scotland) and Germany, most of the fish is now imported. When chefs talk about fresh fish it may be fish imported alive. However, even from a commercial wholesaler of fish delivery may be fast and frequent. Some fish wholesalers for fine-dining restaurants, like Munich company Lurz, do not only import daily but also keep alive the majority of their fish and shellfish in 4,000 litre saltwater and 8,000 litre freshwater tanks. A British supplier of fish, Kingfisher of Brixham, are also proud of the freshness of their products:

We only source fish across the country if it is not available locally: this minimizes our food miles and maximizes freshness. . . . We have a presence at every major UK port, plus strong links with local day boat fishermen. We also maintain relationships with international suppliers. This ensures the best quality, freshest fish on the market. We work with day boat suppliers in ports all around the UK. We are fortunate to be based in Brixham where we have access to a fantastic fleet of day boats who land the freshest and best quality seafood in our waters.[5]

However, not everything sourced from Kingfisher comes from Britain, nor is it always caught 'wild'.

> Aquaculture is now an everyday part of our working lives. We work closely with farms in South Africa, Ireland, Greece, France, Norway, Thailand, India, China, Australia, Canada, Sri Lanka, the Faroe Islands, the Maldives and Holland to ensure consistency of supply and quality.[6]

As regards the sourcing of meat, British chefs like to buy from master butcher's Aubrey Allen, a second-generation family firm. The firm buys the meat in carcass form from farmers who rear cattle ethically. They pay farmers a premium for their produce and ensure that the whole carcass is delivered to Aubrey Allen. The firm has learnt continental butchering practices by listening to chefs who, like Peter Allen himself, had been educated abroad and wanted more from a butcher than the average English butcher was able to provide.[7]

Despite the above reservations, by and large chefs do accord freshness of produce a high priority. One Yorkshire chef, Frances Atkins, even has her chefs rear their own chickens. This probably is due to the fact that free-range chickens—which are bought up mainly by the big supermarkets—are notoriously hard to secure by smaller restaurants. For German chefs, freshness of fruit and vegetables is sometimes attained by frequenting a local market (which additionally provides inspiration for cooking). The majority of my British respondents, in contrast, tell me that their local market is not worth frequenting—another consequence of a high degree of industrialization of food production and an absence of a local food culture during earlier periods. For example, a London chef comments that 'there are no good local markets' and a Birmingham chef expresses the same in stronger terms: 'The Birmingham market is a dead loss.' Shaun Hill, of the *Walnut Tree Inn*, near Abergavenny, is equally forthright in answering my question about visiting local markets: 'No, they are rubbish.' In contrast, even large German towns like Munich maintain markets that chefs find well worth visiting.

A second and very important consideration for chefs is to distinguish their cuisine by acquiring relatively rare or unusual and hence distinctive products. While any chef can serve tomatoes and apples, to include an heirloom variety of tomatoes and a rare breed of quinces on your menu immediately singles you out. According to German chef Johannes King:

> We need the small producers. Producers can give a restaurant its individuality, whereas suppliers offer all high-level restaurants the same thing.

Such distinctive products usually come from specialist suppliers or from producers who circumvent the usual supply chain and make their own craft product. Nearly all of the chefs I interviewed cultivate such specialist small firms and producers, though in very different proportions. The British chefs mainly have a mixed or layered strategy of purchasing, using larger commercial firms, but supplementing them with artisan and/or agricultural suppliers. Three British chefs—two of whom cater for a relatively large number of covers—use mainly commercial firms, and eight source mainly from artisans and farmers. Among German chefs, a very similar pattern prevails, but the use of small farmers and locals butchers is a little more prevalent. Berlin chef Christian Lohse, for example, who has the largest number of suppliers—130—pursues a mixed strategy but for him *most* suppliers are still artisans or farmers.

Using mainly commercial suppliers may be motivated by ensuring greater reliability of supply on the part of larger restaurants. A chef points out: 'Artisan providers cannot always guarantee the volume. But they provide service.' This is confirmed by London chef Brett Graham:

> There may be some fabulous quality produce from artisan providers but you simply can't run dishes based on their produce every day on the Carte because the volume isn't there—from time to time we may be able to support them through specials on the menu.

However, using commercial suppliers may also be prompted by market considerations as small producers tend to be a little more expensive. A mixed strategy, several chefs suggest, would be to balance the higher cost and quality of specialist suppliers with the slightly lower cost, but lesser distinctiveness of most commercial ones.

One type of highly specialist and very small supplier (often only one person) is a forager for wild herbs and/or mushrooms, made fashionable in recent years by Danish chef René Redzepi. According to the trade magazine *Restaurant*:

> the inexorable rise of foraging has led to…a desire to seek out undiscovered ingredients and revive those that had otherwise been forgotten. Chefs wanted to source ingredients that were rare and, even better, practically unheard of.[8]

Foragers are used by eight British and eleven German chefs. A particularly enthusiastic adherent of foraging is British Sat Bains who employs his own Danish forager to get rare herbs and salad leaves from hedgerows in the fairly urban environment of his Nottingham restaurant.

The highest degree of distinctiveness—indeed a singularity—is achieved by cultivating your own garden for herbs and salad crops. Among British chefs, Nigel Haworth, Frances Atkins, and Simon Rogan have developed particularly large and interesting gardens. In Simon Rogan's plot, particular attention is paid to rare, unusual, and top varieties, as well as miniature varieties, such as Russian kale, anise hyssop, and purple cauliflower. Rogan points out that having a garden/farm:

enables us to have complete control over the size of vegetables and the quality. We can use parts you don't usually get from suppliers, such as the roots, leaves and flowers.[9]

Among German chefs, those in a *Landgasthof* commonly have their own gardens, as do Johannes King on the North Sea island of Sylt and Sören Anders (then) in the one-star Karlsruhe restaurant *Oberländer Weinstuben*. Even a two-star chef in the capital Berlin, Michael Hoffmann (not among my interviewees), who specializes in vegetable (vegetal rather than vegetarian) cuisine, runs a large kitchen garden outside Berlin where he grows rare and unusual vegetables.

This 'do-it-yourself' practice is taken even further by chef Stephen Harris of the starred gastro pub *The Sportsman*, at Seasalter in Kent. He cultivates in-house artisan activities, such as curing of ham, air-drying of mackerel, butter churning, and extraction of sea salt. Harris additionally is devoted to local sourcing. A former history teacher, he says:

> It [the area in Kent which contains estuary and saltmarsh] is one of the few genuine *terroirs* in the UK, best thought of as an interconnecting series of geological and geographical facts. You can see a high proportion of the ingredients from the pub—the lamb grazing on the fields outside, we pick our seaweed from the beach, the veges [sic] come from down the road, and the shellfish comes out of the estuary.[10]

Additionally, baking your own bread is a common and very worthwhile practice among chefs in both countries, as freshly baked bread usually gets a meal off to a promising and sometimes intriguing start. Even the butter that goes with the bread may be carefully sourced from a specialist as when two-star chef Sat Bains gets his butter 'made bespoke' by Lincolnshire Poacher Butter. All these practices are clearly not based on a motivation to keep down costs but, by promoting distinctiveness, are closer to the inspired world of worth.

How to Cultivate Suppliers

In addition to finding and selecting distinctive suppliers, chefs have to strive to maintain long and close relationships with them, in order to receive high and reliable value from the relationship. Relations, in most cases, involve daily contact, either by phone or in person. Chefs aim to receive not merely suppliers' produce but also recommendations on what is new or special and, in some cases, advice on what would suit the chef's particular cuisine. British one-star chef Phil Thompson even singles out suppliers when talking about sources of inspiration for creativity, and this is implied also by German three-star chef Elverfeld (see below).

A British supplier of speciality cheeses to eight northern Michelin restaurants makes it clear that he feels as passionately about food as do the chefs: 'It's not about cheese only. They get my passion. I care about the industry.' He also tells me that he often has to act as a quasi-agony aunt and information point for chefs who lack the necessary social skills. In many such relationships the commercial element has receded into the background. Instead, they are more properly located in the domestic or, in some cases, in the inspired world of worth.

Suppliers are often regarded as friends and/or as almost an integral part of the restaurant, that is, as people you trust. British chef Alan Murchison tells me: 'My supplier of fruit and vegetables is my daughter's godfather.' Galton Blackiston's long-time supplier of line-caught fish, the Norfolk Fish Company, describes their relationship 'almost as husband and wife'. And German chef Jacob Stüttgen says: 'The supplier is part of our enterprise. Good relations are very important.' Munich chef Gamba knows how to ensure such reciprocity: 'I invite them to eat in the restaurant so that they can see for themselves what I require.' Scottish chef Tom Kitchin (not among my interviewees) fully engages with his suppliers:

> there are so many things that you have to understand about the suppliers' jobs and it is really grounding to know what these guys do to supply to our restaurants.[11]

Finally, Sat Bains sums it all up when he calls the small artisan suppliers 'the heroes of our industry'.

Sometimes 'domestic' values of trust and respect are born out of a common craft culture. Suppliers, particularly producers, are held in high regard and sometimes are viewed, particularly by German chefs, as fellow craftspersons who share their superior knowledge about certain products with chefs. Chefs, in turn, will advise suppliers on what is in demand or what would be worth adopting or developing. One German chef, Rainer Maria Halbedel, also points out that to retain good relations with suppliers he always pays on time. That this practice is not ubiquitous may be gleaned from a remark by former British restaurateur Nicolas Lander,[12] when he says that relationships can go wrong when a restaurateur treats his supplier as an important source of credit, i.e. he does not pay on time.

That modes of sourcing can be closely connected with culinary originality and innovation is shown by two short accounts of the sourcing practices of first, two-star London chef, Brett Graham of *The Ledbury* (Box 8.1) and, second, of three-star German chef Sven Elverfeld, of Wolfsburg's *Aqua* (Box 8.2). While most of the chefs I interviewed in the two countries have sufficiently small networks of suppliers to maintain such highly personalized relationships, this may prove a little more difficult for those chefs with between 90 and 130 suppliers. In these larger establishments purchasing may also be delegated to a second head chef or to a *sous* chef, and in some hotels there is also

---

Box 8.1 EXEMPLARY SOURCING PRACTICES I

Brett Graham is somewhat unusual among London chefs in that he stays very close to his suppliers. He not merely telephones his suppliers but he *interacts* with them and communicates exactly what he wants. He wants both highly seasonal produce and some unusual ingredients, like, for example, fig leaves, and the root, leaves, and stalks of English wasabi. Graham displays a very high degree of knowledge about produce. Thus he gets his fillet beef from a single farm in Cumbria, utilizing only meat from the top 2–3 per cent of the farmer's herd of Belted Galloway cattle. Furthermore, he specifies exactly what cuts he wants, namely from the narrow end of the chateaubriand for their superior flavour. His intimate knowledge of game—he hunts himself—allows him to buy in exactly the period when meat from male deer is at its best, i.e. before the start of the mating season. It is this combination of the unusual and the carefully selected food at the top of its life-cycle that endows his cuisine with originality, as well as providing exceptionally intense flavours.

Box 8.2 EXEMPLARY SOURCING PRACTICES II

Sven Elverfeld's three-star Wolfsburg restaurant *Aqua* is not large—it has only thirty-six covers. Yet he has invested a lot of time and energy into the identification of a sizeable number of interesting suppliers and unusual produce. Elverfeld has forty-five core suppliers altogether, of whom about twenty are producers.

> There are many suppliers from whom I get only one product. Thus I have five to eight suppliers for meat, including a huntsman, and I have a man who gathers snails in the Odenwald (a forest) for me. One producer is called Edible Landscape—he is quite small, and I have just bought 30 kilos of tips of pine trees from him. I also have someone who plants rare potatoes and another producer who grows very tiny salad plants.

Elverfeld is not sourcing only from the region—Hessen—which does not have a notable food heritage. He selects suppliers and producers from the whole of Germany, as well as having suppliers in France, Japan, Spain, and Greece: 'I myself found very special tomatoes in Spain and have built contacts.'

Elverfeld is concerned to establish long-term relations. He nevertheless changes suppliers when his new ideas for flavours and dishes, such as developing a flavour conveying the essence of fir trees, makes the adoption of a new supplier necessary:

'Around 70 per cent of my suppliers are from when I started here. When I started I travelled round the region [to find interesting suppliers].'

---

a central office for purchasing. In London restaurants, too, relations may be less personal. As one London chef remarks: 'You do not get as much rapport with suppliers as outside London—it is less personal and one is too busy.'

A second way to develop and maintain close relationships is to retain the same suppliers for a long time. Most chefs in both Britain and Germany emphasize that they have had their core suppliers for a long time—usually for as long as they have been head chef or chef proprietor. Tom Kerridge speaks for many other chefs when he says: 'I like not to chop and change but to build a relationship.' German two-star chef Henkel confirms: 'Some of them [the suppliers] I have had for an eternity—fourteen years. It is a very personal relationship.' In several cases, chefs have retained suppliers they have worked with in a previous restaurant or locality, such as British Claude Bosi and German Christian Lohse.

It is interesting that there is no difference between the practices of British and German chefs, concerning the long duration and closeness of supplier relations. For British chefs, such a practice is exceptional in the wider British economy. It departs from the more general British business rule of firms maintaining shorter-term, arm's length relations, as compared with German manufacturing firms.[13] This widespread short-termism in manufacturing is connected with the embeddedness in a financial system which encourages or even compels managers to make quick returns on capital. In this respect, too, the high-end restaurant is 'a very peculiar' business, probably due to the fact that entanglement with financial institutions is uncommon. However, sometimes this loyalty to suppliers may get in the way of the adoption of new ones and thereby may obstruct innovation. Thus, some chefs, despite their long-termism, still look out for suppliers with new produce.

I have so far shown that, by and large, market values are not at the forefront of relationships between chefs and suppliers but that domestic/craft and inspired evaluations are prominent. A higher price may be paid for a quality product from a small producer at the cost of slightly lowering chefs' profit. Many chefs, as argued in Chapter 3, pursue merely 'sufficient profit'. British chef Sat Bains explains:

> We decided that the quality we get far outweighs the financial gains. Don't get me wrong, we all need to make a living but . . . the profit may not be as high as it could be, but I'm willing to take the hit for the sake of flavour.

All this is not to say, however, that chefs abandon any ideas of matching produce buying to the prices they are able to charge for meals. They are very much aware of the fact that keeping the price of produce within bounds must be at the forefront of exercises of cost containment. 'Making a living' does not usually mean haggling over prices but is more about buying judiciously (e.g. to buy when produce is in season and therefore is plentiful and cheaper) and exercising moderation in making indulgent choices of luxury products.

Most chefs carefully judge what proportion of purchased foods may be luxury products, like lobster, caviar, langoustines, or wagyu beef. A few chefs who are deeply concerned to keep prices (relatively) low for customers, such as, for instance, head chef Colin Kelly of *Wild Honey* or Tom Kerridge of *Hand & Flowers*, use a mere 5 per cent of such luxury products, while a few other chefs keep the proportion of luxury products down as a matter of principle.

Overall, however, the proportion of luxury products used fluctuates quite a bit. British chefs, at one end of the scale, estimate a use of luxury products of between 10 and 20 per cent, and, at the other end, of between 50 and 70 per cent. The four highest users of luxury products include two London two-star chefs, as well as two provincial one-star chefs. The picture is very similar in Germany, although the number using a high proportion of luxury products— between 40 and 50 per cent—is slightly higher. As in Britain, the high users are arbitrarily divided between the star categories. The one-star restaurant with the highest use—100 per cent—significantly is situated in one of the hotels that cross-subsidizes its restaurant.

A third strategy to keep down prices (which is unusual among the chefs I interviewed) consists of the adoption of industrial principles of efficiency through scale. This strategy, maintained by some chef proprietors who own more than one restaurant, is bulk-buying for several restaurants at the same time. This, it is believed, makes you a more valued customer who is offered a better price, and, in one case, is said to make haggling possible. Chef Colin Kelly of *Wild Honey* assures me that, despite haggling, he still is getting the best quality:

> We demand the best stuff nevertheless. The quantity of the order counts. We often share food over all three restaurants. So if a supplier offers me twenty poussins at a good price I will take them and share what I do not need with *Arbutus* or *Les Deux Salons*.

However, it seems unlikely that a business practice like haggling keeps intact the special collegial quality of supplier relations aspired to by most chefs. A second chef practising some bulk-buying for three restaurants, Martin Wishart, notes that this strategy has to be applied with care. If you want to retain the distinctiveness of your Michelin-starred restaurant you can bulk-buy only those basic products, like pasta or potatoes, which do not contribute to the individual character of dishes. His Reading colleague Alan Murchison agrees.

Local Sourcing or Locavorism

In addition to shaping the quality, distinctiveness, and price of products, a chef's supplier network also may express his or her overall philosophy or moral values. This is the case with the adoption or rejection of a pronounced localism of cuisine, that is, sourcing mainly in the locality, variously defined. (For definitions, see Chapter 5.) I find a range of attitudes by chefs on the issue of localism, as well as on related ethical questions.

An emphasis on a moral motivation for the choice of a strategy of localism cannot neatly be divided from adopting a market orientation. The adoption of an ethical stance, even if based on sincerely held principles, still serves to create a market niche. The latter was particularly likely when localism, often inspired by Redzepi's culinary philosophy, first became prominent. Once it is quite widely adopted it fails to have this niche-creation effect. Localism, however, is not always a fashionable attitude but, as is the case in some German regionally oriented chefs, expresses older attachments to a particular region's culinary traditions.

In both countries, consumers now are more concerned with the provenance of the food on their plates.[14] According to the 2007 German Apolinaris study of taste, based on a nationally representative sample of 1,000 respondents, provenance is important or very important to 86 per cent of the German population, and German produce is preferred. Norfolk chef Galton Blackiston believes that his customers expect and appreciate local provenance of produce: 'People are interested in provenance; they want to trust when they go out.' My interviews with diners show that people broadly appreciate local sourcing yet many diners no longer expect that chefs adhere to local sourcing. (For details, see Chapter 9.)

It is notable that several chefs, particularly in Britain, define 'local' extremely flexibly, counting as local anything produced in Britain, as, for instance, London chefs Marcus Wareing and Phil Howard respectively:

[Local sourcing is] very important, but by local I mean British . . . You have to support your own country. We have great meat, game, and fish in the UK.

Local sourcing is very important to me. Local means southern England, but also UK supplier/producers.

Quite a few British chefs regard localism as a merely fashionable endeavour which may interfere with obtaining the best-quality produce. Thus one-star Birmingham chef Glynn Purnell comments:

Local sourcing is very important, but I am not blinded by the local product. In the end, Scottish beef tastes better. Quality is the first consideration.

One-star London chef Sriram Aylur agrees: 'Local sourcing is very important as long as one can get the quality required.' One-star Cumbrian chef Colin McLaughlin asserts: 'If it's local and good, great! But if not, I look further afield.' And one-star Welwyn chef Phil Thompson argues: 'Just because it's local it is not the best.' Another British chef who still receives a lot of produce from Paris declares: ' "Local" is a bit of a myth. You have to get quality wherever it is available.'

Local sourcing also makes less sense in the case of Italian or ethnic restaurants. Thus both chefs of British and German restaurants devoted to Italian cuisine do not buy regionally: 'Our suppliers are located all over Britain from

Scotland to the south, including agents in London dealing with Italian goods from Milan'; it depends on 'where you can obtain the best'; 'It has to stay within Europe, but quality not proximity is decisive.'[15]

Several British chefs are somewhat sceptical about the philosophy's relevance to restaurants in a highly urbanized setting. Thus, one British chef who had moved from a relatively rural county to London finds that 'Local suppliers are more difficult in London.' London two-star chef Brett Graham confirms: '[I source locally] as much as possible. You are in London—what can you do?' Even a chef in a southern county close to London finds localism difficult: 'Local sourcing is not important in this location.'

Nevertheless, there are some British chefs who make a point of relying mainly on regional produce. Three examples—significantly all are located in geographically peripheral locations—are Nigel Haworth at Langho, near Burnley in Lancashire (Box 8.3), Galton Blackiston from Morston on the Norfolk coast (Box 8.4), and Tom Kitchin (not in my sample) in Edinburgh.

Box 8.3 A BRITISH CHEF DEVOTED TO LOCAL SOURCING I

One-star chef Nigel Haworth of *Northcote Manor* says: 'Local sourcing is a top priority and drives the whole enterprise.' Haworth has many core suppliers, and a lot of them are located in Lancashire and Yorkshire. He has taken the trouble systematically to develop his network of suppliers/producers, including small, artisanal ones, such as a Whitby supplier of smoked kippers 'who needed a lot of persuasion to become my supplier'. One small agricultural supplier specializes in small cauliflowers (tennis ball cauliflowers) and another is 'a carrot grower who has gained nationwide fame and has built a multi-million business although he can neither read nor write'. What the *Northcote* restaurant cannot get from local suppliers, they grow themselves, 'such as wild herbs—nettle, bitter cress and wild garlic'.

Box 8.4 A BRITISH CHEF DEVOTED TO LOCAL SOURCING II

For Galton Blackiston, who has had most of his twelve core suppliers for around twenty years, local sourcing is 'massively [important]...It makes sense to use what is on your door step...Norfolk produce is up there with the best.'

Local for him means that 'all but one[of my suppliers] are in East Anglia'. Among his suppliers are several agricultural ones, some artisans, some fishermen, a few producers, as well as foragers for mushrooms and wild herbs. Among the produce he sources are:

traditional Norfolk sheep called Norfolk Horns—one of oldest breeds in Britain. A butcher supplies me with game, and a local farm rears a rare breed of pig, while a commercial seafood company deals only in local line-caught fish.[a]

[a] Interview with Galton Blackiston in *The Morston Hall Anniversary Magazine 2012*.

Box 8.5 A GERMAN CHEF DEVOTED TO LOCAL SOURCING

One example of a strongly locally oriented chef is two-star chef Johannes King of the *Soel'ring Hof*, on the north German island of Sylt. He tells me:

> We have over forty suppliers—eight suppliers for fish, twenty-five for groceries, a baker, and eight producers with whom we cooperate directly. We also have our own garden and catch some of our sea fish with our own boat....It is very expensive to go fishing like this yourself. I send employees with the handyman [who runs the boat]. Everything is better understood by them after they have accompanied him—they learn a better appreciation of the fish. All but one of my suppliers are in Schleswig-Holstein [the local state]. The one non-local supplier is for French products. The suppliers are farmers, fishermen, and craftsmen and some are just commercial suppliers. I visit the suppliers twice per annum and the producers once.

Scottish Tom Kitchin adheres to a 'fearsomely local "from nature to plate" philosophy' and champions Scottish produce which he believes to be second to none. He says:

> I have guys who are shooting my hares and venison to order. I speak to the guy who dives for my scallops; I know the names of all the captains on the fishing boats and I'm learning about the weather.[16]

In Germany, localism is more widely embraced by chefs (Box 8.5). Rather than being a recent fashion—although fashion is not absent among German chefs—localism indicates the survival/revival of a more deeply entrenched regionalism in some areas of Germany than in Britain, as already elaborated in Chapters 1 and 6.

The motivations for local sourcing are very diverse: support of the local economy; keeping local growers in business; or ethical motivations, such as reducing the food mileages or supporting sustainability. Hamburg chef Ali Güngörmüs has his own reason for supporting the local economy: 'If the region flourishes, customers will come.' London chef Sriram Aylur favours localism both for 'environmental reasons and to support local business'. London two-star chefs Marcus Wareing and Phil Howard express concern for sustainability: 'Yes, [I support local sourcing for ethical reasons]—we don't use endangered shellfish species'; 'We do have ecological concerns and sustainability is very important, but there's always compromise.'

Berlin chef Christian Lohse takes his ecological ideals extremely seriously: 'We are fighters for sustainability. I went to a tribunal to oppose Monsanto over potatoes and won the case.' German three-star chef Elverfeld also expresses ethical concerns:

> I care where products come from, and local products are preferred. For example, char from fresh, river water and its caviar. I also care about how the animals have been raised. I spend a lot of time with my suppliers.

For some chefs local sourcing is practised simply because local produce is perceived to be best. Martin Wishart sees Scotland excel in its local produce: 'Scotland has the best ingredients.' Bavarian chef Jacob Stüttgen shares this local food patriotism: 'The region offers so many great products.'

The Wider Impact of Chefs' Sourcing Practices

Agricultural and artisanal producers are sought after not only by chefs and their customers but also have a wider beneficial impact. They aim to counteract the industrialization of food production by large companies, as well as the loss of many varieties of vegetables, fruit, and animals. The latter were not deemed suitable for profitable commercialization in the past by these same companies. By providing incentives for the start-up of small niche firms and subsequently keeping them alive and even flourishing, high-end chefs have a positive impact on our food supply which goes well beyond their relatively small customer base. Such producers obviously cannot turn back the clock of the thoroughgoing industrialization of food. They nevertheless keep alive the idea of local, fresh, and high-quality food, as well as, in a few cases, resuscitating varieties of vegetables, fruit, and herbs, as well as animal breeds which otherwise would have been lost to us. They have influenced some high-quality supermarkets and, particularly in Germany, also find outlets in the excellent food markets many cities maintain.

The revival of old, as well as the creation of new, varieties has been particularly prolific in the area of cheese-making. Thus, in Britain, until the late 1950s, most people equated cheese with industrialized cheddar. In contrast, we currently can buy not only many varieties of tasty cheddar but also several kinds of revived regional cheese, as well as completely new varieties. One twenty-five-year-old company has played an influential role in this revitalization of cheese supply. It is a small Cheshire company buying cheese from a network of small producers—mainly family-owned artisan and/or agricultural producers—in the north-west of Britain, to sell on to high-end restaurants and specialist cheese retailers.[17]

A German firm with an entirely different assortment of foods that has capitalized on chefs' search for distinctive wild foods is Essbare Landschaften (Edible Landscapes). The small business, run by a gardener and a former chef/ restaurateur, cultivates long-forgotten herbs and vegetables, as well as wild herbs and edible flowers. It now sells all over Europe. Another producer who has rescued endangered and/or forgotten varieties of vegetable is former teacher Peter Kunze who grows a large number of varieties of tomatoes and peppers, among them many previously forgotten ones.

In Germany, where most rivers now have been decontaminated, freshwater fish is again on the menus of fine-dining restaurants, and small producers have sprung up to supply chefs. One such supplier in southern Germany is Franz von Wiederer who sells freshwater fish, such as several varieties of carp, pike, perch, and tench, from the ponds of his own estate in Franconia.

Another tale of the revival of a forgotten fruit by a small-scale producer—again from Franconia—is that of Marius Wittur. He discovered an overgrown hedge of quince which, since the land consolidation in the 1960s, had become forgotten and totally overgrown. He and his partner then set out to search for other such hedges, and Wittur now cultivates fifty varieties of quince in his orchard and produces wine and juice from them.[18]

Conclusions

This chapter has drawn attention to the fact that chefs in high-end restaurants work in an interdependent manner with their suppliers. They seek out and sustain suppliers who guarantee them quality and freshness of produce which often has an inherent inspirational quality. They thereby also realize the frequently elusive goal of achieving distinction from other chefs. The more chefs can source from small specialist suppliers and particularly from artisan, agricultural, or other independent producers, the greater becomes their scope for originality. On the downside, for chefs, particularly those with two or three stars, this necessitates the building and maintenance of a supplier network which is larger and more complex than their relatively small number of covers makes economic. Deploying such a varied supplier network requires a considerable effort on the part of head chefs on top of, and very much as a condition of, inspired work in the kitchen. Maintaining such a supplier network necessitates the building and cultivation of relationships in which the commercial element often takes second place to a collegial relationship of trust and an exchange of knowledge and expertise. Such a relationship usually is long-term. Selection and maintenance of suppliers additionally require a constant balancing act between choosing cheaper ingredients, which nevertheless can be 'ennobled' by skilful cooking, and luxury produce which some, though by no means all, diners (see Chapter 9) still expect from a Michelin-starred restaurant.

Hence in this part of their work, too, fine-dining chefs are confronted with the demands of competing orders of worth. Market considerations appear uppermost only for a very small number of the chefs; hence most of them manage the opposed demands of the different orders of worth with relative ease. They prioritize considerations of quality, freshness, and distinctiveness over purely market ones, without completely losing sight of the latter.

I have also indicated that some scepticism is in order when confronted with claims about freshness and associated short supply routes in particular. Some basic foodstuffs, such as some varieties of fish and free-range chickens, may simply no longer be available in Britain and Germany in sufficient quantity, and some produce, such as lobster, is still believed to be best if sourced from France. Also often a so-called 'local' supplier is simply an intermediary with their own network of producers, not all of whom are local. Moreover, ordering in French products, for many chefs, is by no means a 'thing of the past'.

British and German chefs alike experience the requirements of keeping up long-term and close relationships with their suppliers, and in both countries such relationships have been forged by chefs. In the British case, such close and longer-term relationships depart from the national business norm, due to the business format of fine-dining restaurants as small and entrepreneurial undertakings with a high concern for quality. A cross-national difference is that German chefs appear to be able to draw on a larger number of producers, reflecting the prominence in German business culture of the notion of 'craft'. The mix of suppliers of British chefs, on average, is slightly more skewed towards commercial suppliers.

Notes

1. E. Barlösius, 'Soziale und historische Aspekte der deutschen Küche', postscript to S. Mennell, *Die Kultivierung des Appetits. Die Geschichte des Essens vom Mittelalter bis heute* (Frankfurt: Athenäum, 1988), 33–44, 440.
2. M. Roux, Jnr., *A Life in the Kitchen* (London: Weidenfeld & Nicolson, 2009); R. Blanc, *A Taste of My Life: One Man's Hunger for Perfection* (London: Transworld Publishers, 2008).
3. *Gault Millau Deutschland* (2013): 13–14.
4. Communication from former Michelin chef Bill Brogan, now catering manager of a Cambridge college, 8 July 2007.
5. Kingfisher's website, <http://www.kingfisherbrixham.co.uk/>.
6. Kingfisher's website, <http://www.kingfisherbrixham.co.uk/>.
7. *Restaurant* (January 2011); Aubrey Allen Ltd., company website, <http://www.aubreyallen.co.uk/>.
8. *Restaurant* (May 2012): 56.
9. Interview with Simon Rogan by *Restaurant* (2012).
10. *Restaurant* (January 2012): 36–41.
11. *Yes Chef! Magazine* 12 (2010): 23.
12. N. Lander, *The Art of the Restaurateur* (London: Phaidon, 2012), 224.
13. C. Lane and R. Bachmann, 'Co-operation in Inter-Firm Relations in Britain and Germany: The Role of Social Institutions', *British Journal of Sociology* 48.2

(1997): 226–54; C. Lane and J. Probert, *National Capitalisms, Global Production Networks* (Oxford: Oxford University Press, 2009).

14. *Restaurant* (September 2011): 71–2; Apollinaris Studie 2007. Geschmack 2006. <http://hottelling.net/2007/09/14/apollinaris-studie-geschmack-2007-deutsche-kuche-bleibt-der-renner/>.

15. *Restaurant* (October 2010).

16. *Yes Chef! Magazine* 12 (2010): 23.

17. Interview with a company representative.

18. *Der Feinschmecker* 10 (2009): 79–80.

9

Diners: In Search of Gustatory Pleasure or Symbolic Meaning?

Eating out has become a widely pursued leisure activity, open to all but the poorest members of contemporary society. This change has occurred in recent decades, from about the 1970s onwards. (See Chapter 1.) It partly reflects the fact that consumers are coming to favour the consumption of experience over that of traditional goods and services.

In contrast to eating out in general, dining in high-end restaurants differs in many respects from the trend described above. Despite a considerable democratization during recent decades, there nevertheless remain important differences between social classes and educational groups as to the form and place of eating out, as well as to its frequency.[1] Both economic and cultural barriers to dining in *haute cuisine* restaurants persist. However, these have become less formidable today than they were even a few decades ago. A tension between elitism and democratization nevertheless permeates all interactions of customers frequenting fine-dining restaurants.[2]

To enjoy a meal in such a restaurant, the French sociologist Pierre Bourdieu points out, the customer has to possess both economic and cultural capital (education, specialist knowledge, and social poise and confidence).[3] The possession of these two types of capital restricts the social milieu from which customers of fine-dining restaurants are recruited. However, contrary to Bourdieu, the social origins of their diners are no longer solely the upper- and upper middle-classes. As a general rule, diners now come from a broader swathe of society, among which the professional-managerial strata are particularly prominent. They do not necessarily own wealth, and many enjoy comfortable, rather than very high incomes. Moreover, their cultural capital often is more important than their economic capital in negotiating the social demands of fine-dining restaurants.

Christopher Driver—a former editor of the *Good Food Guide*—even goes as far as claiming that social division in food consumption

> arrives not where incomes rise and fall, but where some people decide that eating (as opposed to nourishment) is as important to them or their sub-culture as football or golf are to others.[4]

Driver contends that people set different priorities in how they spend their income and that, if only money capital were concerned, even a section of the working-class could afford occasional visits to top-of-the market restaurants. Furthermore, diners in Michelin-starred restaurants are not a homogeneous social group. The main distinction in terms of economic capital possessed may be drawn between the wealthy who dine there fairly regularly (and may not always pay themselves) and those who have lower financial resources and enjoy this pleasure only intermittently.

I also contest Bourdieu's related claim that engagement in fine-dining seeks to establish and signal an exclusive and superior taste. Following other writers in the field of culture,[5] I shall argue that the above-mentioned sections of the middle-class now are cultural *omnivores*, rather than cultural snobs. Omnivorousness in cultural consumption and taste in general is defined by sociologist Tony Bennett and his colleagues as 'an openness to diversity and a cultivated agility with respect to judgements of taste'. [6] Applied to those dining out in top restaurants in particular, omnivorousness suggests that individuals, for a variety of reasons, also visit lower-level restaurants, such as ethnic restaurants, pubs, bistros or middle-level chain restaurants. They have quite catholic tastes although they may still have a scale of preferences. However, I will also suggest that, in contrast to other areas of cultural consumption, such as music, there are limits to omnivorousness, in that the lowest level of eating out, namely in fast-food establishments, generally is not culturally accepted by this social group.

By dining out, sociologist Joanne Finkelstein suggests, individuals 'cultivate and transpose the act of eating into a more socially complex and meaningful activity'.[7] Both diners and chefs I interviewed regard dining in Michelin-starred restaurants as a general cultural experience where bodily sustenance recedes into the background and the symbolic qualities of dining are uppermost. As first pointed out by Bourdieu, the banality of eating is lifted to a higher symbolic level. The symbolic qualities pursued more or less consciously vary between groups of diners, but some common qualities are discernible.

Two main sets of cultural values may be associated with fine-dining. Probably the most important is to gain a pleasurable general experience that takes you out of the ordinary and humdrum everyday life of work and home. It includes enjoyment of the entertainment value and excitement of a meal in an innovative Michelin-starred restaurant, partly derived from the theatricality of the setting and the drama of the presentation of the food. It is constituted not only by the consumption of delicious and often novel foods and wines, but also by the receipt of attentive and friendly personal service, all enjoyed in a pleasant ambience. These elements together act as mood enhancers which transport diners for a few hours into a different and highly agreeable world.

Closely related is the experience of a heightened conviviality, fuelled by the bonhomie generated by excellent food and wine. As noted already at the beginning of the nineteenth century by Brillat-Savarin:

> gourmandism is one of the principal bonds of society; for it is gourmandism which gradually draws out that convivial spirit which everyday brings all sorts together, moulds them into a single whole, sets them talking, and rounds off the sharp corners of conventional inequality.[8]

Whether Brillat-Savarin was a little optimistic about the power of gourmandism to bring together 'all sorts' will be investigated below.

The second important aspect of fine-dining is to achieve the symbolic gratification of social distinction, understood in a variety of ways. This includes being seen in an elegant and expensive restaurant and thus being marked out as financially well-endowed and socially privileged. Enhanced social status also may be derived from appearing socially competent and/or fashionable, as well as displaying fine taste in subsequent conversations with friends and colleagues. Symbolic value additionally flows from being granted superior status by highly attentive service staff and the rituals of deference they enact. Last, diners may seek to acquire new specialist knowledge about food and wine and expand their competence about methods of cooking and serving food which, in turn, may generate social distinction.

The social historian Burnett well sums up some of the experiences provided when he says that eating out in a top restaurant

> is an important aspect of the modern culture of leisure and entertainment, offering a sense of other worlds, desires and fantasies in which people can imagine themselves more empowered, fashionable and sophisticated, more accustomed to superior standards than in their everyday lives.[9]

Last, I wish to critically examine Finkelstein's slightly different argument that dining in a top restaurant encourages a style of social interaction which produces an 'uncivilized sociality'. By this she means that

> the artifice of the restaurant makes dining out a mannered exercise disciplined by customs that locate us in a framework of prefigured actions.[10]

Dining out, she further claims,

> is thoroughly regulated by social prescriptions which relieve us from responsibility of thinking how and why we should act in a certain way.[11]

We simply imitate others and respond to fashion.

Altogether, dining in a top-level restaurant is widely viewed as a highly complex social activity that raises numerous questions about both the social identity of diners and about the social effects connected with fine-dining. It poses basic issues about elitism versus democratization and about exclusive taste versus a more widely diffused access to *haute cuisine*. As the German critical magazine *Der Spiegel* points out: 'He who is on the tracks of the culinary class society, finds material everywhere.'[12]

The above issues concern not only the diners. They are also posed for the providers of the dining experience, that is, for chefs. Many a group of diners spend more on their evening's food and wine than most of the chefs' net earnings per month,[13] and chef patrons' class origins and education mostly put them outside the middle-classes.

To engage in a sustained manner with the issues posed above, I will draw on the material derived from interviews with both chefs (40) and diners (32) in Britain and Germany. These interview data, taken together, provide some insights which confirm other findings on dining out in top restaurants, as well as yielding some new knowledge regarding these issues.

The Social Background of Diners

The Views of Chefs

My question to chefs about the social background of their customers invariably yields answers such as 'all sorts'; 'a complete mix'; 'right across the social spectrum'; 'the social profile is very varied—[customers] range from billionaire to local authority worker'; and '[the social profile ranges] right across society—from members of the DAX (list of German quoted companies) to relatively simple people. They are all keen to eat good food.'

Chefs are not comfortable with admitting that they cater mainly for the relatively socially privileged. Those who acknowledge elitism try to counteract this impression by mentioning measures they have introduced to mitigate an impression of social exclusiveness. The restaurant manager of a large one-star London restaurant tells me:

> It is hard to argue against elitism from the point of view of cost, but the atmosphere is very inclusive. There is no dress code [he wore light jeans], and we offer value for money. Also we try not to intimidate people—we put little cutlery on the table but relevant cutlery is brought for each dish.

British two-star chef Raymond Blanc is similarly trying to play down elitism:

> I hold republican values but was overseeing a restaurant and hotel that apparently catered for the rich. I tried to make *Le Manoir* as inclusive as possible.[14]

German-Turkish chef Ali Güngörmüs is explicit about not liking exclusivity: 'all [of the social categories I specified] come in equal proportions. I do not want only the rich to come.'

A further question about service staff's knowledge of the social status of customers frequently elicits responses such as that no social distinctions are ever made between guests and that all are treated in strictly the same way:

> Intelligent service staff will recognize this [differences in the social background of guests]. They will become aware of it, but they must not betray this awareness. Every guest is equal. (German one-star chef)

> This [differences in social status between diners] is not at all important. Wealth and status are not of interest. (German three-star chef)

The restaurant manager of a British one-star restaurant believes that: 'Yes, staff are aware of different [social] backgrounds, but without being classist.' And two British two-star chefs comment: 'We do not do VIP here but treat all customers the same'; 'Service staff talk to customers without prejudice—everyone is equally important.'

Only when I follow up with a question of which social category predominates among their customers, does a more differentiated and accurate picture emerge. This picture, however, does not totally invalidate chefs' first reaction. The social composition of diners is indeed quite varied, depending both on the time of day (lunch or dinner) and the time of the week (working week versus weekend), as well as according to the geographical location and star category of the restaurant. But it is nevertheless clear that, given the high prices for food and drink, the socially privileged classes predominate. Diners largely belong to the professional and managerial middle-classes who are economically moderately well off, but whose cultural capital usually is higher than their money capital. More exceptionally, diners are small business owners/self-employed on a comfortable income. A German one-star chef sums it up like this: 'They [the guests] are not rich but well-to-do older people, and a very small proportion of younger people.'

Nevertheless, all chefs report also a wider social constituency. While working-class diners rarely patronize fine-dining restaurants, one section of the clientele—chefs—form a significant proportion of their customers. Several chef patrons spontaneously mention that other chefs—their peer group—are among their frequent customers. Seeking inspiration for innovation from 'looking into the pots and pans of other chefs' is a common practice in this trade.

In large urban centres, such as London, Frankfurt, and Munich, business people, often on expense accounts, are said to predominate during lunch-times and during the working week. During other times, less wealthy people also come, though mostly on a more intermittent basis and/or to celebrate a special occasion. Thus a British one-star chef with a lot of corporate business insists that: 'the wealthy are not the majority. Forty per cent are corporate; sixty per cent are individuals, mainly foodies.'

Two further British one-star chefs confirm the socially mixed nature of their customers:

> Business people may predominate at lunch time. In the evenings and at week-ends it is more mixed and more Edinburgh.

> [We get] some business people [but also] elderly retired people at lunch-time and younger people—also from further afield—in the evenings. We also are a destination restaurant for special celebrations.

Two German two-star chefs convey the same picture:

> It [the social profile of customers] is very varied, but 80 per cent are individual guests and 20 per cent business people. We definitely attract also less wealthy people—young people who have saved up for it.

> A lot of business people; many higher-level professionals, but also many younger people who have saved up to come to us.

A longitudinal analysis of the guest list of the two-star Munich restaurant *Tantris* by its owner shows also a predominance of professionals among the guests, albeit high-earning independent professionals, such as doctors and lawyers, as well as independent business owners.[15] As was pointed out in Chapter 2, in Germany the number of customers dining on expense accounts is said to have declined significantly in recent years, due to changed rules for tax relief.[16]

Many restaurants, particularly those in a rural location, have no business diners on expense accounts at all:

> They are not business people, but are food lovers, tourists and, most of all, people who have a family celebration. We also get a lot of grouse shooters. (One-star British chef)

In restaurants situated in smaller or more remote places, the wealthy are more likely to be tourists. Yet even here social diversity comes from the weekenders, as opposed to the longer-stay residents (in the hotel of which the restaurant forms a part). Alternatively, the much more reasonably priced set lunch—in 2012 you could get a two-course lunch (or pre-theatre dinner) below £20 in sixteen British starred restaurants—attracts a wider social constituency of diners. A few chefs express a particular pleasure at attracting also the less wealthy diners who have saved up to be able to afford their prices:

They are very mixed occupationally: businessmen and employed; some rich and famous; bankers; media people; real estate. But this is the profile for weekdays. At the weekend it changes completely, and we get families and even housewives. Lovely! (One-star London chef patron)

Several chefs are trying hard to keep down their prices, so as not to exclude the less wealthy customers. Among them, the two-star *Hand & Flowers* in Marlow and the one-star *Wild Honey* in London stand out, with a two-course and a three-course lunch for £15 and £21.95 respectively served in 2012.

Even if these latter groups of diners are relatively short of economic capital they marshal it in such a way as to be able to afford an occasional treat. Also, as will be further elaborated below, the degree of social sophistication now required to visit a fine-dining restaurant has been greatly reduced. A British one-star chef patron does not exclude the possession of economic capital but rightly adds that it is not the only qualifying factor: 'People [who form the dominant category of diners in his hotel restaurant] are fairly affluent but they also have a passion for food.' One German one-star chef maintains that only cultural capital is relevant: 'People who like to eat well [form the dominant category], it is not a financial matter.'

The degree of social exclusivity also varies with the number of stars the restaurant holds. Whereas one-star restaurants charge prices even members of the moderately well-off professional middle-class can afford, two- and three-star ones require a more substantial economic investment. But even the latter may attract the deeply engaged gourmet tourists—chefs variously refer to them as 'gastro tourists', 'gourmet pilgrims', or even 'food fiends'. Their financial resources are mainly committed to visiting the world's best restaurants and their culinary capital usually exceeds their financial capital. Thus the chef of a prominent German two-star restaurant singles out gourmet tourists as an important constituency among his customers: 'We have more customers who often are guests in highly-decorated restaurants', and his *sommelier* adds a more qualitative comment:

The guests here are incredibly well informed, they are gourmet tourists. I always meet the same people again. All the guests are experienced guests.

German three-star chef Elverfeld talks about 'star pilgrims' among his more frequent guests but does not offer information about their social background. A scholar of food consumption from the University of Göttingen is less reticent about this group of 'fine diners':

There are also extremists in the field of food enjoyment, and they are increasing in number. They do food preparation as a prestige-gathering high-performance sport. Among journalists, advertising people, architects, and teachers there has arisen a cult around fine-dining which frequently borders on the hysterical.[17]

Finally, a British two-star chef provides a very concise definition of his customer base: 'The majority are…middle-class professional high-end earners who like and know their food.'

Clientele also are differentiated by age and stage in the life cycle. Younger people without the financial commitments of a family and older people on good pensions form a significant constituency of many restaurants. Although estimates vary between chefs, the bulk of diners are said to be in the age group of forty years and over; that is, people likely to be in a more senior professional-managerial position. An analysis over several years of the guest list of Munich's restaurant *Tantris* puts the proportion of thirty- to forty-year-old guests at almost 40 per cent.[18] This group includes also the younger retirees on a good pension from such former positions. Chefs welcome also younger people among their clientele. Sven Elverfeld, from Wolfsburg's *Aqua* in the Ritz Carlton, is pleased to count among his customers the young couples who come to collect their first car straight from the VW works, next door to the hotel. One British one-star chef even notes a variation in the social profile of customers according to season of the year:

> This [the social profile of customers] varies with the season. We get the aspiring Welsh middle class during the winter months. Londoners and foodie types come during the holidays. No business people. We also get less wealthy people for family celebrations.

Some of these claims by chefs about a socially mixed customer base are supported, as well as further amplified, by the diners I interviewed. They bear out the claim that diners no longer come solely from the very wealthy and/ or the upper middle-class but from a wider social, but still middle-class, constituency. Thus Mark M., a British professional employee in his late forties on a comfortable salary, who has been dining in top restaurants a few times per year since the end of his university days, sees a change in the social profile of diners over that time towards a wider social distribution:

> Restaurants have changed a lot since we first started eating in fine-dining restaurants. They are not so intimidating now. The middle-classes save up for going on high days and holidays.

Roger, a Londoner in his sixties and a retired small business owner, agrees: 'Television has increased the number of fine diners. It has made it less exclusive.'

Some of my respondents on merely 'comfortable' salaries even seek to distinguish themselves from rich diners and/or business diners on expense accounts. One of the British respondents opines: 'We were less keen on *Le Gavroche* where there is too much stench of money.' Michael, a British barrister, tells me: 'But we do not go to this category of restaurant [where many business people on expense accounts eat]—you find them in Mayfair.'

German diner Inge spontaneously suggests:

> If a restaurant contains too many business people or so-called 'Promis' (famous people) then this is a criterion for us not to go there as we wish to enjoy ourselves undisturbed by their airs and by the press.

German retired teacher Hartmuth dislikes the presence of too many 'financial elites' who can afford the high prices.

While several of my respondents fall into the category of professional-managerial employees with a high income, many others only enjoy a comfortable income. Among the eighteen British respondents, fifteen fall into the category of professional-managerial employees on a comfortable salary or, if retired, on a good pension. Among the younger members of the British sample living in London, the disposable income is not even comfortable. Thus Anna, a twenty-six-year-old managerial employee, puts herself into the category of 'ordinary people who have saved up for a special treat'. She tells me:

> I value this experience enough to sacrifice spending on other things. For instance, I have a very low phone bill, cycle in London etc., so that I save money to be able to eat out.

In the German sample, there are proportionally more respondents on a high income, that is, higher-level civil servants and managerial employees in public and private organizations (*Leitende Angestellte*), as well as one self-employed high-earning professional. My German respondents have a higher average age, and only one of the younger respondents refers to himself as 'ordinary people who have saved up for a special occasion'.

Table 9.1 shows that the relationship to fine-dining differs *within* the same social stratum according to the frequency of fine-dining. Overall numbers are relatively low, but differences in commitment to outstanding food and dining nevertheless may usefully be distinguished in proportional terms. The differing degrees of commitment will be explored in my typology of diners in Table 9.3 below.

Table 9.1 further shows that, in proportional terms, the British respondents visit fine-dining restaurants to a significantly greater extent, as compared with

Table 9.1. Visits to fine-dining restaurants per month as proportion of all restaurant visits

	1–9%	10–25%	33%	50%	70–80%	100%	No answer	Total number
British diners	7	4	2	1	2	2	0	18
German diners	6	6	0	0	1	0	1	14

Source: Author's calculations from interview data.

German diners. Only one person in Germany—lawyer Raoul—devotes more than 25 per cent of all his restaurant visits to fine-dining restaurants. This result, of course, is not statistically significant, given the size and nature of the two samples. But it does fit in well with the concerns voiced by German chefs. They complain that their countrymen do not eat out much at lunch-time and that they generally are loath to spend large amounts of their incomes on dining. This difference in frequency of dining in top restaurants is the case even though there are far more Michelin-starred restaurants in Germany than in Britain and they have, by and large, lower prices. (See details in Chapter 2.)

The above figures point to further divisions between members of the middle-classes in my interview samples, that is, professional-managerial employees and a few self-employed individuals. They depend, on the one side, on the broader social ethos adhered to and the priorities set between dining out in top restaurants and spending on other cultural engagements, such as visiting the opera or theatre. A reluctance to attribute cultural value to fine food often goes hand-in-hand with an economic attitude which regards spending in top restaurants as both wasteful and elitist, even by those earning comfortable salaries. Thus a young German university lecturer who, out of principle, has never eaten in a high-end restaurant, raises the following objection against them: 'One pretends that it would be the best cuisine, including health etc., but as a rule it more likely concerns status differences.'

On the other side, variation within a social stratum is based on a general attitude towards food—whether traditional or not. Among traditionalists, objection to fine-dining may be expressed in the rejection of 'foreign muck' or 'tarted-up' food in preference to more familiar and plainer national dishes. Although not short of cultural capital in general, these two sub-sections of the professional-managerial middle-class have not acquired culinary capital. These within-class differences are further explored below when the symbolic aspects of fine-dining are elucidated. They seem to be more pronounced in Germany.

Snobs versus Omnivores

My interviews with diners confirm what already is well known, namely that most people now eat out very frequently in restaurants (of all kinds). As Table 9.2 shows, the British respondents eat out more frequently than their German opposites, with eight British and four German respondents eating out ten or more times per month. (Two of the younger German respondents, without access to a place of dining at work, include lunch-time visits to cafés, snack bars, and even market stalls in their statement of frequency of eating out.) Cultural factors, already reviewed in Chapter 2, are likely to be behind

Table 9.2. Number of times dining out in all types of restaurants per person per month (in absolute figures)

	1–5	6–8	10	12–16	Total number of respondents
British diners	8	2	5	3	18
German diners	8	2	1	3	14

Source: Author's calculations from interview data.

this British–German difference, as the socio-economic status of German diners is even slightly above that of their British opposites.

Predictably, my question of what kind of restaurant people frequent and how this differs according to occasion, establishes that very few exclusively eat in fine-dining restaurants. The majority of out-of-home meals are taken in middle-level restaurants of various types. (Dining in high-level restaurants in proportional terms is shown in Table 9.1.) The only exceptions are one German (self-employed lawyer Raoul), and four British diners (Peter, Diana, Jonathan, and British-American Nicky) who eat out mostly in top restaurants (70–100 per cent of all restaurant visits). Several respondents—ten out of eighteen in Britain and seven out of fourteen in Germany—indicate that, even if starred restaurants were less expensive, they would not eat there more frequently. Instead, they wish to keep a meal there as an exceptional experience or a treat. Among the eighteen British respondents, most other types of restaurants—middle-level chains, pubs, bistros/brasseries, and other independent restaurants—are regularly visited. The responses from the fourteen German respondents are similar, except that middle-level independent restaurants are more frequently chosen and never pubs, reflecting the different composition of the German hospitality sector. In both countries meals in ethnic restaurants are popular.

Most respondents—seventeen out of eighteen in Britain and thirteen out of fourteen in Germany—are not true omnivores and do not eat in fast-food restaurants. Several respondents in both countries, single out this type of restaurant for explicit rejection. Joe, a young Londoner, does visit fast-food restaurants but it is to fill up in a hurry, rather than being a social occasion: 'I would go to fast-food restaurants when I was in a rush (and typically alone).'

In Germany, Oliver—a thirty-five-year-old recruitment consultant from Frankfurt—also frequents 'fast-food' restaurants at lunch-time. It is interesting that Oliver points out a greater variety of 'fast' food outlets, not all of them serving unhealthy food. In addition to the usual mention of American burger chains, he includes (stand-up) German *Imbiss* stands (snack bars), market stalls, and even a butcher's shop. It is questionable whether the rejection, in both countries, of what might be described as the eating-out preference of the young and of members of the working class, should be described as cultural snobbism, rather than a very rational act of discrimination between good/healthy and bad/unhealthy food.

In both national samples, there is a very small minority—two people in each country—who also reject dining in middle-level chain restaurants. Thus, British-American Nicky, who spends much time in France, says:

> I never deliberately go to a chain restaurant and prefer not to eat in a fast-food restaurant. I am very fussy. The restaurant has to prepare food better than I do at home…I don't like to eat in mediocre restaurants.

Nahee, a Korean-born British university teacher, holds a similar view: 'I never go to fast-food restaurants, and I try my best to avoid the middle market chain restaurants.' Inge, a retired German grammar school teacher, and Karin, a German university teacher, both say: '[we] never [go to] fast-food or chain restaurants'.

In Germany, middle-market chains are, in any case, less common than in Britain, while independent restaurants are more so. As such a rejection of any kind of chain restaurant greatly reduces the choices when dining out, particularly in Britain, it is evidence of strongly held convictions and a certain perfectionism about food and service. But I would hesitate to designate even this attitude as cultural snobbism.

Respondents in both countries further show themselves to have catholic tastes when asked about their preferences regarding type of cuisine. Only a few indicate definite types of cuisine—mostly the French and Italian. In contrast, the majority—fifteen out of eighteen in Britain and ten out fourteen in Germany—claim to be partial to a variety of culinary styles, including Asian ones. Thus Joe, a Londoner in his late twenties says: 'I go for a variety [of styles], but have a preference for Asian cuisine, particularly Thai.'

In sum, the correspondence between taste and class is not as coherent or consistent as the French sociologist Pierre Bourdieu believes,[19] nor do taste preferences fully conform to what the concept of omnivorousness suggests. They have become less fixed and less determined by class, but the influence of class nevertheless still persists. Members of the professional-managerial middle-class, on the whole, neither frequent popular fast-food establishments, nor do members of the working-class, as a rule, visit fine-dining restaurants.

The Symbolic Value of Fine Dining

The symbolic meaning attributed more or less consciously to fine-dining is both varied and difficult to pin down. It is also hard to assess as sophisticated respondents will not necessarily admit to status-seeking of any kind. I distinguish between three kinds of symbolic meaning sought, as well as relate this search to the attainment of social distinction. I additionally examine whether fine-dining constitutes 'uncivilized sociality'.

Seeking a Pleasurable, Exciting, and Memorable Experience

Seeking pleasure and experiencing excitement or fun is a symbolic gratification very much in the foreground of many of my respondents' thinking in connection with a visit to a top restaurant. Karin, a German university teacher, well describes the experience: 'Hours of enjoyment. That the atmosphere and the taste of some of the dishes stay in your memory.' Inge, a retired German grammar school teacher, expects similar gratifications: 'enjoyment, relaxation, good conversations and a good mood'. Hartmuth, a retired German teacher, singles out 'the feeling to have experienced special hours'.

Nicole, a lawyer working for a big insurance company in Munich associates 'a memory of an extraordinary experience' with dining out in a high-end restaurant. Peter, a Londoner, suggests: 'You could spend five hours in a good restaurant, and you would not know that the time has passed.' And Anna, another Londoner tells me: 'Essentially, I want to leave the restaurant with memories of a great evening.'

Respondents welcome the suspension of reality for a short time and seek to prolong the pleasurable experience by anticipatory excitement and remembrance after the event. Alex, a British lawyer in his late twenties, well conveys the enjoyment he and his partner derive from a visit to a top restaurant and the way they manage to prolong the pleasure:

> I expect a wow factor. I want an experience I can talk about afterwards—a treat, a performance. I want a drama but not for it to be dramatic. Every sense is heightened. I talk about it for a long time afterwards. We plan a long time in advance—it is not just a one-night experience. There is anticipation and an after-experience. We get into the mood for it and make it special. I'd hate for it not to be special. You can't put a price on it. In London, I would be able to do a lot for the money— theatre, opera, etc.'

Gunda, the wife of Bavarian Michael, similarly expects 'a beautiful relaxing experience which I like to remember. Also anticipatory pleasure and eager expectation about how he will do the meal.'

Chefs fully realize what diners require and do their best to fulfil their wishes, as expressed by a German three-star chef:

> One wants to surprise the guests and convey to them a total experience which lasts them a long time. One also wants to provoke them, but in a positive manner.

That dining out in a superior restaurant—with its food, service, and ambience—constitutes an uncommonly pleasurable event that lends heightened social significance to an otherwise ordinary day, is borne out by the fact that most of my respondents dine out in this way to mark a special family event such as a birthday. Moreover, many dine out in this way only a few times a year. For most of my respondents the trinity of good food, excellent service, and a pleasant ambience have to come together to create a pleasurable and memorable experience. Some respondents also single out the enhanced conviviality they expect from a celebration in a fine-dining restaurant. British couple Roger and Jean express the added importance of conviviality: 'To get a very enjoyable meal which also is conducive to having a good conversation. Food that puts you into a state of bonhomie.'

But even enjoyment of restaurants is not socially neutral. Preferences and therefore taste in food and dining, often imperceptibly, have been shaped by those we regard as our peer group, and the cultivation of a certain taste serves to distinguish us, more or less consciously, from other social groups, or even from individuals in the same occupational group. However, likes and dislikes in types of food are less amenable to peer group influence than other cultural activities, and family socialization often has a strong lingering impact on the choice of meals eaten.

Seeking Status from Conspicuous Consumption

Deriving social distinction simply from being seen in a starred restaurant or from being able to afford to go there is not mentioned by a single respondent. Such conspicuous consumption in any case is hard to display in a highly anonymous urban society where you would rarely be seen in a particular restaurant by friends or acquaintances. The chance is further lessened by the fact that, in some large cities, particularly in Germany, the number of Michelin-starred restaurants has multiplied significantly in recent years. In this respect, consumption of fine food is much less a public display, than is the consumption of expensive fashion wear or the driving of a car in the luxury class. However, one German respondent, who never has been to a fine-dining restaurant, thinks a visit is 'merely' a matter of seeking enhanced status: 'One pretends that it is the very best cuisine, including health etc. but as a rule it is more likely to be a matter of status distinctions.' A British respondent mentions an incident of 'showing off' vis-à-vis strangers when another customer ordered a very expensive bottle of wine in a loud voice.

In contrast to the showing off involved in conspicuous consumption, several respondents tell me that they would not seek to communicate their dining experience to friends or colleagues because the latter do not share their passion for exquisite and inevitably expensive food. Seven German and two British diners take this stance. Friends, they suggest, would disapprove or think that the diners were showing off. German diners Michael and Gunda well express this reservation about conspicuous consumption: 'We do not have a circle of friends who spend that much for dinners. Our friends would think we are showing off.' British diners David and Sue, living in rural South Wales, are similarly careful with whom they share their enthusiasm about an excellent meal enjoyed:

> If it [the meal] is outstanding we would want to talk about it. But we would select who you talk to—not to the miserly friends…Only some [of our friend have similar interests, concerning restaurants]. Others might say: 'It's alright for you', and they might disapprove.

Interviewed diners are much more likely to share their dining experience with like-minded friends and colleagues and, indeed, derive great pleasure from doing so. But such sharing is unlikely to bestow distinction and is aimed more at reliving the pleasure of an enjoyable evening. However, one German diner communicates her dining experiences more publicly, both within her company, and to a wider Facebook readership: 'Yes, I also talk about it [a dining experience] on Facebook or in a firm-internal newsletter.' But in this case, the dining often has been with clients of the firm and has been chosen and booked by the firm.

A disregard for 'conspicuous consumption' also is expressed by chefs who generally do not aim for a luxurious, but for a more quietly elegant surrounding. Diners similarly do not necessarily look for a luxurious surrounding. None of the interviewees use the word 'luxurious' to describe the ambience and furnishing of their ideal restaurant. Instead words like 'relaxed', 'elegant', 'tasteful', or 'stylish' are used. Great value generally is placed by most respondents on lack of noise, and almost every respondent wishes for sufficient space between tables. A few interviewees specify a table cloth and nice china and cutlery. Only two *German* respondents ask for cleanliness, and a third German suggests that the rest rooms must have fresh towels.

However, among one group of diners—business people entertaining potential or actual clients—the heightened conviviality created by fine-dining is used in a more instrumental way *to impress* in order to 'buy' business loyalty. At least one (German) chef, whose restaurant in a financial centre attracts a lot of such customers, recognizes this need to impress by creating a menu which offers a range of luxury items, such as lobster and truffles. Another (British) chef in a similar business niche is aware that the décor and ambience of his restaurant must appeal to business diners. For them, substantial leather chairs, for example, are seen as conducive to entertaining and impressing clients. Only two German respondents, lawyers Nicole and Raoul, do a fair amount of 'wining and dining' of clients, but they also go out without clients, 'just for fun'. Another German diner, Oliver, visits high-end restaurants sometimes on the occasion of 'company events'. A few respondents mention taking out visiting academic colleagues, or being 'wined and dined' by their publisher.

Distinction Bestowed by Deferential Service Staff

A further avenue of gaining distinction is said to come from interaction with deferential service staff. Even if it not expressed in this stark manner by any respondent it cannot be ruled out. Although highly attentive, indeed, faultless service staff are designated by most interviewees as a necessary and important component of an excellent restaurant this does not necessarily include an expectation of deference. One requirement expressed by nearly all respondents, in both countries, is that service staff keep their distance. They want them to act like professionals, rather than like friends.

However, it is undeniable that, in a high-end restaurant, you receive continuous attention from a large number of staff from the moment you enter to when you leave the restaurant. Where else in modern society would you publicly be treated 'like a king'—as one of the chefs summed up the way he wants his staff to treat customers. Jonathan, one of the British diners, too, singles out such treatment as a criterion for excellent service: 'Even at a relatively simple lunch, you are still treated like a king.'

Joe and Anna, both Londoners in their late twenties, are unusual in rating service even more highly than good food:

> I think service is key—I can accept bad food so long as the service is good...I appreciate the finer details of service as well—it is nice for things to be noticed before you have to point them out (i.e. bringing water to the table as a standard etc.). Overall, I want to be made to feel special—it doesn't matter whether I'm eating in a fine-dining restaurant or a pub; I am still eating out and it is an occasion and should be treated by the restaurant and its staff as such. (Joe)

> First and foremost, superlative service (friendly, efficient, and knowledgeable), but also good food (good quality and good value for money) and a great ambience/atmosphere. (Anna)

While, according to chefs, staff–customer interactions mostly are cordial rather than involving condescending or otherwise offensive behaviour, the nature of the service relationship nevertheless puts the customer into a superior position. A few of my German respondents want to push the power this gives them a little further by asking service staff for special favours, regarding the food served: 'We would like to be able, without a great fuss, to change our order—to change it in terms of composition and quantity of food.' 'But they [service staff] have to be friendly and render a small special service.' A third German diner expects 'a certain flexibility in the face of special wishes'.

Distinction from Possessing Specialist Knowledge

A more frequently implied symbolic value connects the dining experience with an expansion of knowledge about food and cooking. As British sociologist Alan Warde recognizes:

> there is evidence that the habit of talking about food and its qualities, or evaluating it in aesthetic terms, is predominantly a trait of the professional and managerial middle class fractions in Britain.[20]

According to Jeanne, a German radio journalist, the experience she seeks to derive from a top restaurant is: 'New taste experiences, interesting conversations about food.' Daniela, a British university teacher, also approaches the experience with curiosity:

> I want to discover some interesting ideas of what you can do with food and of how they test the limits. If we go out with friends we always end up talking about the food.

A German diner, lawyer Raoul, in addition to relaxation and joy, expects to be 'aesthetically and intellectually stimulated'.

Diners who seek to expand their knowledge will list 'knowledgeable service staff' as one of their requirements of good service. Thus Alex and his partner, for example, seek the following qualities in service staff: 'Friendly, warm and appropriately knowledgeable service'. They try to establish a relationship with staff and to explore their habitat: 'We go back to the kitchen quite a lot and talk to the staff. They are interested in us. All seem to care about what they do.'

German Raoul has extremely high expectations of staff's knowledge (in French and Italian restaurants) when he specifies the possession of 'knowledge of the French language and of Mediterranean culture'.

A few of the 'highly committed' diners, who wish to achieve new taste sensations and to broaden their knowledge of food, emphasize that their main reason for seeking out a top restaurant is the food experience. They profess to be indifferent to ambience and décor or that the latter is secondary. Thus, Ha-Joon, a British university teacher, describes what for him makes an excellent restaurant:

> That they use a combination of the right ingredients. Making ingredients work together. I don't mind going to a hole in the wall if the food is excellent.

Londoner Alex shares this sentiment: 'Décor is lower down on my list of priorities. Food comes first, then service and third, wine.' As does Mark M., another London diner:

> The principal reasons for me for going are the food and the conviviality around it. A beautiful environment, like, for example, in the *Manoir Quatr'Saisons* enhances the experience, but it is not the reason for going.

Even among those valuing a good ambience and décor, spectacular décor or a luxurious environment are not required. Generally, these customers of Michelin-starred restaurants want the food to stand at the centre of attention.

Whether the acquisition of new taste experiences and of culinary knowledge is best viewed as an end in itself, rather than a means to achieve distinction, is a point of contention. Social distinction, according to the German philosopher of food Jürgen Dollase, is not necessarily or primarily the objective a gourmet pursues. Dollase argues that

> to be a gourmet is a state of mind rather than a status symbol...the new gourmet is a sensually perceptive person who has arrived at a positive access to food and its fascinating possibilities by keeping a distance to inferior produce...in all possible culinary places.[21]

One of my respondents, a British university teacher, agrees:

> It [dining in a top restaurant] is, in any case, more about attitude towards food, and not just a matter of money. It has not to do with wealth.

Being a gourmet or foodie in your home environment may be regarded as an end in itself, connected with self-development and satisfaction from and pleasure in the culinary knowledge accumulated. But it may be argued that knowledge acquired from fine-dining in the public sphere contains an implicit drawing of distinction from those lacking this type of knowledge, even where it is not shared with friends or colleagues. Thus British Alex feels he cannot talk to his colleagues about the dining experiences he and his partner have enjoyed, implying their inferiority in terms of taste:

> No, most of our lawyer colleagues have a very strange relationship to food. The opportunity cost is too high for them, and they buy something more tangible which is a status symbol.

When I query what he means by 'a strange relationship to food' he elaborates:

> Food is food to a lot of people. Youngish educated people are often squeamish about particular items of food, e.g. black pudding or mushrooms. They have a pathetic, molly-coddled attitude—they say the sort of thing a five-year-old would say. Even very educated people are scared by fine food and Michelin-starred restaurants.

As a frequent fine diner you may become a connoisseur not only of fine food and dining, but also of the restaurant scene. This may cause friends and acquaintances to defer to your superior knowledge. But equally, being such a connoisseur may be frowned upon or even be despised by other friends and colleagues. This is particularly likely among members of the intelligentsia or highly educated middle-class who often do not regard such expertise in the field of food as a cultural value. What some refer to as 'knowledgeable refinement and discrimination', others merely regard as 'affectation'.[22]

The possession of extensive culinary knowledge finds its apotheosis in the phenomenon of the gourmet tourist who visits three-star chefs in various countries and whose knowledge sometimes becomes paired with arrogance. There is no gourmet tourist among the diners I interviewed. But some chefs spontaneously share with me their opinion on such guests:

> Holding three stars has affected what kind of people come—more foodies, more 'complicated' people. Sometimes I think that it would be better with just one star. Now the guests come to compare, people who throw their weight around.... It is no fun to cook for such guests. They do not behave like guests. Such people have increased with the number of stars. (Three-star German chef)

Uncivilized Sociality

To what extent, if at all, does fine-dining entail an 'uncivilized sociality', as defined by sociologist Joanne Finkelstein?[23] As a social being, you conform to a set of rules of interaction in all social settings. You frequently act in a habitual manner, and often the following of rules can be very beneficial for civilized social interaction. The question concerning Finkelstein's thesis therefore is whether your conduct is regulated by more such rules and/or by more constraining rules, and, if so, whether these render your interactions in a fine-dining restaurant uncivilized.

First, it is true that a stay in a high-end restaurant involves you in more rituals of interaction than say one in a fast-food restaurant or a meal taken at home. However, as was pointed out in Chapter 7, the number of such rules and the degree of formality in fine-dining restaurants have been significantly reduced. A largely relaxed atmosphere mostly leaves it to customers now to decide, albeit within certain limits, how to dress for the occasion and how to comport themselves. Mark M., a Londoner in his late forties, well sums up the transformation:

> I like them [fine-dining restaurants] to be relaxed. All that nonsense about enjoying food like sitting in a church is now gone. Pompous waiters have gone. They were still there in the 1980s—had a class-like snobbery approach. It has become a lot more informal, it has changed. They don't turn their nose up at tap water any more.

Peter, a Londoner in his forties, too, believes it is no longer formal because, unlike in a 'temple of gastronomy', children now are made welcome: 'No, [it is no longer formal]. David [their five-year old son] has been with us at lots of them. They all welcomed him.' Anna, a young Londoner, in common with many other respondents, understands 'formality' to refer mainly to the behaviour of service staff: 'As long as the service is friendly rather than stuffy or arrogant, I don't mind if it is formal.'

Second, although the customer submits to a certain protocol, he or she has actively chosen to do so, rather than passively submitting to a set of rules in an uncivilized manner, in Finkelstein's terms. Consequently customers do not necessarily perceive some of these social rituals as constraining. To the contrary, as several of my respondents spontaneously tell me, they view them as part of the pleasure of fine-dining. They greatly welcome the relative privacy a high-end restaurant facilitates, without depriving them of the 'buzz' that dining in isolation would entail. Diners actively appreciate the absence of loud music which constrains conviviality. They welcome a white table cloth and highly attentive staff which contribute to the sense of occasion they seek to experience as part of the visit of an elegant restaurant. Ha-Yoon, a British academic, answers my question about whether he likes his fine-dining restaurants 'very formal, very informal or somewhere in between' as follows: 'Somewhere in between. They need to keep certain standards to be special, and I pay for them. I like a table cloth, for example.' Richard, a retired British university teacher, says: 'Table clothes are imperative.' Jonathan likes the formality of dressing up for the occasion:

> I like them [restaurants] relatively formal—I like the theatre of a formal restaurant. I like to dress up to mark the occasion. In summer, in France, they often do not wear ties—this shows disrespect to food.

Roger, a retired small-business owner, shares his taste in this respect: 'I actually like a dress code which forbids jeans etc.'

Also the majority of my respondents, in both countries, welcome the advice of a *sommelier*. Mark M., an experienced diner, comments:

> They [*sommeliers*] do have a useful function. They are usually very good at judging how much you want to spend. I often have interesting conversations with them.

Third, respondents actively make choices when they reject restaurants that are too stiff and formal and have waiters who enact rituals of deference such as placing the serviette on the customer's lap. Thus, for example, certain French restaurants in Britain occasionally are ridiculed for making customers wear a jacket and/or for lifting silver cloches from customers' plates in unison. Inge, a retired German school teacher, explicitly expresses selectivity when choosing a restaurant:

> We value a relaxed and hospitable atmosphere, nothing too stiff or ceremonial. We would like to be able to bring children...Arrogant behaviour is a reason for us not to visit such a restaurant again.

Several other German respondents refer to overly formal restaurants they themselves would avoid to dine at.

But selecting only restaurants without constraining rules of interaction has its limits, as some are integral to the concept of fine-dining restaurants. One such custom, singled out by a few respondents for intense dislike, is having the wine placed on a separate table so that only the waiter can refill your glasses. A German food journalist strongly objects to the explanations by service staff of what is on your plate and interprets it in the same way as Finkelstein. He finds it awful 'to have to listen to all the nonsense (*Gequassel*) about what is on the plate. It turns man into a subject of ceremony.'[24]

However, this view is not common among my respondents who, at most, object to such description when it is too frequent and interrupts conversation. But generally, as answers to my question about objections to aspects of fine-dining restaurants reveal, there now exist few socially constraining rituals which are integral to all fine-dining restaurant regimes.

The majority of my respondents—sixteen out of eighteen in Britain and nine out of fourteen in Germany—encounter constraining formality only very occasionally or not at all. But the number of interviewees complaining about remaining formal and/or pompous restaurants is significantly larger in Germany than in Britain. Whereas British respondents report isolated examples of unsatisfactory and/or pompous service a minority of German respondents think they are more common. Whether this says something about German restaurants or about the more vocal consumer attitude found in Germany is impossible to say. Inge, for example, states:

> there still is a tendency towards exaggeratedly stiff and 'distinguished' conduct and too much value is put on external appearance (e.g. cutlery and glasses)...The restaurants we usually visit are not formal. But there still exist some off-putting examples.

Bavarian Michael, too, objects to 'strained exclusivity', and Munich journalist Jeanne responds to my question of whether the behaviour of service staff mostly meets her expectation as follows: 'So, so, [service meets my expectation] rather rarely.' North German retired teacher Hartmut, and Cologne psychiatric consultant Torsten, too, do not always find satisfaction with service staff. It may be that restaurants in some of the luxury hotels, even when their *chefs de cuisine* present them as relaxed, still retain features of 'temples of gastronomy'.

In sum, Finkelstein's connection of the notion of 'uncivilized sociality' with fine-dining, while containing a grain of truth in a narrow sociological reading, largely has lost its applicability, if, indeed, it ever possessed it in an unambiguous way. The much reduced number of social rules and the largely relaxed style of most fine-dining restaurants have made them accessible to a wider social constituency than was the case only a few decades ago. In turn, the presence of a less narrowly defined and less exclusive social stratum makes restaurateurs further relax socially constraining rules. However, some of my respondents draw a line between a relaxed style and a casual approach, and others welcome a minimum of social ritual and refinement to experience that 'sense of occasion' they connect with a fine-dining restaurant.

Attitudes Towards Pricing

One constituent feature of fine-dining restaurants is that they charge comparatively high prices for food and wine. Whereas this feature must deter many people who like good food but are not able or willing to pay these prices, among my respondents objection to high prices for food is not common. Asked to select one of the following statements: *prices are far too high; high but justified; not really high* the great majority of interviewees in both countries—sixteen out of eighteen in Britain and eleven out of fourteen in Germany—feel that the prices for food are 'high but justified'. This does not indicate possession of exceptionally large financial resources, nor the high-spending habit associated with conspicuous consumption. It rather is evidence of knowledge of the costs incurred by fine-dining restaurants and the associated recognition that high prices are a necessity, rather than an attempt to rob gullible customers. (For details on costs and profits, see Chapter 3.) This interpretation also is supported by the fact that most respondents would not go more often if prices were lower, as this would indicate a move away from the high quality associated with fine-dining. Thus Alex, a London lawyer, informs me: 'Price is a factor. But it would not be fine-dining if prices were lower, and I would not go all the time anyway.'

German Inge, a retired grammar school teacher, is the only one who is somewhat nonchalant about prices. Asked what she and her husband are willing to pay for a good meal, she says:

We have not really reflected about this. We pay what is being demanded. And if the enjoyment is worth it, we will return. Generally, it is not insanely expensive, roughly around 80 euros per person.

Only one British and two German respondents find prices to be 'not really high'. The odd respondent—one in each country—who deem the prices to be 'far too high' fall into my category of very occasional diners who are lowly or not at all committed to 'fine-dining'. These findings, it may be objected, are due to the nature of my middle-class sample. This cannot be denied. Yet it is interesting that even those among my respondents who are not high earners accept the necessity for high prices. They manage the situation by going to such restaurants only once or twice per year. Both the highly committed and the more loosely engaged, in terms of the typology introduced below, are sufficiently well informed about the business model of fine-dining restaurants, so as not to criticize the high prices for food.

One interesting difference in responses between British and German interviewees is that a few of the Germans are concerned with value for money or, in a literal translation, the right price–effort relationship. This reflects an attitude found very widely in Germany, said to be the result of highly price-competitive supermarkets. Both Jeanne and Britta only accept high prices 'where the price–effort relationship is right'.

The situation is different where prices for wine are concerned. It is well known that these prices may be up to 300 per cent higher than they are in the retail trade. The mark-up is seen by restaurateurs as a measure to cover the cost of food, staff, etc., but most customers deem the mark-up too high. Mark M, a Londoner, complains:

> Prices for wine are way too high. The mark-up is scandalous, and it is worse in this country than in Europe. It can be up to 300 per cent. There is a limit to what I want to pay for the wine.

Thus thirteen of the British and seven of the German respondents deem prices for wine to be too high. This result partly is informed by the fact that many of them visit high-end restaurants mainly for the food. They are not necessarily connoisseurs of wine who really appreciate rare and highly priced vintages. German diner Michael is an example: '[The prices are] far too high. We do not know how to appreciate expensive wine. We are lovers of wine, rather than connoisseurs.' German diner Inge agrees: 'We are no connoisseurs of wine and therefore do not value senselessly expensive and old wines.'

However, a small number of wine buffs are tolerant of the high prices for wine, too. Thus British barrister Michael finds the prices of wine 'high, but justified': 'You know you subsidize the food.' British university teacher Daniela says: 'A mark-up is taken for granted.'

Two further British respondents—Peter and Nicky—are not outraged about the prices of wine because they know the reason for the mark-up. However, both also point out that charges sometimes are too high for quite undistinguished wine. Six German interviewees think prices for wine are 'high but justified'. In sum, these results show that diners, even those only very occasionally visiting a top restaurant, are well-informed about the business model and therefore tolerant of relatively high prices, particularly for food and, in several cases, also for wine.

Last, some sensitivity about high prices is found also among a few chefs. (I did not specifically ask chefs about price-setting.) They volunteer that they make an effort to keep prices as low as possible, and British chefs stress this more often than their German counterparts:

> There must be a perception of value. Guests do not like to be ripped off. (One-star Alan Murchison)

> We don't want to fleece the guests. They have to feel that they are getting real value for money. (London chef Atul Kochhar)

Further chefs who consciously aim to keep prices down by various means include London chef Colin Kelly of *Wild Honey*, Welsh chef Shaun Hill, and Marlow's Tom Kerridge. A few German chef patrons agree. A restaurateur in Germany's former communist east, Herr König, informs me that, when setting prices: 'I aim for customer-friendly price determination.' And Munich's Mario Gamba has 'the additional consideration to offer value-for-money (a good price–effort relation)'.

The Critique of Fine-Dining from Within or the Ethical Diner

I did not explicitly probe all the different ethical objections held against fine-dining restaurants, as explicated by the media. But I posed a few specific questions which raise ethical issues, namely ascertaining views on local sourcing and healthy eating, as well as probing attitudes towards luxury products. Also my general question about any objections held against aspects of fine-dining restaurants provides an opportunity for respondents to raise ethical issues.

Local sourcing by chefs carries implications not only for the freshness of food but also raises ecological issues, such as the lower damage inflicted on the environment, as compared with importing food by plane from international suppliers. However, ethical issues are not at the forefront of answers to my question of *Are you very concerned that chefs source locally?* Although most diners like the idea of local sourcing they deal with the issue in a fairly flexible manner. Most of my respondents—ten of fourteen in Germany and ten of eighteen in Britain—would ideally like chefs to source their produce mainly locally, but only a handful *demand* local sourcing. One of the latter is David, a retired Welsh farmer, who has the well-being of producers in mind: 'Yes, without doubt—[I am concerned that chefs source locally]. I used to be a producer. It should be sourced within a 25 mile radius.' Another strong advocate of local sourcing is British-American Nicky who says: 'I prefer it. The idea of a plane journey is appalling.' German Inge explicitly seeks out ecologically sourced meat and vegetarian cuisine, and German psychiatric consultant doctor Ute also favours local sourcing: 'I regard it as an advantage if local products assume a definite value.'

But most respondents are very understanding of the problems this may pose for chefs, and few insist on it. They provide no serious criticisms of ecologically damaging sourcing and are prepared to make allowances. Thus Bavarian Michael says: 'It is important that chefs purchase fresh goods but not necessarily in the region.' Or Bavarian Inge: 'Yes, [I am concerned that chefs source locally], if it is possible in view of the fact that certain fish are not local here in lower Bavaria.'

British diners also realize that London chefs, whatever they say about their sourcing practices, cannot really source locally. Alex, a Londoner, observes: 'Yes, [I prefer local sourcing], if it's appropriate. London is slightly different.' For Ha-Yoon, even Cambridge poses limits to local sourcing: 'Not really, as it is not always feasible. Take Cambridge—it would not be a very good meal if you relied on local produce.' Anna, who well knows the London dining scene, picks up on the fact that, for many chefs who profess local sourcing, it is merely a fashionable strategy of market differentiation:

> If it's a sign that they [chefs] care about supporting the local economy, rather than shipping food around the globe, that is a good thing, but I think that it has become a bit of a fad in recent years, i.e. it's done for the sake of the restaurant being able to make such a claim. I'm not certain I could taste the difference in where ingredients are sourced from if they were good ingredients anyway.

Altogether then, most of my respondents, whether British or German, welcome local sourcing if it is done by a chef. But the majority do not see chefs' local sourcing as a pressing ethical issue.

What is diners' attitude towards eating luxury products in fine-dining restaurants? Do they strike an elitist stance? Or do they support the democratic tendency present among quite a few starred chefs that ordinary ingredients can be prepared in such a way as to appear luxurious? Although there is some agreement with chefs that humble ingredients may be 'ennobled' by the right preparation, the majority of respondents do not take this stance. Slightly more diners are in favour of a 'certain amount of luxury products' than are not. Among German respondents, ten unambiguously expect luxury products, two do 'not necessarily' expect them; one did not respond to the question, and only one respondent does not require them. For British interviewees the figures are nine expectancies of luxury products and eight rejections, with one ambiguous reply. Among those welcoming chefs' greater move towards humble products are Londoners Roger and Mark J.:

> It is not too important [that chefs use a certain amount of luxury products], it's more what they do with the ingredients. I actually prefer the slow-cooked [less expensive] meats. They have so much more flavour, and we don't do it at home.
>
> No, [I don't expect a certain proportion of luxury ingredients]. In fact, I particularly enjoy restaurants that can turn the ordinary into the extra ordinary through the way ingredients are used or paired.

German psychiatric consultant doctor Torsten expresses his agreement with this position with a joke: 'No, [I do not expect luxury products], a three-star curry sausage (Germany's favourite street food) would also be OK.' British-Korean Nahee welcomes luxury products more conditionally:

> Fine-dining restaurants should use local, seasonal and fresh ingredients well and creatively. If luxury ingredients help to lift the dish, then that's fine.

As do British Alex and German Ute:

> There is always a foie gras course on the tasting menu. Yes, I do expect a bit of luxury. An eyebrow is raised, but it is not the end of the world. I also enjoy [simpler things like] sweetbreads.
>
> Luxury ingredients should be offered as part of at least one dish, but it does not have to be like this. I also like 'normal dishes' which have been transformed in a special manner.

Altogether, diners are divided about whether chefs should provide a certain amount of luxury products, but even the opponents of luxury products do not expressly articulate this position on ethical grounds.

Nor is eating healthily viewed by most of my respondents in ethical terms or even generally welcomed, particularly in the case of British diners. British diners do not particularly want to eat healthily when they dine in a top restaurant, with thirteen out of eighteen rejecting healthy eating as an objective. British diners Ha-Joon and Alex are representative of several others who, on the few occasions they eat out in a starred restaurant, want to throw health considerations to the wind: ' I can eat healthily at home, I don't want it for a special occasion'; 'At a Michelin restaurant you can't insist on it [healthy food] . . . I care more about the taste. I don't go every day. It's natural and tasty fat on a steak. It's a clean taste.'

In contrast, only one of the German diners shows lack of concern for health. Karin, Inge, and Christian, for example, emphatically endorse healthy dining when they reply: 'without a question', 'of course', and 'most definitely'. Christian, who does not favour high-end restaurants, appears to value 'healthy' food above all other characteristics a dinner might possess.

A concern with health crops up in three of his answers to questions that do not even enquire about health.

But even the German diners do not see this in ethical terms and do not, for example, connect healthy eating with ecological or economic concerns. The only exception is Bavarian Inge who is ecologically conscious and is influenced by her beliefs in the choice of restaurants and of the food she orders.

Finally, my general question of what diners object to in fine-dining restaurants does not elicit a single response voicing ethical concerns. Altogether then, as might be expected, individuals frequenting top restaurants do not place ethical issues high on their list of concerns.

A Typology of 'Fine Diners'

The diversity within the group of middle-class diners I interviewed is usefully captured by devising a typology of 'fine diners'. Table 9.3 shows the distribution of my respondents between the types and sub-types of diners. Individuals may have more than one affiliation. This typology highlights some of the internal differentiation already discussed, as well as revealing new within-group differences.

The Deeply Engaged versus the More Loosely Committed Diner

Here a distinction is being made between those intensely interested in fine-dining and actively following their interest and those less deeply engaged and committing fewer resources to fine-dining. The deeply engaged diner—for cost reasons—may not visit fine-dining restaurants frequently. But this type of diner nevertheless does so regularly (a few times each year) and derives deep satisfaction from doing so. He or she is willing to travel a

Table 9.3. A typology of fine diners

	Britain	Germany
Deeply engaged	7	5
Loosely committed	11	9
Open to innovation	10	7
Actively pursuing innovation	6	3
Traditional	2	5
Cosmopolitan	9	4
Total number of diners	18	14

Source: Author's calculations from interview data.

considerable distance to visit a particular restaurant. Although all but three of British respondents are prepared to travel some distance for a good restaurant, the deeply engaged diners will travel further—between 50 and 100 miles. Among German respondents, all but five will travel some distance, and the deeply engaged will travel between 50 and 120 km (30–72 miles). One German deeply committed diner, Britta, has even travelled 500 km (300 miles), from the north of Schleswig-Holstein to the Black Forest in the south-west of Germany.

Additionally, the intensely engaged diners commit more financial resources to dining out. The British ones are prepared to spend between £100 and £150 per person on food only, and the corresponding figure for the engaged German diners is between 100 (£86) and 500 euros (£430). This type of diner derives strong symbolic gratification in terms of both deep gustatory and other pleasure and also strives to widen their food 'competence'. (The one German diner who will spend between 200 (£172) and 500 euros (£430) on a dinner frequently dines on an expense account.) Such diners often know how many stars have been awarded to all or some of the restaurants they have visited, and they tend to know the chef(s) of their favourite restaurant(s). German journalist Jeanne expresses this attitude of intense engagement when she indicates that no specific occasion is needed to go to a top restaurant but that she and her husband go just for 'interest and the fun of eating'. German office manager Britta shares this attitude: '[We go] for the fun of it.'

The deeply committed 'fine diner' arranges important aspects of his or her life, such as annual holidays, to actively pursue their interest. A fair proportion of both German and British respondents do this regularly. Michael, a British barrister, confirms: 'Yes, [we would usually try to go to a fine-dining restaurant when on holiday]. We would choose the location for the availability of good food.'

Other respondents—a few in each country—do not choose the holiday with restaurants in mind but nevertheless seek out Michelin-starred restaurants if there are any, particularly when on city breaks. Altogether, around a third in each country may be described as deeply committed diners, that is, diners to whom most or all of the above criteria apply, that is seven out of eighteen in Britain versus five of fourteen in Germany.

The 'loosely engaged' diner visits fine-dining restaurants only intermittently, mostly on very special occasions and, in one case, not at all. He or she is neither as knowledgeable about fine food, nor as intensely interested in it. This type of diner will not go to great lengths, in terms of either expenditure or distance, to visit a starred restaurant. Nor does the less deeply committed diner know the chefs of their favourite restaurants, or the number of Michelin-stars awarded.

The Diner Open to Innovation versus the Tradition-Bound Diner

To gauge whether diners are open to innovative culinary styles, I asked whether they enjoy new taste experiences and unusual ingredients and food combinations, that is, food that surprises and even shocks. In cases of positive answers, I followed up with a question on whether they have visited named restaurants—both national and international—known for their innovative chefs. The number of my respondents who are interested in innovative cuisine is relatively high—ten out of eighteen in Britain and nine out of fourteen in Germany. However, only a minority of those who express a liking for innovative food are seriously interested in highly innovative cooking, such as molecular cuisine. (For a description of this type of cuisine, see Chapter 5.) A smaller number actively follow up on their professed adventurousness and seek out highly innovative chefs. Thus of the ten British diners professing an interest in innovative food, four have some reservations and only six have eaten in Heston Blumenthal's restaurant. Of the nine German 'innovative' diners, five express some reservations, and only one respondent has visited an innovative chef within Germany. However, some diners open to innovation express regret about their inability to get a reservation in Copenhagen's *Noma* and/or the restaurants of the Spanish innovators. Thus Mark, a forty-eight-year-old passionate London foodie, says: 'We would have travelled to eat at *El Bulli*'s in Catalonia if we had been able to get a booking.' The same applies for Ha-Joon, a British academic: 'I would like to go to Redzepi's but I hear it is impossible to get a booking.'

Respondents who like innovative food in principle but have not yet tried a restaurant in this category—the majority of my respondents—express a willingness to do so, even if only once. Nahee may be said to fall into this category: 'I wouldn't say I am partial [to innovative food combinations or textures, i.e. food that surprises and even shocks], but I would give it a try.' Or Mark J., a Londoner in his late twenties: 'I am willing to give it a go.' German Britta says: 'I would quite like to try molecular cuisine, but only for once.' German retired small business owner Michael tells me: 'I have never eaten at the Spanish guy's but I am curious. I would not go for enjoyment, I do not like the idea of molecular cuisine.' Joe, a young Londoner, is curious but only wants a second-hand experience: 'I'm interested to learn about it and watch on TV—I'm less interested in trying it.'

In sum, these respondents show an interest in and curiosity about innovative food but they are not fully committed to experimental cuisine, such as the molecular variety and may even express a dislike of it.

Some of the interviewees, like Jonathan, are open to innovative food combinations but show a healthy scepticism about them, as well as asserting different priorities:

267

> Yes, I am [partial to innovative food combinations or textures, i.e. food that sur-
> prises and even shocks], but innovation is less important than some restaurant
> critics suggest...While I like innovation, perfect execution is more important—
> but this is rare.

German diner Michael cautions against innovative excess: '[I object to] eccen-
tric dishes/ingredients, such as termites from South Africa, moistened with
the water of the Yangtse.' Roger, a retired small business owner from London
likes the idea of innovative food but he and his wife did not enjoy their visit
to a restaurant known for it: 'Yes, I [like innovative food] because you don't
do it at home. You go for an experience, not just to fill your tummy.' However,
Blumenthal's *Fat Duck* disappointed them:

> Well, what's the point of egg-and-bacon ice cream? It's just clever. It was an
> interesting experience but not one I would want to repeat. You go there for an
> experience.

These diners thus are resistant to the current hype about innovative chefs
and reassert the value of perfection in execution and taste. Excellent taste,
for them, beats innovation, particularly the introduction of gimmicky kinds,
such as 'egg-and-bacon ice cream'.

The more traditional diners, that is, individuals expressing a dislike for unusual tastes and/or food combinations, sometimes state their preference for
more local or solely for more established styles of cuisine, such as the French
and/or the Italian. Traditionalists and particularly localists form a minority in
my sample. One of the few British localist diners is David, a retired dairy farmer,
who, when asked about preferred culinary styles, expresses these preferences:

> British or French only and preferably British...I would eat Franglais but I prefer
> traditional British food. I like Sunday roasts...I like good traditional food. I do
> not like food that is tarted up.

When he dines out without his wife, he particularly enjoys the *Toby Inn* chain.

Inge, a retired Bavarian school teacher, also prefers local food and is tradi-
tionalist also in other ways: 'We do not especially like Asiatic cuisine...We
very much like German-Austrian cuisine, enriched with ideas from other cuisines.' When asked to define an excellent restaurant, she replies: 'One that is
regional and ecological (bio).' She additionally voices traditional preferences
regarding restaurant decor:

> [We like] well-arranged and aesthetically pleasing furnishings, but they should
> not be especially modern and cool (minimalist) and [we like] good table linen.

Referring to a molecular-inspired German restaurant, she says: 'We have only
heard of it] and consider it all rather over the top. We are not their target
group.'

Among those expressing a preference for only well-established European cuisines, such as the French and Italian, are Ricky, a retired British university teacher: 'We go for French or Italian, not for Sushi, Chinese or Indian', and Germans Ingeburg, Nicole, and Raoul who like only 'French and Italian cuisine', and, in Nicole's case, 'also German cuisine'.

German Oliver likes mainly Asian cuisine. Raoul, a very experienced and intensely engaged diner, wants his meals to come from a defined tradition, as does Geoff, a British university teacher. Geoff additionally specifies traditional recipes: 'I prefer better quality ingredients and traditional recipes to over fussy cuisine using unnecessary ingredients.' British barrister Michael, too, prefers that his food comes from a particular tradition but realizes the problem attached to such an expectation: 'I like food from a particular tradition but realize they all add on touches from other traditions, short of fusion.'

Expressing a preference mainly for an established or traditional cuisine does not necessarily indicate a provincial stance but may well be combined with a cosmopolitan outlook. (For a definition of 'cosmopolitan', see below.) British barrister Michael, who is particularly committed to Italian food, has this to say about innovative food: 'No, [I don't like it]. I once had sardine foam—it was unspeakable.' Nicky, too, who generally adopts a cosmopolitan stance, is not partial to innovative food. When asked to specify what constitutes a good menu, she says: 'It should be fairly conventional and not everything [on the menu] should be outlandish.' She is very explicit in her answer to my question about whether she likes innovative food/food combinations: 'No, they are disgusting.'

Asked about their preferences regarding culinary style, the majority of my customer respondents—nine in Germany and fifteen in Britain—declare that they like a variety of styles. Only three British and five German diners have one or two definite preferences in terms of national culinary style. Of these, only one British diner favours English food and no one mentions regional food. Among German respondents, too, only two diners, Inge and Nicole, include German cuisine among their preferred styles. Inge also singles out regional food. It may be significant that both Inge and Nicole are from Bavaria.

The Internationalization of Fine-dining and the Birth of the Cosmopolitan Diner

Cosmopolitanism, according to sociologists, is a perspective which entails relationships to a plurality of cultures, understood as distinctive entities. A cosmopolitan is expected to have not only a familiarity with one or more other cultures, but also a broad cultural competence in relation to them.[25]

Applied to 'food cultures', a 'cosmopolitan' combines the liking of foreign culinary styles with an experience of sampling these cuisines in their home environment, as well as having an all-round knowledge of the whole restaurant regime around them. Cosmopolitans either regularly travel to a foreign country to eat, or they have lived abroad for a while. Cosmopolitan diners make explicit or implicit comparisons between fine-dining experiences, including service traditions and price, in several countries. Most live in London or in large German cities (e.g. Munich), or they are academics living in university towns.

Thus Peter—a Londoner—has lived for a considerable time in the USA and obviously has that country in mind when he names the qualities he likes and dislikes in service staff:

> They have to be polite; discreet; they should be able to answer questions about the food. I don't need to know their name. Also I get annoyed with over-elaborate explanations.

Nicky—a British-born academic, living in both the USA and in France—is more positive about dining in the US:

> There is more friendliness in the US than in France. In France, it can be very formal, even funereal where you think 'it's like a church in here'.

She continues:

> I have eaten in Spain, France, England, Holland, Turkey, Athens, Tokyo, Mexico, Australia and China...I think I have above average knowledge of different styles. I like Franco-Japanese cooking. I like innovative meals and various styles. Not highly spiced food—if Indian only fine Indian.

Michael, in contrast, has lived only in Britain but regularly visits other European countries for holidays and family visits, particularly Italy (and France and Germany on his way to Italy). He is able to make informed comparisons between French and Italian cuisine, as well as between the pricing policies of British and Italian restaurants:

> There is a class of ludicrously overpriced restaurants, particularly in London. [Provides some names.] In Italy, you do not get this in the same way.

Alex agrees: 'It would be a lower price for such meals in France and Italy.'

Jonathan, a British academic, makes an unflattering comparison between France and Britain, concerning décor:

> I regret the amount spent on design. I wished that instead food was cheaper. Décor in France and Switzerland is not necessarily up to 'star' level. In Britain, it is all desperately modern. Some restaurants I know have had two to three complete changes of décor in the time I have known them.

Some of these cosmopolitan diners, like German lawyer Raoul and British diners Jonathan, Ha-Joon, Peter, and Geoff, name foreign establishments when talking about their favourite restaurant or a restaurant recently visited. Altogether, there are nine cosmopolitan diners in my British sample and only four in the German sample.

Finding Good Restaurants

Customers are keen to learn about good new restaurants, both in their locality and further afield. Several avenues to acquire knowledge about fine-dining restaurants are mentioned by respondents: own local (on foot) exploration; personal recommendations/networks of friends, family, and colleagues; reviews in both the local and the national press, as well as magazines on food and drink; dedicated gastronomic guides; and, finally, search of the Internet (see Table 9.4). Among the diners I interviewed, personal networks are by far the most dominant source of acquiring gastronomic knowledge, probably because trust in this type of source of information has been accumulated over time. It usually involves a judgement of whether the person's taste is similar to one's own—a judgement difficult to make about largely anonymous sources of information. One German diner describes anonymous critics like this: 'Very often it is more about the taste of the critic and less about the needs of the customers.'

Press reviews come second, and local papers seem as likely to offer restaurant information as national ones, particularly in Germany. Perusing guides comes surprisingly low on the list, given that I am dealing with a significant proportion of committed 'fine diners'. However, those who use guides usually consult more than one.

Equally surprising is the finding that the Internet has relatively low salience for these diners as a *primary* source, including the younger ones among them. In Germany, eight respondents use the Internet and for six of them it has become an alternative to using guides. In Britain, seventeen consult the Internet but for only four of them it constitutes an alternative to using

Table 9.4. Diners' sources of information about 'good restaurants'

	Personal recommendations	Press reviews	National guides	Local guides	Internet as complementary source	Internet as alternative source
British diners (18)	12	12	10	0	13	4
German diners (14)	11	8	6	5	2	6

Source: Author's calculations from interview data.

a guide. It is mainly being used to access restaurant sites to check out one or more choices already made. The Internet thus is mostly regarded as a complement by British diners, rather than an alternative to other avenues of accessing information and knowledge. London diner Peter speaks for others when he says: 'Mostly, I cross check when I have discovered a new restaurant.' Dedicated restaurant reviewing sites and food blogs, such as *Trip Advisor*, *Dos Hermanos*, *E-Gullet*, or German *Sternefresser*, *Chefkoch*, and *Restaurantranglisten.de*, *Prinz.de*, and *restaurant-kritik.de* in some cases are less than enthusiastically embraced.

Concerning restaurant guides, only ten of the British and six of the German respondents use them, and even fewer own an up-to-date *Michelin Guide* (*MG*). British foodies are more likely to own and/or consult the *Good Food Guide* than the *Michelin Guide*, and one couple refer to the *Good Hotel Guide*. A few of the cosmopolitan British diners have guides for several countries. Thus Michael, a British barrister, tells me:

> The *GFG* is decent but not great; for France, I prefer the *Gault Millau* to the *MG* because the text is more helpful and it also mentions negative things. The *Gambero Rosso* is great for [Italian] restaurants.

Among the German respondents, only three own national guides—the *MG*, the *Gault Millau*, and *Der Feinschmecker*. However, a clear majority of respondents in both countries—eight in Germany and sixteen in Britain—know about Michelin stars awarded through the papers or through colleagues, even if not for all decorated restaurants. Michael, for example, who does not own a *MG* for Britain, nevertheless finds out about stars awarded every year: 'Yes, [I know about stars awarded], I have a colleague who looks with great excitement at the papers when the results are due.' London diner Alex has a similar strategy: 'I look at the new *Michelin Guide* when it comes out just to see who has gone up and who has gone down.' Ute, a German psychiatric consultant doctor knows about stars through the papers some of the time and 'for some restaurants I am familiar with the [Michelin] evaluations because of their persistently high ranking'.

Londoner Alex also offers a spontaneous and astute evaluation of the *MG*:

> I understand the *Michelin Guide*. It largely is accurate. But the problems are that it is French-heavy and that it is a slightly blunt instrument. Occasionally, they go down too much, e.g. when they gave a star to Hakkasan because Michelin thinks Chinese restaurants ought to get a star. It is a very wide range in the one-star category.

German lawyer, Raoul, also sees the *MG* as a somewhat blunt instrument but, as he values starred restaurants, still buys a copy of it. In sum, gastronomic guides are not the main source of information about good restaurants in either country. However, British diners are more likely to own and/or consult guides, as well as being better informed about stars awarded. This is, of course, congruent with the higher number of deeply committed diners in my British sample.

The disdain for Internet sites and food blogs, particularly among British respondents, comes as a surprise, given the high level of education of the respondents and the hype around Internet use in other areas. Among the British diners, these sites are not accorded sufficient legitimacy and, as they merely display personal opinions, on the whole are not trusted. British diner Mark M., who regularly consults two sites, explains his mistrust: 'No [they are not an alternative to other sources of information], they are probably quite dangerous in that there is no peer review.' Thus while many chefs are deeply concerned about negative 'posts' about their restaurant on the Internet,[26] my results should reassure them that most educated diners make their choices based on information gained in very traditional ways. Restaurant guides are more trusted, and the more 'talkative' guides, like the *GFG* and the *GM*, are more often consulted than the *MG*. This does not render the *MG* irrelevant because its ratings are more widely known and, despite some reservations, trusted. Thus, Ha-Yoon, who does not own a *MG*, volunteers: 'but Michelin approval must be taken seriously'.

In Germany, local culinary guides, such as *Munich Dines Out* or *Frankfurt Dines Out*, are mentioned more often than in Britain, underlining again the effects of Germany's greater political and cultural decentralization. At the other end of the scale, British diners have less confidence in Internet sites than German respondents. While the former consult the Internet mainly to check out the restaurant already chosen or to gain complementary information, for the German diners the Internet serves more often as an alternative source of information. But in neither country is it the main source of knowledge and information about restaurants.

Diners or Chefs as Taste Makers?

Diners' Influence on Taste

Is there still a reigning taste in *haute cuisine* as far as diners are concerned? And to what extent are diners involved in shaping it? The answers are ambiguous. On the one side, a positive answer carries some weight, in that certain general customer expectations about food and dishes set the tone for chefs. They are considered by many chefs anxious to keep their customers, although quite a few—particularly the artists among them—pay no heed to customers' views.

But on the other side, the answer has to be negative, in the sense that a liking for a variety of culinary styles now is prolific. Although some diners still have clear preferences for one or more European cuisines, no particular model of cuisine holds sway among most of my respondents. Also, by and large, although consumers have some influence on chefs, their individual interventions are too episodic and lack authority. Hence diners do not add up to a collective taste-making organ. A German one-star chef comments: 'Guests will not talk directly [about the food], only some very emancipated guests. They don't trust themselves.' A German three-star chef adds: 'Constructive criticism is welcome but is rarely given.'

One of the experienced British diners, Alex, willingly concedes superior expertise to chefs: 'We often do the tasting menu. We rely on the expert—give ourselves over to him.' However, this does not hold true for gourmet pilgrims. Their responses explain the diverging opinion of a long-time German three-star chef who particularly attracts this category of customer: 'The guests have become much more independent (*mündig*), and they have many more possibilities to compare.'

The *Maître de* of a prominent east German two-star restaurant, when asked by an interviewer from *Feinschmecker* how clients have changed in the last ten years, offers a similar evaluation of this type of customer. Moreover, he suggests that German guests are particularly prone to complain—a claim already raised earlier in this chapter:

> Since Witzigmann [pioneering German three-star chef during the late 1970s] woke up the bon-vivant (*Geniesser*), people have learnt a lot about cuisine and try to tell the kitchen how to change things. Germans, in any case, want that the chef cooks what they want. Abroad, the philosophy of the chef enjoys more respect.[27]

This more developed tendency to find something to criticize also is evident from a comparison of German and British respondents to my question *What, if anything, do you object to about fine-dining restaurants?* While the British respondents find little to object to, all but four of the German interviewees come up with a number of very diverse criticisms.

In sum, most customers/guests have neither the inclination nor the authority to micro-manage the chef's cooking. However, a small group of gastro tourists feel sufficiently knowledgeable and confident to tell chefs their critical opinions.

Asked about their preferences regarding culinary style, the majority of my customer respondents declare that they like a variety of styles. Only two British and five German diners have one or two definite preferences in terms of national culinary style, and a further few individuals rule out one or more particular cuisines. Thus Alex would never choose an Indian or Chinese fine-dining restaurant, even though several excellent ones exist in London:

> I would not go to an Indian or Chinese starred restaurant but would go somewhere simpler if I wanted that kind of food. I would see it as a waste. I probably have a very British relationship to Indian food.

Asked whether they object if chefs combine exotic ingredients, such as wasabi sauce or coconut with otherwise European dishes, the majority of respondents in both countries happily accept such usually Asian additions. Thus, at most, diners are endorsing either a multiplicity of styles or an eclectic style, and any basis for taste making seems lacking.

Whereas in the past, French cuisine was a fairly standard taste preference among fine diners, its influence now is less dominant, although by no means negligible. French cuisine still is held in high regard by a significant minority of my respondents. Jonathan, who has often dined in French starred restaurants, rates French cuisine highly:

> [I rate French cuisine] quite highly. In the end, more highly than anything else. It is still top [of the hierarchy]. I am not convinced that the Spanish have anything better to offer.

Jean and Roger—Londoners in their sixties— also are partial to French food: 'We love it—it always looks the best.' Geoff, a university teacher, also counts it 'among the best'. Daniela, a London university teacher in her late thirties, says:

> I think it [French cuisine] probably still is top, given the tradition. I say this because I am a European and I know the philosophy/logic. Japanese cuisine could be rated just as highly, but I don't know its logic.

Peter, a technical employee in London's financial sector, says: 'I think it [French cuisine] is not overrated, but there are other cuisines of comparable value, such as the Japanese.' German lawyer Raoul, too, who often dines in French restaurants, does not think French cuisine is now overrated, and lawyer Nicole also still rates it highly.

A couple of experienced diners pay tribute to the French model as a foundational paradigm for most European cuisines. Alex, for example, who speaks about French food available in London, comments: 'It is a little old-fashioned but French techniques definitely are still at the top of the hierarchy. French still is the basis for everything.' Londoner Mark M., who is very knowledgeable about food and even has acquired a City & Guilds chef's certificate, believes: 'I still think it gives the best training to chefs in terms of structure and tutoring his palate. When it is done well, it is probably still the best.'

Inge, a Bavarian retired school teacher, although not partial to French cuisine nevertheless recognizes its contribution to German gastronomy:

> We think that it [French cuisine], with its insistence on the quality of the basic products and on their exact and good processing, has established important incentives for quality in cuisine in general. We like it when regional dishes are refined with these stimuli. Nevertheless, we do not go into a restaurant that offers only French cuisine.

However, a few of my respondents believe that French cuisine has lost its hegemonic position and that it now competes with other national cuisines for top position in a culinary hierarchy. Robin, a retired business executive, states: 'I don't think it [French cuisine] is necessarily overrated, but there are good alternatives.' Roger agrees: 'It is overrated—other things have caught up.'

Anna, a Londoner in her late twenties, who works in the hospitality industry, well sums up the current situation:

> I think it [French cuisine] remains near the top-end of the hierarchy in terms of fine-dining, but there are other trends that are starting to shake the balance of the restaurant industry in general, e.g. restaurants serving just one type of food (*Chicken Shack* in north London or *Burger and Lobster* in central London) and other chefs giving French cuisine a run for its money.

Ingeburg, from Hamburg, acknowledges the rise of non-European restaurants in Germany: 'The Asiatic cuisine now is highly rated.' Welsh couple David and Susan even detect an emerging competition from British cuisine:

> It [French cuisine] is no longer at the top of the hierarchy, and things are changing. People now are moving towards what British chefs are doing.

In sum, French cuisine still enjoys a lot of support but few diners now view it as hegemonic. Hence it can no longer act as a unifying force laying down what counts as legitimate taste.

Chefs' Influence on the Emergence of a Legitimate Taste

If diners cannot be considered taste makers, what about chefs? Do they mainly reflect diners' preferences, or do they try to shape them? There is a spectrum of attitudes among my respondents towards customers' expectations and wishes in terms of taste. Some chefs try hard to please customers and take any comments or complaints they make into consideration. They recognize that diners now are much more knowledgeable and confident than they used to be:

> We tried to shape people's taste at the beginning, but people are much more sophisticated now and know their Italian dishes. (British one-star chef)

A German two-star chef is prepared to question his own taste if guests consistently reject a particular dish: 'If the resonance from the guests is not positive, we take the item from the menu and re-examine it.'

Other chefs try to appear accommodative but then continue in their accustomed way. A version of this response is that what they are doing is always pleasing to customers, or, put differently, that there is no divergence between their own and customers' taste: 'I am always pleasing customers, but it does not compromise my vision' (British one-star chef).

Yet a third and the largest group of chefs think that customers do not have sufficient expertise to tell them what to do and that, like artists, they are bound to continue with their very own signature style. A one-star Frankfurt restaurateur accords guests little authority: 'I want to present my restaurant to the guests. I do not need creative guests, I am creative myself.' Another German one-star chef also does not expect guests to influence his cuisine: 'The guest does not have sufficient self-confidence to determine standards.'

A German two-star chef explains diplomatically how he guides guests to accept his vision of the food served:

> You have to make some compromises, but quite rarely. In the final resort, I do the cuisine which is fun for me...It is much more important to realize your own vision, without imposing it onto the guests. I try to convince the guests of my own conception and speak with them about it. Guests would rather be advised. One must familiarize guests with one's ideas. We are in advance of the guests.

Berlin two-star chef Tim Raue professes that he does not want to educate the guest or hold him or her in tutelage. However, he then goes on to suggest that he can only take the guest 'on a journey of the senses' if the latter accepts all the details of his dishes. He gets very cross if, after explaining things to the guest, the latter still questions his vision:

> I don't mind explaining things personally, when I see that the guest looks at something sceptically. If I then do not receive respect for our concept it can happen that I put the guest, together with his wishes for change, out onto the street. That this has happened only once speaks for our guests and our service staff.[28]

My own mild criticism of one of several dishes (of a gastronomic menu) served by a British two-star chef was simply brushed aside with the answer that 'taste is very subjective'.

For most starred chefs then their own vision of their culinary style or taste prevails, and they seek to shape, rather than reflect customers' tastes. In other words, they consider themselves taste makers. However, as there is a lot of divergence between chefs' models of cuisine (as shown in Chapter 6), no collective model of legitimate taste emerges. The closest chefs come to accepting a general paradigm is their agreement with the Michelin organization that three-star chefs offer what is best in terms of high-quality creative cuisine. Or alternatively, particularly in Britain, they admire those selected for inclusion in the Pellegrino Top Ten as producing the most advanced/most innovative cuisine. In both cases, they agree on formal, rather than substantive features of cuisine. Also chefs realize that individually they are ineffective in influencing the dining public. A German three-star chefs recognizes this: 'First the chef has to bring the achievement but then he has to be made known by the Guides.'

While the model of French *haute cuisine* still attracts a lot of admiration from both chefs and diners, this model is no longer hegemonic and therefore cannot be understood as the only one constituting legitimate taste.

If neither diners nor chefs may be considered taste makers, who or what can occupy this role? In Chapter 10, I explore the role gastronomic critics and guides try to assume in this area and attempt to gauge the success of different types of critics and guides.

Relations between Diners and Chefs

In both Britain and Germany, a significant proportion of diners are keen to meet the starred chef. However, the British diners I interviewed express their wish somewhat wistfully, knowing that it is rarely fulfilled. Londoner Anna feels: 'I wouldn't necessarily expect this, but it would definitely enhance my dining experience.' Welsh David agrees: '[I would] not necessarily [expect the chef to make the rounds at the end of the main service], but it is very nice if they do.' British Alex and Michael answer in a similar way: 'It is nice but if he doesn't, no fuss'; 'No, [I do not expect it] but it is nice if they do.'

In Germany, the majority of chefs do the round of the restaurant at some stage of the evening. Customers therefore have a much greater chance to find their wish fulfilled. Many of the German chefs view the experience of meeting the customer on their daily round as very valuable. Three-star Sven Elverfeld tells me:

> I fairly regularly come out at the end of the service. It is most important that one keeps the contact with guests to gauge the effect of your efforts in the kitchen.

> Guests love to see the chef, and feedback is very important to me. They tell me more than the service staff.

Hamburg one-star chef Ali Güngörmüs also is keen to keep contacts with customers:

> I have a lot of contact with customers. I need this connection... I put great weight on knowing guests' names. The guest must feel that he is important.

Berlin two-star chef Christian Lohse even walks the floor twice, both at the beginning and then again in the middle of the service. He explains: 'It is too late to take their [customers'] wishes into account at the end of the service.' Three-star Harald Wohlfahrt, who comes out to meet the guests 98 per cent of the time, values the 'direct communication and the exchange of knowledge' this affords.

In Britain, however, most of the chefs have little routine contact with customers. They only meet them if the latter ask to visit the chef in the kitchen. All sorts of excuses are made by British chefs for not entering the restaurant. London two-star chef Brett Graham tells me: 'I do not do the rounds. I think it is artificial.' Two-star Marcus Wareing also does not 'walk around' because 'people do not want this any more. Those who do wish to see me come to the kitchen.' Birmingham's Glynn Purnell similarly only goes out in response to express demand as he does not 'want to impose on them'.

Two-star Tom Kerridge has a different excuse for not doing the rounds: 'I try not to come out... My very big figure coming into the low-ceilinged restaurant would put customers off.' One-star Shaun Hill frankly admits that he finds meeting customers unrewarding: 'I prefer to stay in the kitchen; I don't want to have the same conversation with twenty people every day.'

The excuses offered by British chefs for not doing the rounds do not sound very convincing in the light of diners' comments above. They must cover a deeper social unease about meeting customers. Given that customers really would like to meet with and talk to the chef, British chefs miss a big opportunity. They fail to enhance further the memorable experience a visit to a starred restaurant constitutes for most diners. More important, chefs miss out on vital feedback they do not necessarily capture from intermediaries. The few British chefs who regularly meet customers are very positive about it. French-born London chef Claude Bosi does the rounds once or twice during a service. He says:

> They [customers] like seeing the chef, they are usually very polite... It is rare for customers to complain. They do not seem to notice the problems.

Andreas Antona and Galton Blackiston, who no longer spend a lot of time in the kitchen, also derive a lot of pleasure from meeting customers, as do the two Indian chefs Sriram Aylur and Atul Kochhar.

In Britain, the restaurant manager mostly has become the intermediary between diners and chefs. Also some chefs are willing to receive individual customers on their own ground, in the kitchen. There is yet a third way to find out customers' reactions to the food served. I was taken aback when one chef told me that they have CCTV cameras in the restaurant, in order to ascertain when a course had been finished and the next one ought to come out of the kitchen. This camera clearly also provides information about degrees of customer satisfaction and dissatisfaction. I do not know whether this is more widely practised and only this chef was particularly frank in acknowledging it. The practice clearly is very effective, but it is not on the same level as 'doing the rounds' to gauge, as well as raise customer satisfaction.

My comparison of the degree and kind of contact between chef patrons and their customers reveals a significant difference between British and German chefs. Only the latter consistently make it their business to come out of their kitchens 'to meet and greet' their guests and ascertain their reactions to the food served. One reason for this divergent behaviour, a restaurant supplier tells me, may be that British chefs do not have the social ease required to meet with and talk to customers. But it is not clear why they should differ in this respect from their German colleagues. Social origins of chefs, I have shown in Chapter 4, are similar in the two countries. Another explanation for the different stances is that the vocational training of chefs in Germany explicitly inculcates the need for chefs to act as hosts, together with the service staff—a maxim not known in Britain.

Conclusions

This chapter mainly looks at top restaurants from the point of view of the customer or diner. It throws light on who the diners are and what moves them to eat in such restaurants. Throughout the chapter, I have explored the tension between elitism and democratization. I have suggested that there has been significant movement away from exclusivity, snobbism, and observance of formal etiquette. Although both economic and cultural capital remain important for people visiting fine-dining restaurants, the latter now often exceeds the former in importance. Also there exists considerable social and cultural differentiation within the largely middle-class group that frequents top restaurants. A typology of diners, devised on the basis of my interview data, documents this internal cultural differentiation which is not always mapped onto class differentiation.

Neither diners nor chefs seek to establish social exclusivity, and choices made about eating out point more strongly towards omnivorousness than snobbism. Although dining out now is a frequent leisure activity, dining in up-market restaurants, for most people, is only an occasional pleasure. I have argued against an indulgence in conspicuous consumption. Diners are in search of gustatory pleasure and excitement, as well as symbolic meaning. A quest for an enhancement of culinary knowledge is at least as important as a striving for social status.

I have argued against the claim by the sociologist Joanne Finkelstein that eating in top restaurants necessarily entails 'uncivilized sociality' and have shown that pompous formality of service staff now largely is a matter of the past in most fine-dining restaurants.[29] It is neither cultivated by chef patrons, nor desired by diners. However, some aspects of fine-dining, not necessarily found in lower-level restaurants, such as table cloths, cloth serviettes, and ample space between tables, as well as pleasing décor and highly professional service staff, are still welcomed. They are felt to endow a visit to a top restaurant with the aura of experiencing a special occasion.

In keeping with the point that possession of money capital is not the prime and overriding feature of top-end diners, I have explored attitudes to pricing in high-end restaurants. My finding that diners consider prices in such restaurants 'high but justified' does not point towards the pervasiveness of conspicuous consumption. Instead, it supports my claim that the symbolic value of gaining specialized and complex culinary knowledge is one of the important motivators for repeat diners, even if, due to insufficient economic resources, this is possible only a few times each year. Another facet of diners' views explored is their stance on ethical issues around food. My finding is that indulgence in fine-dining is not compatible with a radical ethical stance on food although diners hold some views which may be considered democratic, as well as sensitive to the ethical implications of fine-dining.

Another aspect of fine-dining I have explored is whether diners or chefs may be considered taste makers. I conclude that diners' tastes are too diverse. Furthermore, they lack the organization and authority to impose their taste preferences as legitimate. Concerning chefs' role as potential taste makers, I point out that many, though by no means all chefs view themselves as artists whose vision has to prevail, rather than as craftspersons whose primary role it is to satisfy customers. However, although chefs are considered more influential in shaping people's taste and contributing to the evolution of a culinary style, collectively they are insufficiently unified to become taste makers.

The final section the chapter has looked at relations between diners and chefs. It establishes that, although 'knowledge-seeking' diners would like to be offered the chance to talk to chefs, British chefs, in contrast to their German colleagues, avoid the close contact involved in 'making the rounds' of the restaurant during or at the end of a service. This is despite the fact that diners are much more likely to bestow praise and enquire about ingredients and techniques, than make complaints. I suggest that vocational training in Britain does not inculcate the requirement that chefs should take a keen interest also in what happens front-of-house and regard themselves as hosts, as well as cooks.

National Comparison

Many of the views and practices of fine diners discussed so far are equally present among both British and German respondents. However, relations to food consumption in general and to fine-dining in particular also vary between the two countries, due to historically founded political and cultural traditions. Economic explanations, however, such as the higher level of GDP per capita in Germany as compared with Britain, have no explanatory value, nor do the generally higher incomes of most of my German respondents. My results are exploratory and suggestive. Nevertheless, some of the findings echo what is established both in other parts of the book and in other literature on eating out.

Although the British sample contains fewer people enjoying a high, rather than a merely comfortable salary (level of education is roughly equal), they dine out more often in all types of restaurant and also, on average, engage more in fine-dining than the German respondents. Conversely, the possession of higher economic and roughly equal cultural capital by the German respondents has not encouraged a more enthusiastic embrace of fine-dining, but rather a more inhibited relation. This, it is suggested here and elsewhere, may reflect features of German culture, such as the lingering Kantian attitude of the highly educated bourgeoisie (*Bildungsbürgertum*) that consumption of good food lacks cultural value. (For greater detail, see Chapters 1 and 2.) Food philosopher and gastronomic writer Dollase is one of several to bemoan these characteristics of the German attitude to food consumption, and it is worth citing him at some length. Given that the cultivation of a discriminating taste for fine food is excluded from high (and valued) culture, together with the deeply internalized picture of 'the economy-minded housewife' who manages with little money and much inventiveness to provide for her family, Dollase suggests,

> any measure to create a meal which exceeds what is necessary could not become an accepted theme, and any preoccupation with good food would not be regarded positively but under aspects like 'superfluous', 'decadent' or as some completely unnecessary excrescence. This evaluation still is very widespread with us and is dissolving only slowly.[30]

This historically moulded 'economy-mindedness' around the purchase and utilization of food became further reinforced from the early 1960s onwards by the availability of very competitively priced food stuffs in discount supermarkets, like Aldi.[31] This endowed relatively expensive meals in top restaurants with an air of extravagance.

This insight about an inhibiting ethos around a strong preoccupation with good food in Germany then explains the comparatively smaller number of German respondents who frequently dine out in both *any* type of restaurant and in top restaurants. This is the case, despite the lower prices in German top restaurants and the greater likelihood in any part of the country, except in the former communist eastern *Länder*, of living near a Michelin-starred restaurant. British diners, in contrast, do not come up against such pronounced cultural barriers although the latter are not absent. In Britain, despite the strong fascination with everything food-related, there also lingers a sense that an interest in food is something to apologize for,[32] or even, as claimed by journalist Steven Poole that it 'represents a kind of perversity or decadence, an inward-turning dissipation of psychological and intellectual resources'.[33] However, such an attitude does not seem as widespread or as inhibiting as the German ethos.

These fundamental cultural differences then underlie further divergences, evident in my allocation of diners to three types. Although the proportion of deeply committed diners is the same in both countries—just over a third— British diners are more open to innovation and also more cosmopolitan in their dining practices. The latter finding may, however, partly be due to the fact that I have a disproportionately large number from a very cosmopolitan city—London—in my British sample. There is no equivalent geographical concentration of respondents in Germany, but more than half nevertheless live in big cities: four respondents live in Munich, one in Frankfurt, one in Hamburg, one in Zürich, one in Bremen, and two in Cologne.

Other cross-national differences found are that British diners are more satisfied with the degree of decline in formality of restaurant regimes and make fewer demands on front-of-house staff. German diners are more likely to expect chefs to source locally and bear health in mind in their cooking. This all fits in well with the fact that Germans are known to be very demanding and very health-conscious consumers, while British consumers are viewed as being more diffident in voicing complaints. This difference also surfaces in the fact that only German respondents demand 'value for money'.

Notes

1. See the study on dining out in Britain by A. Warde and L. Martens, *Eating Out: Social Differentiation, Consumption and Pleasure* (Cambridge: Cambridge University Press, 2000), 90.
2. A focus on this tension replaces the consideration of other competing modes of evaluation of interaction applied in previous chapters from L. Boltanski and L.

Thévenot, *On Justification: Economies of Worth* (Princeton: Princeton University Press, 2006) (translation from the French of *De la Justification: Les Economies de la Grandeur*).

3. P. Bourdieu, *Distinction: A Social Critique of the Judgement of Taste* (London: Routledge, 1984).

4. C. Driver, *The British at Table, 1940–80* (London: Chatto & Windus, 1983), 141.

5. For example, R. Peterson and R. Kern, 'Changing High-Brow Taste: From Snob to Omnivore', *American Sociological Review* 61 (1996): 900–7; T. Bennett, M. Savage, E. B. Silva, A. Warde, M. Gayo Cal, and D. Wright, *Culture, Class, Distinction* (London: Routledge, 2009).

6. Bennett et al. 2009: 31.

7. J. Finkelstein, *Dining Out: A Sociology of Modern Manners* (Cambridge: Polity Press, 1989), 2.

8. J.-A. Brillat-Savarin, *The Pleasures of the Table*. Translated extracts from *La Physiologie du Goût* [1825] (London: Penguin, 2011), 85.

9. J. Burnett, *England Eats Out: A Social History of Eating Out in England from 1830 to the Present* (Harlow: Longman, 2004), 325.

10. Finkelstein 1989: 5.

11. Finkelstein 1989: 12.

12. *Spiegel Online* 44 (2006): 1–9, <http://www.spiegel.de/spiegel/print/d-49378753. html>, U. von Fichter, *Der Klassenmampf*: 2.

13. G. Weber, *Kochen ist Krieg* (Munich: Piper, 2009), 20.

14. R. Blanc, *A Taste of My Life: One Man's Hunger for Perfection* (London: Transworld Publishers, 2008), 31.

15. *Süddeutsche Zeitung* 279 (3–4 December 2011): R16.

16. Gault Millau Deutschland (2013): 34–5.

17. *Spiegel Online* 44 (2006): 6, interview with food scholar Spiekermann.

18. *Süddeutsche Zeitung* 279 (3–4 December 2011): R16.

19. Bourdieu 1984.

20. A. Warde, *Consumption, Food and Taste* (London: Sage, 1997), 108.

21. J. Dollase, *Kulinarische Intelligenz* (Wiesbaden: Tre Torri Verlag, 2006), 76–7.

22. S. Mennell, *All Manners of Food: Eating and Taste in England and France from the Middle Ages to the Present* (Oxford: Basil Blackwell, 1985), 115.

23. Finkelstein 1989.

24. *Effillée* 21 (Summer 2012): 108.

25. U. Hannerz, 'Cosmopolitans and Locals in World Culture', in M. Featherstone (ed.), *Global Culture: Nationalism, Globalization and Modernity* (London: Sage, 1990), 239; J. Urry, *Consuming Places* (London: Routledge, 1994), 167.

26. For example, *Restaurant* (October 2011): 20.

27. Interview in *Der Feinschmecker* 9 (2009): 70–1.

28. T. Raue, *Ich weiss was Hunger ist. Von der Strassengang in die Sterneküche* (Munich and Zürich: Piper Verlag, 2012), 263.

29. Finkelstein 1989.

30. Dollase 2006: 124.

31. M. M. Schwarz, in *Frankfurter Allgemeine* (15 July 2013), <http://www.faz.net/aktuell/lebensstil/essen-trinken/sternegastronomie-es-kann-nicht-immer-kaviar-sein-12281679.html>.

32. As noted by William Skidelsky in *The New Statesman* (12 September 2005), <http://www.newstatesman.com/node/151521>.

33. S. Poole, *You Aren't What You Eat* (London: Union Books, 2012).

10

Taste Makers: The Attribution of Aesthetic and Economic Value by Gastronomic Critics and Guides

Taste makers, by imposing a canon of rules and standards, establish an aesthetic trend and determine what is legitimate taste. They may strongly influence aesthetic identifications and economic practices among both consumers and producers of cultural products, such as *haute cuisine* meals. Arbiters of taste have far-reaching symbolic effects and material consequences for the whole culinary field.

This chapter examines the roles played in the process of taste making by gastronomic critics, guides, and gastronomic competitions. A second and related question I seek to answer is what role gastronomic guides play in upholding or prolonging the cultural hegemony of French (classical and modern) cuisine in the early twenty-first century.

After a brief consideration of theoretical conceptualizations of the role of taste makers, I examine three important gastronomic guides in the 'fine-dining' restaurant industry—the international *Michelin* (or *Red Guide*), the British *Good Food Guide*, and the German *Gault Millau*. This is followed by an examination of one ascendant international culinary competition which competes with guides; namely, the Pellegrino Awards. I conclude with a brief analysis of gastronomic critics, writing in national and local newspapers and magazines, as well as of Internet food blogs.

How Do Taste Makers Evolve and What Makes Them Influential or Powerful?

How is taste—that is the capacity to be discerning and discriminating vis-à-vis a variety of objects or experiences—developed and communicated, and what effects may be attributed to taste makers in the cultural field of fine-dining restaurants?

The quality of aesthetic goods, such as 'fine-dining' restaurant food, is not signalled by price alone and needs to be experienced and tested by a qualified analyst. There exists an asymmetry of knowledge between seller and buyer, and the market is not self-regulating. Hence economists mainly focus on the task of gastronomic arbiters to convey specialist knowledge, in order to ease the functioning of the market. They speak of 'devices to provide the information which removes uncertainty and opacity, as well as signal out-of-the ordinary creativity'.[1]

The device in the market for *haute cuisine* is the restaurant guide. It has to have access to an extensive knowledge of the products and services involved and be able to give an accurate and reliable account of them, in order to gain the confidence of its readers. By stimulating producers to compete with each other for the patronage of an informed public, guides also set benchmarks within an industry. Over time, these benchmarks expand the top restaurant market, as well as raising the level of food served in the restaurant industry as a whole. (See Chapter 1.)

Sociologists enquire also about the consequences of such market regulation in terms of the establishment of aesthetic trends and legitimate tastes. They explore the mechanisms which lend legitimacy and render some critics/guides more influential than others. Critics' possession of a large amount of aesthetic experience and of specialized knowledge allows them to rank restaurants and thereby establish and make public a cultural hierarchy.[2] They may also consider the material preconditions and consequences of taste making and place emphasis on the power implied by them. Gastronomic arbiters' critical discourse therefore is both a mediator between chefs and diners *and* a determinant of aesthetic and/or symbolic value.[3]

The establishment of a hierarchy turns gastronomic arbiters into gatekeepers who, by establishing symbolic boundaries, include some and exclude other chefs.[4] All these functions combined can make arbiters extremely influential and sometimes even powerful. They simultaneously structure the experience of both diners and chefs. Like art critics, gastronomic critics are not objective referees. They become participants in a stream of discourse that defines the social hierarchy, established by their evaluations.[5] The objectivity of the reviewing process claimed by some gastronomic critics is put into question.[6]

A core problem for guides is to construct credibility. The credibility of critics may depend on their *connoisseurial* knowledge and/or on their reference to rules, principles, or standards. Standards imply rule-based judgement or evaluation in terms of aesthetic criteria. Such systems of rules are said to render critics' judgement legitimate.[7]

Connoisseurial reviews are presented by the American sociologist Blank as relying solely on the skills, sensitivity, and training of a single reviewer; they are almost entirely discursive and put a premium on sensitivity to nuance and complex understanding of mostly single restaurants/chefs. His *procedural* review, in contrast, is based on well-defined procedures that allow reviewers to rank performance of a product or cultural object compared to similar products.[8] The resulting rating system uses mainly numerical rating, rather than text. Both kinds of reviews are analytical types and actual rating systems usually have aspects of both types.[9]

For the British sociologist Stephen Mennell,[10] a second dichotomy is relevant when dealing with critics—that of elitism versus democracy (a theme also running through this book). For Mennell, the democratizing tendency emerges from a wider dissemination of aesthetic knowledge and judgement, assisting critics in reaching beyond a narrow elite. I follow Mennell but additionally consider strategies of inclusion of readers in the judgement of taste, as well as highlight inherent tensions between democracy and elitism in guides' strategies. My study highlights the different ways in which guides attempt to shed an elitist image, as well as judging how their promotion of democracy may enhance or reduce legitimacy.

Depending on the degree of credibility they command, the extent of influence and power of the critics varies. The ability to acquire moral authority is enhanced by the financial means guides can deploy in the rating process. Hence there occur struggles between different arbiters of taste to render their approach more legitimate than those of others.

The number of guides, critics, and competitions affecting British and German restaurants is too large to cover them all in detail. Concerning guides, the focus therefore is mainly on the *Michelin* or *Red Guide*, but two other guides with considerable influence, particularly among consumers—the *British Good Food Guide* and the *Gault Millau Germany*—also will be analysed to pinpoint competing strategies employed to gain legitimacy. The culinary competition selected—the Pellegrino Awards—has been chosen because it tries to challenge established guides. Gastronomic critics in the press and on Internet sites are too numerous to select any specific ones and will be covered only in general terms and with greater brevity.

Gastronomic Guides as Arbiters of Taste

The Michelin or Red Guide

The *Michelin* (MG) or *Red Guide*, due to its high degree of professionalism, is considered to be the most widely referred to restaurant guide in the world.

The *MG* is held to have greatly raised both standards of quality and creativity in the top layer of the restaurant industry.[11] It enjoys legitimacy and remains a reference point particularly among chefs, and less so, among the dining-out public. Prospective diners do not usually consult the *MG* itself but nevertheless take cognizance of its ratings, widely discussed in both the British and German press at the time of their annual announcement by Michelin Publishing. (See Chapter 9.)

The *MG* has been referred to as a 'chefs' guide'. The remark by a British one-star chef is representative of many other chefs' opinion: 'The *Michelin Guides* are still the benchmarks for a lot of chefs. For the public they are not necessarily the best guide.' All but one of the forty chefs I interviewed consider the *Michelin Guide* as the most important in the field and see it as their main point of reference. The one British one-star chef who strenuously denies the *MG* any importance—'I don't really pay much attention to it [the *MG*]. It is not important to my business'—later partially contradicts herself by saying 'We would want a second star, we absolutely deserve it.'

What has lent the *MG* this aura of professionalism and reliability and hence credibility among chefs? First, as a subsidiary of the French tyre-manufacturing company Michelin—who see the *Guide* as a marketing device—it is financially supported by the company and does not have to make a profit.[12] In recent years, the *Guide* has had to be subsidized by its parent to the tune of 15 million euros annually but nevertheless has been able to maintain editorial independence.[13] This indicates both the considerable material resources the *MG* can devote to its ranking exercise and the degree of financial independence from interests in the food industry it is able to maintain. The command of a large budget permits the *Red Guide* to employ a large cadre of professional inspectors—it has around 100 full-time inspectors throughout western Europe and thirteen inspectors in Germany.[14] This greatly increases its legitimacy among chefs. According to a German one-star chef: 'Michelin is more important than the rest. They are a large enterprise—they can afford it. The others just copy—they do not have the means.'

Michelin inspectors are required to have an industry background and receive six months of training. Their salaried status and their anonymity are said to safeguard their independence from chefs and any other interested parties in the food industry.[15] The deployment of this large cadre of inspectors in the evaluation and judgement process facilitates multiple visits (up to twelve in difficult cases) by different inspectors before a decision is taken,[16] the geographical and sometimes cross-national rotation of inspectors,[17] and the collective nature of the final accreditation process.[18] Concerning repeat visits, the editor of *Michelin Germany* tells me: 'We get about 150 meals a year where at the very least, a second opinion is required.' Decisions about elevation to three-star status are said to be taken at the European level: 'There is the "Stars Conference" in which France participates.'[19]

These financial and organizational features safeguard the integrity and reliability of the *MG*. Paradoxically, the Michelin company's large financial investment cannot be recouped by selling a large number of copies of the *Guide*. It is the inclusion of chefs and the order they are ranked in, not the discursive evaluation, which is of interest to chefs and diners, and these results can be ascertained free from the quality press and from Internet sites.

Selection of restaurants for starred status is claimed to be objective by the *Guide* in that it is the result 'of a strict use of a system of evaluation oriented to *objective* measurement criteria by all'.[20] The *Red Guide*'s criteria for assessment of restaurants have been constant over a long period of time. All these attributes serve to create confidence in the *Guide* on the part of its readers and render its rankings legitimate in the eyes of (the vast majority) of ranked chefs. The following representative extracts from my 2010/11 interviews illustrate the highly positive views of the *Michelin Guide* held by starred chefs:

> Michelin inspectors are professional, they understand the basis of food...The *MG* sets standards for the guest and the chef. (British one-star chef, 2010)
>
> *Michelin* is still the most revered guide in the world. (British one-star chef, 2010)
>
> The *MG* is a trustworthy guide. (British one-star chef, 2010)
>
> *Michelin* is the preserver of the holy grail...the court of last instance...At the international level, only starred restaurants count. (German three-star chef, 2011)
>
> Michelin people are informed about cooking. The rest are mere journalists. (German one-star chef, 2011)
>
> Michelin watch out but do not wish to prescribe, like Gault Millau. They are the court of last instance. They preserve anonymity and are incorruptible. (German three-star chef)

Unlike the other two guides, the *Michelin Guide* does not offer *connoisseurial* reviews. It is much closer to Blank's *procedural* reviews in that it relies extensively on what it considers easily legible 'unambiguous, objective and unbiased symbols'.[21] They provide star ratings as well as general information (e.g. on price, opening times) that is said to facilitate comparison across a large number of restaurants and even countries. The *Red Guide* also details three representative or signature dishes, selected by the chef. Since 2000, the procedural type of rating has been followed by a very short text of about six lines. This provides a more *connoisseurial* review that evaluates the food offered, as well as describing the specificity of the kitchen's expertise and the restaurant's ambience. But it remains too short to convey a restaurant's special character to the dining public, in the way both the *GFG* and *Gault Millau* do. Hence prospective diners, as shown in Chapter 9, do not usually acquire their own copy, even though they often know and value the ranking information.

The *MG*'s judgements refer to standards, said to be grounded in carefully established procedures of reviewing restaurants. Stars are awarded on five criteria: the quality of produce; the mastery of flavours and cooking; the creativity of the chef; value for money; and the consistency of the kitchen's achievement.[22] But the requirements differ according to category. The symbolic boundaries between the categories are firmly drawn, in that ascendance to a higher star category is extremely difficult and is achieved only by a comparatively small minority of chefs. In the one-star category, only the quality of the food and the wine list is judged, whereas in two- and three-star restaurants originality or a personal signature of the chef is an additional requirement. To become eligible for three stars, Derek Bulmer, the editor of the *MG Britain* until 2010, stated, all-round excellence is expected, and elegant surroundings and faultless service are added to the other demands.[23] In contrast, both the Michelin representatives I interviewed insist that for all three categories only the quality of food is considered, and not the quality of the ambience or service.

Despite its pre-eminent position among gastronomic guides, the *MG* has been criticized on a number of points. First, chefs are not provided with any information on *why* they gained or lost one or more stars. Inspectors still make their judgements without discussing the grounds for reaching them in particular cases. The vagueness and opacity which cloak the actual evaluation process in secrecy are proudly referred to by the Michelin organization as its mystique.[24] But it is less approvingly remarked upon by the British inspector I interviewed who sees this secrecy 'as a French thing'. The opacity and secrecy rule-out a challenge of the *MG*'s judgements of taste, as well as making it difficult for chefs to learn from them. Michelin themselves, however, justify it by stating that they wish to prevent a slavish adoption of their criteria which would result in unwelcome homogenization of culinary styles. Also chefs can visit the central office to get the information on which they were judged, but never any advice on how to improve. According to the editor of *Michelin Germany*:

> I receive many chefs and speak to them openly about dossiers. I explain the reasons for the withdrawal but do not give advice, just analysis. I rarely have had an unpleasant conversation.

Second, to enhance its image of reliability and consistency, the *Guide* eschews risk-taking. Hence, it is relatively slow both to promote new talent and originality in chefs and to demote highly ranked chefs who have ceased to be innovative. This criticism has been voiced by many other authors, and it also is remarked upon by some of the chefs I interviewed. A comparison by the author of British and German three-star restaurants in the years 2005 and 2009[25] shows no downward movement among three-star restaurants during that period, though the number of two-star restaurants had increased significantly in both countries between the two dates. (For more detail on stars awarded in different years, see Chapters 1 and 2.) The *Michelin Guide* does not want to risk undermining readers' confidence in its authority as a taste maker by frequent changes in evaluation of chefs. In the process, however, it forfeits a reputation for 'discovering' radically innovative chefs and the capacity to spot new directions in chefs' taste.

However, Michelin have slightly relaxed their conservatism in recent years, particularly in relation to the award of the second and even the third star where a few swift promotions have occurred in recent years. The number of two-star chefs increased dramatically in Germany in 2013, though not in Britain, from eighteen in 2010 to thirty-six in 2013, with ten new awards in 2013 alone. Examples of rapid promotion in Germany are Sebastian Zier who received his second star in 2011 although the restaurant *La Mer* in the Sylt A-Rosa Hotel had only opened in 2010. Even more dramatic, Travemünde chef Kevin Fehling was awarded his third star in 2013, only two years after having received his second star. Overall, however, the *MG* still is more conservative than other guides.

Third, the *MG* is still considered very elitist in its stance towards the dining public, as well as in the type of restaurant it picks for the award of stars. The *MG* actively encourages responses from diners but still uses inspectors' judgement as the main criterion for the classing of restaurants. The considerable customer feedback—around 45,000 letters and e-mails from European readers each year—is said to provide useful indications but is never considered a substitute for the work by inspectors in the field.[26] Customer feedback therefore constitutes a check on, rather than a basis for inspectors' judgements. However, in 2013, Michelin finally introduced an online portal where comments sent in by members of the German public will be published, once they have been selected by a special committee for publication.[27] Democratizing tendencies in other aspects of its judgements have emerged fairly recently and are still comparatively modest.

The Michelin organization has lately becomes anxious to distance itself from the elitism many still associate it with. Thus the British inspector I interviewed correctly points out that, in terms of the number of entries into each guide, non-starred establishments are a much larger proportion than starred ones. Also, since 1997, the *MG* has expanded the range of restaurants it classes, with the introduction of the award of *bib gourmand* that rewards 'value for money'. Additionally, prices of starred restaurants are scrutinized to penalize over-pricing. A British Michelin inspector tells me:

> We have taken restaurants out of the *Guide* because they are too expensive. There are restaurants we would not recommend because of the price.

This appears to be a new policy direction. It constitutes a nod towards consumers without huge funds to spend on fine-dining. It therefore constitutes an important move towards democratization.

Michelin additionally has responded to diners tired of 'stiff and formal' restaurants. Since 2009, they have awarded a star to more modest restaurants with an informal style. Among these, one may count Chinese Dim Sum shops in Hong Kong, as well as a small number (thirteen in 2012) of gastro pubs in Britain and of bistro-type establishments in Germany (meriting the symbol of only one set of knives and fork for ambience). At the public announcement of the 2013 awards in Berlin—another Michelin innovation—the editor-in-chief made a special mention of the fact that 'many small restaurants had been found, where the atmosphere is relaxed, unrestrained and cheerful. And they offer value for money.'

Although elitism thus has been significantly reduced (interviews with chefs 2010–12), the tension between democratic impulses and continued elitism remains. Both the knowledge of good food—the ability to cultivate good taste—and the financial means to eat in Michelin-starred restaurants are available only to a relatively small section of diners in advanced societies, even if this stratum has broadened considerably in recent decades (see Chapter 9).

The fourth criticism of Michelin relates to the appropriateness of applying the same criteria to evaluate different national cuisines. The *Red Guide* has traditionally defined itself by its classical taste.[28] Once it started judging restaurants also in other countries, it has emphasized its neutrality towards cooking philosophies and its impartiality and even-handedness between countries.[29] In the words of the editor of the British *Red Guide* in 2009:

> We're aiming to get *one* consistent standard for entry into the guide, for one star, two stars and three stars, around the world. It's the same standards *throughout*.[30]

It is, however, widely believed that, as each cuisine has its own standards, it is most appropriately judged by what it tries to achieve.[31] Hence different genres of cuisine require judgements based on different criteria, and it is difficult to evaluate, as the Michelin organization claims to do, European and Japanese or Chinese cuisine by the same standards. This point is not conceded by my Michelin interviewees who both insist that cross-national comparison is possible with the current criteria for evaluation.

Fifth, due to its resources and exalted position as described above, the *Michelin Guide* has had enormous influence over the definition of culinary culture and the making of taste. The *Guide* has exerted its power discreetly and often imperceptibly. In answer to questions about the substance of the culinary style or taste it has institutionalized, I claim that it has prolonged the dominance of French *haute cuisine* over much of western Europe and, perhaps less so, over US metropolises. It thereby has perpetuated what is still regarded by many as a highly complex, expensive, and therefore elite taste.

The French origin of the *Guide*, together with its integral position in French culture and identity and the extended period (from the beginning of the nineteenth century onwards) of hegemony in Europe of French *haute cuisine*,[32] raise some doubt about whether strict impartiality of evaluation between culinary styles of different countries is attainable in practice. Moreover, the standards of excellence for *haute cuisine* were originally systematized in Escoffier's 1907 *Guide Culinaire*, and in Europe French culinary techniques, passed on during initial vocational training, are still widely taken for granted. Moreover, so-called star conferences, where the award of higher-level stars is discussed, still take place in Paris. As noted above, a rating system is very much influenced by the institutional and cultural environment in which it has arisen, and critics are participants in a stream of discourse that defines the social hierarchy. Thus the *MG*'s standards have been shaped not only by critics themselves but also by producers and diners who, historically, have been, and still are, predominantly French. However, the *Guides* of both countries insist that it is possible to be even-handed in the cross-national comparison of different culinary styles.[33]

The Michelin award system is regarded as an exceedingly important influence on culinary culture and on the socio-geographic identity of chefs and their cooking. Although it is never articulated that to get two or three stars chefs must adhere to the basic principles of French *haute cuisine*, many British and German chefs have drawn their own conclusions from the pattern of stars awarded. The overriding importance of the award of stars to both chefs' financial success and professional reputation therefore has prolonged French culinary dominance among them.

At the same time, it is suggested, the prolonged hegemony of French cuisine has prevented the emergence of both a plurality of culinary styles and of an eclectic global mélange in which boundaries between different types of cuisine have been largely eroded.[34] However, chefs no longer rigidly adhere to the rules of French classical cuisine and are very open to influences from other world cuisines, as well as from their own national and regional traditions. Yet the *basis* of their cooking for a large number of chefs remains the cannons of French classical and *nouvelle cuisine*.

I do not allege conscious discrimination in the rating process in favour of French cuisine. Instead I point out that the deep cultural rootedness of the Michelin organization may have resulted in a tacit bias. This is, however, disputed by most chefs, regardless of their national origin. Only five, mainly British chefs, of the forty chefs I interviewed question the *Guide*'s apparent French bias in fairly mild terms, detecting an 'unknowing bias':

> In France, the *MG* is so important, it is a big part of their culture … Not all French three-star restaurants deserve their three stars. (British two-star chef)

> There could be a few more stars in Britain at every level and a few less in France. (British one-star chef)

> There are very few two-star restaurants [in Britain] that are not French. (British one-star chef)

A German one-star chef also thinks that 'Michelin may be a bit chauvinist—most of the stars remain in France.'

In contrast, the following representative extracts from my interviews illustrate most chefs' beliefs in the impartiality of the *Michelin Guide*:

> They are very strict, there is no compromise. They are no longer influenced by French standards. (British one-star chef)

> No way is there any bias. First, it [French cuisine] is the mother of all cuisines, and second, the *Guide* has opened itself to other ways of cooking. (German three-star chef)

> Michelin are not biased now, not during the last five years. Under Naret they became less French. (German one-star chef)

Chefs and, indeed, the Michelin staff I interviewed rightly point out that, in recent years, Michelin have become a more encompassing and international organization by including also various Asian cuisines in their rating processes.

> No, there is no bias. They have been brave to recognize ethnic cuisine although it has taken them a long time. (British one-star chef)

> No, they don't have a bias. Pubs have stars and so do all different types of cuisine, i.e. Japanese, Indian, Chinese, Italian, etc. (British one-star chef)

> There is no tacit bias now. The *MG* has changed in the last ten years. Molecular gastronomy and other changing gastronomic styles have intervened. (British one-star chef)

> No [there is no tacit bias], Michelin now have a much broader outlook than in the past...Michelin have become more attuned to current time. (German one-star chef)

However, this attempt to repudiate French dominance is still too recent to have had a decisive impact on the general pattern of award of stars. Moreover, outside the world of chefs it has not yet been widely recognized.

A close study of the results of the *Michelin Guide*'s ranking in present-day Britain and Germany readily reveals that it upholds the dominance of either classical or modern French cuisine at the top of the restaurant pyramid, i.e. among two- and three-star restaurants. The first source of support for this claim lies in the very high proportion of two- and three-star chefs in both Britain and Germany who still adhere to the classical or modern French style of cooking, albeit individually adapted by considering also other genres. This is indicated by chefs themselves in interviews and by other public definitions of their cuisine. (The main exceptions are a handful of restaurants in each country, wholly or partly following Ferran Adria's molecular culinary style.[35]) At the same time, there prevails a corresponding absence at this higher level of styles oriented towards other national or ethnic cuisines, such as the Indian, Chinese, Thai, or Turkish. Even Italian, not to mention English/German cuisine, is underrepresented *above* one-star level. This is not to say that elements of German and British national/regional culinary heritage respectively are completely absent on the menus of two- and three-star chefs but merely that they do not *define* their general style. Ethnic restaurants may attain one star, but to date they have not managed to go beyond this in either Britain or Germany. Thus Britain has several Indian and Chinese restaurants, as well as a Japanese and a Thai restaurant, in the one star-category. In Germany, the 2011 award of one star to a Japanese restaurant still was considered a minor sensation.[36] This lower reward of ethnic restaurants in both societies may be interpreted as undermining any attempt by the *MG* to develop a more inclusionary process of judgement.

When confronted with the fact that there are no two- or three-star Italian restaurants in either Britain or Germany, the Michelin inspectors I interviewed explained that none were good enough to be awarded multiple stars:

> I know of no Italian restaurant in Britain that would deserve a second star. We do not want to widen the goal posts just to let in Italian restaurants. (British Michelin inspector)

A second and related piece of evidence derives from the fact that German regional cooking, although very popular and alive among German one-star chefs and in hotel brasseries, as well as in German restaurants more generally,[37] remains somewhat marginal to the culinary styles of most two- and three-star chefs in terms of actual dishes prepared, despite the rise of *Neue Deutsche Küche* in recent years. This is the case even though Michelin now actively welcome refined regional cuisine. This is explicitly stated by my British Michelin interviewee. The lack of response on the part of two- and three-star chefs portrays their lack of confidence in testing the veracity of Michelin's pronouncement on this point.

The continued observation of the French classical and modern canon of taste—either as a whole or in part—is fairly equally pronounced in Britain and Germany. This is the case, even though German two- and three-star chefs are now largely second-generation and are mainly (93 per cent) German-born.[38] They have been trained by German chefs. German chefs long have adhered less rigidly to French *haute cuisine*, with many practising a Mediterranean cuisine, i.e. they have complemented French with elements of Italian cuisine. Also in very recent years, they have begun to show a new confidence in engaging in more far-reaching new departures. While all these developments are fairly new and constitute nascent, rather than fully formed trends, they do demonstrate a waning of loyalty to French *haute cuisine*. However, one German French-born chef, proud of his French cuisine, also connects the influence of French cuisine firmly with Michelin. When I ask him what he regards as the main function of the *Michelin Guide*, he replies: 'That the vision and tradition of a grande cuisine remains; and that one takes cooking also as a form of art' (two-star chef Eric Menchon).

Among British chefs, with the notable exception of Heston Blumenthal, there does not exist a comparable basis for the discarding of French culinary tradition. The revival of *haute cuisine*, in the early 1980s, had been spear-headed by French-born chefs who trained a whole generation of younger chefs. Even today, French nationals still constitute 39 per cent of two- and three-star chefs;[39] and vocational training remains weak. Hence in British fine-dining restaurants, the French paradigm of cuisine ought to hold greater sway than in Germany. However, as shown in Chapter 6, this is not the case among the twenty chefs I interviewed (the majority were one-star chefs). There is greater diversity among them in the way they perceive their cooking and the number owning up to French styles even is slightly lower than in Germany.

In view of these recent and still inchoate developments, one might conclude that the still considerable influence of the *MG* on chefs acts as a taste maker, upholding the slightly diminished but still high status of French classical and modern cuisine. The *Red Guide* may not impose its taste preferences on chefs, but chefs deduce them from actual patterns of starring. They may exercise self-censorship and not develop, for example, a regional cuisine because they *believe* the *Michelin Guide* would not reward the adoption of such a cuisine. Hence the perpetuation of the French culinary paradigm may be primarily a consequence of its deep internalization by chefs, even though it sometimes runs counter to principles the Michelin organization now claims to uphold. When I asked the German editor-in-chief of Michelin Publishing whether the principles of classical cuisine still provide the measure of quality and whether the French origin of the *MG* shapes selection criteria in any way I received the following reply:

> I am not at all content with your question. The opposite is the case. We have been criticized for preferring modern cuisine...The only French influence is that one values good food. You can see how cuisines have changed.

The above analysis of the *Michelin Guide* as a taste maker has highlighted both the characteristics which lend it credibility and virtually unchallenged legitimacy among chefs and the features which might be connected with the enduring influence of French cuisine over both British and German chefs, even if the latter has weakened in recent decades. My analysis additionally has highlighted the merely modest moves towards greater democratization, in terms of both including diners in the evaluation process and in terms of becoming more inclusive in the culinary styles considered for award, particularly of two and three stars.

The Consequences of the Michelin Ranking System for Fine-Dining Restaurants

This section investigates the ways in which the dominance of the *Michelin Guide* as a taste maker and its exercise of symbolic power simultaneously exert material power over fine-dining chefs. This power is exercised through the several positive and negative implications the ranking system holds for chefs, rather than being overtly imposed. Gaining Michelin stars has many highly positive effects on both chefs' reputation, their business, and on their professional career. (For details, see Chapter 4.) This explains why the majority of chefs would give anything to become starred or increase the number of their stars. A recent article in *Restaurant* sums up the situation as follows: 'Like it or not, the accolade [of receiving one or more stars] remains the benchmark for high-end restaurants.'[40] A British two-star chef agrees: 'The *Michelin Guide* does more to fuel the ambition of younger chefs than other guides.'

It is now widely documented that each star greatly increases the level of a restaurant's business and that the award of two or more stars thrusts chefs into the public limelight in a way unimagined at the beginning of their careers.[41] The reverse side of this is that Michelin chefs can never relax and instead have to show constant vigilance that their standards of excellence do not slide and risk the loss of one or more stars. The pressures become particularly acute at the level of two-star restaurants (aspiring to the receipt of a third star) and among those in the 'three-star' category. Contrary to the protestations of the Michelin inspectors, chefs still believe that, at the three-star level, fine wines, faultless service, and elegant surroundings have to be supplied in addition to excellent and creative food.

The achievement of these qualities by both aspiring and actual three-star chefs calls for considerable financial investment into the restaurant, the wine cellar, and into a large body of well-trained staff, as well as requiring a larger and more complex network of suppliers. Such restaurants, for many chefs, become economically unsustainable. Two of the chefs interviewed do not aspire to a higher star ranking because they consider themselves unable to obtain the funds necessary for the new investment they see as associated with two- or three-star status. Whether or not their estimations of the expenditure involved are realistic—my British Michelin interviewee categorically denies that they are—it nevertheless shapes many chefs' strategy of business development.

The loss of one or more stars also means a serious loss of business, jeopardizing the chef's reputation and income and therefore his or her ability to repay the loans taken out to upgrade the restaurant. The ranking thus has very real material consequences for high-level chefs, going well beyond its symbolic value. Consequently, the *presumed* rules and requirements of the *Guide* are taken extremely seriously by chefs.

French sociologist Lucien Karpik and his US colleague Rick Fantasia go even further and plausibly suggest that the financial pressures on restaurant owners, faced with increased expenditure to attract a second or third star, eventually may change the whole fine-dining restaurant industry.[42] Currently a significant proportion of fine-dining restaurants in Britain and Germany are relatively small, owner-managed businesses, started with own savings, a small loan from a bank, or, more often, a business partner. Financial pressures to make very large investment have been conducive to the establishment of ties with financial groups and large industrial food producers.[43] By risking increasing commercialization, both Fantasia and Karpik suggest, craft or culinary art is surrendering to big business. While both authors are referring to French Michelin restaurants, I have been struck by the emergence of a similar trend in the British industry. (See Chapter 11.)

Two Major Contemporary Gastronomic Guides

The British *Good Food Guide* (*GFG*) was founded in 1951 by Raymond Postgate (an academic, writer, and gourmet), to advance appreciation of good food in Britain. In that year it sold 5,000 copies which, by the early 1980s, had increased to 50,000.[44] But formal ranking was introduced only in 1970. By then, according to Mennell,[45] there was confidence that there was a sufficient consensus about what counts as good taste.

My analysis of the *GFG*'s distinguishing characteristics draws on information published in the *Guide* (various years) and on the Internet. The *GFG* contrasts with the *Michelin Guide* in several important respects. Its ranking of restaurants is based on a large number of readers' evaluations (25,000 in 2010), combined with reports by employed, anonymously working inspectors. Inspectors are people with experience in the field of restaurants or gastronomic criticism, but no mention of training is made.[46]

It is not clear from the *GFG*'s own publicity material how much weight is being accorded to each source of judgement, nor how many inspectors are employed.[47] An interview with the editor reveals that, although only food is benchmarked by readers and inspectors according to uniform criteria, service and ambience are given some consideration in the ranking. However, the editor remains deliberately vague on what weighting each of the three receives.[48]

Restaurants have been ranked, since 1996, on a scale of 1 to 10, and only categories 6–10 overlap with those referred to for starring by the *Michelin Guide* (9 and 10 are very rarely given, with only one of 10 and two of 9 awarded in 2012). The long list of criteria for ranking are made public in the *GFG*.[49] They are left sufficiently general so as to require some individual judgement. In addition to numerical scoring, a substantial discursive evaluation is provided. The *GFG* is what Mennell calls a talkative guide,[50] that is, it comments at much greater length than the *MG* on the particular strengths and weaknesses of restaurants' cuisine, wine, and ambience. This feature makes it more popular with consumers, as compared with the *MG*. A chef comments: 'The *Good Food Guide* probably brings more people through the door than anything else.'[51] This is borne out by my interviews of diners, discussed in Chapter 9. However, its method of evaluation and the resources for ranking at its disposal endow it with less legitimacy compared with the *MG* among chefs, as illustrated below.

In contrast to the *Michelin Guide*, the *GFG* is located at the democratic end of Mennell's continuum between expressing elite taste and trying to democratize that taste.[52] It operates under the umbrella of the British Consumers' Association. To be sure, the *GFG* covers the same high-level restaurants as the *MG*, but it also ranks quality establishments in the middle price band and ethnic restaurants and has been one of the first to champion gastro pubs. It ranks highly a range of culinary styles or tastes and is not beholden only to the French genre, and therefore is judged to be more inclusive or democratic. The *GFG* recognizes that contemporary diners are omnivores, that is, they may seek to act out more than one canon of taste.

The *GFG* also is more democratic than the *MG* in that the opinions of its readers, made known to the *Guide* by their reports, provide a stronger weight in the ranking process than the views of its relatively small cadre of paid inspectors. To rebalance the *Guide*'s orientation from being too '*haute cuisine*' to taking account of readers' views, the *GFG* introduced totally reader-led Annual Awards in 2008. The *GFG* therefore promotes a somewhat confusing mix of a democratic ethos with elitism.

The *GFG* cannot be said to *impose* a canon of taste as it aggregates and claims to reflect those of its readership. Whether the *GFG* therefore is more objective and hence legitimate than the *Michelin Guide*, however, is open to debate. As Blank has pointed out, whether taking readers' views into account adds objectivity and reliability depends totally on the sampling process adopted.[53] In the case of the *GFG*, which relies on unsolicited readers' letters, a sampling process is non-existent.

The *GFG* views itself as both the representative and the advocate of the dining public. Yet it also tries to shape the public's taste in a very general way. It does this overtly by informing the users of the *Guide* of certain trends that are said to be embodying exemplary taste. Over the years, different editors have pursued different campaigns. During the 1980s, there was an attempt to champion a Modern British cuisine which, during the 1990s, gave way to celebrating the cosmopolitan diversity and eclecticism of high-level restaurants.[54] In the 2010 *GFG*, the local sourcing of fresh and seasonal produce by restaurants predominantly located outside the metropolis was rewarded in the ranking process.[55]

Is the *GFG* then an arbiter of taste? The answer is both 'yes' and 'no'. Yes, the *GFG* rewards both high creativity and highly priced quality, thereby appealing to elite diners, as well as setting obligatory standards for chefs. In its campaigns, the *Guide* theorizes trends it claims to have found in both readers' communication and in certain highly rated chefs' culinary styles. At the same time, however, the *GFG* aims to reach beyond a small elite and be more inclusive. It may be argued that it acts as a mere mediator between chefs and the increasingly diversified 'fine-dining' public.

Furthermore, the *GFG* rewards more than one contemporary culinary trend or taste, and it ranks highly 'refined' ethnic cuisine. The *Guide* also has distanced itself from the allegedly formal French style of dining and tries to cultivate a more informal style of sociability. Despite the *GFG*'s greater efforts to become more inclusive and democratic, the tension between elitism and a democratic approach remains unresolved.

All of the above-noted objectives/practices must be considered as attempts to 'propagate a taste', albeit an internally differentiated taste. Yet the periodic changes of objects of campaign, the championing of a range of genres and hierarchical levels of cuisine, as well as the representation and targeting of multiple readerships, weakens or even blurs symbolic boundaries. It has robbed the *GFG* of a distinctive voice. These orientations and practices obviate the representation of one dominant taste. The *Guide* would not be able to, nor would it want to, privilege French cuisine. All this endows it with less legitimacy and authority among chefs, as compared with the *MG*. This is well expressed in the words of a British one-star chef:

> I could not care less about the *GFG*. It is written by the people who read it…Michelin inspectors are different—they are intelligent and subtle. Michelin inspectors remember dishes. They have integrity and commitment. Michelin inspectors *really* know the food. They are really professional people. They have all worked in the business. Most of the time they are right, even if they criticize.

A London one-star chef has a different criticism: 'The *GFG* do not update enough, they do not have enough inspectors.'

Yet, due to its more discursive style, the *GFG* is very popular with the British fine-dining public. They are reputed to sell more than double the number of copies of the *Michelin Guide*.[56]

The second guide to be contrasted with the *MG* is the *Gault Millau Germany*. The *Gault Millau* (*GM*) was started by the journalists Gault and Millau at the end of the 1960s in France to propagate their ten commandments about *nouvelle cuisine*. It was introduced into Germany in 1983. It thus resembles the *Michelin Guide* in that it is of French origin and has become European, though not yet fully international. Yet in most other respects the *GM* differs decisively from the *MG*. *Gault Millau* is a much smaller and less well-resourced organization than Michelin Publishing. It is forced to raise some of the necessary financial resources by including advertisements for drinks and luxury goods, though never foods, in the annual publication, even though *Gault Millau* relies on an unpaid inspectorate (who only get their expenses refunded). From initially using mainly part-time editors and inspectors, in 2010, it further scaled down its expenditure and changed to using only locally recruited agents. Its inspectors, in contrast to those employed by the *Michelin Guide*, are not trained industry insiders but come from journalistic and other professional backgrounds. They rely on their knowledge as engaged gourmands who try not merely to inform but also to entertain and provoke. The editor of the *GM* until spring 2012, Manfred Kohnke, used to be a reporter for the critical socio-political magazine *Der Spiegel*, while his successor, Patricia Bröhm, is a journalist writing in a less polemical manner on culinary matters mainly for *Süddeutsche Zeitung*.

In common with the other two guides, *GM* uses both numerical ranking and text, but its discursive evaluation is much more substantial than that even of the *GFG*. *GM* rates a restaurant only on one aspect—its food—on a scale of 1–20. It awards outstanding restaurants, rated between 13 (one toque) and 20 (four toques).[57] No restaurant in Germany has ever been given 20 points, and only four German chefs have received 19.5 and nine 19 points in 2013. Their longer rating scale allows finer gradations in judgement, getting over the *MG*'s huge bunching in the one-star category. *GM*'s criteria for rating are more specific and more adequate to the task than those of the *MG*: quality and freshness of produce; creativity and professionalism of preparation; harmony between dishes; menu sequences; exactness of timing in cooking (*Garzeit*); and presentation.[58] *GM* also provides criticisms in lengthy reviews of each restaurant so that chefs implicitly are given justifications for the number of points awarded. Colour photos of some restaurant exteriors or interiors further enliven the *GM*. In contrast to the other two guides, the editor concedes that their criteria are applied according to 'our personal taste', i.e. there is no claim to objectivity.[59]

Where the *Gault Millau* differs decisively from the *Michelin Guide*—something which goes back to its origins in the late 1960s as a promoter of *nouvelle cuisine*—is that it sees itself as more avant-garde and not beholden to the French classical tradition. In contrast to the *MG*'s traditional conservatism in awarding multiple stars, the *GM* distinguishes itself by being more adventurous. It seeks out innovative chefs who have moved the goalposts in their culinary style and rewards them with a high ranking well before the *MG* has dared to promote them. (However, the gap between the two guides, as shown above, has been somewhat reduced in recent years, and in 2013 the *MG* was even held to be more daring by some commentators.) *Gault Millau* actively attempt trend setting by making extensive comments on the Chef of the Year chosen by them. In 2013, for example, they selected two-star Bavarian chef Christian Jürgens for his skilful integration of the local and the global. Their often witty and polemic comments on restaurants—'the sharp tongue is our trade mark', said Kohnke—are designed to provide interesting reading matter. Its engaging style partly seeks to compensate for the fact that their verdicts on individual restaurants are not always spot on.[60] In its appeal to highly educated readers, the *GM* is unashamedly elitist.

The *Gault Millau* therefore must be considered a taste maker but not in the sense of *upholding* a culinary tradition, as does the *MG*. It is more akin to an art critic who continuously seeks out new talent, rather than trying to establish unswerving confidence in its readers. The *GM* is more intent on indicating a new direction of taste, than on preserving a culinary tradition. Its success in this endeavour, however, is reduced by the fact that chefs consider it to be less consistent and reliable. The *GM*'s restricted financial resources, precluding frequent restaurant inspection before the award or withdrawal of points, have reduced its credibility among chefs. A German two-star chef, interviewed in 2011, comments:

> Gault Millau is not respectable. One man only covers the whole of Schleswig-Holstein [a state in northern Germany]. He comes at the same time every year. He is very personal in his evaluation.

Another two-star chef from the state of Rhineland-Westphalia confirms this practice. A one-star chef interviewed in the same year adds that, because *GM* cannot command a sizeable inspectorate, it sometimes merely copies other reviewers' views. Even worse, he holds that

> the *GM* is very dishonest—one of the least honest in Germany. I took them to court and won. They sell the least number of copies. *Michelin* are more careful.

The legitimacy of the *GM* among chefs therefore has become impaired. It is not considered a strong competitor to the *MG* by chefs themselves. In sum, although the *GM* aspires to being a taste maker, its other roles—those of trend-spotting and entertainment, together with its inadequate resources for reliable evaluation—have impaired its legitimacy among chefs and undermined its capacity to 'make a taste'. Whether its greater audacity, lesser self-righteousness, and its lengthy critical and entertaining descriptions of restaurants endow it with more popularity among consumers cannot be answered by this research.

Other gastronomic guides held to be influential by several British chefs are the *AA Guide* and for London, *Time Out.* Some German chefs mention *Der Feinschmecker* as an additional influential guide.

Other Types of Gastronomic Arbiters

In addition to gastronomic guides, competitions between chefs, organized by a variety of more or less self-interested organizations, also offer a set of evaluations of what has value in the area of *haute cuisine* and establish ranking orders on this basis. Hence they, too, become gastronomic arbiters and may even become taste makers. Such national and international competitions proliferate, and only one will be discussed in detail here—the Pellegrino Awards to the World's 50 Best Restaurants. It is sponsored by the drinks producers San Pellegrino and Acqua Panna and has been run by the British trade magazine *Restaurant* since 2005. I have chosen this particular competition because its highly ranked chefs have acquired international fame and unheard-of success. Thus, Danish René Redzepi of *Noma*, after election to the first place in the list in 2010, found that the number of guests on his reservation list went from 14 to 1,204. The competition is of additional interest because the Pellegrino Awards are very internationally oriented, as well as embracing a more casual ambience. They thus unwittingly compete with the Michelin awards in areas where the latter have often been criticized.

How are chefs assessed and selected for placement in their hierarchy of the world's 50 (now grown to 100) best chefs? Selection works according to the following methodology. The list of the 50 best restaurants is compiled from the votes of the World's 50 Best Restaurants Academy, a virtual organization of twenty-seven panels established to make the ranking. The world is divided into regions, with a chairperson in each region appointed for their knowledge of their part of the restaurant world. Some regions span more than one country. The regions are designed to represent fairly the global restaurant scene at the time. The chairpersons of each elect a voting panel of thirty members, who are selected from among chefs, restaurateurs, food photographers, travel journalists, and 'well-known gourmets' who are not further defined. Chairs of panels, according to a German food writer, are not even well known in the region.[61] These panels of around 800 judges together cast a total of 5,859 votes. Each panel member votes for seven restaurants of their own choice, which may include up to two restaurants from their own region and must include three from another region. No one can vote for their own restaurant, and they must have eaten in the restaurants of their choice in the last eighteen months—but it is not possible to ensure that they have. There are no set criteria on which voting must be based. According to the editor of *Restaurant*, William Drew, 'the list has no criteria for the voter other than this is one of their seven best restaurant experiences of the last 18 months'.[62] The rationale for this open-endedness is said to be to ensure the widest possible consideration of restaurants, wherever they are located and whatever low quality of service and ambience they offer. Food alone is to be judged. It has allowed for the inclusion of such totally informal restaurants like *Momofuku Ssam Bar* in New York's East Village which is said to serve superb Korean-American comfort food and has 'about three' informally attired waiting staff.[63] (No equivalent British or German restaurants are in the list.)

This, at first sight, seems an ingenious methodology which, through mainly peer review, can cover most of the up-market international restaurant scene in the world, at relatively low cost. By not laying down voting criteria a wide range of restaurants become eligible, regardless of their type of cuisine, their level of refinement, or their location. This approach expands the catchment area well beyond Europe and takes in parts of the USA, Hong Kong, Australia, South Africa, South America, and Singapore, but does less well on Japan and China. According to the sponsor of the competition, *Restaurant*, the list of 50 in 2012 represented twenty-one different countries.[64] It is additionally reputed to go well beyond the types of restaurants Michelin visit and is said to include also places without excellent service staff, table cloths, and other refinements. It thus squarely puts food at the centre of attention. According to *Restaurant*, the announcement of the list now is regarded 'as one of the most important events in *world* cuisine'.[65]

A closer analysis reveals a number of flaws in the selection process involved, particularly in its voting system. First, selection of restaurants for inclusion in the Top 50 List depends on snapshot preferences at one point in time, rather than on a process of careful repeat assessment, considering also consistency of performance. Second, it is based on the judgements of chefs and other people familiar with the global restaurant scene but does not consult consumers, many of whom value good service and ambience in addition to, though not in place of, food. (See Chapter 9.)

Third, the system makes the same assumption as the Michelin organization that cuisines can be compared across different culinary styles and food traditions. The Pellegrino competition takes this assumption even further in inviting an equal consideration of say, street food and food in the classical French *haute cuisine* tradition or the infinitely careful and intricate Japanese *Kaiseki* culinary style, based on years of training of the chefs involved. One of the diners I interviewed comments: 'The Pellegrino list is rubbish. The idea of a global list is absurd. How can you compare *Noma* with *Senderin* in Paris?' And a British one-star chef also is dismissive: 'But the problem is that the criteria for choice vary from region to region so that they have to correlate different points of view.'

This difficulty of comparing across food traditions and styles may also explain the low representation of Japanese restaurants on the winners' list, despite their extremely high evaluation by the Michelin organization.

Fourth, and perhaps worst concerning in its impact on legitimacy, there is no safeguard against somewhat haphazard voting, largely connected with the voters' travelling patterns and likes and dislikes of various nationalities. As judges simply have to declare that they have eaten in the restaurant of their choice during the course of the preceding eighteen months, chefs from highly visible places like New York and London are more likely to be voted for than those cooking in a small village or in a geographically remote place, less well connected by public transport. Some chefs also tell me that the Pellegrino Awards operate in a way similar to the European Song Contest, where voting for performers from neighbouring countries occurs not always strictly according to the quality of the song, but is influenced also by likes and dislikes of certain countries. Furthermore, larger countries designated as a region fare less well than smaller ones.

Last, although no stipulations are made about the style of cuisine, highly innovative styles, which catch the attention of food tourists, fare particularly well in the competition. A German food writer, M. Rolf, calls the Pellegrino Awards system a 'bizarre system' and sums it up in a contemptuous manner as:

> an arrogation of judgement where one did not know whether one should smile dismissively about their naïve audacity/presumptuousness, or admire them for an imaginative marketing idea.[66]

The impression of setting the latest trend arises because chefs who one year have figured among the top ten a few years later may have descended twenty or thirty places, or may even have disappeared from the list of the World's 50 Best Restaurants altogether. For example, British Heston Blumenthal's *Fat Duck* descended from first place in 2005 to place 33 in 2013, while American Thomas Keller's *French Laundry* which topped the list in 2004, in 2013 only just managed to squeeze in at place 47. British two-star restaurant *Hibiscus* went from place number 43 in 2011 to place 94 in 2012. British one-star chef Fergus Henderson, whose 'nose to tail' concept of using animals once was the flavour of the moment and gained his restaurant inclusion in the top fifty, now no longer appears. A British one-star chefs notes with irony: 'They go for the freshest thing on the shelf.'

These dramatic shifts occur although none of these chefs have changed their cooking. They simply are no longer perceived as cooking in the latest fashion or as standing out by a particular technique or approach. Also most recent top runners have been engaged either in molecular/techno-emotional cuisine, or, like the current and recent chefs in first place, practise molecular cuisine together with extreme localism. (For an analysis of changing fashions in food, see Chapter 5.) In contrast, Michelin have rewarded German chef Harald Wohlfahrt's persistent quality and perfect execution with three stars since 1992. Likewise, the British *Waterside Inn* in Bray, first run by Michel Roux senior and now by his son Alain, have held three stars in perpetuity since 1985.

In sum, the Pellegrino list certainly has caused a big stir. It has usefully brought issues like elitism and democratization in restaurant ambience and service to the forefront of debate, as well as providing a less Euro-centric focus. But its voting system has too many serious flaws to lend the list widespread legitimacy. The lack of criteria for selecting restaurants is unable, and does not even want, to promote any one single culinary trend. It thus lacks the basic characteristics of a taste maker. However, its voters' focus on the 'flavour of the moment' has intensified the bias towards extolling innovation above all, already present on the culinary scene. (See chapter 5.) It thus may serve to undermine more traditional cuisines where perfection in execution and taste still count as the prime markers of excellence.

From a system ranking a wide range of globally dispersed restaurants in an imperfect manner, I now switch to a more local system with a fairly narrow focus; namely, restaurant reviews in the national or local press. Their advantage, my interviews with diners have revealed, is that reviewers know the local scene, provide a connoisseurial review and aim to both inform and entertain. Furthermore, critics of the national and local press review a restaurant usually when it is fairly new and may never return to do a repeat review. Access for diners thus is easy and cheap. As such reviews deal in the main with only one restaurant at a time, they do not rank, nor do they aim to establish a trend or engage in cultivating a taste. Critics usually are journalists or engaged gourmets without any specialist training. Like the *Gault Millau*, critics try to seek out novelty and/or delight the reader by the occasional outrageous remark.

Newspaper Critics

Whereas the gastronomic guides can make or break a restaurant and the Pellegrino Awards can raise a restaurant to previously unimagined, though often impermanent, fame and financial rewards, newspaper critics generally enjoy a more limited impact. Well-known national critics can raise the profile and income of a well-reviewed restaurant to a significant degree for a period of time and, conversely, a bad review can lower the reputation of a restaurant for a while. But they generally do not have a lasting impact, nor can they turn consumers off a well-loved restaurant or raise a restaurant with low standards by an off-beat positive review. Critics themselves feel that restaurateurs are taking insufficient notice of criticisms which come up again and again in reviews—e.g. the importance of not over-filling wine glasses.[67]

However, the influence of critics varies between countries, with, for example restaurant critics of the *New York Times*, like Ruth Reichl, having become almost a demi-god during her long tenure. But the situation is more pluralistic in Britain and Germany. In Britain, there are as many national critics as there are quality newspapers. As one British chef remarks: 'There is no major national crusader among the journalists.' In Germany diners will more often also consult regional/local critics. Thus, although the critics who write newspaper and magazine gastronomic reviews do not become taste makers, they may nevertheless have some influence on developments in the culinary scene. In the words of *The Guardian* critic Marina McLoughlin: 'We disseminate trends, we don't dictate them.'[68]

How then do chefs and diners view gastronomic arbiters of this kind? Chefs, on the whole, see them mainly as a temporary irritant and do not pay a huge amount of attention to their reviews. They view newspaper critics as having a less systematic and thorough knowledge, as compared with guides and even regard some well-known critics as totally idiosyncratic. They realize that the worth of critical opinion depends on the precision gained from repeat visits and successive observations. Thus a British one-star chef who highly values Michelin is dismissive of 'mere' critics:

> Critics are all a waste of time. I am not bothered by them. I have a strong relationship with my guests. I have never seen any detrimental effect from a food review—this is an 'out-of-London' location.

Another British one-star chef is equally derogatory: 'Critics need to get a [proper] job. They are very subjective, and there is no control over them from within the industry.' When I demurred and raised the name of a very influential and often acerbic national critic he responds: 'A complete nutter!'

However, not every chef dismisses critics. One London two-star chef tells me: 'London's restaurants at this level need the big critics. A review in a paper such as the *Sunday Times* makes a big difference.'

Customers, according to the people I interviewed, rate newspaper critics more highly. This is primarily because of the low-cost access and easy availability they afford but also because they usually draw attention to a new restaurant before the guides have had an opportunity to do so. Some customers also enjoy their connoisseurial approach and sometimes witty and/or polemical style. The majority of respondents in both countries mention newspaper reviews as either a first but more often a second source of their knowledge about good restaurants. They certainly prefer them to bloggers.

Internet Bloggers

Most of my respondents would agree with the view expressed by journalist Fay Maschler:

> Bloggers aren't replacing critics, it's a whole different world. Why would you pay any attention to their opinion? It would be like walking up to someone in a crowd and asking them what they thought of the *Ivy*.[69]

Bloggers, with the exception perhaps of British Andy Hayler and *E-gullet* and German *Sternefresser* (Star Consumers), do not enjoy a good reputation among the majority of either chefs or diners. A London one-star chef responds: '[I do] not particularly [consider Internet sites important in shaping my market]. They are squabbling people who have no work to do.' Another British chef views bloggers mainly as an irritant: '*Trip Advisor* is a pain but not worth worrying about.' A third British chef accords them some importance but also realizes the danger they may pose:

> There is a negative side to the Internet. People can post a negative comment on your restaurant with impunity...[but] they keep dining as a topic of conversation.

One London two-star chef, however, takes bloggers very seriously:

> My office will read all the food blogs, and we adapt accordingly. But we only actively respond to very misleading comments which constitute damaging allegations.

In contrast, another London two-star chef countered unfavourable comments by a blogger with a stream of abuse on the web, as well as enlisting the help of other chefs to reinforce his displeasure. This chef clearly *is* sensitive about critical blogs.

Few of the diners interviewed regularly consult bloggers. Those who do, view them as complementary, rather than as alternatives to gastronomic guides. Bloggers, whatever their ambitions, thus are widely recognized for what they are—individuals or a small group of individuals whose expressions of taste are no more authoritative than those of other individual diners.

Conclusions

This chapter has shown the highly influential roles gastronomic guides play in the process of taste-making. Among the various guides, the *Michelin Guide* occupies a particularly powerful position. It has been portrayed as exercising both symbolic and material power, particularly over chefs. It constructs a hierarchy of chefs and restaurants, and, within the hierarchy, draws strong symbolic boundaries between various categories of value, i.e. between one, two, and three Michelin stars. High symbolic value then is readily translated by chefs into both reputational and economic value. Furthermore, the material effects of the *MG*'s symbolic classification are beginning to reshape chefs' economic strategies and thereby the structure and ethos of the industry.

I have illuminated how guides acquire legitimacy as taste makers. It is not sufficient merely to have professional knowledge and expertise. Guides additionally have to possess the material means to use and apply their knowledge widely and reliably to attain legitimacy. The ability to achieve these objectives requires the investment of considerable material resources. Standards of evaluation are constructed in an emotionally freighted cultural and even political field (particularly in France) where tradition has elevated certain sets of rules and procedures above others. A critical analysis of the process of taste making has illuminated how a particular cultural context has introduced a specific bias in judgements of taste, namely a bias towards French *haute cuisine*. This bias, however, is no longer imposed but is unconsciously internalized and reproduced by the producers of cultural products.

The above way of interpreting taste making has been applied to the empirical analysis of a variety of other gastronomic arbiters: national guides, critics of the press, competitions, and food blogs. The British *Good Food Guide* and the *Gault Millau Germany* have been examined as points of contrast to the *Michelin Guide*, deemed the most influential of the three, particularly in the eyes of chefs. While relatively few diners now buy the *MG*, its award of stars, widely reported in the press, still preserves its considerable, albeit mediated, influence also over diners.

Gastronomic guides are widely seen to mediate between producers and consumers. However, I have shown that the degree to which guides take the views of consumers into account differs considerably. The stances of guides are variously distributed on a continuum between elitism and democratization. Better resourced and more elitist guides base their judgements mainly on the evaluations made by internal inspectors and editors and do not see it as their primary aim to widen access to the evaluation process. Democratically inclined guides take the opposite position. Paradoxically, more elitist guides, because they apply more unified standards in a more consistent manner and therefore generate less ambiguous ranking orders, enjoy a greater legitimacy among chefs than guides which aim to take the views of diners into account. However, more democratically inclined guides, like the British *GFG*, enjoy greater loyalty from the readers they profess to serve.

In addition to the main gastronomic guides, the Pellegrino Awards, bestowed in a high-profile international competition, has been interrogated as a potential taste maker. Some of its features, such as its developed international orientation and its highly democratic bent, should be regarded as a challenge to the more elitist *Michelin Guide*. However, other aspects of this competition, like it flawed voting system, prevent it from becoming a serious competitor to the still fairly elitist, but nevertheless modernizing and democratizing *Red Guide*.

Connoisseurial gastronomic reviews in the local and national press, although not without influence, nevertheless largely lack the features which could render national critics taste makers. Finally, it is noteworthy that, despite all the hype about the Internet, it has not sufficiently empowered individual bloggers to exert significant influence. Some chefs and diners alike may consult certain Internet blogs, but they rarely endow bloggers' verdicts on taste with strong authority.

Notes

1. B. Surlemont and C. Johnson, 'The Role of Guides in Artistic Industries: The Special Case of the "Star" System in the *Haute-Cuisine* Sector', *Managing Service Quality* 15.6 (2005): 577–90.
2. G. Blank, *Critics, Ratings and Society: The Sociology of Reviews* (Lanham, MD: Rowman & Littlefield, 2007), 18.
3. W. M. Shrum, *Fringe and Fortune: The Role of Critics in High and Popular Art* (Princeton: Princeton University Press, 1996); L. L. Schücking, *The Sociology of Literary Taste* (London: Routledge & Kegan Paul, 1966; orig. 1932, Teubner); Blank 2007.
4. R. E. Caves, *Cultural Industries: Contracts between Art and Commerce* (Cambridge, MA: Harvard University Press, 2000); P. DiMaggio, 'Classification in Art', *American Sociological Review* 52.4 (1987): 440–55.
5. Shrum 1996: 10.
6. Blank 2007: 10.
7. Blank 2007.
8. Blank 2007: 7.
9. Blank 2007: 2, 7, 103–4.
10. S. Mennell, *All Manners of Food: Eating and Taste in England and France from the Middle Ages to the Present* (Oxford: Basil Blackwell, 1985).
11. I. Terence, *Le Monde de la Grande Restauration en France* (Paris: L'Harmattan, 1996); Surlemont and Johnson 2005; P. Bröhm, 'Die neuen Sterne', *Süddeutsche Zeitung* 260, Panorama (10 November 2010): 10.
12. Interviews with Michelin inspectors, 2011 and 2012.
13. J. Boxell, 'Star-Crossed', *The Financial Times Magazine* (16/17 July 2011): 16.
14. Interviews with *Michelin Britain* (2011) and *Michelin Germany* (2012).
15. *Michelin Germany* (2009): 6.
16. Interviews with *Michelin Britain* (2011) and *Michelin Germany* (2012).

17. The current editor of *Michelin France* is a German woman.
18. Interviews with *Michelin Britain* (2011) and *Michelin Germany* (2012).
19. *Michelin Germany* (2009): 7.
20. *Michelin Germany* (2009): 6, author's addition of emphasis.
21. *The History of the Michelin Guide 1900–2011* (Clermont Ferrand: Michelin Tyre Company Ltd 2011), 41.
22. *Michelin Germany* (2009): 7.
23. Interview with the then editor of the UK *Michelin Guide* (2005), <http://www.fine-dining-guide.com/Michelin/Derek_Bulmer_Michelin.html>.
24. *The History of the Michelin Guide 1900–2011*: 5.
25. C. Lane, 'The Michelin-Starred Restaurant Sector as a Cultural Industry: A Cross-National Comparison of Restaurants in Britain and Germany', *Food, Culture and Society* 13.4 (2010): 493–519.
26. <http://www.fine-dining-guide.com/Michelin/Michelin_Background_2009.html>, accessed 31 January 2010.
27. *Süddeutsche Zeitung* 258, Panorama (8 November 2012).
28. Terence 1996: 169.
29. <http://www.fine-dining-guide.com/Michelin_Derek_Bulmer_Editor_interview>, accessed 31 January2010.
30. <http://www.fine-dining-guide.com/Michelin_Derek_Bulmer_Editor_interview>, accessed 31 January2010. Emphasis added by author.
31. For example, Blank 2007: 59, 165.
32. Mennell 1985; P. Ferguson, *Accounting for Taste: The Triumph of French Cuisine* (Chicago: University of Chicago Press, 2004).
33. *Michelin Germany* (2009): 7; *Michelin Great Britain and Ireland* (2011): 4.
34. C. Lane, 'Culinary Culture and Globalization: An Analysis of British and German Michelin-Starred Restaurants', *British Journal of Sociology* 62.4 (2011): 696–717.
35. In Britain, Blumenthal is a strong follower, and in Germany Amador has been counted as one in the recent past. But several chefs, such as Germans Elverfeld and Wissler and British chefs Bains and Rogan work with some of Adria's techniques. Moreover, the German restaurant, Juan Amador, gradually has retreated from molecular cuisine in recent years, and several German chefs told me that this cuisine had run its course (interview notes, 2011).
36. Bröhm 2010: 10.
37. T. J. Bless, *Erfolgreich in der Gastronomie. Entwicklungen und Trends in der deutschen Esskultur* (Hamburg: Diplomika Verlag, 2008), 90–1; R. Lücke, 'Die Rückkehr des Rustikalen', *Süddeutsche Zeitung* 66, Panorama (20/21 March 2010): 13.
38. Author's archive, 2010–12.
39. Author's archive, 2010–12.
40. J. Lutario, 'Reach for the Stars', *Restaurant* (December 2010): 27.
41. Terence 1996: 162 footnote; Surlemont and Johnson 2005: 583–4; Lutario 2010: 27; interview notes, 2011–12.
42. L. Karpik, 'Le guide rouge Michelin', *Sociologie de Travail* 42 (2000): 369–89; R. Fantasia, 'Cooking the Books of the French Gastronomic Field', in E. Silva and A. Warde (eds.), *Cultural Analysis and Bourdieu's Legacy* (London: Routledge, 2010), 28–44.

43. Karpik 2000; Fantasia 2010.
44. C. Driver, *The British at Table, 1940–80* (London: Chatto & Windus, 1983).
45. Mennell 1985: 283.
46. <http://www.the goodfoodguide.co.uk/how-we-choose-our-inspectors>, accessed 9 March 2011.
47. <http://www.the goodfoodguide.co.uk/how-the-entries-are-scored>, accessed 9 March 2011.
48. <http://www.the goodfoodguide.co.uk/news/meet-elizabeth-carter>, 26 January 2011, accessed 9 March 2011.
49. <http://www.which.co.uk/the-good-food-guide/about-the-good-food-guide/how-the-good-guide-is-compiled>, accessed 9 March 2011.
50. Mennell 1985: 282.
51. <http://www.thestaffcanteen.com/the-staff-canteen-meets/marc-wilkinson-chef-patron-restaurant-fraiche-oxton-the-wirral/>.
52. Mennell 1985.
53. Blank 2007.
54. A. Warde, 'Imagining British *Cuisine'*, *Food, Culture and Society* 12.2 (2009): 151–71.
55. *Good Food Guide* (2011): 7, editorial introduction.
56. T. Naylor, 'Star Wars: Michelin at 100', *The Guardian* (18 January 2011), <http://www.guardian.co.uk/lifeandstyle/2011/jan/18/star-wars-michelin-at-100/print>, accessed 20 January 2011.
57. *Gault Millau Deutschland* (2011): 48.
58. *Gault Millau Deutschland* (2013): 72.
59. *Gault Millau Deutschland* (2013): 72.
60. <http://www.suedeutsche.de/leben/restaurabtkritiker-manfred-kohnke-in-vielen--lokalen-sind-die-produkte-drittklassig.http>, accessed 10 August 2012.
61. *Süddeutsche Zeitung* 103 (4 May 2012): 11.
62. <http://www.afr.com/p/lifestyle/life/_leisure/san_pellegrino_awards_show_appetite_gn>.
63. <http://www.afr.com/p/lifestyle/life/_leisure/san_pellegrino_awards_show_appetite_gn>.
64. *Restaurant* (May 2012): 57.
65. *Restaurant* (May 2012): 57.
66. *Süddeutsche Zeitung* 103 (4 May 2012): 11.
67. Debate among critics in *Yes Chef! Magazine* 13 (2010): 9–10.
68. *Yes Chef! Magazine* 13 (2010): 10.
69. *Yes Chef! Magazine* 13 (2010): 9–10.

11

The Transformation of the
Fine-Dining Sector

The beginning of the twenty-first century has been a time of flux in the high-end restaurant sector. Both established and aspiring chef proprietors have faced economic and cultural challenges. While economic recession has not yet seriously reduced their clientele, a shortage of credit, together with rising property prices/rents in London, has affected both business expansion and new entry into the sector by younger aspiring chef patrons. The shortage of bank lending to first-time entrepreneurs has coincided with and reinforced a cultural change among chefs and diners alike; namely, the turn away from sumptuous and formal dining towards a more relaxed and even slightly casual style. This style does not sit comfortably with the notion of 'fine-dining'. Young but experienced chefs, brimming with ambition to realize their new ideas for dishes in their own restaurant, are turning towards somewhat basic, transitory business premises as a stepping stone towards realizing their dream of a restaurant of their own. At the same time, established and more mature chefs have come to a stage of their career where 'kitchen toil' no longer appears so attractive. Alternatively, inspirational qualities may have dried up and/or the development of their reputation has stalled. For them, inventiveness in the realm of aesthetics has often given way to business creativity and an urge to expand.

Whereas aspiring chef proprietors seek to create a business base to realize their values in the inspired order of worth, established chefs often jettison these values for the sake of self-realization in the market order of worth. Both tendencies—albeit in different ways—are affecting conceptions not only of 'fine-dining' but of the restaurant itself. Although the viability of the fine-dining restaurant and its chef proprietor is not seriously threatened both these developments challenge and influence their identity and practices in several ways. In this chapter, I trace these two distinct developments and their intersections in the market for high-end dining and draw out their various implications, as well as the motivations behind them. I will additionally explore why both these developments appear to be much more pronounced in Britain than in Germany.

From Artistic Craft to Big Business

Industry Context and Models for Expansion

Michelin-starred restaurants are mainly small independent enterprises or form part of a hotel, and their organization closely approximates traditional craft-type small businesses. (See Chapter 3.) These entrepreneurial businesses are typically set up with the owner's capital or at most together with that of one or two close partners. Where a bank loan has been secured—and this is the more exceptional case—the chef patron has to give his or her residential property as security. Once the restaurant is established, outside financing becomes slightly easier, though, since the financial crisis of 2008, not very easy.

This model of business start-up and expansion is not at all common in the restaurant sector as a whole. The wider restaurant sector follows a mode of financing which is more typical of advanced economies, namely external financing of various kinds. Also the business model/concept differs in that food, décor, and ambience in middle- and upper middle-level restaurant chains are more standardized, and the food offered is simpler, as well as (sometimes slightly) cheaper. (I do not consider fast-food large chains which are too far removed from the fine-dining type.) Companies running these chains have built business empires. One may distinguish between smaller groups where standardization, by and large, is avoided and an approximation to an independent restaurant (in both food and décor) is aspired to and the larger chains where standardization is the norm. Examples of the first type are Caprice Holdings (*Le Caprice*, *The Ivy*, *J. Sheekey*, *Scott's*, and at least six further sites in London), Russell Norman's Group, which includes *Polpo*, or the group assembled by Ratnesh Bagdai which has twenty-seven units in London. The second type of restaurant chain is represented by the Côte Group or Jamie Oliver's *Italian* chain.

A cross-over of the two types of chain also exists where a large public hospitality company becomes involved in the world of fine-dining. An example of this is Restaurant Associate Group (RAG), the fine-dining arm of the Compass Group, a food service and support services organization, offering contract catering and facilities management. RAG asks Michelin chefs to supply a menu for private catering for business functions, develops concepts for fine-dining restaurants, and even manages and runs a Michelin restaurant—*Gary Rhodes*

27 in Tower 42, City of London. (Rhodes himself, by the way, owns other restaurants to form his own British business empire.) The latter gives RAG the fine-dining credentials for private catering and is a powerful marketing tool. This picture of the middle- and upper middle-level restaurant chain sector is typical mainly of the UK. It is much less significant in Germany where independent restaurants have survived much longer.

The first model of business empire—the smaller chain striving to retain individuality for its component restaurants—often has its restaurants mistaken for independent restaurants by the dining public. It is also this business type which, coming closest to a fine-dining restaurant, is its strongest competitor. Not surprisingly, it often serves as a model for starred chef proprietors who are seeking to expand. A short description of Ratnesh Bagdai's group of restaurants serves to illustrate this type of business (Box 11.1). It is this latter type of a relatively small restaurant group/chain which often forms the model for starred chefs who seek to build their own business empire.

Box 11.1 THE BAGDAI GROUP OF RESTAURANTS

Ratnesh Bagdai (R.B.), an accountant who first worked with Caprice Holdings, has twenty-seven restaurants in his group which has been expanded gradually mainly by drawing on retained profits. He seeks to invest only in start-ups and small independent restaurants. Bagdai is an active shareholder in just a small number of the twenty-seven, in particular in the six restaurants owned together with Mark Hix. (Hix's training partly took place in fine-dining restaurants.) In these restaurants, R.B. is also operationally involved, even down to walking the floor. He consciously aims to give each new restaurant its own distinctive concept and personality, while still setting out to benefit from economies of scale and cross-establishment managerial expertise. The number of covers is larger than in starred restaurants, and the standard of quality attained is lower, ranging between the award of 4 and 5 points in the *Good Food Guide*'s ranking scale of 10. Achieving a distinctive ambience is usually more important than maintaining food quality at the highest level. They aim for a relaxed style, with a buzz, resulting from the overall concept, staffing, as well as from the type of customer attracted, i.e. the younger and usually less well-off. Bagdai says:

> Whilst Mark and I are not in every location every day, we are very intense on dialogue through meetings, emails, and telephone and each head chef and manager are shoulder to shoulder with us, and that's what keeps them feeling the pulse of the operator/owners, and I am not sure that's the case in other groups. It's not a chain scenario but each restaurant is like an independent restaurant. I don't like the words 'chain' or 'brand' or 'empire', I don't want any of those.[a]

Acquired or opened restaurants may either come under the Group umbrella, or they will be turned over to their tenant or closed after a few years. It is a London phenomenon, and examples are much rarer in the rest of Britain.

[a] <http://www.ft.com/cms/s/2/70fab5a8-f762-11df-8b42-00144feab49a.html>.

While many readers may be familiar with such early and high-profile empire builders among Michelin chefs as Marco Pierre White (during the 1990s) and Gordon Ramsay (2000s and still ongoing), it is less well known that business expansion is gaining ground in the Michelin sector. It has become the practice or aim of a majority of starred chefs. Of the twenty starred chefs I interviewed in Britain, twelve already own one or more additional restaurants, and thirteen are either planning (with greater or lesser certainty) to open their first additional restaurant or are pursuing further expansion of their existing group. In Germany, only two chefs have opened a second restaurant, and one of these restaurants is run by the wife of my respondent. A slightly bigger number—nine—have plans to either open their own restaurant or to expand, but in most cases the plans are rather vague and often are mere dreams.

Strategies and Motivations for Business Expansion

HORIZONTAL EXPANSION

Some of the chef patrons/proprietors adopt a strategy of horizontal expansion (see Table 11.1). They set up one or more additional restaurants of the same kind, that is, fine-dining restaurants that are intended to achieve Michelin status. Several of my respondents have already achieved this goal. One such 'fine-dining' entrepreneur is Alan Murchison, of one-star *L'Ortolan* in Berkshire whose company Ten in Eight (consisting of him and a business partner) aims for a group of ten starred restaurants within eight years. Currently three of his

Table 11.1. Types of business expansion (1)

Type of strategy	Examples	Mode of control	Motivations for expansion	Mode of financing	Likely impact on flagship restaurant/chef
Horizontal I (establishing other free-standing f-d restaurants).	Murchison's Ten in Eight; Howard's investment in *The Ledbury*.	Delegated operational control, with central financial control.	Providing outlets for creativity of younger chefs.	Mostly retained profits.	Low to medium. Potential financial risk.
Horizontal II (establishing other f-d restaurants in hotels).	Michael Caines and partners' Abode Group.	Partial personal control in early stages.	Market orientation. Building up capital.	Requires some external financing.	Medium-high impact.
Horizontal III (developing a concept for other f-d restaurant in hotels).	Blumenthal's *Dinner* and Ramsay's reopening of *Savoy Grill*.	Operational control mainly at the opening stage. No financial control.	Seeking inspired worth with concept creation, as well as supplementary earnings.	No financial stake required.	Low impact.

four restaurants hold one star, while the fourth won a star and lost it again. A similar model has been adopted by two-star chef Phil Howard and his business partner, Nigel Platts-Martin, though without such a highly ambitious statement of their overall goal. Phil Howard, in addition to running *The Square*, is also the co-owner of two-star *The Ledbury*, where his former *sous* chef, Brett Graham, is at the helm and has become a co-owner. Platts-Martin—a former lawyer and wine connoisseur, rather than a chef—has a stake in three further London starred restaurants—*Chez Bruce*, *The Glasshouse*, and *La Trompette*, all three of which are co-owned with Bruce Poole—the *chef de cuisine* of *Chez Bruce*. In both restaurant groups, the *chefs de cuisine* have not deserted the stove in their original restaurant. As Alan Murchison puts it: 'You cannot be part-time passionate.' Howard, unlike Murchison, is not intent on building a big business empire. He explains: '[Expansion] has always been organic. I don't need a complicated life any more.' In both cases, the most important reason for expansion is to tie talented young chefs to the business, by placing them in their 'own' restaurant. In the words of Murchison:

> Eventually you run out of things you can teach these experienced people in the kitchen, and without an opportunity for them to stretch themselves there's no doubt in my mind that a lot of them would have gone.

Both chefs realize that they cannot micro-manage a second restaurant and at most give advice and help. A second motivation is to gain economies of scale in some areas. In the Ten in Eight holding, they are beginning to pool staff and do joint purchasing for dry goods, bottled water, and also crockery. As the head office looks after the financial side of all the restaurants, Murchison and his partner have reduced the risk of excellent chefs turning out to be poor financial managers. The Platts-Martin Group also pools some resources. All constituent restaurants have access to Platts-Martin's legal advice, as well as to his valuable expertise on wine.

A related strategy of expansion is to open an additional fine-dining restaurant in a high-end hotel where the chef is only the tenant/licensee or has some other contractual arrangement. He or she mainly develops the restaurant's concept and spends only some of the time in seeing that it is faithfully and efficiently executed. In such cases the head chef—usually from his or her original brigade—is usually in full-time charge. The most celebrated examples here are Blumenthal's restaurant *Dinner* in the Mandarin Oriental Hotel, Marcus Wareing's bistro in the renovated St. Pancras Hotel, as well as Gordon Ramsay's reopening of the *Savoy Grill* in 2010 and, more recently, Simon Rogan's opening of the *The French* in Manchester's Midland Hotel.

These latter cases, after an initial intensive set-up engagement, involve the chefs more in consultancy services than in cheffing. They enable them to increase their income in a risk-free expansion of their business activities.

Furthermore, they are left free to devote the bulk of their time to their original or flagship restaurants or, in the case of Ramsay and Blumenthal, to additional business ventures. As Wareing explains:

> You can have your name only over one door, over one kitchen. External activity is possible as a concept—you can influence and guide it but you cannot be in two places at once.

But the starred chef also may be the owner/co-owner of the hotel and its restaurant (see Box 11.2).

VERTICAL EXPANSION

Another popular strategy aims for vertical expansion, i.e. one where chefs add one or more lower-level types of restaurant to their intended empire, such as a bistro/brasserie or a gastro pub (see Table 11.2). These chef proprietors still aim to produce very good food but no longer try to achieve the inspired creations of their starred restaurant. They retain their craft identity but swap their artistic inclination for a market orientation. These chefs choose the additional restaurant(s) because the business model—such restaurants have more covers and/or more sittings and do simpler food—yields a higher profit. Thus a one-star chef who makes little profit in his starred restaurant says this about vertical expansion: 'A second operation has to be a money-driven operation, rather than a passion-driven operation.'[1]

Box 11.2 A HOTEL CUM FINE-DINING RESTAURANT GROUP

An example of a chef-cum-hotel owner is two-star Michael Caines of Gidleigh Park in Devon. Caines, who together with Andrew and Christina Brownsord, owners of the Abode high-end hotel group, has opened (and partly co-financed) several hotels-cum-restaurants. These hotels are on a relatively small scale and outside London, but the empire built up is quite large and has been assembled rapidly during the last ten years. It has involved Caines in what has been described as the second biggest collection of high-end restaurants overseen by a British Michelin star chef, after Gordon Ramsay. While Gidleigh Park remains Caines's main focus, he also travels extensively between the various Abode Group restaurants, located in such far apart places as Exeter, Canterbury, Glasgow, Manchester, Chester, and Salisbury, in order to train and oversee their head chefs. Rather than being tied to one stove, he prefers rotating between many. Caines has different motivations for expansion from other chefs covered so far. He is unashamedly attached to the 'market' order of worth and is prepared to jettison the 'inspired' guiding principle—which gained him Michelin status—in the process. Michelin fame and ensuing economic reward, he fears (not unreasonably), may be inconstant, while a business empire has lasting value. He explains: 'It's the accolades that would have to give way...I'd choose the business every time. Those stars can be withdrawn whenever they want. That business is truly yours.'[a]

[a] Caterersearch (2009).

Table 11.2. Types of business expansion (2)

Type of strategy	Examples	Mode of control	Motivations for expansion	Mode of financing	Likely impact on flagship restaurant/chef
Vertical (establishing more casual restaurants).	Gastro pubs of Bosi and Haworth; Purnell's bistro.	Mainly financial control but also some operational oversight.	Building up capital, perceived as less risky.	Requires some bank finance.	Medium-high impact.
Mixed (both horizontal and vertical expansion).	Martin Wishart's bistro, plus 2nd starred restaurant.	Financial control, plus part-time operational control.	Building up capital and reputation.	Combined strategy.	Medium-high impact.

Examples of this strategy are *Purnell's Bistro* of Birmingham one-star chef Glynn Purnell and the brasserie *Les Deux Salons* of the London team of chef-restaurateurs Anthony Demetre and Will Smith (*Arbutus* and *Wild Honey*). Another prominent example is Raymond Blanc's company Brasseries Blanc, an upper-middle market chain, with investors and a board. It is managed by a person with experience in the mid-market segment and has an Executive Chef who used to be head chef at the *Manoir*. Blanc is making mainly a creative input. The people centrally involved do not want to project the image of a chain but view themselves as a group of restaurants built around people. Whether this can be achieved with a central management structure must remain an open question.

Often the venue for this more casual type of restaurant is cheaper to acquire as is the case when former pubs are transformed into gastro pubs. (Also they already have a licence to sell alcohol.) Adherents of this vertical strategy of expansion are Nigel Haworth (with four gastro pubs in Lancashire and Yorkshire), chef Brett Graham (one London gastro pub), and French-born Claude Bosi. Bosi has taken to the idea of an English pub, with the opening of two London pubs that serve superior food to a larger number of customers. Although his second pub restaurant with rooms, *The Malthouse*, is leased to him by the company Brakspear, a family pubs company, Bosi nevertheless has contributed a very sizeable sum to the renovation of the pub.

Atul Kochhar, too, is a chef with many irons in the fire. He recently added the *Colony Bar and Grill*, devoted to mid-market Indian street food, to his one-star Indian-British restaurant *Benares*. After a disagreement with his business partner, Carlo Spetale, he withdrew from this venture, only to open his own similar restaurant, *Atul's Kitchen*. The current economic situation has held him back from introducing the format of *Atul's Kitchen* on multiple London sites. In addition, Kochhar has been involved in a pop-up restaurant in *Meza*,

Tooting, following the same concept. Also part of his business empire are two further fine-dining restaurants outside London. Atul Kochhar clearly is as much a business entrepreneur as a chef and, to paraphrase Marcus Wareing, is happy to have his name over many doors or stoves.

Vertical expansion is designed to generate a higher and more certain income than a Michelin restaurant alone can yield. It requires new investment which mostly cannot come from retained profits in the starred restaurant. But the vertical strategy of expansion is also more difficult because both the start-up and the day-to-day running require new skills, and these skills are not necessarily held by chef proprietors' former *sous* chefs in the Michelin flagship restaurant. Glynn Purnell, for example, found that putting chefs from his Michelin restaurant in charge of the bistro did not work. He had to choose a new top team for the bistro. Nigel Haworth tells me that his gastro pubs require a lot of attention and cause sufficient financial worries to keep him working harder than ever. Moreover, as the vertical empire grows, dilution of individuality and originality is always a danger.

MIXED STRATEGY

Several chefs have adopted a mixed strategy (Table 11.2), acquiring both further fine-dining restaurants likely to become starred, as well as a gastro pub and/or bistro. One example is one-star Edinburgh chef Martin Wishart who runs both a second starred restaurant and a brasserie and is planning further expansion. While the brasserie is co-owned with a partner who also is its head chef, Wishart has a contractual relationship with Hotel Cameron House, Loch Lomond. This obliges him to personally oversee the fine-dining restaurant which also gained a Michelin star. He drives there—about an hour's drive—twice a week. Heston Blumenthal owns a one-star gastro pub, located in Bray, in addition to the three-star *Fat Duck* and his contractual obligations for *Dinner*.

Another intriguing example of this strategy is where a company, owning a string of non-starred restaurants, establishes a new restaurant with the express aim of gaining a Michelin star. This is the Living Ventures Group—with twenty-seven sites and a turnover of £40 million—which *Manchester House*, in Manchester. The Group has already hired a chef with ample Michelin experience—he will become a shareholder in the business.[2]

MULTINATIONAL EXPANSION

While all the above cases of expansion have occurred *within* Britain, we are also beginning to see the emergence of multinational restaurant empires (see Table 11.3). Among them, that built by Gordon Ramsay is the most developed and best known. Ramsay not only has other restaurants in London (besides his three-star *Gordon Ramsay* opened in 1998) but has opened restaurants in

Table 11.3. Types of business expansion (3)

Type of strategy	Examples	Mode of control	Motivations for expansion	Mode of financing	Likely impact on flagship restaurant/chef
Multinational expansion	Ramsay's and Atherton's empires	Ceding operational control to others but retaining financial control.	Pure market orientation, plus seeking enhanced business reputation.	Requires significant external finance and/or a partner.	Considerable impact.

several countries and on several continents, including the USA (New York, Florida, Los Angeles, and Las Vegas), France (Paris), Tuscany, South Africa, and Dubai. All of these foreign ventures are fine-dining restaurants and several of them hold a star. As if this cross-border horizontal strategy of expansion were not demanding enough, he recently adopted also the vertical strategy, opening a more casual place in London, *Bread Street Kitchen*. (His earlier foray into the more casual end of the sector failed when his gastro pub, *The Devonshire*, had to be closed.)

Ramsay's empire has achieved both extraordinary success and many setbacks. His empire has expanded and contracted with amazing speed and makes a charting of all the twists and turns hazardous. He has gained stars for, amongst others, his restaurant in *Claridge's* and for the *York & Albany*, as well as for his New York restaurant (this was lost again in 2013). He not only has lost stars again, but also has closed sites and lost a lot of money—coming close to bankruptcy in 2008/2009. Ramsay and his then partner Hutchinson, in 2008, were forced to renegotiate a £10 million loan from the Royal Bank of Scotland.[3]

Given the size of his empire, the earnings of Ramsay Holdings in 2011— reported by Bloomberg to be only £1.46 million—are not spectacular. His rapid and daring, if not reckless, way of building up a restaurant empire has become legendary and is referred to within the industry as 'Doing a Ramsay'. While Ramsay has been savaged by the press with epitaphs such as a 'hubristic chef' and 'warped by celebrity culture', many of his colleagues in the industry (among my respondents) still admire his high level of culinary craft and artistry. They additionally acknowledge his contribution, along with that of Marco Pierre White, to the recovery and expansion of the British high-end restaurant sector from the middle 1990s onwards.

Ramsay himself sees no incompatibility between being an international business entrepreneur and running a three-star restaurant. You simply put another chef with three-star qualities in charge. In the case of *Gordon Ramsay*, Royal Hospital Road, it is Clare Smyth who, in March 2013, was made a partner in the business and devotes herself full-time to it. Ramsay himself argues:

> We have restaurants on five continents, although the charge I often hear—that we are spreading ourselves too thin—is total rubbish...Everything we open has its own identity with talented individuals at the helm.[4]

Another builder of a multinational empire is Ramsay's former executive chef—Jason Atherton. Within the last two years or so, Atherton has opened nine establishments in four different countries, several of them in Asia. Atherton belongs to a younger—though not the youngest—generation of chefs. He partly trained abroad (including a spell in Ferran Adria's kitchen in Catalonia) and has travelled widely to develop his career, largely facilitated by Ramsay. A significant exposure to the international restaurant world came when Ramsay appointed him as an Executive Chef, tasked with setting up Ramsay's various foreign outposts. At first, in 2001, he ran his restaurant *Verre* in Dubai. After having launched Ramsay's London restaurant *Maze* in 2005, Atherton helped Ramsay to set up offshoots of *Maze* in Prague (2007), Cape Town (2009), Melbourne, and Qatar. In 2010, he left Ramsay and set up his first independent restaurant venture in Shanghai where he has since opened a second restaurant, *Social Tapas*. This was followed, in 2011, by *Esquina*, a gastro tapas bar in Singapore and, later, three further Singapore ventures. These more casual restaurants inspired him to develop the new concept for his London restaurant *Pollen Street Social*, set up with much fanfare in 2011. (For further discussion, see below.) His latest venture is *Social Eating House*, opened in March 2013 with Paul Hood, one of his former employees.

Atherton initially chose the vertical strategy of expansion, but his culinary skill and imagination soon gained him Michelin stars and turned the strategy horizontal. He first received a star for *Maze* (now no longer operated by him) and then for the more relaxed and innovative format of *Pollen Street Social*. To finance his rapid expansion, Atherton has drawn on both his own resources and on partnerships with experienced and wealthy Asian partners. Singapore's *Esquina* and later restaurants were set up in partnership with Singapore hotelier Loh Lik Peng and journalist-investor Geoffrey Eu. For *Pollen Street Social* (*PSS*) Atherton used his life's savings, plus a large bank loan, with his own house as collateral. But Atherton also has a financial backer, called Mavis Oei (hotel owner and scion of a Singaporean banking dynasty) who acts additionally as an informal business adviser and mentor. She not only has a 25 per cent ownership stake in *PSS* but also in his Asian restaurant company JC Tapas Limited.[5] In Hong Kong he has partnered with entrepreneur Yenn Wong to open a tapas bar, *22 Ships*. Further London openings are forthcoming.[6] Like most empire-builders, Atherton now installs trusted former head chefs in his various ventures. He has made *Pollen Street Social* his flagship restaurant to which he gives his primary commitment. Atherton explains:

> I only ever cook day-to-day at *Pollen Street Social*. It's where I want my name to be attached to, it's where I live and die by the food...I'd like, eventually, for *Pollen Street Social* to go even higher in the UK guide books.[7]

However, even if he principally exerts financial control of the various restaurants in his empire, that, together with his extensive consulting activity, must require a large amount of mental energy and extensive travelling. According to Atherton himself, he spends three to four months annually travelling overseas. Despite his best intentions, all these ventures combined must make it difficult to give *Pollen Street Social* his full and continuous attention.

But it is not only British chefs who build restaurant empires abroad. American chefs and, more so, French chefs have expanded their empires into Britain, thereby transforming the high-end dining scene. Ducasse, Danny Meyer, Robuchon, and Wolfgang Puck are only the most prominent examples.

Business Expansion in Germany?

How does the British picture of expansion contrast with that in Germany? As already indicated, the situation among German chefs differs drastically. Only two among my respondents had expanded—one very modestly and the second, three-star chef Juan Amador, on nearly as grand a scale and with even more turbulent outcomes than those associated with Ramsay's expansion (Box 11.3).

Box 11.3 JUAN AMADOR'S BUSINESS EMPIRE

At the time of my interview in 2010, in his Langen restaurant, near Frankfurt, Amador had a second Michelin-starred restaurant in Mannheim, *Amesa*, and he had just closed his development kitchen in Wiesbaden. He was in the process of setting up a limited company (Aktiengesellschaft or AG) and told me: 'We must find our sponsors ourselves. We will issue shares and go to Frankfurt. If you do not have a sponsor you create one.'

He was also in the process of opening a restaurant in Bucharest, as well as planning a chain of licensed restaurants in Moscow and Dubai. Additionally, he acted as consultant in several other places around the globe. Three years on, the original restaurant in Langen has been sold, and Amador has moved to the Mannheim site. His international ventures have failed, and, in 2012, he went through insolvency procedures. His AG of four partners has been dissolved. However, he is determined to soldier on and keep his three stars shining in Mannheim.

Amador is a highly exceptional case in the German restaurant landscape. Even among the larger group of *all* two- and three-star chefs in my database, the building of restaurant empires has been rare. As two-star Johannes King observes: 'In Germany, gastronomy is rather chef-dependent.'

Moreover, the large proportion of chefs with only employed status in top hotels are prevented from building up the capital needed to set up on their own and/or have become too risk averse to go down the ownership route. At most, German chef proprietors will open a second restaurant in the same house, and it is mostly vertical expansion away from Michelin-perfect food. Examples are two-star Bavarian chefs Alexander Herrmann in Wirsberg and Hans-Stefan Steinheuer in Bad Neuenahr. They each own small hotels which have both a starred gourmet restaurant and a restaurant or rural pub (*Landgasthof*) serving regional fare.

However, a few very recent developments indicate that business expansion is at last catching on also in the German fine-dining sector. The motivation of chefs is mainly to secure extra finance to secure their survival in the starred restaurant. Examples from the last three years are the vertical expansions of three-star chef Klaus Erfort in Saarbrücken and that of two-star chef Wolfgang Becker, planned for 2014 in Trier. The latter is to be financed by issuing micro bonds to Becker's customers. Also of note is that Berlin two-star chef Tim Raue is supplying the concept for the planned Thai–Japanese restaurant *Sra Bua*, to be opened in the Berlin luxury hotel Adlon. The Adlon hotel is part of the Kempinski Group whose chief shareholder happens to be the Thai royal family.[8]

Nevertheless, nine German chef patrons among my interviewees have plans to set up their own restaurant. However, these are usually rather vague plans, with chefs waiting for the appearance of a wealthy patron of the culinary arts. Some of the chefs who have plans to set up their own business note, with a mixture of envy and resignation, that the business atmosphere in Germany, unlike that in the USA and France, does not really support such entrepreneurialism. Three-star employed chef Joachim Wissler tells me that he would like to build up a small restaurant group in the vertical mode:

> Between a bistro and one star would be just right. People look for a brand—they have brand formation in the USA and in France. We in Germany have not understood this [brand formation]. Asia could be open to such expansion, the Europeans do not like Germans.

His models are American Thomas Keller, as well French Joel Robuchon. Wissler is convinced that empire building need not undermine the quality generated by the 'craft' mode, nor compromise his 'inspired' approach:

> If done well, expansion can work, and the chef does not always have to be present....Robuchon is far in advance of what is done in Germany...he is able to manage the expansion, as far as quality is concerned.

This brief outline of the virtual absence of empire building in the German high-end restaurant industry shows that, due to the lack of an entrepreneurial model in this industry, as well as of a model for the 'brand' building which usually accompanies expansion, restaurant empires have not emerged. Despite comparatively greater risk averseness in the German business world, this conspicuous lack of entrepreneurialism cannot be generalized to German business in general. Many small and medium-sized industrial enterprises (SMEs) have recently engaged in multinational expansion. This perceived absence of support for business expansion instead must be connected with a restaurant industry structure which is still strongly marked by the dominance of small independent and hotel restaurants. It additionally is influenced by the attitudes towards and expectations of fine-dining restaurants and their chefs by the German dining public. An article in the *Frankfurter Allgemeine* newspaper, based on a number of interviews with chefs, concludes that 'the personal handshake by the starred chef should be at least in the realm of possibility',[9] thereby limiting expansion to only in-house additions, as outlined above. As I will show below, German chefs themselves do not necessarily think that they must *only* 'mind their own stove'. Nevertheless, the only very recent emergence of business expansion and its as yet fairly exceptional character mean that that much of my discussion dwells disproportionately on the British case.

In Germany, inward investment by entrepreneurial foreign starred chefs is fairly new. The announcement that Pierre Gagnaire is coming to Berlin's newly opened Waldorf Hotel has been greeted with excitement and pride about Berlin's newly gained attractiveness as a European capital in one of the food magazines, *Der Feinschmecker*. Germany's three-star chefs, however, already hard pressed for customers, will probably greet his arrival with less enthusiasm.

Financing Expansion

All this expansionism by Ramsay and other chefs raises the question of how expansion is being financed. Are financial pressures being added to the business headaches of running a diverse business empire? Finance for second and further restaurants is easier for chefs with both a sound business record and a high reputation as a chef. It is noteworthy, however, that in most of the cases discussed above, chefs have expanded gradually and have mainly relied on capital from retained profit. Additionally, in several cases, they have looked towards a business partner or backer with knowledge and a sympathetic understanding of the industry. Bank lending has not been popular among either British or German chefs, either because of banks' unwillingness to lend to restaurants or because of their onerous terms. Two British chefs tell me: 'Banks are the worst kind of people to be involved with. They are the worst kind of business'; 'I considered a bank loan last year. Banks are incredibly unwilling.' And a German chef agrees: 'It is not worth it asking banks. It is even more difficult if it is a starred restaurant.' A British one-star chef talks about the onerous condition involved:

> I funded this restaurant myself, I had no financial backers. I looked for investment capital from a bank against my house as security. It is very difficult getting a sizeable bank loan, especially for restaurants.

Once expansion becomes rapid and occurs on a grand scale, like Ramsay's, huge bank loans have to be taken out. Alternatively, chefs can turn towards private equity. However, both bank loans and private equity investment come with a relatively short time horizon for repayment, and private equity firms expect high margins. They would expect to recoup two-and-a half times what they invest, as against a bank's margin of 2 or 3 per cent.[10] Such conditions are likely to pressurize chef patrons into finding more and more savings, or they have to gain income from complementary activities, just to meet repayments on time. Both create the kind of pressure which is not conducive to the immersion required to remain creative.

My expectation of family financing in such a small craft-type enterprise is not borne out by my interviews in either country. However, within the larger German industry there are known to be a significant number of second-generation owners of rural inns (*Landgasthöfe*). This type of debt-free ownership enables chefs in independent restaurants to break even at the two- and three-star level, widely believed to be impossible otherwise. Thus two- and three-star chefs Hans Stefan Steinheuer in Bad Neuenahr and Helmut Thieltges in Dreis, respectively, are both second-generation chefs who have taken over their parents' relatively simple inns (*Gasthof*) and have turned them into high-level restaurants with rooms. In Britain, we now have second-generation chef proprietors in the two restaurants owned by members of the Roux family.

The Impact of Expansion on the Flagship Restaurant

Is empire building antithetical to chefs' creativity and the preservation of quality? Notwithstanding Ramsay's protestations, the building of restaurant empires, whether adopting the horizontal, vertical, or mixed strategy, requires the confrontation of important questions. Can the artistic craft, rewarded with Michelin stars, withstand the intrusion of market rationality, entailed by the building of business empires? Should Michelin-starred chefs stay behind the one stove or become serial founders of new restaurants and mere business people? Answers to these related questions have to take into account both the strategy and speed of expansion, as well as chefs' motivation for embarking on it. It is clear that Ramsay's strategy stands at the extreme end of a continuum of modes of expansion and that other, less ambitious attempts have been effectively combined with continuing culinary perfection in the flagship starred restaurant. To evaluate the consequences of empire building, I shall consider the views of chefs, diners, and of the Michelin organization in both countries.

The Views of Chefs

There are plenty of industry voices claiming that expansion is antithetical to the preservation of the values and practices of the inspired order of worth and to the maintenance of high quality. Running a starred restaurant, I have shown in previous chapters, requires passion and a high level of devotion. Hence objections to business expansion often are phrased in motivational terms: 'Nobody quite gives a restaurant the love and attention as its owner, and an owner can be only in one place at a time.'[11]

Two-star chef Marcus Wareing says:

> Yes, the presence [of the chef in the kitchen] is very important. You can have your name only over one door, over one kitchen. External activity is possible as a concept—you can influence and guide it but you cannot be in two places at once.

Two-star Brett Graham of *The Ledbury*, London shares this view:

> This restaurant has to be my main focus. This is where I cook…Running around opening other restaurants and pubs won't allow *The Ledbury* to reach its full potential.[12]

At the same time, there is an implication that taking on new ventures is bound to dilute the quality and creativity of the original restaurant's food. British one-star chef Frances Atkins thinks her creative input is indispensable: 'Roger [her *sous* chef] is very capable. Roger is a good technician but does not supply creativity.' Three-star German chef Harald Wohlfahrt strongly believes: 'My image would not be very high if I did not constantly exert upward pressure on achievement.'

His two-star colleague Christian Jürgens has a slightly different reason for thinking his presence in the kitchen necessary for success. Due to relatively frequent turnover in the kitchen, he considers himself indispensable to integrating new staff into the team. One-star German chef Sören Anders agrees: 'Yes, it is a matter of leadership. I have to convey to my staff an understanding of my own actions.'

Some chefs also think that they owe it to their guests to be present in their kitchen, particularly if the restaurant has become totally identified with the name of the chef. Among these chefs is German one-star chef Rainer-Maria Halbedel: 'I have no other restaurant. The guests buy the presence of the chef; they have the right to see me.' British Claude Bosi agrees: 'Customers want the chef's cooking.'

Nicolas Lander, a former restaurateur, suggests that the importance of the patron's presence in the restaurant goes far beyond kitchen work. It affects the overall restaurant ambience and the character of all restaurant operations, and these aspects cannot easily be communicated to staff where further places are owned:

> Opening more restaurants...is also the time when everything that is attractive about opening a restaurant slips out of the restaurateur's personal control—forever...the warmth and welcome received by the customer—the restaurant's sense of style—has to be encapsulated and delegated to a trusted team.[13]

But equally, a few chefs—including some German ones—deny that exclusive control and constant creative input by the chef proprietor are required:

> I am not the sun king without whom nothing runs. Greatness instead means when you have distributed functioning restaurants over all continents. If people have worked at your place and pass on your philosophy, that is greatness.[14]

Two-star German Hans Horberth shares Tim Raue's views on team building:

> I agree only conditionally [that the chef's presence in the kitchen is necessary for the restaurant's success]. A strong team is evidence of the strength of the chef de cuisine.

Other chefs very reasonably point out that businesses should be built up in such a way as to obviate the need for constant personal control by the chef proprietor. Delegation to a second-in-command—the *sous* chef or a second head chef—is necessary for the personal well-being of the chef proprietor. It is additionally held to be fully compatible with maintaining a high level of excellence in the flagship restaurant. Thus:

> They [critics of the chef's absence] are to an extent right. But a chef also has to balance family life and preserve his sanity. I have trained the kitchen well. I like to say that the kitchen is only as good as the number two.

Alan Murchison, one of the chefs who has built up an as yet small restaurant group and spends four out of five days in his original kitchen, agrees with this position:

> You have to delegate to your team. People have to feel involved. It's a balance. There is a system and a process, even if I am not here. I have a head chef who controls.

Several chefs support their tolerance of the occasional absence of the chef proprietor/patron from the kitchen by pointing to high-profile chefs who continue to keep up standards in their flagship restaurant even while building/maintaining a large and multinational restaurant empire. The names of Ducasse and Robuchon crop up particularly frequently. German two-star chef King tells me:

> Alain Ducasse is the perfect counter-example. But people like him probably are exceptional. If the restaurant has become very much identified with one person, it is very difficult to be absent. If the concept is right, it works in either case.

The general pattern among my respondents in both countries is that a majority of the chefs believe that the chef's relatively constant presence in the kitchen is necessary for the success of the restaurant. In Germany, only six respondents think that a good *sous* chef or team is an adequate substitute, while in Britain a mere five chefs take this position. This relatively high degree of commitment to maintaining a constant presence in the kitchen is not astonishing when one considers that the success of their restaurants is due to winning one or more Michelin stars. This requires the presence of a creative individual and leader of the team. It is, however, somewhat surprising that chefs in Britain express the same commitment as German chefs, given that so many more are engaged in empire building. They obviously delegate a lot of control over their additional restaurants to appointed head chefs.

At the same time, one should not dismiss the minority response that a good team can make up for the absence of the chef proprietor. One German chef tells me that the evening they had the Michelin inspection which resulted in the award of a star he was in hospital for the removal of his appendix. It is evident that many restaurants continue their record of excellence even when the chef patron is not constantly present, as long as he or she continues to provide the 'inspired' input. Moreover, the low level of profit associated with the business model of the Michelin-starred restaurant (see Chapter 3) makes business expansion, particularly the adoption of the vertical strategy described above, very compelling. (In Germany, it was pointed out in Chapter 3, chefs are more often employed and cushioned by the luxury hotels in which they are situated.) It is only when empires grow large very quickly that creative leadership may become undermined and constant high-level performance can no longer be guaranteed in all constituent restaurants. Quality may also be compromised when the conditions for the repayment of the expansion loan are accompanied by very onerous short-term repayment pressures and/or high interest demands.

The Views of Customers

How do restaurant customers view this issue? Do they, as some chefs suggest, actually expect the chef's constant presence in the kitchen? Do they feel that their high expenditure buys them the right to the chef patron's presence? The majority, though by no means all diners, expect the chef patron to be present when they visit a fine-dining restaurant. A few customers, though, are remarkably tolerant of his absence. Although they welcome the chef's presence they no longer necessarily expect it. Thus London diner Roger comments: 'It's nice if they are present but I would not expect it.' London lecturer Daniela and Cambridge academic Ricky agree: 'No [I do not expect them to be present]. I somehow trust them that they do it alright, but it is nice when the chef comes and is friendly'; 'I would be delighted if they were present but they seldom are.'

Cambridge academic Ha-Yoon, too, believes that delegation is possible as long as the *chef de cuisine* remains the creative head of the business:

> No [I do not expect the chef of the restaurant to be present most of the time]. If they have a competent deputy, I don't mind. The role of the chef, in any case, is more the inspiration, the creativity, not the execution.

German academic Karin similarly suggests that quality should be guaranteed by the whole team: '[The chef patron does] not necessarily [have to be present]. In a high-level restaurant all the chefs should uphold quality standards.'

Altogether, seven out of fourteen German diners expect the chef patron to be present when they visit a restaurant. In Britain, an even higher proportion have this expectation—twelve of eighteen respondents. Among them is David, a retired Welsh farmer, who feels: 'Yes, [I expect the chef to be present] if you are paying fine-dining prices.' Mark, a London professional, agrees, particularly as far as three-star chefs are concerned: 'In a three-star restaurant, I want them to be there. I want them to be cooking for me.' Jonathan, a Cambridge academic, concurs: 'I think it is a good sign if he is present and vice versa.' German diner Inge is concerned that quality might suffer if the chef is often absent: 'Yes, [the chef patron should be present], he should watch that quality is being maintained.'

These customer responses indicate that, on balance, diners expect the chef patron to be present most of the time. As starred chefs now are very high profile and often covered by the media, prolonged absence from their flagship restaurant probably would become known to customers. British chefs, among whom many are engaged in business expansion, should take note. They should be careful to not expand too much too quickly, and they need to adopt a strategy of expansion which still ensures their presence in their flagship restaurant most of the time.

The Views of Michelin Inspectors

The Michelin organization has never expressed a public view on expansion, but the pattern of their awards demonstrates that they do not penalize expansion by itself, as long as quality in the flagship restaurant remains upheld. Thus Ramsay's three-star restaurant *Gordon Ramsay* in London's Royal Hospital Road still has its three stars, now mainly preserved by the efforts of head chef Clare Smyth, rather than by Ramsay himself.

My interview with a British Michelin inspector confirms that no general policy of penalizing expansion exists and that the latter may even be associated with a positive outcome: 'Expansion enables the mother restaurant to promote its talented chefs and hence can be worthwhile.' The evaluation of expansion, though, is case-sensitive: 'Some do not have the infrastructure to carry it off, but some do it very well.'

My interviewee cites the positive case of the Platts-Martin Group but cannot be drawn to disclose a negative example. This inspector is right to emphasize the fact that the strategy of horizontal expansion has been one of the ways to promote young talented chefs without the financial base to the highly visible position of chef patron and sometimes part-owner. Some noteworthy benefactors of this strategy have been two-star chef Brett Graham of *The Ledbury*, two-star Marcus Wareing at *Marcus Wareing at the Berkeley*, and one-star Jason Atherton of *Pollen Street Social*, formerly head chef at Ramsay's *Maze*.

Cultural Change in the Top Restaurant Sector

Cultural change among top restaurants has accelerated in recent years and is connected both with the worsening economic situation (mainly the difficulty in obtaining credit) and with a broader cultural trend towards democratization. The latter is manifest mostly at the level of dining *style*, but, in some cases, also in increased affordability. The two developments, in many ways, are interrelated but are usefully analysed separately.

Cultural Change Due to the Financial Crisis

As already indicated, high-level chefs who want to start their own restaurant now face considerable financial hurdles. Banks in the UK are not lending anymore unless substantial collateral is available—a condition very few young chefs can meet. Finding a generous backer is also difficult before chefs have become distinguished by the award of their own star. With prices for real estate now sky-high in London, a start-up there seems almost impossible. Berlin real estate prices are significantly lower. Yet keen and ambitious young chefs have found ways to accumulate the necessary finance and/or attract the attention of potential backers. They have started a supper club in their own homes, have offered sophisticated street food from a market stall, or have opened what is referred to as a 'pop-up' restaurant on a shoe-string in simple temporary premises. Indeed, young chefs with prior training in one or more Michelin-starred restaurants have become quite inventive in presenting what they regard as outstanding food in extremely modest surroundings.

The physical environment inevitably influences the aesthetic side of the restaurant—its food, its ambience, and the style of sociality it encourages in its customers. Cultural change has emerged out of economic necessity. However, the new culture would not have been possible if there had not been a prior embrace of a more relaxed and democratic style of dining by both customers and chefs, as highlighted in earlier chapters. A second aspect of this cultural transformation is a consequence of economic and cultural globalization and our greater familiarity with the food of other nations on more distant continents. Britain's 'street food' revolution of the last five or so years is one example of this culinary transformation. It entails the adoption of foods, offered by stalls in the streets of Asian cities, such as Hong Kong, Singapore, and Bangkok, and upgrading them to restaurant standards. It is thus inspired by a humble Asian culture of food consumption, but also by American southern cooking. Street food has advanced from stalls in middle-class food markets, such as London's Borough Market, via pop-up or temporary restaurants into more conventional restaurants. A third new cultural current is born out of a coming together of both 'small plates' eating and of health considerations in an affluent society. With the emergence of this trend, traditional British 'meat, potatoes, and two vegetables' meals have given way to tapas-style dining, inspired by a variety of foreign dining cultures. This permits the combination of diversity with a reasonable overall quantity of food consumption. While the ingredients constituting these 'tapas' are not necessarily Spanish or Asian, they often are. This trend therefore, at the same time, permits diners to sample a range of globally dispersed foreign dishes and styles of preparation. It is no longer bound to the French heritage and the custom of eating three or more clearly distinguished courses from an à la carte menu. This trend finds its logical conclusion in the elimination of this style of menu altogether, as recently carried out by one Michelin chef, Daniel Galmiche, of the *Vineyard*, Stockcross, near Newbury.

Moreover, chefs can now reasonably expect that, if their food is of a consistently high quality, a Michelin star may be awarded, even if the food is served in a somewhat basic environment, with more relaxed service, and with only minimal resemblance to French classical cuisine.

While in the past it has been easy to know what constitutes excellence in food and dining, now excellence is pitched at many different levels with each equally effective but usually addressing different social constituencies. It is no accident that most new concepts are introduced in cosmopolitan London and less so in Berlin, Munich, or Frankfurt. Significantly, ideas for conceptual innovations come mainly from New York and from Asia and no longer (directly) from France.

Too few young chefs in both countries have taken the option of acquiring premises in low-rent areas, away from the capital and other expensive large urban centres, particularly in regions of much lower property prices such as in the north of England. While there may be fewer customers with higher incomes in its counties, chefs would also meet much less fierce competition from other fine-dining restaurants, and in some counties there is none. For Germany, the equivalent would be opening a restaurant in one of the *Länder* of the former German Democratic Republic or in a less developed part of Berlin in the former communist East, and both have happened to a modest degree.

New Forms of Gastronomic Dining

The gradual transformation of the fine-dining sector started about ten years ago, well before the current economic recession. It nevertheless was born out of economic hardship for younger aspiring chef patrons, faced with prohibitive prices for real estate. This economic stimulus for change became united with a general cultural impetus towards a more relaxed and less formal style of fine-dining. The latter was first embraced by customers and chefs and, somewhat later, became accepted also by the Michelin organization. The first wave of change occurred along fairly conventional lines, appropriating and making use of already existing lower-level formats of dining, namely those cultivated by pubs and by bistros and brasseries.

A relatively early strategy adopted by aspiring chef patrons in Britain was to buy, rent, or become a licensee in a former pub. (These are typically free houses, rather than being owned by breweries.) The widespread closure of drinking-only pubs and the usually lower price/lower rent of this type of real estate has made this approach a feasible one. It accounts for the considerable growth in Britain of gastro pubs. But their attraction goes beyond their lower price/rent. Their long-held central place in British culture, particularly their informality and relative classlessness, constitute an additional plus for both chefs and a segment of fine-dining customers. The concept of gastro pub is a contested one, and some chefs, such as two-star chef Claude Bosi, for example, reject the label. Brett Graham, owner of the London gastro pub *Harwood Arms,* defines it by pointing out the old pub features it has retained: 'It has been a pub. There is no *sommelier*. It still has bar seats, with beer on tap, and you can go just to drink.'

Tom Kerridge's definition of a gastro pub goes further when he describes his two-star *Hand & Flowers* in Marlow also in cultural terms: 'We serve real ale; you can sit outside; the general low-key feeling of the place. There is no dress code; everyone is welcome.' But except for the availability of real ale, these characteristics do not really distinguish his establishment from some of the simpler restaurants. What sets Kerridge's place apart, however, is the sum of these attributes, together with the kind of food he serves. He describes it like this:

> [It's] food people understand and [which they can eat] in a non-intimidating environment. It is not elitist. It is where I would like to eat on my day off.

Kerridge is aware of the ambiguity attached to a starred gastro pub but does not unduly worry about it:

> Some customers come and expect a kind of *Manoir aux Quat'Saisons* experience and leave disappointed. Others see the restaurant as a small pub in a market town, and we exceed their expectations.

Germany has no equivalent of a British pub. But in Germany, too, two types of simpler dining establishments have risen to prominence in recent years. The first type is found in large urban centres, and the second is the old-established rural inn, the *Landgasthof*, already described in Chapter 2. The first type is a very simple restaurant, referred to in the *Michelin Guide* as 'standard comfort' and earning no more than one knife and fork for ambience/physical appearance (Box 11.4). What these places lack in physical comfort they often make up for by creating a 'young' and/or quirky atmosphere. There were ten such one-star places in the 2012 German *MG*, of which three are in Berlin, three in Munich, and the rest, with one exception, in other big cities.

Box 11.4 A GERMAN EXAMPLE OF THE NEW TYPE OF 'RELAXED' STARRED RESTAURANT

An example of a German 'standard comfort' restaurant is Munich's *Tramin* where 'unpretentiousness has reached almost extreme proportions', both in furniture and décor and in its very relaxed style of service, with no proper menu. Service staff wear jeans and trainers. *Tramin* also provides exciting contemporary music. Chef Daniel Schimkowitsch turns out flavoursome and sometimes innovative quality food, and the wine list offers reasonably priced bottles. His partner Holger Baier—the host and *sommelier*—is 'a real life actor with the calibre of a rock star'. One does not often hear, in descriptions of starred restaurants, 'that the atmosphere rocks'.[a]

[a] <http://www.deliciousdays.com/archives/2011/08/23/tramin-our-culinary-grail>, accessed 27 July 2012. <http://www.anothertravelguide.com/eng/europe/germany/munich/destinations/restaurants>, accessed 27 July 2012.

Another increasingly popular concept, also embracing a greater simplicity and a more relaxed style, is the fine-dining bistro. Like a gastro pub, the bistro offers a less elegant and more casual environment but still serves refined, Michelin-standard food. Additionally, it has usually more covers in a less spacious environment. Although it is a quintessentially French institution,

British chef proprietors seeking to add a bistro or brasserie to their fine-dining restaurant no longer look for inspiration to France. Instead, they look towards New York and particularly to Daniel Boulud and his expanding empire.

The dividing line between Michelin-starred bistros and restaurants sometimes is hard to draw. Thus restaurateurs Anthony Demetre and William Smith call their London place *Wild Honey* a bistro. While its slightly simpler food and lower prices remind the diner of a bistro, its leather banquettes and general atmosphere—it was once a members' club—cancel out this impression.[15] In contrast, the German two-star bistro *Le Moisonnier* in Cologne has certainly the simple wooden furniture, slightly cramped space, and buzzy atmosphere of a bistro. Yet its food is very much fine-dining restaurant food.

We therefore have to distinguish the new fine-dining, stand-alone bistros serving food of Michelin standard from bistros within hotels. The latter are separate establishments (from the Michelin restaurant) that both afford an alternative dining experience for hotel guests and improve the level of profit for owners. The latter type of bistro serves simpler, more standardized food, still recognizably of French origin, to a larger number of people. They do not aspire to a Michelin star.

More recently, as banks have further curtailed their lending, less conventional and more novel forms of fine-dining have evolved, particular as start-ups by younger chefs. They are responses to both economic and cultural change and permit chefs a more gradual limbering up to the status of chef proprietor (Boxes 11.5 and 11.6).

Both concepts, in different ways, satisfy the current demand for more democratic dining. There are no table cloths and no waiter service, but there is a lot more social mixing than in the traditional fine-dining restaurant. At the same

---

Box 11.5 THE CLOVE CLUB: A NEW INVENTIVE FINE-DINING RESTAURANT

The amalgam of economic hardship and cultural inventiveness is illustrated by the case of a young British chef called Isaac McHale. Together with the Young Turks collective, he has made the transition from a supper club to a temporary restaurant above a pub to the relative luxury and permanency of the *Clove Club* restaurant, opened in March 2013 in the old Shoreditch Town Hall, East London. The final finance required was procured through crowd-funding on the funding Internet site *Crowdcube* where the collective raised £250,000 in six weeks from many small investors. Crowdcube investors do not expect much of a financial return but get several minor perks—such as priority booking, as well as the satisfaction of being associated with a business whose output they know how to appreciate. The restaurant design and food served at the *Clove Club* are as modern and experimental as the funding method. McHale previously worked at Copenhagen's *Noma* and, more recently, at the two-star *The Ledbury*, London. Vegetables and wild herbs are given pride of place on his set menu which is strongly influenced by his spell at *Noma*.[a]

[a] *Restaurant* (January 2013): 30–3; *Observer Food Monthly* (17 March 2013).

Box 11.6 ANOTHER INVENTIVE FORM OF A FINE-DINING RESTAURANT

Another aspiring and inspired chef who has given a new twist to what constitutes a fine-dining restaurant is James Knappet. He previously worked in the London restaurants of two-star chefs Marcus Wareing and Brett Graham. He recently opened a restaurant which combines, in one building, a crowd-pleasing and therefore lucrative dining concept with one oriented to a smaller number of people seeking a gastronomic experience in a relaxed environment. Behind Knappet's restaurant *Bubbledogs*, which sells up-market hot dogs with a large selection of champagnes, there is another culinary space. It consists of a modern kitchen, surrounded on all sides by a bar, and it seats only nineteen diners. Here diners may consume a no-choice, thirteen-course gourmet menu, prepared in front of their eyes by Knappet and his chefs. (Knappet has worked at both Keller's *Per Se* in New York and at Copenhagen's *Noma*.) Examples of dishes from his gastronomic menu are 'Home-made tagliatelle with a truffle butter sauce, topped with black truffle shavings and garnished with foraged chickweed' or 'Crispy pieces of chicken skin, topped with mascarpone and bacon jam'. This new venture thus combines the by now well-accepted idea of the fine-dining chef's table with the format of a sushi bar. As journalist William Skidelsky suggests, this flexible format presents two of the new cultural trends in dining out: 'street food's incursion into the restaurant and top-end's partial escape from it'.[a]

[a] William Skidelsky, 'Today's Specials', *Prospect* (November 2012): 74–5.

---

time, the two concepts are compatible with the pressure on the chef patron to keep down expenditure. The format of *Bubbledogs* helps Knappet also to cross-subsidize his craft-based and aesthetically more elaborate cooking for small numbers in one space, by providing highly standardized 'fast food' to a larger crowd in another space. Furthermore, the low-class image of hot dogs has been given a social lift by serving them with select champagnes of the diner's choice, thus making the gustatory and social discrepancy between the two formats less apparent.

Another novel format which meets the requirements of diners for more flexibility and a more relaxed dining style, is the concept embodied in Jason Atherton's *Pollen Street Social*. Predating *Bubbledogs* and described by the 2012 *Good Food Guide* as 'utterly brilliant,' it was one of the first radical departures from the standard fine-dining format. *Pollen Street Social* offers a high degree of flexibility and movement to make it appear very lively and 'social'. It facilitates both the more casual type of 'bar' dining and the more traditional idea of 'separate table' dining. It promotes also the idea of 'small bites' eating (first introduced in *GRH*'s *Maze* in 2005). Its 'desserts' bar offers the possibility of ordering one or more desserts only. They are assembled by chefs as you wait and are described by the *GFG* as 'sushi for the sweet-toothed'.

Atherton has travelled widely internationally and has spent a fair amount of time in Asia. But like other younger chefs, he, too, looks towards the USA for inspiration and to empire builders like Danny Meyer and Thomas Keller.[16] Despite its appearance of relaxed casualness, the restaurant's 'mixed' concept actually is very demanding for the chef patron and requires huge organizational and culinary flexibility. Atherton soon realized that the diversity of dishes offered had to be carefully controlled.

Are such innovative restaurant concepts only to be found in Britain's capital, or are they also being devised in Berlin? While the financial requirements are somewhat less onerous for aspiring start-up chefs in Berlin (due to lower prices for real estate), setting up a fine-dining restaurant is not easy for a young chef even in the German context. Although Berlin is by no means comparable to London as an entertainment centre—it has competitors in several other German states—it has recently developed a more diverse and vibrant dining-out scene. In contrast to London, there is a stronger focus on regional food (of the surrounding Land Brandenburg), but this is combined with an openness to world cuisines. Berlin, too, has many foreign communities, and this has manifested itself in the presence of Asian (particularly Vietnamese), Latin American, Italian, east European and Russian, and also Jewish cuisines. An article in the *Guardian* on Berlin's ten best high-end restaurants included also two relaxed traditional brasseries, namely *Ganymed Brasserie* and the old-established *Lutter & Wegner* (Berlin Mitte),[17] with both offering regional and German cuisine.

Young start-up chefs have found properties in the less select districts of Berlin, such as parts of Kreuzberg or areas in the formerly communist East Berlin. Restaurants in these parts necessarily require a slightly different concept, adapted to the less illustrious environment. Berlin's continuing attraction to people with an orientation to an 'alternative' culture (which dates back to the time when the city attracted young people trying to avoid military conscription), as well as to a growing stream of tourists, make new restaurant formats or simply more quirky environments for fine-dining also more acceptable. Two relatively recent openings which have gained stars illustrate the trend towards a less select and more relaxed environment (Boxes 11.7 and 11.8).

Box 11.7 A NON-TRADITIONAL BERLIN RESTAURANT

One example is the *Wine Bar Rutz*, in a non-central part of Kreuzberg (a former working-class district). *Rutz*, an establishment with only one knife and fork (standard comfort category) in the *MG*, combines a wine shop, wine bar, and a gourmet restaurant in one building. Chef Marco Müller offers two very different menus. One is a fairly conventional gastronomic menu, while the other—called 'Saving the German Dining Culture'—contains more robust regional dishes, sometimes rendered in Berlin dialect: examples are a main dish of '*gebratene blutwurst aus berlin, lauch-kartoffelpüree & jemüse* [sic]' (fried black pudding from Berlin, a puree of potatoes and leek & vegetables) and a desert called '*Petras zwetschgenblechkuchen, zitronenmelisseneis*' (Petra's tray-baked damson cake, lemon balm ice cream).[a]

[a] Rutz's website, <http://www.rutz-weinbar.de>.

Box 11.8 AN EXCITING NEW BERLIN VENTURE

A more exciting new venture is Daniel Achilles's *Reinstoff* which gained a star the year it opened and has been awarded a second star since. Three friends, who had worked together at three-star Juan Amador's restaurant, converted the fire station of the old AEG light bulb factory into a restaurant. It is situated in the so-called Edison Court Yard, in the formerly Communist East Berlin. In addition to using their own pooled financial resources, their business plan also won a regional competition staged by the Berlin Volksbank (People's Bank) for start-up companies. This supplied the rest of the capital the three friends needed. Because of their nevertheless 'restricted means', they renovated the space simply, but with stunning results. Advised by an architect among their relatives, they managed the creation of the restaurant with some input by themselves. The three young owners left some of the exposed brickwork and the broad metal pipes and focus attention, by means of lighting, mainly on the tables. The whole, somewhat high, ceiling is hung with glistening metal balls, hung at different heights. There is no dress code for either guests or serving staff. According to Bloomberg, they have created 'fire-station cool'[a]. Achilles, who has worked for a while in the kitchen of Ferran Adria, has developed two interesting menus, called 'Close By' and 'Further Afield'. The first offers regional Brandenburg products and dishes, while the second is a gastronomic chef's menu which uses also global, and some traditional luxury, products. Although Achilles is strongly influenced by molecular cuisine—he does imaginative deconstructions and reconstructions of German dishes—he does not want to be known as a molecular chef. He senses that his Berlin customers would not accept 'only foams and jellies on their plates'. Achilles clarifies: 'The cuisine is avant-garde but this does not necessarily mean molecular cuisine.' The three friends thus have evolved a very modern and restrained style and a relaxed ambience, as well as a flexible menu concept. But unlike their young London counterparts, they have not necessarily evolved an inventive new restaurant concept. To the contrary, they deliberately set out 'not to be trendy, hip or in . . . We want to be honest, both on the plate and in the glass[b].'

[a] <http://www.bloomberg.com/news/2010-o9-20/berlin-s-classiest-new-eatery-has-bisected peas-fire-station-cool-review.html>, accessed 26 March 2013.
[b] *Sommelier Magazin* 5 (2009): 12; <http://www.centurion-magazine.com/nc/sections/post/a-taste-of-berlin.html>; <http://www.bloomberg.com/news/2010-09-20/berlin-s-classiest-new-eatery-has-bisected peas>, all accessed 26 March 2013.

Conclusions

The harder times of the twenty-first century, together with new cultural trends, have begun to transform the high-end restaurant industry. Fine-dining has received a modern twist. On the one side, we have seen the evolution of business empires by established and usually older chefs. While some have exchanged an inspired stance in the kitchen for inventiveness in the business world, others attempt to juggle the demands of the inspired and the market orders of worth with more or less success. Their business expansion, if handled well, creates a more solid financial basis for all their restaurants. They provide also an opportunity for younger chefs to head their own kitchen, at the same time increasing the choice for customers of the high-end restaurant sector. This phenomenon of creating national and international business empires is, however, mainly one embraced by the more entrepreneurial British chefs. Unlike their German colleagues, they have more models to follow in the restaurant industry at large, as well as in the general economy. Expansion for its own sake receives a very positive cultural endorsement in the British business world. In Germany, such expansion is only hesitantly being accepted and has not advanced very notably.

Cultural change in the fine-dining restaurant sector is present in both societies, particularly the turn away from the old format of pomposity, stiffness, and exclusivity. Transformation, however, has gone significantly further in the British fine-dining industry where entirely new restaurant concepts have been developed. This is probably due to the influence of the more vibrant second-tier restaurant sector, as well as to the greater size and cultural openness of London to the world. Against this, it is worth remembering that in Germany change is not merely confined to the capital but also has influenced the restaurant scene in Munich, Frankfurt, and other large regional urban centres. In the large British provincial cities, in contrast, no equivalent high-end dining scene has developed.

However, the new concepts of British chefs are not going to oust the traditional fine-dining restaurant. Indeed, most of these chefs still aim for a Michelin star in the longer run. Their new restaurant concepts are likely to be attractive to younger, single-sex groups of diners, while couples, family groups, and business diners will continue to look for the privacy of separate restaurant tables. The traditional high-end restaurants have not stood still but now combine a more relaxed and democratic style of service with the retention of some of the more refined trappings of dining, such as starched white table cloths, comfortable chairs, waiter service, and lots of space between tables. As my interviews with diners, presented in Chapter 9, make clear, most diners still look for the trappings of fine-dining restaurants, only barring pompous and/or arrogant staff. These, they believe, elevate a meal taken there to a special occasion and/or to a memorable experience all-round. It is clear that chefs, too, remain attached to the notion of a Michelin-starred restaurant even at the same time as they are engaged in empire building. Thus Jason Atherton has gone on record stating that he is working towards gainer higher awards—probably a second star—for *Pollen Street Social*.

In sum, despite much journalistic carping at Michelin-starred restaurants, often based on an outdated image of what they represent, the majority of the various stakeholders are agreed that fine-dining restaurants are here to stay. In both countries, a wider trend towards democratization has created a new definition of fine-dining. While most of the trappings of fine-dining endure, a more relaxed style of service and, in many venues, also a less luxurious, though still very comfortable, environment, create the impression of a lower degree of exclusivity. However, high prices for high-quality food, original and often very elaborate combinations and plate arrangements have remained, particularly in three-star restaurants. They continue to preserve a degree of social exclusivity, now based more often on income, rather than on cultural sophistication. Despite current economic hardship, the pleasure of eating out will still be pursued, and the cultivation of taste, now experienced in (more democratic) fine-dining restaurants, will continue to thrive.

Notes

1. Interview with Marc Wilkinson, <http://www.thestaffcanteen.com./the-staff-canteen-meets/marc-wilkinson-chef-patron-restaurant-fraiche-oxton-the-wirral/>.
2. *Restaurant* (July 2012): 24–6.
3. <http://www.guardian.co.uk/lifestyle/2010/nov/14/gordon-ramsay-chef-business>.
4. W*aitrose Food Illustrated* (March 2010): 85.
5. <http://www.catererandhotelkeeper.co.uk/Articles/12/03/2012342663/The-Caterer-and-Hotelkeeper-Interview-Jason-Atherton.htm>.
6. *Restaurant* (April 2013): 36–8.
7. <http://www.catererandhotelkeeper.co.uk/Articles/12/03/2012342663/The-Caterer-and-Hotelkeeper-Interview-Jason-Atherton.htm>.
8. Patricia Bröhm, 'Doppelt schmeckt besser', *Süddeutsche Zeitung* 79 (5 May 2013): 9.
9. M. M. Schwarz in Frankfurter Allgemeine (15 July 2013), <http://www.faz.net/aktuell/lebensstil/essen-trinken/sternegastronomie-es-kann-nicht-immer-kaviar-sein-12281679.html>.
10. *Restaurant* (January 2013): 30–3.
11. S. Wright, *Tough Cookies: Tales of Obsession, Toil and Tenacity from Britain's Culinary Heavyweights* (London: Profile Books, 2006), 183.
12. *Restaurant* (November 2012): 62.
13. N. Lander, *The Art of the Restaurateur* (London: Phaidon, 2012), 117.
14. T. Raue, *Ich weiss was Hunger ist. Von der Strassengang in die Sterneküche* (Munich and Zürich: Piper Verlag, 2012), 13.
15. At the time of this chapter's completion, the interior of *Wild Honey* was being completely redesigned.
16. <http://www.catererandhotelkeeper.co.uk/Articles/12/03/2012342663/The-Caterer-and-Hotelkeeper-Interview-Jason-Atherton.htm>.
17. <http://www.guardian.co.uk/travel/2011/aug/17-10-best-restaurnts-berlin>.

List of Chefs Interviewed

Britain

Chef's name	Name of restaurant	Stand-alone or in hotel	Town and county	Employment status	No. of stars in 2012
Alan Murchison	L'Ortolan	Stand-alone	Reading, Berkshire	Proprietor	One
Frances Atkins	Yorke Arms	Restaurant with rooms	Ramsgill, Yorkshire	Proprietor	One
Colin Kelly	Wild Honey	Stand-alone	London	Employed head chef	One
Glynn Purnell	Purnell's	Stand-alone	Birmingham	Proprietor	One
Andreas Antona	Simpsons	Restaurant with rooms	Birmingham	Proprietor	One
Nigel Haworth	Northcote	Restaurant with rooms	Langho, Lancashire	Proprietor	One
Ruth Rogers	River Café	Stand-alone	London	Proprietor	One
Atul Kochhar	Benares	Stand-alone	London	Chef patron	One
Sriram Aylur	Quilon	Connected to Taj hotels	London	Chef patron	One
Martin Wishart	Restaurant Martin Wishart	Stand-alone	Edinburgh	Proprietor	One
David McLaughlin	Holbeck Ghyll	Part of hotel	Windermere, Cumbria	Employed head chef	One
Galton Blackiston	Morston Hall	Part of hotel	Morston, Norfolk	Proprietor	One
Shaun Hill	Walnut Tree Inn	Stand-alone	Llandewi Skirred, Wales	Chef patron	One
Phil Thompson	Auberge du Lac	Part of Brocket Hall hotel	Welwyn, Hertfordshire	Employed head chef	One
Tom Kerridge	Hand & Flowers	Stand-alone	Marlow, Buckinghamshire	Proprietor	Two
Claude Bosi	Hibiscus	Stand-alone	London	Proprietor	Two
Phil Howard	The Square	Stand-alone	London	Proprietor	Two
Marcus Wareing	Marcus Wareing at the Berkeley	Part of hotel	London	Chef patron	Two
Sat Bains	Sat Bains	Restaurant with rooms	Nottingham	Proprietor	Two
Brett Graham	The Ledbury	Stand-alone	London	Joint proprietor	Two

Appendix I: List of Chefs Interviewed

Germany

Chef's name	Name of restaurant	Stand-alone or in hotel	Town and Land	Employment status	Number of stars
Rainer Maria Halbedel	Halbedel's Gasthaus	Stand-alone	Bonn, NRW	Proprietor	One
Jacob Stüttgen	Terrine	Stand-alone	Munich, Bavaria	Chef patron	One
Ali Güngörmüs	Le Canard Nouveau	Stand-alone	Hamburg	Chef patron	One
Herr Brzinski	Osteria Enoteca	Stand-alone	Frankfurt, Hessen	Proprietor	One
Herr Wannhof	Français	Frankfurter Hof	Frankfurt, Hessen	Executive Chef for hotel	One
Mario Gamba	Acquarello	Stand-alone	Munich, Bavaria	Proprietor	One
Raik Zeigner	Haus am See	Hotel Haus am See	Krakow, Mecklenburg	Employed head chef	One
Sören Anders	Oberländer Weinstuben	Stand-alone	Karlsruhe, BW	Employed head chef	One
Markus Nagy	Zum Löwen	Stand-alone	Eggenstein, BW	Proprietor	One
Christian Lohse	Fischer's Fritz	Hotel Regent	Berlin	Employed head chef	Two
Hans Horberth	La Vision	Hotel Wasserturm	Cologne, NRW	Employed head chef	Two
Dirk Luther	Meierei	Hotel Alter Meierhof	Glücksburg, SH	Employed head chef	Two
Niels Henkel	Restaurant Schloss Lerbach	Hotel Schloss Lerbach	Bergisch Gladbach, NRW	Employed head chef	Two
Christian Jürgens	Überfahrt	Hotel Überfahrt	Rottach-Egern, Bavaria	Employed head chef	Two
Johannes King	Söl'ringhof	Hotel Söl'ringhof	Rantum/Sylt, SH	Chef patron	Two
Eric Menchon	Le Moissonier	Stand-alone	Cologne, NRW	Employed head chef	Two
Sven Elverfeld	Aqua	Hotel Ritz Carlton	Wolfsburg, Niedersachsen	Employed head chef	Three
Juan Amador	Restaurant Amador	Stand-alone	Langen Hessen	Proprietor	Three
Joachim Wissler	Vendôme	Hotel Bensberg	Bergisch Gladbach, NRW	Employed head chef	Three
Harald Wohlfahrt	Schwarzwaldstube	Hotel Traube	Baiersbronn, BW	Employed head chef	Three

Interview Schedule

Date:

I'd like to start with your own career and some questions about this restaurant.

I. CAREER AND EDUCATION

If owner

1. For how long have you owned this restaurant?

If employed

How long have you been working in this restaurant?

If not British

2. When did you come to Britain?

Education and training

3. Please briefly describe to me your education and training, starting with your highest level of *general* education.

Prompts

    a. GCSE or equivalent
    b. A-level or equivalent
    c. Tertiary

4. Basic vocational training:
    a. Chef's training (NVQs, City & Guilds, apprenticeship)

5. What type of course was it and how long did it last?
    b. Hotel management (what kind of diploma?)
    c. Other or no training

6. How would you assess the quality of the basic vocational training you received?
Excellent
Good
Average
Poor

On-the-job training/stages

7. In which kitchens did you work after completion of your basic training (as *stagaire* or paid work)?

Please name the three most important work stations for your subsequent professional development?
(For each of the three ask 'Important, in what sense?')

Prompt

8. Have you worked in any kitchens abroad?
9. Who has influenced you most during your career?
10. In whose restaurant would you most like to have a meal or have recently had a meal? Name your top three choices.

II. NOW TURNING TO THIS RESTAURANT

1. Who is the owner? If restaurant part of hotel, ask about ownership of that as well.

If interviewee is owner (If not owner, turn to Q. 5)

2. Are you the sole owner?
3. If not, are other family involved?
4. If a partner, what are his (her) responsibilities?
5. How many covers do you have, and how many services do you do per day?

III. PROFESSIONAL IDENTITY

Could I ask you a question about how you identify yourself?

1. Would you consider yourself, above all, an entrepreneur or business person, an artist, an artisan, or what?
2. Do you consider yourself a British chef, or do you view yourself as cosmopolitan?

IV. IDENTITY OF CUISINE

I'd like now to turn to the type of cuisine you do.

1. Does your cuisine have a particular national or regional reference? Or is it internationally eclectic?

(If regional turn to Q 5)

2. If *national*, which particular national cuisine?

Prompt

If French, ask whether classical, modern, or *nouvelle cuisine*.

3. Are there any other culinary traditions that have an influence on your dishes and cooking?

If mentions another foreign cuisine/country:

4. Do you borrow mainly some of the ingredients/spices, the techniques of preparation, or the actual dishes?

If regional:

5. What does 'regional cuisine' mean to you?

Prompt: geographical/cultural context, culinary tradition, or local supply network?

6. What are the characteristics of this region's food that you include in your repertoire?

7. Do you employ any specific techniques which distinguish your food from that of other chefs?

Prompt

a. What about the use of molecular techniques?

b. Do you do sous-vide preparation?

c. How high- or low-tech is your kitchen?

V. THE CULTURAL DIMENSION

I am interested in what you might call the 'cultural dimension' of restaurants. By this I mean what kind of culinary experience you seek to provide.

Prompt with flash card

1. Which of the following experiences do you attempt to provide for diners and how much weight do you give to each?

a. Convey visual beauty	important	some importance	no importance
b. Evoke delight	important	some importance	no importance
c. Use humour	important	some importance	no importance
d. Evoke magic	important	some importance	no importance
e. Create excitement	important	some importance	no importance
f. Create surprise	important	some importance	no importance
g. Create shock	important	some importance	no importance

2. How important is an aesthetically pleasing presentation to you?

   Very important

   Important

   Not important

VI. TURNING NOW TOWARDS TASTE

1. How do you balance your emphasis on these visual aspects with the taste of food?

2. In terms of the taste of food, do you have any particular approach?

Prompt with flash card

a. Try to create deep flavours	Very Important	Important	Not Important
b. Try to create clear flavours	Very Important	Important	Not Important
c. Bring out the taste of main ingredient	Very Important	Important	Not Important
d. Try to create unusual flavours	Very Important	Important	Not Important
e. Invent new taste sensations	Very Important	Important	Not Important
f. Contrast flavours	Very Important	Important	Not Important
g. Contrast textures of food	Very Important	Important	Not Important

VII. CHARACTERISTICS OF CUISINE

I'm interested in the particular characteristics of your cuisine.

1. Which of the following culinary contrasts characterize your cuisine:

   a. Tradition or innovation?

   b. Simplicity or complex/elaborate style?

   c. Authenticity or eclecticism?

   d. Economy or extravagance?

2. What proportion, very roughly, of the ingredients you use are luxury products, such as lobster, truffles, caviar, etc.?

3. What about healthy eating? Is it:

   Very important

   Somewhat important

   Not important to you?

4. If very important, what concrete measures are taken to achieve healthy eating?

5. How much do you use exotic ingredients (not counting spices)?

   Extensively

   Frequently

   Occasionally

   Never

6. How much do you use Asian/Middle Eastern spices and sauces?

   Extensively

   Frequently

   Occasionally

   Never

VIII. INNOVATION/CREATIVITY

1. Do you consider your cuisine to be innovative?

2. Could you say something about the form innovation takes?

Prompt if necessary
Are you constantly searching for new original dishes, or do you seek to stay close to a particular style and introduce changes within that style?

3. What or who inspires you to be creative and innovative?

Prompt if necessary: clients, critics, employees, or other chefs? Anyone/thing else?

4. Is the flow of new ideas/concepts now national, international, or global?

5. How much do you network with other restaurateurs/chefs?

6. Where are these chefs located?

Prompt: locally, in the UK, or abroad?

IX. THE MENU

1. What considerations come into play when making your menu?

2. What do you try and convey to diners when making your menu?

3. How often is the menu changed?

4. Could I receive a copy of a menu?

X. RESTAURANT AMBIENCE

Restaurants do not merely serve food but also provide an ambience. How would you describe the ambience of this restaurant?

Prompt with flash card

1. Which of the following do you *mainly* aim for?

   Luxury

   Elegance

   Sophistication

   Artistic surroundings

   Comfort

   Intimacy

   Tradition

   Relaxed atmosphere

   A particular national or regional style

2. Which are the most important of these?

XI. SERVICE

1. What qualities do you seek to cultivate in your service staff in their relations with customers?

Prompt with flash card

Good manners

Being well spoken

Confidence

Amiability

Empathy

Worldliness

Efficiency

Intelligence

Knowledge of social standing of customers

2. Which of these are the three most important?

3. Do the front-of-house staff present themselves as equals, or do they show deference to guests?

4. How formal would you say your restaurant is?

5. Do you have explicit or implicit rules that clients must adhere to? What are these rules?

Prompt if necessary: about dress code, table manners

6. How do you enforce them?

XII. ECONOMIC ASPECTS

So far we have discussed the culinary and cultural side of the restaurant business. But the economics of the restaurant also are important.
If employed (If owner, go to Q. 2):

1. How much *operational* autonomy do the owners leave you in what you do

   a. Regarding your work in the kitchen:

      No autonomy

      Some autonomy

      Complete autonomy

   b. Regarding the restaurant:

      No autonomy

      Some autonomy

      Complete autonomy

   c. On the cost and profit side of the restaurant

Prompt with flash card

> Owner does *not* see the restaurant as a business
>
> Owner tolerates the occasional loss
>
> Owner demands that sufficient profits are made
>
> Owner demands that good profits are made

2. What level of profit do you aim for? Sufficient or maximum?

3. Are there any other business goals you pursue?

For both chef patrons and employed chefs:

4. What measures, if any, do you take to achieve cost containment?

5. What considerations do you (or the owner) apply when you set your prices?

6. Do you take into account the prices of your competitors?

7. Do you/does the owner own any other restaurants?

If yes, how many and what kind?

If owner:

8. Are you planning further business expansion? Why? In which country?

9. How did you finance the setting up and improvement of this restaurant?

> With own savings
>
> A bank loan
>
> External investors

10. How difficult or easy is it to get a sizeable bank loan?

11. *For non-owners:*Do you have plans to open your own restaurant?

12. How difficult or easy is it to get a sizeable bank loan?

XIII. CHEFS' VARIOUS ROLES

Many chefs now have other roles. For instance they appear on TV or write for magazines or even write books or undertake other business activities.

1. Do you engage in other income-generating activities?

Prompt if necessary: keep hotel rooms, merchandising, consulting, cookery book writing, television appearances, run other restaurants

2. What proportion of your time is spent on what activities?

3. What proportion of your income do you derive from them?

4. Do you see these external business activities as enriching for your restaurant activities? Or do you find them irksome and are only doing it for the money?

Tensions between creative and economic side of running a restaurant

5. What do you regard as the main economic pressures you experience in this business?

6. How do these economic pressures and demands impact on the creative aspects of your work?

7. What do you regard as the main psychological pressures of this business?

8. How many days per week do you aim to be in the kitchen?

9. How many hours per day do you usually work?

10. How would you answer critics who claim that the presence in the kitchen of the chef himself or herself is crucial to the restaurant's success?

XIV. STAFF EMPLOYED

First, the kitchen

1. What is the size of your brigade in the kitchen?

2. How many work full-time?

3. Is there another Head/Executive Chef?

4. How do you recruit kitchen staff?

Prompt: advertising, use of agencies, personal networks

5. What do you look for when appointing kitchen staff?

6. How much training do you yourself provide?

7. How many of your kitchen staff are

   a. British

   b. What countries do the foreign staff come from?

8. Many traditional terms, regarding work in the kitchen, such as the word 'brigade', hint at a military-style, highly disciplined form of work organization. Is this still the case today?

If not, how would you describe the organization of work in this kitchen?

9. If still highly disciplined, etc., how can this be reconciled with eliciting creativity from staff?

10. How would you describe your management style?

11. How long, on average, do kitchen staff stay with you?

Now to the restaurant

12. What is the size of your brigade in the restaurant?

13. How many work full-time?

14. How do you recruit restaurant staff?

Prompt: advertising, use of agencies, personal networks

15. What do you look for when appointing restaurant staff?

Training

Experience

Personal characteristics

Other

16. How much training do you yourself provide?

17. How many of your front-of-house staff are British?

18. What nationality are the others?

19. What are the main problems you encounter with front-of-house staff?

20. How difficult is it to recruit a good restaurant manager or *Maître de*?

21. How difficult is it to recruit a good *sommelier*?

XV. RELATIONS WITH CUSTOMERS

1. How would you describe the social profile of your customers?

2. Which social category is dominant—business people, tourists, wealthy individuals, other less wealthy food lovers/families celebrating a family anniversary, who come only occasionally.

3. What proportion of customers are

   a. from the town or county/region

   b. the UK?

   c. from abroad? (Which countries?)

4. How much contact do you personally have with customers? Do you do the rounds after service?

5. How do you assess customers' reactions to the food, service, and ambience this restaurant provides?

6. What problems, if any, do you encounter when meeting your customers?

Prompt: problems over price, quality of service, dissatisfaction with the food

7. If you have a dish on the menu you personally (or your head chef) consider really great but it is infrequently ordered, do you take it off the menu?

8. Do you try to shape your customers' taste or do you reflect it?

XVI. RELATIONS WITH SUPPLIERS

Let's now turn to your suppliers of produce for the restaurant.

1. How many core suppliers of produce do you have?

2. Where are they geographically located?

3. What type of firm are they? Are they artisanal, agricultural, or what?

4. How important is local sourcing to you?

    a. Why?

Prompt: do you have ecological concerns?

5. How long have you worked with your core suppliers?

6. Do you regularly go to a local market? What kind?

7. Do you experience any problems with suppliers, as compared with chefs in other parts of Britain?

8. Do you employ foragers for wild ingredients, such as herbs or mushrooms?

XVII. THE ROLE AND INFLUENCE OF GASTRONOMIC CRITICS *(both individual ones and Guides)*

1. Who, in your view, sets the standard in the fine-dining restaurant scene?

Prompt if necessary: the restaurants themselves, the guides, the customers, or some other organization?

    a. Do you consider Internet sites important in shaping your market? If so, which ones?

    b. If considered important, are they now seriously undermining restaurant guides?

2. Which purely British guides do you consider as influential in shaping your market and the customers you attract?

3. Are the national guides *as* important to you as the *Michelin Guide*, or are they even *more* important than the *Michelin Guide*?

4. When did you:

   receive the first star?

   the second star?the third star?

If one-star

5. What are you doing to achieve a second star?etc.

6. How would you describe the impact of your Michelin star(s) on the restaurant?

7. What impact on:

   a. your revenue did you experience on receipt of your first (second; third) star?

   b. on investment?

   c. on type of diners frequenting the restaurant?

   d. on prices?

8. How would you describe the impact of your Michelin star(s) on yourself, psychologically and physically?

Prompt if necessary

   a. on levels of anxiety

   b. the hours you work

9. In more general terms, what main functions, in your view, does the *Michelin Guide* serve in the 'fine-dining' industry?

10. How would you describe its influence?

11. What would you do differently if you did not have to heed inspectors?

12. Do you think the *Michelin Guide* has any tacit bias?

XVIII. THE NATIONAL PICTURE OF HAUTE CUISINE

1. In a comparative European perspective, this country has a relative low number of Michelin-starred restaurants. Why do you think this is the case?

2. Do you consider British culture supportive of fine-dining restaurants and their chefs?

3. How many German chefs do you know by name/in person?

Recommended Reading

On British Restaurants and Chefs:

Blanc, R. 2008. *A Taste of My Life: One Man's Hunger for Perfection*. London: Transworld Publishers.

Burnett, J. 2004. *England Eats Out: A Social History of Eating Out in England from 1830 to the Present*. Harlow: Longman.

Driver, C. 1983. *The British at Table, 1940–80*. London: Chatto & Windus.

Lander, N. 2012. *The Art of the Restaurateur*. London: Phaidon.

Mars, G. and Nicod, M. 1984. *The World of Waiters*. London: Allen & Unwin.

Mennell, S. 1985. *All Manners of Food: Eating and Taste in England and France from the Middle Ages to the Present*. Oxford: Basil Blackwell.

Roux, M. Jnr. 2009. *A Life in the Kitchen*. London: Weidenfeld & Nicolson.

Warde, A. 2009. 'Imagining British Cuisine', *Culture, Food and Society* 12.2: 151–71.

Wright, S. 2006. *Tough Cookies:Tales of Obsession, Toil and Tenacity from Britain's Culinary Heavyweights*. London: Profile Books.

On German Restaurants and Chefs:

Barlösius, E. 1988. 'Soziale und historische Aspekte der deutschen Küche', postscript to S. Mennell, *Die Kultivierung des Appetits. Die Geschichte des Essens vom Mittelalter bis heute*. Frankfurt: Athenäum, 33–44.

Drummer, C. 1997. 'Das sich ausbreitende Restaurant in deutschen Grossstädten als Ausdruck bürgerlichen Repräsentationsstrebens 1870–1930', in H.-J.Teuteburg, G. Neumann, and A. Wierlacher (eds.), *Essen und kulturelle Identität*. Berlin: Akademieverlag, 303–22.

Eckhardt, M. 2002. *Kochköpfe. Dreizehn Köche hinter den Kulissen*. Bremen: H. M. Hauschild GmbH.

Horbelt, R. and Spindler, S. 2000. *Die Deutsche Kueche im 20. Jahrhundert*. Frankfurt am Main: Eichhorn AG.

Jenn, A. 1993. *Die deutsche Gastronomie. Eine historische und betriebswirtschaftliche Betrachtung*. Frankfurt: Deutscher Fachverlag.

Raue, T. 2012. *Ich weiss was Hunger ist. Von der Strassengang in die Sterneküche*. Munich and Zürich: Piper Verlag.

Teuteberg, J. 2003. 'The Rising Popularity of Dining Out in German Restaurants in the Aftermath of Modern Urbanization', in M. Jacobs and P. Scholliers (eds.), *Eating Out in Europe*. Oxford and New York: Βerg, 281–300.

Weber, G. 2009. *Kochen ist Krieg*. Munich: Piper.

On Gastronomic Guides:

Blank, G. 2007. *Critics, Ratings and Society: The Sociology of Reviews*. Lanham, MD: Rowman & Littlefield.

Karpik, L. 2000. 'Le guide rouge Michelin', *Sociologie de Travail* 42: 369–89.

Mennell, S. 1985. *All Manners of Food: Eating and Taste in England and France from the Middle Ages to the Present*. Oxford: Basil Blackwell.

Michelin Tyre Company Ltd. 2011. *The History of the Michelin Guide 1900–2011*.

Surlemont, B. and Johnson, C. 2005. 'The Role of Guides in Artistic Industries: The Special Case of the "Star" System in the *Haute-Cuisine* Sector', *Managing Service Quality* 15.6: 577–90.

Warde, A. 2009. 'Imagining British Cuisine', *Culture, Food and Society* 12.2: 151–71.

Index

Index